A HISTORY
OF
JAIPUR 1503-1938

A HISTORY OF JAIPUR 1503-1938

JADUNATH SARKAR

GYAN

Published by

Gyan Publishing House
5, Ansari Road
Daryaganj, New Delhi-110002
Phone: 011-47034999, 9811692060
E-mail: books@gyanbooks.com

Distribution Network
gyanbooks.com
India, USA, Canada, UK, Australia

ISBN: 978-93-7097-016-8 (HB)
First Published, 1935

2nd Impression 2025

Printed at: Gyan Press, Delhi.

A HISTORY OF JAIPUR 1503-1938
Author: JADUNATH SARKAR

A History of Jaipur

c. 1503 - 1938

A History of Jaipur

c. 1503 - 1938

Sir Jadunath Sarkar

Contents

I	The Land, Its Features and Produce	1
II	The People	9
III	The Early Kachhwa Kings	20
IV	How Akbar Won the Kachhwas Over	31
V	Akbar's Wars Against the Maharana of Mewar	45
VI	The Kachhwas as Wardens of the North-Western Frontier	63
VII	Man Singh in Bengal, Bihar, Orissa and the Deccan	75
VIII	Interlude and Mirza Raja Jai Singh (First Phase): 1614-1637	97
IX	Jai Singh in the War of Mughal Succession	113
X	Jai Singh and Shivaji	123
XI	The Last Campaign and Death of Jai Singh I	135
XII	Ram Singh and Bishan Singh, 1667-1700	145
XIII	Sawai Jai Singh's Early Career	156
XIV	Sawai Jai Singh's Dealings with the Marathas	174
XV	Sawai Jai Singh and Rajputana	187
XVI	Sawai Jai Singh's City and Observatory	205

XVII	Sawai Jai Singh's Achievement and Character	218
XVIII	Ishwari Singh, 1743-1750	229
XIX	Sawai Madho Singh, 1751-1768	242
XX	The Jaipur State and the Imperial Delhi Government, 1778-1785	259
XXI	Mahadji Sindhia Invades Jaipur: the Lalsot Campaign, 1786-1787	270
XXII	The Last Rajput Struggle against the Marathas: the Battle of Patan, 1790	285
XXIII	The Last Years of Sawai Pratap Singh, 1791-1803	299
XXIV	The British Alliance	315
XXV	The Last Days of the Ancient Regime in Jaipur	330
XXVI	The Reign of Ram Singh II: The First Half	338
XXVII	The Reign of Ram Singh II: An Era of Progress	353
XXVIII	Sawai Madho Singh II	365
XXIX	Sawai Man Singh II: Education and Share in Administration	379
XXX	Jaipur Administrative Activities Today	386

Plates

Appendices

1. From Nizam-ul-Mulk Asaf Jah I's letter to Sawai Singh II
2. Captain J. Pillet's account of Sawai Pratap Singh

Index

I

The Land, Its Features And Produce

Area

The Jaipur State, with its now independent offshoot of Alwar, occupies the northern half of the eastern side of Rajputana, while the State of Mewar (with Bundi-Kota) fills up the southern half, with the British district of Ajmer-Merwara as the dividing line between these two sections.

With Alwar included, Jaipur looks like a rough rectangle on the map, 200 miles long and 140 miles wide. Since the north-eastern quarter of this area is excluded on account of the separation of Alwar (3380 square miles) from its parent stock, the figure now formed by Jaipur State is that of a huge letter L, the base line of which is much thicker than the vertical line, and which is further mutilated by a small triangle on the lower right hand end, cut off by Kerauli (1260 square miles), and a similar oval area (1688 square miles) appropriated by the newly sprung Muslim State of Tonk, just below the bend of the letter.

The Jaipur Kingdom now extends over 16,681 square miles,[1] third among the States of Rajputana in terms of mere superficial area, as the sandy deserts of Marwar and Bikaner exceed it in this respect. But, from the most vital standpoint of population, Jaipur easily occupies the first place in Rajputana, as it includes 24 per cent of the total population of this region, with Marwar (19 per cent) and Mewar (14 per cent) far behind. In the wealth of its government, people and culture, Jaipur has enjoyed an undisputed first place in Rajputana for more than two centuries. Above all, the rulers and statesmen of this kingdom have played a part in the shaping of Indian history unparalleled by any other State or clan, as the following pages will show.

Natural Features

The centre of Jaipur State is an elevated table land of triangular form, 1400 to 1600 feet above sea-level, bound on the south by a base-line running west from the City of Jaipur; the eastern boundary consists of hills running north and south along the Alwar border; towards the north and west this plateau is bound by a broken chain of hills, a portion of the Aravali range, the apex of the triangle being near Khetri in Shekhawati. This range of hills on the north-west forms a natural boundary between the sandy desert tracts of Shekhawati and Bikaner on the one side, and the more fertile soils of Jaipur on the other.

To the east of Jaipur, beyond the range of hills close to that city, there is a rapid fall of some three or four hundred feet in the first two or three miles, after which there is a gradual fall along the valley of the Banganga river to the Bharatpur border (in the extreme east) and the country becomes gradually more open. The eastern portion of the Jaipur State has many ranges of low hills in it, and near the Kerauli border (in the south-eastern corner) is much cut up with ravines.

From the base of the central plateau (i.e., south of the latitude of Jaipur City) the country slopes gradually to the south-east towards the Banas river, only a few isolated hills appearing above the plain; but in the extreme south the hill-ranges reappear, and in the neighbourhood of Rajmahal, where the Banas river has forced itself through the (Toda) range, the scenery is exceedingly wild and beautiful.

Westward from Jaipur City the country rises gradually towards the Kishangarh border and consists of a great measure of broad open treeless plains, dotted with occasional hills. The hills for the most part rise very abruptly from the plains and many of them are peaked; others are flat at the top with the edges steeply scraped for some way down the hillside, thus forming natural fortifications.

Water In The Soil, Rainfall And Rivers

In Shekhawati, the north-western division of the State, water is found only at a great depth, from eighty to hundred feet below the surface, and it is brackish in most parts, where the soil is highly impregnated with salt, especially throughout the districts west of the capital. In the central and eastern divisions of the State territory, water is fairly near the surface, varying from a few feet in low-lying ground to 30 or 40 feet.

The soil of Jaipur, immediately west and north of the capital, is generally sandy; in some places there are tracts of mere barren sand. Eastward along the Banganga valley, the soil is usually a rich firm loam; and in the extreme east, towards Hindaun, it is still sandy, though not unproductive. Southward from Jaipur the soil is, for the most part, rich and fertile; and the tract to the extreme south, enclosed by the bend of the Banas river (i.e., Sawai Madhopur), consists of a rich alluvial loam, and is the most fertile portion of the State. Shekhawati, to the north of the Aravali range, consists almost entirely of shifting sands, and the great scarcity of water prevents the growth of any other than the October or *kharif* crop (*moth, bajra* and *guwar*) raised during the rains. 'Should there be a bad rainy season, and the supply of water be cut off, these parts of Shekhawati would be exposed to all the miseries of scarcity and starvation, as in 1812.' (Lt. A.H.E. Boileau, *Narrative of a Tour Through Rajwara in 1835*, Calcutta, 1837.)

The annual rainfall for the whole State averages a little less than 23 inches, of which 20 inches are received in the three months of July, August and September. The rainfall is 15 to 18 inches in the north, about 25 inches in the capital and more than 31 inches in the south-eastern district. The climate is dry and healthy, and malarious fevers are rare. The mean temperature in Jaipur city is 77°, varying from 59° in January to 91° in June. But in 1904, the maximum was 114° (May) and the minimum 37° (January), so that the yearly fluctuation ranged over 77°. In the cold season the climate is very agreeable, but in Shekhawati it is often unpleasantly cold. During summer, the hot winds from the west blow with great force in Shekhawati and the northern portions of Jaipur; but the sand soon parts with its heat, so that the nights are generally pleasant and the mornings very cool.

The mighty Banas river has all its lower course (110 miles) and the last two of its northern feeders (the Masi and the Morel) within the limits of this State, and it joins the still mightier Chambal at a point where the north bank belongs to Jaipur and the south bank to the Gwalior State. The Banganga, later known as the Utangan, flowing east towards Agra, and the Sabi flowing sharply north-east towards Delhi, originate in Jaipur territory.

Irrigation Works

Since there is no perennial river in the State, the crops are watered by means of wells, many of which are very deep, as well as tanks formed by raising embankments (*bunds*) and damming up water across the lower slopes of the valleys and across the beds of rivers. The larger of these irrigation works are the following:

The Crosthwaite Sagar, across the Banganga at Jamwa-Ramgarh, consists of an enormous sand dam, 90 feet high, entirely overlaid with rubble stone. When full, it covers an area of six square miles and the greatest depth of water over the sluices is 61 feet. The main canal issuing from it is 20 miles in length with 210 miles of distributaries.

The Tori Sagar has a catchment area of 320 square miles, and when full, the tank covers an area of six square miles with a capacity for irrigating 27 square miles. Its bund is an earthen dam with a masonry core-wall, 6,400 feet long, which impounds water to a depth of 40 feet.

The Chaprwara Bund is an earthen embankment more than three miles in length, with a central masonry escape and core-wall. The tank, when full, covers an area of four and three-fourth square miles.

The Bund Moran is an earthen dam 3308 feet long, with a masonry core-wall and escape on rock closing a gap in a range of hills. When full the tank covers an area of two square miles to a depth of 17 feet.

The Bund Boochara on the river Sota, is a solid masonry dam 75 feet high and 480 feet long, in a rock-girt hollow.

The Kalekh Bund, across the river Bandi, impounds water to a depth of 31 feet.

Crops And Tillage

Agricultural conditions vary in different parts of the State. Shekhawati consists almost entirely of shifting sands, and generally produces only one harvest in the year, which is grown in the rainy season and which ripens in October and November. This crop consists chiefly of *bajra* (spiked millet), *mung* and *guwar, moth* (lentil).

Camels, not bullocks, are usually yoked to the plough. In the immediate neighbourhood of the capital and to the west and north, the soil is generally sandy. The rain crop is the same as in Shekhawati, and a little wheat and barley are grown in the cold season (the *rabi* crop). To the east of the capital, along the Banganga valley and in the northern districts, the soil is for the most part either black cotton or a rich alluvial loam. Here *jawar,* maize, cotton and *til* (oil seed) are grown in the rains, while the cold season crops are wheat, barley, gram, sugarcane and poppy. A small quantity of rice, of a coarse variety, is grown in Gangapur on the eastern border.

Crop area and yield: Agricultural statistics are available only for the Crownland portion of the Jaipur territory, but not for the baronial fiefs and other alienated lands. The cultivated area in the Crownlands totals 13,54,500 *bighas* (165 chains each), out of which 1,53,500 *bighas* are under wheat cultivation, (average yield for the quinquennium 1934-38 was 15.35 lakh maunds of grain); 1,80,500 *bighas* under barley (yield 21.65 lakh maunds); 2,24,800 *bighas* under gram (yield 8.96 lakh maunds); 61,870 *bighas* under maize (yield 5.56 lakh maunds); 2,25,000 *bighas* under *bajra* (yield 5.62 lakh maunds); 1,86,200 *bighas* under *jawar* (yield 5.58 lakh maunds); 2,40,000 *bighas* under *moth, masina* and *chaunla* (yield 4.79 lakh maunds); 74,100 *bighas* under oil seeds, and 34,600 *bighas* under cotton (yield 1,38,352 maunds).

Cities And Villages

The entire territory of Jaipur State is now divided for administrative purposes into eleven districts, each under a magistrate and collector; namely, Shekhawati on the north-west or Bikaner frontier, followed as we move southwards, by Sambhar and Malpura (which includes Toda Rai Singh and Newai also). Then, along the middle line north to south, come Torawati, Amber and Sawai Madhopur; Jaipur in the heart and Dausa, Hindaun and Gangapur on the east. Kot Qasim forms an isolated district (really a sub-division) in the north-east, entirely surrounded by 'foreign' territory.

The total number of villages in the State in 1938 was 6,379 and that of the towns with a population above 2,000 was 39. Out of the latter, the capital with its suburbs contained 1,44,179 people, Sikar 26,297, and six other towns from 10,000 to 20,000; while the remaining 31 had less than 10,000 inhabitants each.[2]

Forests And Minerals

The forests cover an area of 283 square miles, of which only 71 square miles are reserved. There are but few valuable timber trees.

A considerable part of Jaipur State is covered with alluvium. But in the northern and eastern districts large areas are occupied by schists belonging to the Aravali system, resting on gneiss and overlaid by quartzites of the Delhi system. Intrusive granite is common with the Torawati hills of the north-eastern corner. Copper is found at Khetri and Singhana at the northern end of the Aravali range. Nickel and cobalt are found at Babai (seven miles south of Khetri) in association with copper pyrites disseminated through the slates. At Karwar near Hindaun, iron occurs in jaspideous shales of the Gwalior series.

Apart from salt, the minerals of the State are now hardly worked at all. Good building stone (chiefly sandstone and marble) is plentiful. Huge slabs of foliated mica schist are quarried and are used for roofing and flagging purposes. Coarse grey marble comes from Raiwala[3] near the Alwar border; and a black marble, used for inlaying work, is obtained near Kot Putli.[4] An abundance of excellent lime stone is available at Rahori, 14 miles north-east of the capital. Garnets of the best kind are fairly common in the Rajmahal hills near the river Banas in the south-eastern corner of the State.

Sambhar Salt Lake

A depression within the lines of the Aravali hills, about 40 miles north-west of Ajmer and 36 miles on the west of Jaipur city, forms a great basin with no outlet, covered with a shallow sheet of water, which spreads or contracts according to the season. This is the Sambhar lake. In the height of the rains the water extends to a length of 18 to 20 miles with a breadth varying from three to ten miles. In very hot and dry summers the wet bed is little more than a mile in length and less than half a mile across. The lake's deeper portion which never dries up and which is locally called 'the treasury',[5] is situated near its centre, almost opposite a bold promontory (*Mata-ki-devi*),[6] which juts out from the southern shore. In the dry season, the view of the lake is very striking. Standing on the low sandy ridges in the south, one may see what appears to be a great sheet of snow, with pools of water here and there, and a network of narrow paths marking the near side of it. As the railway skirts one side of the lake and then crosses it by a causeway, the traveller notices in the middle of it a huge white mountain, from which waggons are being loaded with this precious mineral, while at his feet stretch rectangular shallow beds of darker colours from which the water is evaporated. The annual yield of the Sambhar lake was 1,26,000 tons in 1915. The net income received by the government from all sources was Rs. 88,00,000 in 1915.[7]

Game, Large And Small

The Sawai Madhopur district is the hunter's paradise. Here one can find the tiger, the panther and the bear (and a rare lynx now and then). There are also wild boars, *nilgais* (blue bulls), wolves and hyenas, with a stray wild dog or two. The *Sambhar*, the spotted deer, the black buck and *chikara* (small deer) abound. Among game birds, the sand grouse, the rock grouse, partridges, painted partridges, (black partridges being rare), quails, green pigeons and wild fowls are plentiful. Peacocks are numerous, but shooting them is not allowed out of regard for Hindu religious feeling.

During the cold season, in the lakes of the State and the two great rivers, the Banās and the Chambal, many varieties of migratory birds (especially teals, spot-bills, mallards, pochards and the bar-headed geese) in addition to snipes and ducks, afford very good shooting. Carp and other varieties of fish common in north-western India abound. Crocodiles haunt the rivers and large lakes within the State.

In the central part of the State (that is Jaipur district) as well as the hilly regions of other districts, we have tigers, panthers, the *sambhar* deer and the wild boar, with black bucks and blue bulls in the plains. Here too most varieties of the above game birds occur, with the exception of wild fowls. In the sandy tracts of the west, bordering Bikaner and Jodhpur, imperial sand grouse, and more rarely bustards, are found during the season. There are two large game preserves, one near Sawai Madhopur and the other near the capital.

Notes

1. In p. 274 of the authoritative Government of India publication *Memoranda of the Indian States, 1940*, the area of Jaipur State is '15,601 sq. miles'. *Ed.*
2. These figures relating to population etc. are based on the 1931 Census. *Ed.*
3. The correct name is Rayanwala. *Ed.*
4. 'At Bhainslana.' Bhainslana is situated 27° 24′ N and 76° 6′ E; 8 miles south-west of Kot-Putli. *Ed.*
5. The terms used locally are *khazzana* and *bhandar*. *Ed.*
6. For Devi read Doongari (Hill). *Ed.*
7. The average annual revenue of Jaipur State in 1939 was Rs. 1,44,67,000. (*Memoranda, 1940*, p. 274). *Ed.*

II

The People

Sects And Castes

Jaipur has by far the largest population among all the States of Rajputana, its inhabitants numbering 26,31,775 or nearly one fourth of the total population of the entire Rajputana province. Here the density of population is 169 to the square mile on an average, ranging from 247 inhabitants in Kot Qasim to 88 in Shekhawati and Malpura, which may be contrasted with five persons to the square mile in Jesalmer, and is exceeded only by the average of 210 for Alwar.

Of the population, less than one in twelve (or exactly 8.1 per cent) profess Islam. The Jains number 29,492 or just over one per cent of the total; the Christian and other minor denominations contribute a few thousands, while the Hindus form the great bulk of the population, numbering about 90 per cent of the country's inhabitants within their fold.

The *jat* or agricultural caste, as may be expected, number over three lakhs (or 12 per cent of the population) and allied caste of *gujars*, i.e., cattle-breeders and cultivators, contribute a little short of two lakhs (exactly 7.3 per cent). But, surprisingly enough, the highest of Hindu castes, the *brahmans*, number over two and three-fourth lakhs or 10.5 per cent of the total, clearly showing how the Kachhwa State has been the asylum of Hinduism when persecuted elsewhere, and how the Rajput sword has protected the priesthood of the nation even from beyond the frontiers of Jaipur. It speaks equally eloquently of the Jaipur rajahs' boundless charity to the pious and their patronage of the sacred learning of their faith.

The third in numerical importance among the tribes are the Minas or the aboriginal holders of the Dhundhar country, with their present strength of two lakhs and 60,000 or just under one-tenth of the total. Then, in the decreasing order of numbers come the leather-dressers and scavengers called *chamars* (just below nine per cent), the *gujars* (7.3 per cent), the *banias* or the trading and the banking caste (1,62,520, or a little above six per cent), the *malis* or gardeners (5.2 per cent) and the Rajputs (4.3 per cent).

In the Rajput population of 1,13,389, as many as 59,095 (or above 52 per cent) belong to the ruling clan of Kachhwas. A large body of the clan has been lost to Jaipur through the separation of Alwar, where the Naruka branch of this clan has formed an independent State since 1780; but there are still over 3000 Narukas in Jaipur territory.

Aboriginal Minas

The Minas are a non-Aryan tribe who occupied and ruled Jaipur territory till they were dispossessed of their lands and reduced to subjection by the advancing waves of Rajput colonization in the thirteenth century, as the Gaels of Scotland were ousted by the more civilized Saxons and driven away from the plains to the Highlands. Ethnologists hold that the Meos of Mewat and the Minas of Rajputana and the Punjab are really of a common origin—the Meos are at least nominally Muhammadans by religion, while the Minas are Hindus. Philologists derive the name of their cradleland Mewat from the Sanskrit *Minawati* or 'rich in fish'. The term *matsya-desh* or fish-country was applied to this region up to the north-eastern part of Jaipur in the ancient Hindu epics. Russell writes,

> It is recognised that the Minas are a caste of the most mixed and impure descent (probably from Rajput immigrant fathers and aboriginal mothers) . . . Another piece of evidence of the Dravi-

> dian origin of the tribe is the fact that there exists even now a group of *Dehdia* or impure Minas, who do not refuse to eat cow's flesh. The *Chaukidari* Minas, dispossessed of their lands, resorted to the hills, and here they developed into a community of thieves and bandits recruited from all the outcastes of society.

But whatever may be their true ethnic origin, today 'the Minas of upper Rajputana are Hindus of the straitest sect; all castes of Hindus (except *brahmans* and *banias* only) will partake of food which has been prepared by them, and even these two castes will drink water which has been drawn by a Mina'. (Col. Hervey)

Sir Denzil Ibbetson wrote in 1881,

> The Minas are the boldest of our criminal classes... In Marwar they are armed with small bows which do considerable execution. They travel great distances in gangs of from twelve to twenty men, practising robbery and dacoity as far as the Deccan. They have agents in all the large cities of Rajputana and the Deccan who give them information... The criminal Minas are now said to inhabit a tract of country about 65 miles long and 40 broad, stretching from Shahpura (some 40 miles north of Jaipur) to Guraora in the Gurgaon district on the Rohtak border.

Before the Rajput penetration, the central region of the present Jaipur State was ruled by a number of petty Mina chieftains each living in his fort, carrying on depredations on the trade caravans, and owing a very loose allegiance to the Mina Rajah of Amber, who was nominally the head of the clan. The incoming Kachhwas, under their Rajah Dulha Rai and his successors, conquered the forts of these aboriginal chiefs and reduced their race to subjection; but the chiefs were given *jagirs*, which their descendants still enjoy. Originally, these tribal chiefs reduced to landlords were twelve in number, hence they are known as the *Bara Mina Baragaon*.

The lands they enjoy were given on service tenure; the condition was that one man was to be produced for the service of the Jaipur rajah for each 'plough', or 120 *bighas* of land. As the descendants of the original grantees multiplied with time, their lands were minutely fragmented, the period of service of each shareholder being proportionately reduced. The number of such men has increased to 1712 at present. These Minas now perform watch and ward duties in the palaces and offices of the State. They also serve as guards in forts such as Nahargarh, Jaigarh and Ambagarh. Formerly they were so highly trusted that they were charged with the duty of escorting the palace ladies when they made a journey. Even the *tika* or red mark on the forehead of every Amber-Jaipur rajah at his coronation was originally made by the leader of the Minas, with blood drawn out of his big toe. But when the Mughal Emperors themselves agreed to anoint the new Kachhwa Rajahs with their own hands (in sandal paste), this function of the Mina headman was discontinued.

The Mina tribe in Jaipur is split into two sections that do not marry with each other. The first consists of cultivators by hereditary profession (called *kheter* Minas), who are considered trustworthy. The second, called *chaukidar* Minas, are treated as a criminal tribe, and the name of each individual among them is entered in the criminal register of the police. They are called *chaukidars*, because, following the principle 'Set a thief to catch a thief', many of them are employed as watchmen in houses and stores, and held responsible for all thefts within their charge. They have deservedly won the reputation of being the cleverest and most daring thieves in India.

A story characteristic of the daring, resourcefulness and cunning of the Mina race is current in Jaipur. A rajah of the place had heard of the wonderful miracle-working power of the idol installed in a famous temple in the far off Tamil country. He tried in vain, with all his treasures, to induce its priests to transfer the deity to him. Then he called to his aid the crack thief among his Mina subjects. This man went to the Tamil country in disguise, spent some time in the temple, and found it always double locked at night and guarded by sentinels at the front porch. So, one dark night he climbed on the roof from the rear with some mason's tools, lime and mortar, and food and drink for three days, removed the stones of the top of the tower slowly and carefully and on the last night, let himself down by a rope into the locked sanctuary. He stole the idol, went up hand over hand to the roof, filled up the hole with stone and mortar, and on getting down fled to Jaipur with the image tied round his waist. The stolen deity now adorns a temple outside the Kachhwa capital. The story may or may not be true; it is certainly *bon trovato*.

Peasant Life

The peasantry form the backbone of the nation, and the more so among a purely agricultural people like the Rajputs, *jats* and Minas. A study of their normal life is necessary if we are to understand the economy of the nation, and it is described below from the observations of a recent British traveler, F. Stewart.

Only a very small proportion of the peasants in Rajputana are actually Rajputs. The majority of those in Jaipur State and Haraoti are Minas, while the *jats* form the greater part of the cultivators in Marwar. There is also a fair proportion of *gujars* and *malis* in all the States. The *gujars* on the whole are not good cultivators, and prefer to keep cattle.

Few villages consist entirely of one section, and are, rather, made up of several groups, who though they do not eat together or intermarry, live on the best of terms. The *chamars*, who in the past have been outcastes, earning their livelihood by skinning animals and making leather water buckets, harness and shoes, for the higher caste people of their village, have also taken to agriculture, proving to be excellent cultivators.

Each village, besides the actual tillers of the soil, has a number of village 'servants', among whom the most conspicuous are the village blacksmith or *lohar*, the carpenter and the *nai* or barber whose duties also include that of a surgeon.

In late years a great deal has been done to help the peasant of Rajputana, to teach him the use of manures and various remedial and preventive measures against pests and insects. He has been given the chance of procuring better seed. Much has been done to improve the cattle as well.

By the stars his ancestors planned their labours, and by the stars he will continue to do so, be he *jat*, Rajput or Mina. In the *nakshatra* corresponding to part of our October, he will sow his cold weather crops. In November you can see him cutting his *makki, til*, and the rest of his hot weather crops. In November too, comes the washing of the walls and doorsteps in preparation for the Diwali festival.

In December, the *jawar*, one of the staple crops of Rajputana, is cut. Up to the end of February, every man is busy harvesting, cleaning and selling. The women, children and old men in the meanwhile, look after the young wheat, barley and linseed which were planted early in the cold weather. In March when the festival of Holi is over, the cutting of these cold weather crops begins, and their harvesting, husking, storing and selling goes on until the end of May. The second half of April as well as May and June are allotted for building, cutting bamboos, rethatching and making earth bricks. In these months, when there is not much to do upon the land, the marriage ceremonies take place, and from every village comes the sound of drums and the high pitched voices of women singing.

The cold weather crops sown on soil that needs irrigation, have to be watered two to five times from November to the end of March. With the breaking of the rains, *jawar* is sown.

While their parents are busy in the fields and at the well, the children are not idle. From the age of five or six they make themselves useful. Their special work is the care of the flocks and herds. In the grey dawn the cows, goats and great black buffaloes leave the house of their owners and wander unguided to the meeting place outside the village, where they are herded by their youthful guardians and driven out into the jungle to graze.

Through the long hot hours the almost naked little boys, and the girls with swinging red skirts and bare pigtailed heads, laze in the shade of *babool* or *peepal* trees, or sprawl full length upon the broad back of some favourite buffalo. In the evening, a blue haze of dust marks the return of the herds (hence the Sanskrit name for the evening twilight, *go-dhuli* or cow's dust). A blue smoke in the tree-tops shows where the women, after working in the fields all day, are busy preparing the evening meal.

The lot of the peasant of Rajputana is not an easy one. In many parts rainfall is scarce. Wells have often to be dug to a depth of a hundred to two hundred and fifty feet before water level is reached. Wild animals too are common. Cultivation has to be protected by high barriers of thorn or mud walls, and constant watch has to be kept to frustrate the invasions of herds of wild pig, black buck and *sambhar*. In Rajputana there are more peacocks to the square mile than anywhere else in India, and half a dozen peacocks can, in as many hours, play havoc with a field of young wheat or gram.

There are compensations, however. The Indian of the peasant class, as everyone knows, loves a *tamasha*, and what finer *tamasha* could anyone see than the magnificent processions and festivals for which Rajputana is famous? At the time of the festival of Gangaur,

Ram Navmi, Teej and Dassehra in Jaipur and Kotah, peasants from distant villages journey for several days to come flocking into the city, the bright colours of their clothing adding to the brilliance of an already brilliant spectacle.

Life for the peasant is not all work. There are the evening gatherings round the fire or under the village *peepal* tree, listening to travelers' tales, or the reminiscences of the oldest inhabitant. There are the visits of the traveling monkey men, or the *bhat* who sings of Rajput chivalry in the days of Prithvi Raj, the last king of Ajmer, or Rana Pratap Singh of Mewar, who defied the Mughal armies after the fall of Chitor. Then, too, there are market days and the visit of the nearest town, when news and gossip as well as goods and money are exchanged. But best of all, there are the great annual camel and cattle fairs of Rajputana to which country-folk from far and near come flocking, every one dressed in his or her best; the Rajput peasant and his wife, when in holiday clothes, are truly a magnificent sight.

The Trading And Professional Castes

But the history of Jaipur is not the work of the Rajput caste only; other sections of the population have contributed, each in its own way, to the evolution of the State as we find it today, in its political or economic life. No picture of Jaipur would be complete unless we keep in view its trading and banking class, which is most famous and influential in India, though they overlap the boundary of the Kachhwa kingdom and have great branches in the neighbouring Rathor and Bhati States also.

It is a mistake to imagine that all the Hindu traders and bankers of Rajputana belong to the *bania* or *vaisya* caste. The class is professional and includes *brahmans* also; its members belong to the Hindu and Jain faiths alike. Some of these traders deserve special notice.

During the decline of the Mughal Empire, throughout the eighteenth century and for some decades later, Jaipur was the asylum of capitalists in North India. It was also the chief exchange house and distributing centre for the trade of the Punjab, Kashmir and Central Asia in one direction, and the merchandise of the Gangetic valley, Malwa and Gujarat on the other. Even today, the bankers whose original homes lie in Jaipur territory, though their business is scattered all over British India, are among the richest and most widely ramified banking houses of the Hindus. Jhunjhunu, Khandela, Singhana, Khetri and Kanud (now under Patiala) are cities of the Kachhwa State whose sons hold the foremost rank among the Hindu bankers and public benefactors. Their charitable institutions adorn many Indian cities, and in the service of man, no appeal to them goes unheeded.

The banking class, styled *mahajans*, are principally Jains, and the traders or *banias* are mainly Hindus; but there are exceptions to this division. The Oswal section of the Jains (originating in Rajputana) form the largest community among the merchants. The Khandelwal branch of the *banias* came from Khatu Khandela in Jaipur State, though their principal *gotra* is the Bajolia, in Nabha State. They are devotees of Bhagwandas Mahatma of Tikha, in Bawal *thana*.

The professional name *bohra*,[1] derived from the Sanskrit word *vyavahar* through the Prakrit form *beohar*, is borne not only by a Muslim sect (whose chief colony is in Ujjain), but also by a sub-caste of *brahman* moneylenders in Rajputana and the Punjab, who spread out from Marwar.

Other Castes And Sects

The ruling community of Jaipur is *kshatriya* by caste, but many of the hereditary official families—including ministers, financiers, diplomats, treasurers and secretaries—belong to the *bania* and *kayastha* castes, as one would expect among a primarily military and agricultural people. Some of these official families are descended from persons of these two castes, who accompanied the earliest emigration of the ruling chiefs to the Dhundhar country. Among the notable *bania* families engaged in administrative work are the Natanis, the Haldias, and the Kotharis, in Bharatpur. At the same time the *kayastha* Pancholis have supplied eminent and faithful envoys, court agents and reporters for many generations in the past. Examples of these two supposedly non-military castes supplying leaders of armies and governors of cities to the State are not unknown either.

Only one religious sect deserves special notice here; the Dadupanthis had their origin in this State, and their headquarters are still at Naraina[2] (on the Jaipur side of the Sambhar lake), where a monastery and a temple mark the residence of Dadu. The Naga troops of the Kachhwa *raj* (i.e., fighting monks) belong to this sect.

National Festivals

Diwali or the Festival of Lamps, which takes place on the *Kartik amavasya*, near about the end of October, is one of the most brilliant and popular festivals in India, especially in Rajputana,

> ... when every city, village and encampment exhibits a blaze of splendour. The potters' wheels revolve for weeks before solely in the manufacture of lamps (*diwas*), and from the palace to the peasant's hut, every one supplies himself with them, in proportion to his means, and arranges them (round his house) according to his fancy. Stuffs, pieces of gold, and sweetmeats are carried in trays and consecrated at the temple of Lakshmi, the goddess of wealth to whom this day is consecrated. The agricultural community place a corn-measure filled with grain and adorned with flowers, as the representative of this goddess. (Tod)

But the festival *par excellence* of the fighting castes throughout the country is the Dashahare (Dassehra) on the tenth new moon of the month of *Ashwin* (early October). All Hindus try to make a beginning of their most cherished work on this auspicious day. According to primeval Hindu tradition, on this day the god-king Ramchandra set out on his conquest of Lanka, and therefore we can easily imagine the supreme importance of Dassehra in the eyes of the princes of Mewar and Amber who claim direct descent from Rama. Its essence is the combination of worship and military display: all the arms, accoutrements and paraphernalia of royalty and the State forces are inspected, and divine blessing sought on them by the Maharaja as the supreme commander of the troops and the chieftain of the clan.

The old ceremony as observed in Udaipur more than a century ago, has been described fully by Col. Tod. A change was introduced in the details by Maharajah Sawai Madho Singh of Jaipur in 1913, when all the State forces were assembled together at the Fatah-Tiba or Mound of Victory outside the capital. There, after offering worship to the gods, the colours were taken down and re-hoisted, and a salute fired by the entire artillery. But this collective celebration was discontinued in 1924. Since then every unit of the army performs the Dassehra rites at its headquarters, conducting the *puja*, changing the colours and firing the salvo on the local scale. At Jaipur, His Highness the Maharajah rides at the head of the Sawai Man Guards to Amber, and offers adoration to the flag of this *corps d'elite* of his army before the Shila Mata, the goddess enshrined in that ancient capital in the days of the great Maharajah Man Singh I.

In the afternoon His Highness with his own hands performs *puja* to the arms and the throne in the Chandra Mahal Palace, while one vassal noble stands behind the throne holding in his hand the feather of a *huma* (a most auspicious bird)—which has been an heirloom of the Kachhwa dynasty for many centuries. Three other vassal nobles hold up the royal umbrella and the fly-whisks of the yak cow's tail (*chamar*). Afterwards a public durbar is held, usually in the pillared Hall of Public Audience (Diwan-i-Am). The Maharajah sits on a chair of gold and silver; dancing girls sing songs specially composed for the occasion; bards and *brahmans* chant their odes in glorification of the dynasty or to invoke Heaven's blessings on the ruling prince; the nobles, officers of State, and the leading merchants present *nazar* in gold or silver coins according to their status.

Then the Maharajah, as the head of his people, does *puja* to the paraphernalia of State, such as the chargers, palanquins, *takht-i-rawan* (throne carried on the shoulders of porters), carriages, *raths*, elephants and transport oxen.

Next at sunset comes the chief attraction for all and sundry. His Highness rides through his capital in procession and as he reaches the Jai-pol gate the auspicious bird *nilkanth* (blue throat) is let loose on his right hand. The procession goes on, via the Sireh Deorhi to the Vijai Bagh park on the Amber road. Here the Maharajah adores the *khejri* tree and presents one gold *mohar* and one coconut to the abbot (*mahant*) of Balanandiji's temple. The cortege now returns to the palace. Salutes of 80 guns are fired both at the beginning and at the conclusion of the procession, with the chariot of Sitaramji, the guardian deity of the dynasty, going before the Maharajah throughout.

The rejoicings conclude on the day after Dassehra with a military parade and a *fue de joie* (known by the Persian name *shallak*). In the evening H.H. Maharajah Madho Singh used to ride out to the 'Mound of Victory', review all his forces there and receive a salute of five discharges from each of his 42 cannons, and three volley-firings from the rifles of his infantry. But since 1932 the present Maharajah Sawai Man Singh II has been performing this ceremony in the Chaugan field behind the City Palace and below the Nahargarh Fort. He inspects all the forces on horseback in military uniform in his capacity of their Chief Commandant. The old practice of firing artillery salutes and rifle volleys is continued in a greatly improved manner, since the present troops are better organized and carefully trained. In 1939 this review was held at the Bhagwant Das Barracks,[3] the headquarters of the Sawai Man Guards.

Notes

1. Its more correct derivation is from *bahurin*, which in *apbhramsa* becomes *bahuria*, and in common parlance *bahura* or *bohra*. *Ed.*
2. Naraina, situated 26° 48′ N. and 75° 13′ E., is 41 m. west of Jaipur city and 43 m. north-east of Ajmer. *Ed.*
3. After Independence, when Jaipur State was merged to complete the formation of the present State of Rajasthan, Jaipur City became its capital, and then these Bhagwant Das Barracks were turned into the Secretariat of the Rajasthan Government. *Ed.*

III

The Early Kachhwa Kings

The Age Of Demi-Gods

The ruling dynasty of Jaipur State and most of its landed barons belong to the Kachhwa clan of the *kshatriya* or the fighting and the governing caste among the Hindus. They are included, along with the people of the States around them and many more families thinly spread throughout northern India, in the general ethnic division called Rajputs, meaning 'sons of kings', a name which philologists have traced back to the *rajanya* class of the Vedic age of India when the caste system was in the process of formation.

The Kachhwas claim descent from Kush, a son of the demi-god Rama whose life the epic *Ramayan* celebrates. The Maharanas of Mewar (Udaipur) and their clansmen the Sisodias, claim descent from Lava, the twin-brother of Kush. Both tribes are called *surya-vamshis* or 'the progeny of the sun' because in the epic, Rama's line stretches backward to that luminary of the sky, *Surya*, whom antique man regarded as the most powerful and visible form of the God-head. Similarly, sun-worship was an important part of the ancient Egyptian religion, and their kings claimed descent from that divinity, who bore there the cognate name of *Ra*.

The minstrels and family priests who stand for the College of Heralds among the Hindus, have supplied the house of Jaipur with a genealogical tree which fearlessly goes back even further than Rama, to the very Creator Brahma, the first member of the Hindu trinity.[1] In the sixty-third generation from the Creator was born the epic hero or god-man Rama, the husband of the tragic heroine Sita and the conqueror of the demon-king of Ceylon (Sri Lanka), who had abducted this Indian Helen and stood a siege as long as that of Troy. Every year at the *Dassehra* festival (in October), millions of Hindus all over Northern India and even in Maharashtra, act a miracle-play dealing with Rama's life and deeds, and many more millions listen to his story as immortalized by the Hindi poet Tulsidas, in a book which Sir George Grierson has rightly called the Bible of the Hindus.

The Romance Of Prince Dhola

A modern historian dare not trespass into the sacred precints of such mythic lore. Nor can he feel sure that he is treading on solid earth even for nearly a hundred generations after Rama, which are covered by kings of epics and heroes of ballads. It is only with Sodo-dev, who was ninety-fifth in descent from Rama, that the first gleams of history begin to break through the thick mist of poetic invention and oral tradition, and we get a little more reliable light on the fortunes of the Kachhwa rulers and the origin of their connection with the land they now hold.

But in this epic period, one scion of the House of Kachhwa has been immortalized in poetry. He is Dhola,[2] son of that Nala-rajah (the eponymous founder of Narwar city in Malwa), whose adventures form a well-known episode in the great epic, the *Mahabharat*. Dhola is the hero of a popular ballad in the Marwari tongue which celebrates the chequered love-life of this king and his beloved Maruni, a princess of the western desert of Rajputana. The story, with many variants in different local versions, beautifully paints the first dawning of love in the virgin heart, the maiden's dream of the Prince Beautiful destined to be her mate, the fantastic devices by which the high-born maiden in her palace tower soothes in secret her love-laden soul, the jealous watch of the wife against 'the other woman' who would steal her husband's heart, the sturdy villain's chase of the reluctant beauty, and a faithful wedded love that can triumph over death and bring the beloved back from the realm of Pluto. All this is poetry—sweet poetry no doubt—but it is not history, and the historian must regretfully pass on to things more prosaic but less unreliable.

The Story Of The Kachhwa Migration To Rajputana

The tradition runs that Dhola's great-grandson founded the fort of Gwalior in an expansion of the Narwar *raj*, and that Sodi-dev, who came thirty-one generations after Dhola, migrated from his ancestral home to Rajputana.[3] These migrations of tribes, so well-known to ethnologists as 'wanderings of the peoples', were really due to the growth of population in excess of the local food supply or the drying up of the soil.[4] But in Rajput tradition this natural cause has been buried under pretended commands of the stars, domestic feuds or political revolutions in the homeland. Among the many conflicting versions of the origins of the Kachhwa settlement in the land they now hold, written down from oral tradition only in the eighteenth century,[5] the following course of events seems to be the least improbable.

Sodo's father, Ishwar Singh, gave away his ancestral estate of Narwar to his younger brother and Gwalior to his sister's son, and retired to the life of a religious recluse in the Karauli territory northwest of the Chambal river, on the route from Malwa to Rajputana. On his death, his son Sodo crowned himself at Nadarabari,[6] but he seems to have been already aged, and continued as a *roi faineant,* while all the activities of his State were guided by the insatiable ambition, dauntless spirit, inborn leadership and organizing genius of his heir Dulha Rai, the real conqueror of Dhundhar. He was a youth of remarkable beauty and valour, for which he was called Dulha Rai or 'the Bridegroom Prince'. His fame attracted to his banners the voluntary support of all the spirited chiefs in that neighbourhood. Dulha married the daughter of Ralhan-si, the Chauhan rajah of Lalsot district, and received as his wife's dowry half the share of the fort of Dausa (and its adjacent district) which his father-in-law owned. The other half belonged to a Bar-Gujar family.

At this time the country south-east of the present city of Jaipur was parcelled out among five family groups of ruling Minas, known as the *Panch-wara* or Confederacy of Five, who prided themselves on being of the purest blood among their fellow castemen. But these people were not united into one political body. Each fort with the hamlets grouped round it for protection lived its isolated life and warred with its neighbours even when peopled by men of the same blood. A vague and ineffectual headship of the Mina caste was nominally acknowledged in the Mina lord of Amber hill. Here and there the Mina holdings were dotted with the forts of the Bar-Gujars, and as these Rajputs represented a somewhat higher order of civilization than did the aborigines, the Minas used to appeal when in distress, to the Bar-Gujar rajah of Deoti, as a suzerain.

The Kachhwa occupation of Dhundhar land, like all tribal migrations, could not have taken place in one lifetime nor been completed by one stroke, as the cock-and-bull story circulated by Tod asserts. And there were also temporary fluctuations in the fortunes of the conquerors. We can readily believe in the tradition which tells us that Dulha Rai, after his first success over the Minas, was defeated by them and left for dead on the field, and that he retrieved the disaster by the miraculous grace of goddess Jamwa Devi, as the simple medieval people believed. Lastly, the Kachhwa leader made a statesmanly compromise with the vanquished race by granting to such of the aboriginal chiefs as offered him allegiance and promised loyalty for the future, some landed estates, which have been held in hereditary succession ever since. Dulha also kept the rank and file of the Mina youths out of mischief, by employing them as watchmen and permanent servants of the State. Bearing these facts in mind, we can reconstruct the history of the Kachhwa settlement in Jaipur territory.

The Kachhwa Conquest Of Dhundhar

After securing half of Dausa fort by marriage, Dulha Rai, with the armed help of his wife's kinsmen and no small amount of guile, expelled the Bar-Gujars from their portion of Dausa, and that city became the first capital of the Kachhwas in Dhundhar land. The ousted Bar-Gujars appealed against the usurper to their tribal head, the 'proud and lofty' rajah of Deoti, but their army was defeated by Dulha.

The youthful victor next cast his eyes westwards, on Manchi, a Mina stronghold, 14 miles north-east of Jaipur city. His first campaign failed, with heavy losses, but he renewed the enterprise by attacking Manchi on a festive day when its Mina defenders were drinking themselves to fury and quarrelling with and killing one another. As a result the remnant of the garrison who made a sally against the Kachhwas were easily put to the sword. The goddess whose blessings alone had given him this crowning victory, was not forgotten. A temple to her on the Banganga river, at Jamwa, six miles from Manchi, stands today as the symbol of Dulha Rai's gratitude. Manchi was newly named Ramgarh, to represent the Kachhwa claim of descent from the epic hero Rama.

Dulha now turned to crush the greatest threat to his infant power; he stormed the Bar-Gujar fort of Deoti and became master of its accumulated treasure of ages. Next in succession came the conquests of two other Bar-Gujar forts,[7] each achieved after obstinate fighting and heavy loss on both sides, for the Rajputs were here matched against each other. We can truly say that the Kachhwas have purchased every inch of their present home with their life-blood. Khoh, five miles east of Jaipur city, was taken from its lord, a Mina named Chanda, and it became Dulha's capital after his father's death. Then Getor, two miles north-east of Sangner, formerly held by Geta Mina, was annexed, followed by Jhotwara, the stronghold of Jhota Mina, three miles west of the modern city of Jaipur. Thus the region round the future capital of Amber was well nigh cleared.

Kakil succeeded his father Dulha about 1070 A.D. He continued the expansionist policy of that great conqueror, and took Amber from Rao Bhatto, a Mina of the Susaot family; the villages held by Nandla Mina; and the *parganahs* of Med-Bairath which belonged to the *yadava* Rajputs. Kakil removed his capital to Amber and laid the foundations of its fortified walls, founded a new fort at Kakilgarh and built the temple of Ambikeshwar Mahadev at Amber. His short reign was troubled by frequent Mina revolts, but all of which were in the end, suppressed.

Raja Pajvan, The Right Hand Of Prithviraj Chauhan

With Pajvan, the great-grandson of Kakil, we come to the most celebrated hero among the Kachhwa kings before the Mughal age. He married a cousin of Prithviraj Chauhan, the renowned king of Ajmer and Delhi,[8] who fell while making the last stand against the Muslim invasion from Afghanistan in 1192. Pajvan[9] was his most devoted friend and constant companion, and he led many an expedition in his brother-in-law's cause.

The bard Chand Bardai, who was no retainer of the Kachhwa rajahs, has sung in his famous epic, *Prithvi-Raj Raso,*[10] how Pajvan was the bravest among the many brave warriors who had gathered around this last champion of Hindu independence, and how Prithviraj would invariably call upon Pajvan in his sorest need, and how Pajvan nobly responded to the call and saved his friend and sovereign on every occasion.

The Kachhwa prince defeated Bhimdev the Solanki king of Gujarat and Parmal the Chandela rajah of Bundelkhand (1182), and took Mahoba from the latter.[11] He was appointed commandant of the dangerous frontier posts of Nagor and Mahoba, and held them fast against enormous odds. The story runs that Pajvan was by the side of Prithviraj in the first battle of Tarain, where the invader from Afghanistan was defeated by the combined Rajput princes. He did not live to take part in the second and more disastrous battle at the same place, because he had fallen a year earlier, while guarding Prithviraj by fighting desperate rear-guard actions when pursued by the overwhelming forces of Jaychand during the Chauhan's gallant elopement with princess Sanyogita. In almost every one of the countless battles that filled Prithviraj's reign, some Kachhwa prince or the other poured out his life-blood. In Pajvan's last battle alone, three brothers and one son accompanied him to the heroes' Elysium.

The poet Chand bursts into lyric rapture when he describes the deeds of Pajvan: 'Prithviraj fought many big battles and he had many valiant warriors under him, but Pajvan was the bravest among them'. And again, 'As the wind sweeps through a garden uprooting trees, so did Pajvan move killing *Mirs* and forming heaps of the Slain. The enemy captains that he killed remained in the field, all others fled away'. Or, 'Pajvan moved about in the army of the Muslims like an intoxicated elephant uprooting and scattering with ease a dense tangle of lotus leaves'.

Such rhapsodies might move a modern reader to a smile, but they produced unspeakable enthusiasm among the gaping throng of rustics and blunt soldiers gathered round the market square or the baron's courtyard, where the minstrel used to sing his yarn. These ballads at least prove that the royal house of Jaipur was no mushroom growth of the Imperial Mughals' patronage. Its princes were recognized far beyond the limits of their territory as 'the bravest of the brave' among Rajput warriors centuries before Akbar ascended the throne of Delhi.

The Descendants Of Pajvan And Their Deeds

On the death of Pajvan (*c.* 1191 A.D.), his eldest son Malesi, with wounds received in his father's last fight not yet healed, ascended the throne. He raised his State to greater heights than ever before. The wholesale destruction of Rajput princes and nobles in the recent wars of Shahbuddin Ghori and Jaychand, left Malesi pre-eminent among the surviving Rajput royalty, as we can clearly see from his marrying six princesses of the highest families, Khichi, Devda (of Abu), Solanki, Bar-Gujar, and Chauhan.[13] Malesi had 32 sons. (The daughters do not come into the count.) His successors were nearly as prolific, and the whole country was dotted with the appanages of their offsprings, each bearing the distinctive name of the first princely founder of that branch, followed by the patronymic suffix *-ot* or *Pota*, exactly like the Scotch prefix *Mac* and the Irish *O'*.

Two of these offshoots of Udaikaran deserve to be remembered for the mark they have made on Jaipur history. Bar Singh (the second son of Udaikaran) received the appanage of Mojad (Mozamabad),[14] and founded the Naruka branch of the clan who now hold Alwar, Uniara, Lawa and some smaller estates. Baloji, the youngest brother of Bar Singh, held Barwara and was the progenitor of the very powerful Shekhawat branch of the Kachhwas. Baloji's eldest son Mokal was childless for a long time, but at last got a son through the blessings of a miracle-working Muslim saint, Shaikh

Burhan. The child was named Shaikhji after the saint, and the district that this prince afterwards conquered and colonized is known as Shekhawati. The saint's tomb stands six miles from Achrol.

As for the progeny of Pajvan, during the ten generations that lay between him and Babur, it is necessary to note only the forts and palaces, temples and tanks, that owe their origin to their rajahs and their queens. The Kachhwa capital seems to have been transferred from Manchi to Amber by Raj-dev (fourth in succession from Pajvan), who completed the fortifications of Amber. The next two kings, Kilhan and Kuntil, founded Kilhanpur and Kuntilgarh (in Amber), while Narsigh-dev (the great-grandson of Kuntil) built the temple of the god whose name he bore. Raj-dev made the Rajola tank and planted the village below the hill of Amber. Banvir made the Ban tank and Udharam laid out the Naulakha park in the same city. The Chauhani Rani of Chandrasen built the inner shrine of the Mahadev temple in Amber; and another wife of the same king built a temple in Mahar. This Chandrasen's daughter-in-law, Apurva-devi (popularly called Bala Bai[15] for her extreme devotion to the god Krishna) constructed the Laxmi Narayan temple in Amber.

An Illustration Of Lt. Col. Tod's Imaginative Writing

Tod's account of the Kachhwa conquest of the Minas is the classic howler in his *Annals of Rajasthan*, and illustrates alike his method of work and attitude towards the House of Jaipur. On the strength of a tradition which he admits is 'tinged with romance' but which he unhesitatingly accepts on the ground that it 'does not violate probability,' he tells us that after Sodo Singh's death, his infant son Dhola [*sic*]—who 'subsequently married the daughter of Ajmer, whose name was Maroni,'—on being robbed of his patrimony by his uncle, was conveyed by his widowed mother to Kho, where she became a menial servant in the kitchen of the Mina rajah, Ralunsi [*sic*]. This rajah later learnt of her history, adopted Dhola as his nephew, and sent him to Delhi with the tribute of Kho. Dhola, on his return after five years at that capital, treacherously massacred his unsuspecting benefactor's family en masse when they were performing the ablutions of Diwali, and thus made himself master of Kho.

Here Tod confounds Dulha with Dhola who lived *eleven centuries earlier*. He also supports the story that at the time of the Kachhwa conquest, which he admits took place five generations before Prithviraj Chauhan (i.e., about 1030 A.D.), 'the Tomar tribe were supreme lords of India', and that Delhi was the metropolis of a Hindu empire getting tributes from distant Rajputana, as under the Mughal Empire!

We can now understand why the best modern historians have nothing but condemnation for Tod's work. Major Raverty denounced his 'usual highly imaginative way of writing' (*T.N.*, 458 *n*), and Vincent Smith his 'inaccurate rhetoric' (*Akbar* 149 *n*).

Notes

1. These early genealogies up to Rama and a few of his descendants including Atithi are based on the lists and details given in the *Puranas*, and except for minor differences of names, they are the same relating to the Kachhawas, the Rathors and the Guhilots of Mewad and Dungarpur. *Ed*.
2. The famous folk tale of the romance of Dhola or 'Salha kumar' of Narwar and Maru was compiled in Jaisalmer by the Jain poet, Kushalabh, in about the middle of the 16th century A.D., entitled *Dhola-Maru ra Duha*. Its older manuscripts extant are dated 1651 and 1657 V.S. But the clan to which Dhola belonged is not mentioned anywhere. In one of its later recensions Dhola is mentioned as a Chauhan prince.

   Narwar first became associated with the Kachhawa House of Amber only in the reign of Akbar, when he gave Narwar in *jagir* to Raja Askaran Kachhawa, the dispossessed son of Raja Bhim and grandson of Raja Prithviraj of Amber.

   On the basis of their mistaken belief that the famous *Kachchhapaghat* rulers of Gwalior and Narwar belonged to the Kachhawa clan, their names have been mistakenly included in the genealogies of the Kachhawa clans 'no less than 21 generations or reigns anterior to Dulha Deva' according to Alexander Cunningham. Thus Dhola or 'Salha kumar' of Narwar was in the course of time taken to belong to the Kachhawa clan. *Ed*.

3. The year of this migration from Gwalior towards Rajasthan has generally been given in the Kachhawa *khyats* or genealogists' annals as 1023 V.S. (966 A.D.), the year when Sodh-Dev's father, Ishwar Singh, is said to have died. But all these dates and years have obviously been assigned only later when these genealogies were reduced to writing, and cannot possibly be deemed to be authentic unless supported by epigraphical or any other similar, trustworthy contemporary evidence. *Ed.*
4. This truth is clearly set forth in an old Anglo-Saxon poem describing the Saxon colonization of Britain, in which Hengist, the leader of the Teutonic immigrant band, tells the Celtic King of Kent:

   We are from Germany,
   The noblest of countries.
   There is in our place
   A strange custom:
   Every year a child comes into the family,
   As in the case of animals,
   Every fourth year lots are cast
   And he on whom the lots fall
   Must emigrate from the country. *J.S.*

5. This was, more probably, during the last quarter of the sixteenth century A.D., when Abul Fazl began collecting detailed information about the historical past from the grandees and dignitaries of the Mughal Empire for his own historical works. *Ed.*
6. In *Vamsa*. (P. Har. Mss. p.3.) This place is called Nidaravari. There is one Ninder (20° 19′ N, 77° 10′ E, three miles west of Mondrael and five miles north-west of Chambal in Karauli. Hence the correct name seems to be Nidaravari. *Ed.*
7. This is named in the Persian manuscript *Kafandar-ghati* (?) and *Jhotwari*, the latter being three miles west of Jaipur city. *J.S.*
8. On the testimony of Persian as well as other Indian sources, including the numismatic evidence of the Tomar coins of that period, it is now accepted that Prithviraj Chauhan III never ruled over Delhi, which continued to be under Tomar rulers till it was finally conquered on March 17, 1192 A.D., by Shahbuddin Ghori, the victor of the second Battle of Tarain (February, 29, 1192 A.D.) while returning from his conquest of Ajmer. See *Dilli ke Tomar* by Harihar Niwas Dwivedi, pp. 275-298 (1973). *Ed.*
9. There is no mention of Pajvan Kachhawa in any of the contemporary or early later sources relating to the reign or times of Prithviraj Chauhan III. All this account is based on unauthentic heresay which seem to have originated some time in the sixteenth century A.D., and thereafter included only in the later recensions of *Prithviraj-Raso*. In its oldest and shortest recension in the Dhar-

noj manuscript, copied out in 1610 A.D. from the original (transcripted possibly in the last decade of the sixteenth century at Bikaner), Palhan Dev is mentioned as the Kachhawa ruler. See *Prithviraj-Rasau*, ed. by Mataprasad Gupta, verse 20, p. 196. *Ed.*

10. This account of Pajvan is based on the last and largest recension of the *Prithviraj-Raso*, prepared in Udaipur about 1665 A.D., and published by the Kashi Nagari Pracharni Sabha (1887-1913 A.D.). The text of the manuscript was finalised and copied at Udaipur on Monday, January 17, 1704 A.D. See Raghubir Sinh's *Samaharanatmak Prastavana*, pp. i-xxxviii, in *Prithviraj-Raso; Itihas aur Kavya*, by Rajmal Bora (1974). *Ed.*
11. There is sufficient reliable evidence about Prithviraj III being involved in Chauhan-Chandel and Chauhan-Chaulukya wars after 1180 A.D., but there is no mention at all about Pajvan having taken any such prominent part there. See *Early Chauhan Dynasties*, by Dashrath Sharma (1959), pp. 75-77; *Chaulukyas of Gujarat*, by Ashok Kumar Majumdar (1956), pp. 140-141, 458. *Ed.*
12. The English poet who wrote the ancient ballad *Chevy Chase* does not shrink from this quaint conceit:

    For Witherington must I wail,
    As one in doleful dumps,
    For, when his legs were smitten off,
    He fought upon his stumps.

    The Rajput bard, who wrote *Prithviraj-Raso* in the opposite hemisphere but in the same age, goes one better and sings of how even after the head of Balbhadra (Pajvan's son) had been cut off, his two hands continued to play their swords and kill enemies 'for full two gharis' and only then did his trunk fall down! Chand Bardai's dates, too, are extremely shaky. *Ed.*
13. The Kachhawa *khyats* have greatly exaggerated the regional importance of Malesi. He married the daughters of Anil Khichi of Gagron and of Deva or Patal, after whom his descendants were called the 'Devdas', and who were then merely struggling to gain a footing in their respective regions. *Ed.*
14. Mojad (Mozamabad)—35 m. south-west of Jaipur. *Ed.*
15. She was the daughter of Rao Lunkaran (1505-1526), of Bikaner. *Ed.*

IV

How Akbar Won The Kachhwas Over

Kachhwa Rajahs Before Akbar's Time

With the coming of the Mughal Emperors and their highly civilized court in the middle of the sixteenth century, Rajput history emerges from the delusive mists of oral tradition and bardic exaggeration, into the clear light of authentic contemporary record. The holiest Muslim shrine of Hindustan had been erected at Ajmer in 1236,[1] and since then the new lords of Delhi had felt bound to keep the pilgrim route to it open. That route lay through the territory of Jaipur, and butted the dominions of Marwar on their eastern side. Hence the eternal friction between the Muslim rulers of Delhi and the rajahs of Marwar, which ended only with the complete imposition of Akbar's suzerainty over Rajputana. Hence, too, the precarious position of the lords of Amber, whom inexorable geography had placed between the upper grindstone of Delhi and the nether grindstone of Jodhpur.

Prithvi Raj Kachhwa (the son of Chandrasen) sat on the throne of Amber from 17th January 1503 to 4th November 1527. Maharana Kumbha of Mewar, in the course of his campaigns for establishing hegemony over Rajputana, swept the Kachhwa territory and probably exacted tribute from Amber. This is the most likely meaning of the epithet 'Trampler of Amber hill' (*Amrad-adri-dalana*)[2] given to him in a Sanskrit eulogy. Prithvi Raj, along with other Rajput princes, had fought Babur, under the banner of Rana Sanga, on the fatal field of Khanua (17th March, 1527),[3] when for the first time gunpowder triumphed over Rajput chivalry. He survived the disaster for barely six months, dying on the 4th of the following November.[4]

Prithvi Raj was a great devotee of Krishna, and his spiritual guide was an ascetic who had taken the name of 'the slave of Krishna' (*Krishna-das*). This guru lived on milk alone, and was called *pai-hari*. He bestowed on the rajah two sacred idols, Narasimhaji (whose temple is still in Amber) and Sitaramji (who was later removed to a new temple in Jaipur.) The image of the latter is carried at the head of the Jaipur army at the time of battle. This rajah made a pilgrimage to Dwarka in Kathiawar, where he was initiated into the monastery as a monk (*bhagat*).

He had nine wives from different clans, by whom he had eighteen sons and three daughters. Twelve of these sons reached man's estate. To nine of these and to their successors in perpetuity he assigned appanages. They are styled along with the fiefs of three descendants of collateral lines, the *bara kotri* or 'twelve chambers' of the Kachhwa house,[5] who form the highest aristocracy of Jaipur. Their names are:

1. Puran-mal (son of his Tonwar queen),
   seat: Nimera,
   name of sub-clan: Puranmal-ot
2. Sanga (son of his Rathor queen),
   founded Sanganer, which lapsed to the parent State on his death without issue.
3. Pachayan (son of the Rathor queen),
   seat: Samriya,
   name: Pachayan-ot.
4. Gopal (same mother as No. 3),
   seats: Chomu and Samod,
   name: Natha-ot.
5. Balbhadra (same mother),
   seat: Achrol,
   name: Balbhadr-ot.
6. Surtan (same mother),
   seat: Surothe,
   name: Surtan-ot.
7. Jagmal (same mother),
   seat: Diggi,

name: Khangar-ot.

8. Chaturbhuj (same mother),
seat: Bagru,
name: Chaturbhuj-ot.
9. Kalyandas (son of Sisodia[6] queen),
seat: Kalwar,
name: Kalyan-ot.

The other three were:

10. Kumbha (son of Junsi, who had come to the throne in 1317),
seat: Bans Khoh,
name: Kumbhani.
11. Sheobrahma (son of Udaikarn, who had come to the throne in 1367),
seat: Nidar,
name: Sheobrahma-pota.
12. Naro (son of Banvir, who had come to the throne in 1429),
seat: Watka,
name: Banvir-pota.

Prithviraj was succeeded by his son Puranmal, who ruled from 5th November, 1527 to 19th January, 1534. This rajah fell in battle on the side of Humayun's brother Hindal.[7]

After him came his step-brother Bhim (the eldest son of Prithviraj's Rathor queen), who reigned for three years and a half (dying on 22nd July, 1537), and was succeeded by his eldest son Ratan Singh. The new rajah, '...from the turbulence of youth and bad company, insulted men. Some instigated Askaran his step-brother to attack his life in the hopes of the chiefship, and with the help of wicked men the idea became fact'. Ratan Singh was killed on 15th May, 1548, and Askaran was crowned the next day, but enjoyed power for sixteen days only, after which the nobles joined to depose him. Bihar Mal, the fourth son of Prithviraj and his Rathor queen Apurva Devi or Bala Bai, was crowned on the first of June, 1548. Later, Askaran rose high in Akbar's service and was given the vacant succession to Narwar,[8] where another branch of the parent Kachhwa had so long been in possession.[9] (*Ak.*, iii, 925-926).

Rajah Bihar Mal: The Problems Facing Him At The Beginning Of His Reign

With the accession of Bihar Mal, a completely new chapter opens in the history of Jaipur as well as all of Rajputana. He was an old man by this time, verging on fifty. He had already passed through stirring times, and was to see and assist a total revolution in India's destiny before he closed his eyes on 27th January 1574. The Chaghtai Turk had founded an empire in Delhi in 1526. That empire was subverted by an Indian-born pathan and the Turks were kept out of India for sixteen years. During this interval, the armed power of Delhi had impinged upon Rajputana more thoroughly than ever before, except under Ala-ud-din Khilji two centuries and a half earlier. Sher Shah invaded Maldeo's country and fought him for some time, making Ajmer his base. The death of Rana Sanga, shortly after Khanua, was followed by a succession of minor or weak kings in Mewar. In Amber too, there were disputes for the throne and short reigns. The new Mughal lord of Delhi was entangled with the Pathan upstart. Seizing this eclipse of his possible enemies, the ruler of Marwar suddenly sprang to the first place in Rajasthan and made himself 'the greatest of the rulers of Hind' (*Tabaqat*, ii, 104). He extended his sway on both the right and the left, and seized the lands of friends and foes alike. As Maldeo, this Rathor conqueror, had taken four districts of the Amber Kingdom, the Kachhwa rajah had necessarily to side with the pathan.

After the death of Sher Shah, his son Islam Shah ruled for eight years, during which Bihar Mal became rajah and joined the Sur king's governor at Ajmer. After Islam Shah's death (1554) his empire broke up and Humayun returned to Delhi. On the death of Humayun (24 January, 1556), Akbar, a boy of thirteen, inherited the very much shrunken and unsettled dominions of Delhi. In the confusion now raging on all sides, the old servants of Sher Shah's dynasty began to seize territories for themselves from the local agents of the Mughal sovereign. One of these, named Haji Khan (a former slave of Sher Shah), besieged Narnol and drove its Turkish commandant Majnun Khan Qaqshal to hard straits. Bihar Mal, then in the train of Haji Khan, interposed his good offices, secured the peaceful surrender of the fort on condition of life and liberty to the garrison, and helped Majnun Khan to reach Akbar's Court at Delhi in safety.

In the meanwhile, the Mughal empire in India had been placed beyond challenge by the victory at the second battle of Panipat, on 5th November, 1556. Soon afterwards, Akbar came to Delhi. There Majnun Khan told the young Emperor of the excellent loyalty which Bihar Mal had displayed at the siege of Narnol. Akbar accordingly sent for the rajah. Bihar Mal came to the court at Delhi and was rewarded.

> One day after robes of honour had been presented to the rajah and to his sons and other relatives and they had been brought to the Court to receive their *congee* (farewell), His Majesty was mounted on a mast elephant which in its intoxication was rushing in every direction. People were all going to a distance. Once it ran towards these Rajputs, but as they were fast in their loyalty they remained standing firmly. The steadiness displayed by them pleased the lofty glance of His Majesty and he made inquiries about the Rajah and told him 'We will cherish you'.

They were then sent back to their homes. (*Ak.*, ii, 69-70).

This happened in December, 1556, and the promise then made was to be fulfilled six years later. These six years were a period of great distress and anxiety to the Kachhwa rajah. Suja, the son of the former king Puranmal, had been denied the throne because he was a mere child at the time of his father's death in 1534 and the succession had gone to his Uncle Bhim Singh as the *heir per capita*. The dispossessed Suja had taken shelter with his mother's family, the Rathors. He now came to the court of Mirza Muhammad Sharfuddin Husain, Akbar's governor of Mewat, and bought his support for winning the Kachhwa chieftainship for himself. The Mirza led a large army to Amber, which Bihar Mal was in no position to resist. He came to terms, promised a fixed tribute to the Mirza and handed over his own son Jagannath[10] and his nephews Raj Singh[11] and Khangar Singh[12] as hostages for its due payment.

Bihar Mal Seeks Akbar's Protection

But Mirza Sharfuddin Husain was not really satisfied. He made preparations, with a larger force, for renewing the invasion next year

(1562) and 'extirpating the family of Bihar Mal and annexing Amber'. (*Ak.*, ii, 241) In this state of extreme peril from both domestic and foreign foes, Bihar Mal made Chaghtai Khan his intercessor with Akbar, who had now arrived at the town of Kirauli on his way from Agra to Ajmer. The Khan pleaded with his master:

> The Rajah is eminent in wisdom and valour and has always been loyal to the Imperial family and rendered excellent service. At Delhi he was granted audience. For a long time he has been in fear on account of Sharfuddin Husain's bad treatment of him, and has taken refuge in the hills. If a ray of the royal grace fell on him and he was raised from the dust, he could probably render services that would be pleasing to your Majesty.

Akbar agreed, summoned Bihar Mal to Court. On the way to Ajmer, Bihar Mal's brother Rupsi,[13] the baron of Daosa, and his son Jaimal,[14] waited on the Emperor at Daosa, and so did Bihar Mal himself at Sanganer (about 20th January, 1562). Chaghtai Khan introduced Rajah Bihar Mal together with many of his relations and the leading men of his clan to the Emperor.

> His Majesty with his discerning glance read devotion and sincerity in the behaviour of the rajah and his relatives. He captivated his heart by kindness and exalted his rank. The Rajah, in order to bring himself out of the rank of (mere) landholders and to make himself one of the grandees of the Court, proposed to give his eldest daughter in marriage to the Emperor.

Akbar consented, and from his camp at Sanganer, sent Bihar Mal with Chaghtai Khan to make the necessary arrangements and quickly bring the bride.

On the return journey from Ajmer, when they reached Sambhar, Mirza Sharfuddin Husain surrendered his hostages—Jagannath, Raj Singh and Khangar Kachhwa. Here Bihar Mal brought his daughter and she was married to Akbar (circa 6th February) amidst proper festivity. At Ratanpura (8 miles east of Jaipur), Akbar's newly made kinsmen again came to his camp to take formal leave of him (10th February). Here Man Singh, the son of Bihar Mal's eldest son Bhagwant Das, was presented to the Emperor. His transcendent genius was instinctively perceived by the sagacious Akbar, and he was forthwith enrolled in the permanent service of the empire. While Bihar Mal was loaded with gifts and favours and given leave to return to his capital, Bhagwant Das, Man Singh and a number of their relatives and officers were attached to the Emperor's train and accompanied him to Agra. (*Ak.*, ii, 240-244)

Akbar's Rajput Marriage Policy Critically Studied

The giving of Hindu princesses in marriage to Muslim kings had been known long before[15] the union of Akbar and Bihar Mal's daughter. As early as 1176, we read of the queen of the Rajah of Uchh (a town now in Bahawalpur State)[16] having affianced her daughter to Shihabuddin Ghori. In more recent times a Bhati Rajput princess, Naila (the daughter of Rana Mal of Dipalpur), had been married to Salar Rajab. She later became the mother of Firuz Shah the Tughluq Sultan of Delhi. More instances may be found in the lives of the Muslim kings of the Deccan.

But Akbar's mingling of blood with the Hindu ruling houses, of which this marriage at Sambhar was the beginning, stands on a different footing altogether from all previous instances of such unions. It introduced in its effect a complete revolution in the policy of the Muslim monarchy in India. In the earlier Hindu-Muslim marriages the bride was thenceforth lost to her father's family as fully as if she had been kidnapped or killed. Her Hindu kinsfolk ceased to have any further communication with her or her husband. But Akbar's policy was to make such unions the starting point of a new order of relations in which his Hindu kinsfolk by affinity would stand on an equal footing with his Muslim father-in-law and brothers-in-law. They would hold their heads as high in his Court, differing only in that they could not dine with him, pray with him, or reciprocate by taking Muslim girls as their lawful wives.[17] Thus the giving of a daughter in marriage to Mughal royalty, ceased to be a mark of degradation for the Hindu father within the Court circle and the polished Hindu society of that age, although orthodox Hindus still looked down upon it as a humiliation. For these Hindus still clung to the primitive tribal theory of hypergamy, or the ideal of marrying one's daughter to a man of higher social status or bluer blood than oneself, with the effect that the mere fact of being the father-in-law necessarily implied an inferiority of rank in comparison with the son-in-law. (See Prof. Rivers on hypergamy in *J.B. & O.R.S.*, 1924.)

Under Akbar's enlightened rule, the political effect of these marriages was immeasurably great. True, the Rajput ladies who entered the Delhi royal harem became Muslims and were buried in Muslim cemeteries; they could no longer visit their parents' houses or dine with them. But, after all, blood is thicker than water, and the Hindu point of view in every question—that is the weal and woe of the immense majority of the subject population—could not henceforth go by default in the councils of the Mughal sovereigns. Hindu ability was made available for the highest service of the State under a policy which granted religious toleration to all[18] and threw careers open to talent irrespective of creed. This policy immensely multiplied the strength and man-power of the Indian empire. As Hindu and Muslim nobles met on terms of equality in the Imperial court and camp, an exchange of thought and a blending of the two cultures took place very rapidly, which supplied the moral basis of a common Indian nationality. Akbar could trust the Rajputs because he held their dearest hostages in perpetuity. They too could trust him fully for the same reason and they stood round his sons and grandsons because the newer generation of princes represented the mingling of their blood with his.

How Akbar Won Rajput Devotion

The thoughtful mind of Akbar had been impressed very early by the valour, truthfulness and devotion of the Rajputs. In them he could find the one sound prop of an empire, when threatened by the rebellion of the half-subdued Afghans in the east, the treachery of his Uzbak and other Muslim generals, the selfish greed of his brother in the west and the deadly hostility of the Mirzas who shared his Timurid blood. Here was a race which could supply him with personal guards and a royal war-band whose courage and fidelity were proof against every temptation, who would never be his rivals like the men of his own race and creed. The Rajputs would prove the one steadfast star of hope and strength in the clouded political firmament of the new-born empire, if only he could win their hearts.

He won their hearts, and how we shall soon see. But his Rajput policy not only won for him the loyal devotion of the Hindu fighting castes. The house of Kachhwa also supplied him with something infinitely more rare and precious: the cool penetrating brain-power, the unfailing political insight, the great administrative skill and the inborn power of leadership of a Man Singh, a Mirza Raja Jai Singh and a Sawai Jay Singh.

Rajputana had already begun to see that in Akbar, India had got an altogether new type of sovereign. During the course of this very journey of Akbar (though it was avowedly a pilgrimage and he was lightly escorted), his cavalcade reached Daosa to find that so great was the terror left behind by the earlier Muslim rulers that most of the inhabitants were found to have fled away in fear. In the evening the local headman's son[19] paid a visit as a preliminary survey, and when he reported that the new sovereign was not a tiger, Rupsi and other notables came to see Akbar. But the royal entourage had still to be broken of their old predatory habits and that was soon done. A day later, an Imperial *chita*-keeper was found to have robbed a villager of his shoes. 'By Akbar's orders his feet were cut off. It became known in the country and afterwards no one thought of running away.' (*Ak.*, ii, 242.) One such draconian sentence had the desired effect.

More humanitarian edicts were soon to be issued and enforced by the young master of India's destiny. The historian of the reign writes,

> Muslim troops who came into India used to make prisoners of the wives and children and other relatives of the people of India, and used to enjoy them or sell them. But Akbar in his 7th regnal year (1562-63) forbade this enslavement of the captives of war. (*Ak.*, ii, 248)

In 1563, he remitted the tax on Hindu pilgrims throughout his dominions, though it used to yield many lakhs of rupees every year. Next year the humiliating poll-tax on the Hindus (*jaziya*) was abolished.

This liberal policy, far ahead of his time, whether we cast our eyes on contemporary Europe or Asia, was initiated by a youth not yet twenty, out of his inborn humanity and originality of thought, without the prompting of any minister or preceptor. We can now understand that it was not oriental flattery but the remembrance of the state of their country since the second battle of Tarain that made the Hindu world of the time hail Akbar as a god, *Dillishware va Jagdishware va*.

The Kachhwa Rajputs whom Akbar had thus drawn to his bosom, soon justified his choice. They supplied the bravest and most devoted 'war-band' for his personal defence in every battle. A year had not passed since the momentous marriage at Sambhar, when Akbar owed his life to Rajput loyalty. The Emperor made a forced march from Agra with a small force to attack the village of Paronkh (in the Mainpuri district), which was held by 4000 rebels and plunderers. He charged recklessly at the head of 200 men only, and a hot engagement followed. The front side of the village was unassailable, and 'a number of imperialists took shelter under the trees and looked out for a safe corner'. In anger, Akbar went alone to the back of the village, with no other attendant except Bhagwan Das and Rajah Bidi Chand (of Nagarkot).[20] As he drove his elephant against a house held by the rebels, his elephant's forefoot went into a grainpit and the bump threw the servant in the rear seat upon His Majesty's back. But Akbar extricated the elephant from the hole and continued his attack. When he suffered from thirst, Bhagwant Das served him with water from his own flask. Then he broke down the wall and entered the rebel stronghold. (*Ak.*, ii, 251-254.) The same unfailing Kachhwa support in his sorest need was given to him in the Battle of Sarnal during the Gujarat campaign of 1572.

Rajputana Before Akbar: Disunion, Internecine Wars And Constant Disorder

In studying Akbar's Rajput wars, we cannot forget two leading facts. First, that the encroachments and raids by Mewar and Marwar, two of the important states in Rajputana, under their recent expansionist policy, had driven other Rajput chiefs to Akbar's side for self-protection. Second, that Mughal communication with Gujarat and the west coast, and the defence of the western border of Malwa, could not be assured while any potentially hostile chief was left in Rajputana. Akbar was determined to annex Gujarat and reach the famous ports on its coast, so vitally important for his empire's foreign trade and intercourse with Persia and the holy cities of Islam.

The eclipse of Mewar following the defeat of Rana Sanga by

Babur (1527), was the opportunity for Marwar, whose enterprising and unscrupulous ruler Maldeo had through a long reign (1532-1562) made himself, from the lord of two barron districts (*parganas*) 'the greatest of the Rajahs of Hind', with an enormously expanded territory, and crushed all of his refractory usurping vassals. Maldeo had not been friendly to the fleeing Humayun in 1541. Twenty years later, when Humayun's son had firmly planted himself on the throne of Delhi, Maldeo had prematurely aged and grown into a sluggard. His death (on 7th November, 1562) let loose a fratricidal contest for his throne. His third son[21] Chandrasen crowned himself and held the capital. The eldest son, Ram Rao, naturally joined the Mughals to win his patrimony, while another son, Udai Singh, set up for himself and began to raid many parts of the country.

The Marwar balloon which had been so enormously inflated in the course of one lifetime, was soon pricked, and it collapsed in the dust. Merta, known as the Gateway of Marwar, fell to Mughal arms early in 1562, and the capital itself next year, its new rajah having vacated it. This Chandrasen lived as a wandering fugitive and troubled Akbar's local officers for a long time. But he was hunted out of one place after another, and died in January, 1581. His brothers Ram Rao and Udai Singh remained in Mughal service. After its conquest in 1563, Jodhpur was kept under Imperial control. In 1571, it was placed in charge of the chief[22] of Bikaner, to be held on behalf of the Emperor. From 1581 to 1583,[23] this State was made a crownland directly administered by Imperial officers. It was only in August, 1583, that its own prince Udai Singh (*Mota Rajah*) was given the long-vacant throne with the title of Rajah by his Imperial suzerain. He had to pay the usual price for it: his daughter Mira Bai[24] was married to Prince Salim in June, 1586.

Notes

1. Khwaja Muinuddin Chishti died at Ajmer in March, 1236 A.D., and his remains were interred in the cell in which he lived. Sultan Ghiyasuddin Khilji, son of Sultan Mahmud Khilji of Mandu, gave large donations to Khwaja Makhdum Hussain. Hussain was a descendant of Shaikh Hamidudin of Nagor, the chief disciple of Khwaja Muinuddin Chishti. The donation was spent in building a brick mausoleum on Khwaja's tomb at Ajmer. But the building of the mausoleum was not completed till 1537 A.D. (See *Ajmer*, by Har Bilas Sarda, 1941, pp. 86, 88, 90).
   Akbar was the first Mughal Emperor to visit the shrine. He visited it first in January, 1562, and after the conquest of Chitor, he proceeded to the shrine in Ajmer on foot (February-March, 1567). (*Ak*., ii, pp. 240-243, 476-477, 510-511). *Ed.*
2. Ojha, *Ud*., i, 247. *J.S.*
3. The correct date of the Battle of Khanua is Saturday, March 16, 1527, or Jamadi-us-Sani 13, 933 A.H. Bevridge failed to take note of the specifically mentioned day of the week on which the battle was fought. (*Babur Nama* in English, II, p. 558). *Ed.*
4. Thursday, Kartik Sudi 14, 1584 or Safar 12, 934 A.H. The correct date and place of Rana Sanga's death have been the subject of great controversy. According to *Vir Vinod* (I, pp. 366-367), Rana Sanga died at Baswa (8 m. north of Bandikui Rly. Station and 23 m. north-west of Dausa). There is a *chauntra* at Baswa, which is said to been built on the cremation place of Rana Sanga. *J.S.*
5. Though usually described as such, their number as well as their lists have varied from time to time. *Ed.*
6. This Sisodia Queen was the daughter of Maharana Raimal of Chitor. (*Vamsavali*, p. 13.) *Ed.*
7. Evidently against Tatar Khan, at Mandrail, which is 20 miles south-east of the capital of the Karauli State. (*Ak*., i, 299) *J.S.*
8. This statement is based on the then accepted (but in fact mistaken) assumption that the Kachhapghat rulers of Narwar, Gwalior and Dubkund (tenth and eleventh centuries A.D.) were in fact the predecessors of the Kachhawa clan of Amber, particularly because the names of all these Kachhapghat rulers had been duly included in the genealogies of the Kachhawa House of Amber-Jaipur. *Ed.*
9. This is the authentic contemporary history as recorded by Akbar's official historian Abul Fazl from the best sources of information. But on the strength of an anonymous and undated work which

he admits to be obscure. Tod asserts, 'it would appear that Askaran, the son of Bhim, was instigated by his brethren to put their father to death and to expatiate the crime by a pilgrimage.' But as Askaran went on pilgrimage *eleven years after* his alleged act of parricide, the casual connection between the two is incredible, and so the story of the unnatural crime loses its credibility. In the same credulous strain, the tradition asserts that Prithviraj was murdered by his son Bhim, though it is an admitted fact that Bhim did not ascend the throne after his father's death. The throne went instead to his step-brother. *Qui bone? J.S.*

10. Jagannath was the younger son of Raja Bihar Mal from his Solanki wife, Champavati, daughter of Rao Ganga. *Ed.*
11. Raj Singh was the son of Askaran, the deposed Raja of Amber (*Ak*., ii, p. 241). *Ed.*
12. Khangar was the son of Jagmal and the grandson of Raja Prithviraj of Amber. *Ed.*
13. Rupsi was the younger son of Raja Prithviraj from his Gaud queen, Sohag Devi, daughter of Gyan Rao Gaud. He is generally referred to as 'Rupsi *Bairgi*'. He was granted the Porbatsar pargana as *jagir*. Nainsi gives a list of his sons and grandsons, but ultimately his line became extinct. (Nainsi, *Khyat*, RPP, I, pp. 312-313; *M.U.*, E.T., II, pp. 617-619). *Ed.*
14. Jaimal was granted Fatehpur pargana in *jagir*. *Ed.*
15. Shihabuddin, in *Firishta* (Lucknow ed.), i, 56. Rajah in *Afif*, 37. *J.S.*
16. Now a part of Pakistan. *Ed.*
17. They could however, and did, drink with him and join his Su i seances, when so inclined. *J.S.*
18. Abul Fazl repeatedly describes Akbar's policy to the same effect: e.g., 'It is my duty to be in good understanding with all men...'. 'My mind is not at ease in this diversity of sects and creeds.' 'A king's gratitude to his Lord should be shown in just government and due recognition of merit.' (Sayings of Akbar, in *Ain*, iii.) See the account of *sulh-i-kul* in *Ak*., iii, 398-400. *J.S.*
19. Rupsi Bairagi Kachhawa was the head-man of the district Daosa. His eldest son, Jaimal, first visited Akbar. (*Ak*., ii, p. 241). *Ed.*
20. Raja Bidhi Chand was the son of Raja Jai Chand of Nagarkot (Kangra). In view of the fact that Bidhi Chand was thus on active service in 1562, the remark in *tabqat* (E.T. II, p. 399) of his being 'of tender year' in 1572 A.D., when he rebelled at Nagarkot after his father's arrest at the Imperial Court, seems incorrect. (*History of the Panjab Hill States*, by J. Hutchison and J. Ph. Vogel, I, 1933, pp. 140, 154)

    Nagarkot or Kot Kangra, now known as Kangra town, is situated in 30° 3′N. and 76° 16′E. *Ed.*

21. According to Bishweshwar Nath, Chandrasen was the sixth son of Rao Maldeo. (*Marwar ka Itihas*, I, pp. 144, 148). *Ed.*
22. Rai Singh (1574-1612 A.D.) of Bikaner. *Ed.*
23. Rai Singh was sent to Jodhpur c. Nov. 1, 1572 (*Ak.*, iii, p. 8). According to *Dayaldas ri Khyat* (II, ed. by Dashrath Sharma, 1948, p. 118). Rai Singh was in Jodhpur for a year only. Persian sources do not indicate the year when Rai Singh was relieved of the control over Jodhpur. *Ed.*
24. The correct name given in *Jodhpur ki Khyat* (Ms., I, p. 103) is 'Mani Bai, her second name being Jodh Bai'. *Ed.*

V

Akbar's Wars Against The Maharana Of Mewar

Causes Of Hostility

Thus, after 1563, Mewar remained the only large independent State in Rajputana, while all the other States were ruled by smaller princes, already vassals of the Delhi throne. Akbar found in the Maharana the only obstacle still standing in the path of the unity and peace of his empire, or, in the pompous rhetoric of the conventional 'dignified' style of Persian historical prose, 'to overthrow the neck-stretching rebel is to establish one-ness, which is the choicest worship in the fore-court of plurality, and to make current the coin of peace and tranquillity' (*Ak.*, ii, 441). Already Sakta Singh, the son of Udai Singh, the reigning Maharana, had joined the Mughal camp like so many other Rajput princely adventurers in the hope of some chance of military service which would enable him to win a new principality as his reward, but he had been waiting in vain.

Early in 1567, Akbar, then at Dholpur, asked Sakta what service he would render in his intended campaign against Udai Singh, who alone among the princes of India, had refused to pay his respects to the Imperial throne. The Mewar prince very diplomatically gave promises of help, but soon escaped to his own country. In the following September, the Emperor launched his attack. After taking smaller places he sat down before Chitor on 20th October[1] (1567) and sent detachments to devastate the enemy's country. Udai Singh had deserted the historic capital of his house, and with the fall of its gallant defender (Jaimal Rathor, ex-governor of Merta), Chitor fell, on Tuesday, 24th February, 1568. Ranthambhor (under Surjan Hada) capitulated a year later on 22nd March, 1569. [*Ak.*, ii, 442, 464-476 (Chitor); 484-496 (Ranthambhor)]

At Ajmer,[2] towards the close of 1570, the Emperor received the homage of the chiefs of Bikaner, Jesalmer and Jodhpur. In October, 1572, he began his invasion of Gujarat. The soft Maharana Udai Singh had died in the preceding February, and his legacy of Mewar and defiance of Mughal suzerainty had descended to his son Pratap Singh, the noblest prince of a noble race. But the new chieftain was merely on the defensive, his ancestral capital was in the enemy's hands, Udaipur had been sacked[3] and the fertile eastern part of his territory occupied by the Imperialists, thus greatly reducing his resources. In June of the next year (1573), Man Singh paid a visit to Mewar by order of the Emperor, on his way back from Gujarat after conquering Dungarpur.

> The Rana came out to welcome him and the other officers (of that army), and received him with respect and put on the royal *khilat* (sent for him). He brought Man Singh to his house as his guest, but... proceeded to make excuses (about going to Court), alleging that his well-wishers would not suffer him to go. He made promises about going to the sublime Court (later)... and gave Man Singh leave to depart, while he himself stayed and procrastinated (*Ak.*, iii, 57).

But months passed and still the Maharana kept aloof from the Imperial Presence. So in October of the same year, Bhagwant Das, on his way back from Gujarat, passed through Gogunda, which was now the Maharana's residence. Here Pratap came out and visited him, expressing regret for his past conduct and prolonged failure to go to the Imperial Court.

> He also took him (Bhagwant Das) to his house and treated him with respect and hospitality. He sent along with him his son and heir Umra (i.e. Amar Singh), and represented that... he now presented his petition (to Akbar) through Rajah and was sending his son as a mark of obedience. When his desolate heart should become soothed by the lapse of time, he (i.e., Pratap) too would come and do homage in person.

Bhagwant Das arrived at the Court at Agra, about the first of November, 1573, and presented Amar Singh to the Emperor.[4] Shortly after this, Rajah Todar Mal, also on his way back from Gujarat, was visited by the Maharana, who spoke to him gently and professed submissiveness. (*Ak.*, iii, 92–93) The young Amar Singh was soon afterwards sent back to his father.

Years passed and the Maharana did not keep his promise of coming to the Imperial Court. At last on Monday, 2nd April, 1576, Akbar sent Man Singh from Ajmer in command of a strong force with detailed instructions for bringing Pratap Singh to his presence. It was hoped that this demonstration of force would cow the Maharana into submission, but Man Singh was also told to be prepared to resort to arms if peaceful persuasion failed. This latter alternative turned out to be the case. Pratap refused to bow before Akbar's might. He despised Man Singh as a mere landlord, whose forefathers had been subordinate to the Ranas of Mewar, and talked of beating him out of the town of Mandal where the Mughal expedition was assembling. But the wiser ministers of Mewar held their Chief back from venturing so far into the open country against a better armed and better mounted foe. (*Ak.*, iii, 236, 244)

Tod's Gossipy Annals Proved To Be Incorrect

These contemporaneously recorded facts and dates refute the opium-eater's tale given currency to by Tod that

> Raja Maun was returning from the conquest of Sholapur [*sic* !!!] to Hindustan when he invited himself to an interview with Pertap, than at Kolmulmeer, who advanced to the Oody-Sagur to receive him. A feast was prepared for the prince of Amber. The board was spread, the Raja summoned,... but no Rana appeared... The Rana expressed his regret; but added that he could not eat with a Rajpoot who gave his sister to a Toork. Raja Maun was unwise to have risked this disgrace... Raja Maun left the feast untouched, observing as he withdrew, "If I do not humble your pride, my name is not Maun": to which Pertap replied, "he should always be happy to meet him;" while some one, in less dignified terms, desired he would not forget to bring his *Phoopa* Akbar. (i. Mewar, ch. II)

Now, Man Singh paid this visit to the Maharana in June, 1573, and if he had been insulted by his host in the manner alleged by Tod's bardic gossip, would Bhagwant Das have courted a similar rebuff by visiting the Maharana only four months later, before the insult was atoned for?[5] We must not forget that the greatest humiliation that can be offered to a Hindu family is for its caste-brethren to refuse to dine with it, and Man Singh was Bhagwant Das's son and heir. Prince Amar Singh's visit to the Emperor, as his father's representative along with Bhagwant Das in October 1573, proves that the Maharana could not have been so contumacious only four months before, for Haldighat was fought in 1576, and not immediately after the insult to Man Singh in June, 1573, as Tod would have us believe.

Haldighat Described

Akbar arrived at Ajmer on 3rd April, 1576[6] and ordered Man Singh to lead out an army for bringing the Maharana to terms. Chitor had been lost to the Mughals by the Sisodia Chieftain in 1568 and the lord of Mewar had been driven into the hills to take up his residence at Gogunda, 16 miles north-west of Udaipur as the crow flies, surrounded by a network of hills and jungles, and standing 2757 feet above sea level.

This Gogunda was Man Singh's objective. Starting from his own base at Mandal, midway between Ajmer and Chitor, he could have turned a hundred miles south-west to Udaipur, and then worked his way north-west through a maze of tangled broken country which Tod has likened to Oberhasli of Meyringen in the Oberland Bernois. Or he might have left the road to Udaipur half-way and proceeded south-west over the level country, with help from the perennial Banas river till he reached Khamnor, sixteen miles north-east of Gogunda. Here the hills began and barred his path. He chose the latter route as shorter and more promising of adequate water supply.

As the traveller from the east leaves the holy city of Nathdwara,[7] 30 miles north of Udaipur, he crosses the snaky Banas river twice, and at the end of seven miles reaches on its southern side the large village of Khamnor,[8] a revenue Collector's seat[9] in the Mewar Kingdom. Proceeding three miles further south by the winding paths

over an almost treeless stretch of uneven rocky soil, he comes to a square shaped plain embosomed among the hills and dotted with the mango and the *babul* whose green shades refresh his eyes after the glare from the sand and rock that he had just passed over. A perennial spring tumbles down from the hill on his left and waters many small corn fields on the lower ground to the right of the path. In this plain a force of 2000 or 3000 men can easily encamp. Just beyond it, the hills almost close the square round, then recede a little for a few hundred yards and at last approach very near so as to form the Haldighat pass, three miles in length. This defile is so narrow that two horsemen cannot ride abreast in it, and at places even men can walk only in single file. The hillside on the right and left rise abruptly, covered with thorny grass and scrub or exposing the bare jagged rock. The track is uneven and made rough by the irregular heights of the stones that form nature's roadway under foot. Within the defile the rocks, when crushed, yield a bright yellow sand which looks exactly like the turmeric (*haldi*) powder with which Indians spice their dishes. Hence it is fittingly known as Haldighat. After three miles the pass ends, the hills recede, and a wide undulating path leads to Gogunda.

Hearing that Man Singh had reached Khamnor, Maharana Pratap Singh left Gogunda in order to strike the first blow, instead of waiting to see his last capital attacked and taken. In the morning of 18th June, 1576, his army debouched from the Haldighat and marched upon the enemy's camp. Man Singh immediately took up the challenge, and then followed a battle which will always be remembered in Indian history.

The Rival Armies At Haldighat

A force of 5000 men had been assembled under Man Singh's command, including a picked body of mounted archers from Central Asia—Uzbaks, Qazzaqs (the same race as the Cossacks of Russia), and Badakhshis, noted for their skill in shooting arrows with precision while fleeing or whirling round and round. A more obstinate class of fighters were the Sayyids of Barha, whose steadfastness in battle had given them the hereditary honour of occupying the right wing of the Imperial army in every battle. The core of the invading force was formed by the clansmen of Man Singh and these Rajputs fought with a degree of valour which matched that of the Sisodia defenders. Above all shone the Kachhwa prince's cold calculating brain, ever alert eye, and power of prompt action at every change in the tide of the combat, against which the primitive weapons and disjointed individual valour of the Rana's followers dashed themselves in vain. The Mughals had, no doubt, a numerical superiority of five to three; but a single stricken field could not have been decisive of the entire campaign in that difficult terrain and against the most reckless fighters in India, were it not for the consummate generalship of Man Singh, who guided every section of his troops so as to draw the fullest advantage from their superior training and tactics.

Man Singh marshalled his ranks in the highly methodical Turkish order. Besides the five regular and closely interlocked divisions—the vanguard, centre, right and left wings, and rearguard—there was the useful *iltmish* or 'advanced reserve', a picked body of troopers placed between the centre and the right wing (immediately before or behind their point of junction). This body was kept ready to be hurried up in support of any point in the battle line that seemd about to give way under enemy pressure. Man Singh himself took his position in the centre, seated on the back of a huge elephant, from which elevation his eyes swept over the entire field. His right wing was under the Sayyids of Barha, his left under Ghazi Khan Badakhshi with his Central Asian mounted archers, and Rao Lunkarn Shekhawat, the baron of Sambhar, and his followers. The vanguard was led by Jagannath Kachhwa, Ghiyas-ud-din Ali and Asaf Khan; the rear by Mehtar Khan, and the advanced reserve by Madho Singh (the younger brother of Man Singh). In the very front spread a thin screen of skirmishers, formed by 80 high-spirited warriors, who advanced before the compact army like chickens before the mother hen. Hence their significant name, 'the chickens of the vanguard'—*juzha-i-harawwal*.

Maharana Pratap Singh was brave as a lion, and so were his clansmen and wild Bhil auxiliaries. But he was unfit to lead in a modern war, which is in effect a game of chess. He had no plan of battle (as Abul Fazl points out); the moves of his separate divisions were not carefully timed and combined so as to produce a united result. He followed the exploded old tactics of making a simultaneous headlong charge by two solid columns of cavalry and then pursuing the enemy if they broke and fled at the first impact. If, however, the enemy divided into small self-contained units, facing round or revolving on his flanks, he became helpless as soon as the initial impetus of his charge was exhausted and his men were unprotected against the rain of missiles from three sides of them. His cavalry thrust, resembling the 'wild-boar rush' of General Petain, and condemned in Liddell Hart's *History of the Great War*, was to be followed up by an elephant charge carrying the debris of the shaken enemy before it, as in the mythic age of the Hindu epics. But Alexander and Babur had shown that elephants are more of a hindrance than a help to their owners when confronted by disciplined sharp shooters on horseback. This was to be proved once again at Haldighat.

In the Mewar army, the Maharana himself led the centre, as was the invariable rule with the Commander-in-Chief. His right and left wings were respectively commanded by Ram Sah Tonwar (the dispossessed Rajah of Gwalior) and Bida, the Jhala Chieftain. The post of the greatest danger at the head of the vanguard, was fittingly taken by Ramdas Rathor, the seventh son of Jaimal, the martyred defender of Chitor. But as the Maharana had staked his all on a desperate frontal charge, he kept no rear-guard and no reserve for any emergency. Indeed his total strength was too small to permit him these precautions without hopelessly weakening his attacking columns and taking the sting out of his attack. Hence his initial success could not be followed up, nor his early check overborne.

The Battle Of Haldighat: Man Singh's Exploits

It was three hours after sunrise on Monday the 18th of June, when the two advancing armies first clashed against each other. From the mouth of the pass rolled out a raging torrent of Mewar horsemen led by Ramdas, the son of Jaimal. The impetuosity of their charge swept away the Mughal line of skirmishers in a twinkle and rolled them up upon the vanguard, which itself was shaken. In the broken narrow paths hedged with thorny bushes, the men of the Imperial van became hopelessly mixed together and sustained a complete defeat, as the eye-witness Badayuni reports. Many of the imperialists gave way, as the official historian admits, and fled away without drawing rein for miles.

The confusion here was made worse by a severe reverse sustained by the Mughal army on its left wing, where Ghazi Khan and Lunkarn Shekhawat of Manoharpur were broken and pushed back by Ram Sah, simultaneously with the attack on their front division. The fugitives from this wing burst through the Mughal vanguard and fled for shelter to their right wing, there the obstinate valour of the Sayyids of Barha alone upheld the Imperial cause in spite of heavy slaughter by the Sisodia left wing (under Bida Jhala). But even the Sayyids seemed about to give way when the advanced reserve (under Madho Singh) arrived in support of the sorely pressed wing. Ghazi Khan also came up with the broken remnants of the left wing.

At this crisis of the battle Man Singh hurried to the front and plunged into the fight. Behind him came Mehtar Khan with the Imperial rearguard, beating his kettle-drums and shouting to hearten his comrades. This spread the rumour that Akbar himself had arrived, in one of his lightning marches, to lead the battle. A 'cry went up from the combatants, and the enemy (i.e., the Rana's troops), who were continually becoming more and more predominant, lost heart'. By this time the momentum of the attack had been spent and the battle line was stabilised. The rival hosts were now locked together in a death embrace, and hand to hand fighting raged all over the field. 'The warriors on both sides yielded up their lives and preserved their honour.' (Abul Fazl, *Ak.*, iii, 245)

The deadlock could be removed only by employing four-footed artillery. The Maharana sent his famous elephant, 'the rank-breaking Lona', to clear a path. Man and horse quailed before it. But the imperialists countered the move by driving forward their own 'pearl among elephants' (*Gaj-mukta*), to oppose it. 'The shock of these two mountain-like forms threw the soldiers into trepidation, and the Imperial elephant was wounded and about to fly when a bullet struck the driver of the enemy's elephant and he turned back. But just then Pratap Tonwar[10] brought forward Ram Prasad, the head of their elephants, and threw down many gallant men. At this time of wavering, two of the Mughal elephants, Gajraj and Ran-madar, were brought up to oppose Ram Prasad. But the driver of Ram Prasad was hit by an arrow in a vital place and thrown down to the ground by the shock of the charge. Then the driver of the Imperial elephant, with the greatest agility, leapt from his own elephant on to the back of Ram Prasad and secured that noted elephant (which had often been a subject of conversation in Akbar's Court), among the spoils of the Imperial victory.

The hand-to-hand combat was now resumed. Kachhwa and Sisodia grappled together in deadly rivalry. Ram Sah Tonwar (the ex-King of Gwalior) with his three gallant sons, who always kept in front of the Rana, 'performed such prodigies of valour against the Rajputs of Man Singh as to baffle description. Similarly, the young heroes who acted as the bodyguards of Man Singh performed such exploits as were a perfect model.' This is the grudging testimony extorted from the bigoted Al Badayuni, an actor in this fight. In the heat of their onset, the two supreme commanders once approached each other, but happily never came within reach of their spears. The Maharana was for the main part opposed to Madho Singh Kachhwa, who led the all-important reserve. 'Showers of arrows poured on the Rana who was wounded' by arrow and spear.

It was now midday. The contest had raged obstinately for three hours, and the Sisodias who had been under arms and moving for six hours began to faint from the intense heat of midsummer in that treeless plain shut round by hills.[11] There were woeful losses on their side; Ramdas Rathor met with his father's heroic end by falling on the field. Ram Sah of Gwalior with his three sons, Salivahan, Bhan[12] and Pratap Tonwar, perished 'after showing extreme obstinacy of resistance, and there was none left to be his successor.[13] (*Al Badayuni*) There were many others among the noble slain, of lesser note but of no less valour than these.

One act of the purest Rajput devotion was to light up the closing scene of Haldighat. By this time the tide of battle had turned irretrievably against the Maharana, his wings had been crumpled up and crowded upon his centre, which was hemmed round on three sides by the exultant imperialists. In the confusion the hope of Mewar himself was all but surrounded by the enemy and about to be cut off. But it was not to be, so long as there remained a single Rajput true to his chieftain. Realizing the crisis, Bida[14] the Jhala baron promptly snatched away the royal umbrella from over the head of Pratap Singh and rushed forward with it shouting that he himself was the Maharana and defying the imperialists to face him. The ruse succeeded; the Mughal captains, each eager to win the honour of being the Maharana's captor, crowded round Bida. The pressure on Pratap Singh was released, and his faithful adherents seizing his bridle turned his horse's head and led their bleeding chieftain out to safety through the pass in their rear. Bida met with the death he had coveted. With his fall the struggle ended; the remnant of the Mewar army dissolved and fled through the pass or up the hillsides, leaving 500 of their number to consecrate with their life-blood the Thermopylae of Rajasthan. On the generally accepted calculation that the wounded number three times the dead, the Mewar army on that fatal day bore casualties to the extent of fully two-thirds of its total strength. From this we can judge the fury of the fight. The imperialists lost 150 men besides the several hundred who were wounded.

There was no pursuit. The victors, no less than the vanquished, were worn out by the heat of the sun and the fatigue of the long-drawn struggle, and they could not be sure that the Mewar troops had not planted any ambush in their path of advance among these intricate and unexplored hills. The next day the route was reconnoitred. Man Singh crossed the Haldi defile and took unopposed[15] possession of Gogunda which the Maharana had vacated.

Haldighat Battle Seen In A Historical Perspective

At Haldighat, Man Singh won and Pratap Singh lost. The Maharana staked his all in a hopeless contest with the Imperial crown of Delhi in the full flush of its youthful vigour and the swelling tide of its conquests in the east, west, north and south of India. After a life-long struggle, he closed his eyes as a cityless fugitive, an almost landless king, a dweller in grass-covered huts, a father of famished children.[16] But the highest human endeavour is not measured in terms of pounds, shillings and pence. The laurel-crowned poet of Asia has sung:

> What voice is this from the land of dawn
> Proclaiming, "Fear not! fear not!
> He who gives up his life, retaining nothing,
> Shall never perish, never perish![17]

Fame after death has made ample amends for Pratap's sufferings in life. The name of the general who lost the battle of Haldighat will live to sustain and uplift the spirit of man at every arduous call of duty so long as the history of India is read. It is the losing side who have made that yellow defile a haunted holy ground for pilgrims of Indian patriotism.[18] Rana Pratap is still a name to conjure with.

But the historian of Man Singh may plead that the Kachhwa prince too had chosen no ignoble part, that he was the greater statesman of the two. He lent his help to uniting India under one sceptre and imposing an Imperial peace upon the hundreds of petty potentates, eternally wrangling and raiding one another's territory, each eagerly cherishing the independence of his small plot of land as the sole object of his life. Pratap was an independent prince. Man Singh was a servant; but the servant of a master who had set out to give India's millions a long unknown peace, justice, universal toleration and 'careers open to talent'. It was only by sweeping away the obstacles in the path of such a policy that a united India could be rendered possible, and an Indian nation could be dreamt of. Man Singh devoted his life to the first honest and conscious effort at realizing such a dream. The history of India since that day has shown which of the two chiefs in confrontation at Haldighat was the more far-sighted patriot.

Unsuccessful Attempts To Occupy Mewar After Haldighat

From the lost field of Haldighat, Maharana Pratap Singh fled, abandoning his capital Gogunda and taking refuge among the steep hills and dense jungles of the Aravali range near Kumbhalgarh. The chiefs of Jalor and Sirohi yielded, soon afterwards, to the Imperial generals penetrating into their countries. Nadot[19] was occupied in force, which 'made the strife-mongers of that country obedient, and the roads of ingress and egress from the Rana's country were closed'. The strategic encirclement of the portion of Mewar still in Pratap Singh's possession was completed. (*Ak.*, iii, 267) But the Mughal detachment had to entrench itself at Gogunda in self-defence and to subsist on their draught cattle and the mango-fruit, as the region was sterile and grain-porters found the roads from the plains quite unsafe. Following the Rana into his unexplored Aravali fastnesses was impossible. Hence Man Singh and Asaf Khan, after exhausting the scanty local supplies within reach of their daily foraging parties, 'came out of that stony land into the open plain' and joined Akbar who had arrived at Ajmer on 26th September[20] (1576). For this hurried withdrawal they fell under Imperial suspicion, but soon cleared themselves. (*Ak.*, iii, 260; *Bad.*, ii, 241, 247)

Thereafter Akbar himself marched towards Gogunda on the pretext of hunting, but really to overawe all rebelliously inclined people. This was specially necessary, as the retirement of the Mughal detachments was followed immediately after by the renewed disturbances of the Maharana, the chief of Idar and other princes. Akbar started from Ajmer on 11th October, 1576, and the Maharana again went into hiding. But the Emperor detached Bhagwant Das, this timed with Qutbuddin Khan and Man Singh, 'to penetrate into the hollows of the hills and lay hands on the dweller in the ravines', while a second force was sent to pacify Idar. These two bodies also acted as escort to a very numerous party of Mecca pilgrims (including many ladies of the Imperial family) who proceeded *via* Haldighat, Gogunda, Banswar[21] and Idar to Ahmedabad.

Akbar halted for some time in the village of Mohi (on the north bank of the Banas river, a few miles from Kankroli[22] (in the south of Raj Samundar lake); and set up military posts at Mohi, Madar (midway between Udaipur and Gogunda)[23] and some other places to keep watch and intercept the Maharana when he next descended into the plains. In the meanwhile, Qutbuddin and Bhagwant Das, finding no trace of the Maharana in the Gogunda district, hastily returned to Mohi, without following him into the western hills and jungles. For this abandonment of their post without orders, they incurred the Emperor's displeasure and were refused audience; when they showed penitence they were pardoned. (*Ak.*, iii, 267-275.)

On 27th November, 1576, the Emperor left Mahi and started for Malwa, via Udaipur and Banswara, and the Maharana at once resumed his raids into the plains. From Banswara, on Wednesday, 26th December, Akbar sent Bhagwant Das, Man Singh and some other officers who restored order there. But it was found by painful experience that Imperial peace in Mewar or Idar could at best be only a precarious armed truce. It was impossible for a small detachment to maintain its predominance at Gogunda, not to speak of overwhelming the hill region, and equally impossible for a large army to subsist long in that barren country for want of provisions and fodder. It will not be out of place to mention that the poor success of Man Singh in the Gogunda district and in restoring calm in this area had been represented to Akbar by his enemies at the Court as being due to his sympathy for the Maharana. But after his stay for some months in this country, Akbar realized that all these complaints on the part of his courtiers were due to envy at a Hindu's rise to the foremost rank of the peerage. (Abul Fazl rightly calls these calumniators, 'tricksters and time-servers,... evil-inclined wordspinners'. *Ak.*, iii, 250)

Shahbaz Khan Devastates Mewar

When the campaigning season opened again in October 1577, it was found that the renewed disturbances of the Mirzas in Gujarat demanded immediate attention. Hence, the expedition for the conquest of Khandesh was diverted to Gujarat and effective steps were devised for safeguarding the communication with the latter province through Rajputana. On 2nd October,[24] Akbar left Ajmer for Merta, where ten days later he appointed Shahbaz Khan (Mir Bakshi) commander of an expedition for suppressing the Maharana. Bhagwant Das and Man Singh were deputed with him. Shahbaz Khan, warned by the failure of his predecessors, set to work in grim earnest. He wrote to the Emperor asking for reinforcements which would hold the passes, and a fresh force was sent under Shaikh Ibrahim which took post at Nadlai[25] (in the open country near the mouth of the Desuri pass), so as to cut off the Maharana's communications with the Godwar province (west of the Aravali). This was exactly the strategy followed later by Aurangzib against Maharana Raj Singh in 1680.

Then Shahbaz Khan proceeded in full force to beat the Maharana out of his last home, the hill-fort of Kumbhalgarh (also called Kamalmir), standing 3568 feet above sea level and commanding the Ghanerao (or Hathigura) pass lying 700 feet below it. But first of all he sent back to the Court Bhagwant Das and Man Singh, 'lest from their feelings as land-holders they might delay in inflicting retribution on that vain disturber' (the Maharana). With the rest of this campaign we are not concerned, as no Kachhwa troops took part in it. By a night march, Shahbaz surprised the town of Kelwara lying at the head of the pass and advanced some six miles northwards up to the very gates of Kumbhalgarh. The next night the Maharana, further disheartened by the bursting of a large gun and the destruction of much of his munitions, slipped out of the fort and made for the hills of Banswara, and Kumbhalgarh was stormed by the Mughals in the morning (4th April, 1578). Shahbaz hastened in pursuit of him, taking Gogunda and Udaipur on the way and obtaining immense booty. (*Ak*., iii, 307, 339-340)

The Last Efforts Of The Imperialists Against Maharana Pratap Singh

It was a relief for Man Singh to be recalled from the Mewar campaign. His reluctance to go to extremes with a defeated opponent amply proves the nobility of his character. He was an Indian and a statesman, not a Khurasani *condottiere;* he knew that it was not by massacring their peasantry and sacking their villages that the Sisodias could be made willing partners of the Delhi Empire. Shahbaz Khan's policy of frightfulness had no effect except to stiffen the Mewar resistance, and as soon as Akbar's forces were diverted to far off Afghanistan or Deccan, the Maharana returned and recovered much of his lost dominions. It was not coercion but conciliation that won from Pratap's successor homage to the Imperial Crown, and that was under the mild Jahangir.

Shahbaz Khan's suspicion that the Kachhwa chiefs were capable of double-dealing in favour of a brother Rajput had not the slightest basis in fact. Bhagwant Das and Man Singh would have openly refused to go out against the Maharana if they were really so inclined. They were transferred from Rajputana only because a more pressing danger required the presence of such doughty and trustworthy warriors for the defence of India's north-western frontier. The Kachhwas were again employed in the pacification of Mewar some years later. On 5th December 1584, Jagannath (a son of Rajah Bihar Mal) was sent, along with Sayyid Raju and many other captains, to suppress the Maharana who had resumed his annual raids but shifted his ground too quickly to be caught by the imperialists. Jagannath, leaving Sayyid Raju in Mandal, penetrated into the western hills and attacked the Maharana's residence there, but finding no one to fight with, returned to his base.

In the autumn of the next year, Pratap Singh reappeared in the course of his guerilla warfare. On 15th September,[26] 1585, Jagannath made a forced march, and at the end of the day reached the village where Pratap had been living since the loss of Udaipur and Gogunda. 'Apparently one of the companions of the Rana gave him information and he took refuge with his family in the defiles. His house and household were plundered.' (*Akbarnamah*, iii, 661, 705-06)

The Kachhwa share in Akbar's Mewar wars has been treated here in ample detail, because its nature has been hitherto imperfectly understood and much adverse criticism of Bhagwant Das and Man Singh has been made by popular writers ignorant of the facts.

Notes

1. The correct date is Thurdsday, October 23, 1657 A.D. (*Ak.*, ii, p. 464). *Ed.*
2. This should be Nagor, where Akbar arrived on Friday, November 15, 1570, and stayed for some time (*Ak.*, ii, pp. 517-519). *J.S.*
3. Udaipur was occupied for the first time by the Mughals only after the Battle of Haldighat when Akbar himself arrived there sometime in November, 1576, and was recovered by Rana Pratap within a short time after Akbar's departure for Malwa via Banswada. *Ed.*
4. This statement of Abul Fazl about Rajkumar Amar Singh being sent to the Mughal court is not corroborated even by other contemporary Persian sources. On the other hand Jahangir's statement 'Rana Amar Singh... had never seen... any kings of Hindustan...' (*Tuzuk*, Bevridge, I, p. 274), fully contradicts Abul Fazl's said statement. *Ed.*
5. It is rather difficult to agree to this view that nothing untoward happened between Man Singh and Rana Pratap at their meeting in June 1573, near Udaipur, though Tod's exaggerations cannot also be accepted. Even a non-partisan historian like Muhnot Nainsi records that at dinner something *viras* (unpleasant or disagreeable) happened (*Khyat*, RPP edn., I, p. 39). Akbar realized that the unpleasantness created by the visit of the youthful Man Singh must necessarily be assuaged before long. Hence the experienced factful worldly-wise seasoned statesman Raja Bhagwant Das was deputed to meet Rana Pratap. Though not a very palatable assignment, Bhagwant Das could not have declined it.
   Abul Fazl's obvious exaggerations of Rana Pratap 'putting the

royal *khilat'* on the occasion of Man Singh's visit and about Kunwar Amar Singh being sent along with Bhagwant Das to the Mughal Court are apparently to cover the unpleasantness of the former and the infructuousness of Bhagwant Das' visit to Rana Pratap. *Ed.*

6. This is an inadvertent mistake. The correct date is Tuesday, March 6, 1576 (*Ak.*, iii, p. 233). *Ed.*
7. This holy city of Nathdwara came into being after 1571, when the image of Krishna (*Shri Nathji*) from Govardhan was installed in the village till then known as Sihara. *Ed.*
8. This description is based upon a journey which I (J. Sarkar) made on foot from Khamnor through the Haldighat pass in October, 1934. My account of the battle has been taken from Abul Fazl's *Akbar-namah*, written from contemporary official records, (iii, 236, 244-247), and Al Badayuni's *Muntakhab* (ii, 236-239), the report of an actual fighter in the battle. Col. Tod's wild gossip and baseless imaginings have been corrected.
(After Independence the historical Haldighati pass has been disfigured and completely altered beyond recognition by building a motorable road through it. *Ed.*)
9. The headquarters of the *hakim* of the Khamnor Pargana. *Ed.*
10. He was the youngest son of Raja Ram Shah Tanware, the deposed Raja of Gwalior. His eldest brother Shaliwahan is said to been married to one of the daughters of Rana Udai Singh of Mewad, hence Abul Fazl calls Pratap Tanwar 'a relation of the Rana' (*Ak.*, iii, p. 246; *Gwalior ke Tomar*, by Harihar Niwas Dwivedi, p. 197). *Ed.*
11. When I traversed the Haldighat in 1934, though the month was October and the time afternoon, the water in a metal flask which I was carrying with me turned hot. (J. Sarkar.) Badayuni, who fought in this battle, writes, 'It was so extremely hot—being during the forty mid-summer days—that the very brain boiled in the cranium.' (ii, 239.) *J.S.*
12. The correct full name is 'Bhawani Singh' (Ojha, *Udaipur*, I, p. 431). *Ed.*
13. Al Badayuni was obviously unaware of the two sons of Shalivahan, Shyam Sah and Mitra Sen, who took service under Akbar probably soon after the death of Rana Pratap in 1597. For further details about them see *Gwalior ke Tomar*, by Harihar Niwas Dwivedi, pp. 256-271; *Shah Jahan ke Hindu Mansabdar*, by Manohar Sinh Ranawat, pp. 79, 80, 103. *Ed.*
14. The son of Sultan Jhala. His other name was Man Singh. (Ojha, *Udaipur*, I, pp. 440-441 f.n.). *Ed.*
15. At Gogunda there was a token yet stiff opposition from the guardians of the Rana's palace, and some inhabitants of the temples

at Gogunda who were all killed to a man fighting against the Mughal Army. *Al-Badayuni*, ii, pp. 239-240. *Ed*.

16. This descripiton sums up succinctly the condition of Rana Pratap as given by Tod in his *Annals* (i, pp. 397-398, 405-407), which, however, is historically not true. By the time of his death Rana Pratap had recovered much of his former domains except the historic forts of Chitor and Mandalgarh. His last capital, Chawand (an old village about 26 m. south of Udaipur) had become a flourishing *kasba* and the remains of Rana Pratap's residential palaces still exist. He had, however, to suffer extreme hardships during the years 1578-80 and 1584-85 because of Shahbaz Khan's invasions and Jagannath Kachhawa's lightning attacks and hot pursuits. (Ojha's *Udaipur Rajya ka Itihas*, I, pp. 39-40, 455-458, 463-466; Raghubir Sinh's *Maharana Pratap* (Hindi), pp. 47-51.) *Ed*.
17. Tagore wrote:

    उदयेर पथे शुनिकार वाणी

    भय नाइ ओ रे भय नाइ

    नि: शेषे प्राण ये करिवे दान

    क्षय नाइ तार क्षय नाइ ।।
18. In 1934, the governor of Chitor told me that during his term of office almost two hundred educated people (mostly from Bengal) had visited Haldighat. *J.S.*
19. Nadot—This incorrectly written place-name has been wrongly identified by Bevridge as 'Nandod' in Gujarat (36 m ENE of Broach). It is 'Nodol' the then headquarters of the 'Godwad district' of Mewad, which was taken over by the Jodhpur state during the reign of Maharana Ari Singh (1761-1773) of Mewar. From Nadol the historic Desuri or Jhilwara pass, below the Kumbhalgarh Fort and also known as *Paglia-Nal*, could be fully controlled. *Ed*.
20. The correct date is Friday, September 28, 1576. According to *T.A.* (ii, pp. 492-493) Akbar arrived in Ajmer on 5 Rajab 984 A.H., which corresponds to this very date, though he wrongly mentions Thursday as the day of the week of that date. According to Badaoni (ii, p. 246) Akbar arrived at Ajmer on 6 Rajab (Sept. 29, 1576). *Ed*.
21. This should be Panwara, the headquarters of the Rana of Panwara, a Bhil Bhumia. *Ak.*, III, p. 272; *Rajputana Gazetteers*, Vol. II-A, *The Mewar Residency*, 1908, p. 115; (also Tod's *Travels in Western India*, pp. 32-33). *Ed*.
22. Kankroli kasba came into being after 1676, when the image of Dwarkadish, brought from Mathura in 1671, was installed in the present temple on the occasion of the inauguration of the Rajsamand lake formed in the reign of Maharana Raj Singh between 1662 to 1667. *Ed*.

23. Madar mentioned here is 6 m north-west of Udaipur, which is obviously a wrong identification, as Abul Fazl calls the place 'Madaria', which can not be same as Madar. Madaria, mentioned by Abul Fazl, should be some village on or near the route of Akbar from Mohi to Udaipur. *Ed.*
24. The correct date is Saturday, October 5, 1577. *Ed.*
25. The correct name is Nadol, the headquarters then of the Godwad pargana. *Ed.*
26. The correct date is Friday, September 17, 1585. *Ed.*

VI

The Kachhwas As Wardens Of The North-Western Frontier

Bhagwant Das And Man Singh Defend The Punjab Against Afghan Invasion

The Kachhwa Rajahs, after being recalled from the war in Rajputana, were sent at the end of the same year (about the 10th of December, 1578) to the Punjab, to defend that province under its *subahdar* Said Khan. In the north-western frontier of India, and even beyond it in what now forms the kingdom of Afghanistan, this Rajput tribe was destined to play a very important and glorious part during the next eleven years. 'The year 1581 (really 1580-1581) may be regarded as the most critical in the reign of Akbar', as the historian Vincent A. Smith has shown. A dangerous conspiracy to overthrow him was formed in the name of Islamic orthodoxy. His Muslim officers in Bihar and Bengal rose in triumphant revolt against him and his authority was almost extinguished in those eastern provinces. On the west, his brother Mirza Muhammad Hakim, the ruler of Kabul (which then did not form part of Mughal India) was being tempted to invade India and oust Akbar from the Imperial throne. But Hakim had neither brains nor character; after the eastern rebels had shown their hands, he delayed launching his attack for ten months, and even then acted languidly.

On 26th November, 1580, Haji Nuruddin (a general of Hakim) made a raid into the Punjab by crossing the Indus, but was repulsed near Peshawar after receiving a wound. Muhammad Yusuf Khan, the Mughal fief-holder of Peshawar, had shown his incompetence, and Man Singh was transferred from Sialkot to take charge of the danger point in India's defence line. The Kachhwa prince hastened towards the frontier. At Rawal Pindi he heard that a second and very large force from Kabul had arrived on the bank of the Indus, led by Shadman Beg, 'whom Hakim regarded as the sword of his army', and so he quickly proceeded to oppose him. On 17th December, Shadman crossed the Indus and laid siege to the fort of Nilab, 15 miles south of Attock. Zain-ud-din Ali and other servants of Man Singh defended it. When Man Singh arrived at the place, he at once attacked the enemy, 'who were in the slumber of neglect, but being aroused by the sound of the kettledrums, sought to engage'. Evidently no artillery had accompanied Man Singh in his forced march. On 23rd December, an obstinate hand to hand fight took place, the Kachhwas leading the all important van, centre and advanced reserve. Shadman fled after being mortally wounded by Rajah Suraj Singh Kachhwa[1] (a brother of Man Singh). The 'Afghan army's sword' broke under the Rajput *talwar*. 'From his bravery and success in war, Shadman was highly regarded among the Afghan tribes.'

Three weeks after the fall of Shadman, Prince Hakim himself invaded the Punjab. This news reached Akbar at Agra on 23rd January, 1581, and he started for the Punjab on 6th February, after sending orders to his generals in the Punjab to wait for him and not to give battle to Hakim unless compelled in self-defence.

Hakim descended into the north Punjab plains, and not one local officer or noble joined him. Every fort in his path loyally held out against him. The Imperial officers gathered together at Lahore and put its old fort in some sort of defence. The Prince encamped before Lahore for 22 days (6-27 February), engaged in 'shooting arrows at an imaginary target' as Abul Fazl poetically puts it, because the *subahdar* Said Khan, aided by Rajah Bhagwant Das and other officers, offered a brave defence. Several assaults by the Afghans were beaten back. When the news came of the approach of Akbar (who had reached Panipat on 23rd February and hanged Shah Mansur, the arch-traitor and pivot of the pro-Hakim conspiracy), terror and confusion seized the invaders. Hakim at once broke up his camp and fled back to Kabul, losing large numbers of his men in crossing the Chenab and the Jhilam. (*Ak.*, iii, 492-494, 500-508.)

Akbar himself marched into the Punjab, and by way of Fort Rohtas reached the bank of the Indus on 23rd May, 1581. As Hakim did not respond to his brotherly messages, the Emperor in the middle of June despatched Man Singh 'and other brave and loyal men', across the Indus to Peshawar. The nominal command of this army was given to his young son Murad, and the most dangerous position, the leadership of the vanguard, was entrusted to Man Singh. Madho Singh and many other Kachhwa captains were posted to different divisions of the army of invasion. They were sent on Thursday, 22nd June, with orders to cross the Indus and to proceed to Kabul if necessary. (*Ak.*, iii, p. 518.)

But the Indian army at first recoiled from the idea of penetrating into the hills of Afghanistan, 'some owing to their dread of a cold climate, some to considerations of health and love for India, some to reluctance to face the inconveniences of travelling'. Among the murmurers was Rajah Bhagwant Das, who like all Hindus of that age clung to the belief that he would lose his caste if he crossed the boundary of the holy land of Aryavarta. Abul Fazl, as instructed by his sovereign, met the officers, took down their objections and placed the paper before Akbar, who at first tried to reason with them. It was on this occasion that he worte to Bhagwant Das (and not to Man Singh, as Tod alleges) the fine verse:

> The whole world is God's
> In which lies this Attock that you dread.
> He who has some impediment (*atak*) in his mind,
> Will regard Attock as an *atak* to himself.[2]

At last on Wednesday, 12th July, the Emperor by strict order enforced a crossing at Attock. A bridge was thrown over the river to ensure their communication with their base in India. (*Ak.*, iii, 518-523.)

Man Singh Forces The Khyber Pass And Occupies Kabul

But as Hakim showed no sign of coming to an agreement, Akbar advanced towards Afghanistan, reaching Bagram on 24th July.[3] At this Hakim fled from Kabul to Badakshan, and Akbar found it necessary to hasten to the masterless capital of Afghanistan. On the 26th,[4] leaving Prince Salim in charge of his main camp at Bagram, with Said Khan, Rajah Bhagwant Das and other officers, to follow him by more easy stages, he pushed on to Jamrud, crossed the Khyber pass the next day, and reached Jalalabad the day after.

In the meanwhile, the Mughal advanced division under Man Singh (with Prince Murad in charge) while marching from Barik-ab towards But-khak, had some baggage and stragglers in the rear cut off by Hakim's men under his chief officer Faridun (Monday, 31st July). A second engagement took place near Chinartu, in which Shaikh Jamal Bakhtiari beat back Faridun and fought his way to Khurd Kabul, where prince Murad was then encamped. But isolated Imperial troops and one treasure party were cut off by the hillmen. At last Hakim appeared and gave battle in the darkness of the night, on the first of August, but was defeated and forced to flee. The next day Faridun renewed the contest by falling on the isolated Mughal vanguard near the mouth of a ravine and killing some brave men. This emboldened Hakim to debouch on the plain, and at first the Afghans seemed to get the best of it. 'At this time, Rajah Man Singh came forward with a rush. First Madho Singh, Surat Singh[5] and a number of brave men formed platoons and went into battle, sending the rank-breaking elephants ahead and firing the swivel guns mounted on their backs', which shot down prominent leaders of the enemy. The Kabulis broke and fled away with their prince. This victory was a source of great encouragement to the Imperial troops, because before it the Kabulis had predicted, that 'the Turanis and Persians who are in the Imperial army will join us without fighting, and the brave Rajputs will perish, and the other natives of India in the Imperial army will be made prisoners'. Hakim narrowly escaped capture near Kotal Minar and fled to Ghorband.

On 7th August, when Akbar reached But-Khak, Man Singh and many other officers came to see him and they accompanied him in the march to Kabul, where they arrived on the 11th. Hakim now wrote a submissive letter, and Akbar withdrew with his army from Afghanistan, leaving Kabul a week after his entry[6] into it, and crossing the Indus back into India on Monday, 4th September. Here 'the guardianship of the Indus province was entrusted to the activity of Kumar Man Singh'. At Sarhind the Emperor gave Bhagwant Das and other Punjab officers leave to return to their fiefs in that province. (*Akbarnamah*, iii, 527-548.)

The Kachhwas kept the peace on the north-western frontier so well that for the next four years Akbar was relieved of anxiety about that frontier and left free to subdue Bihar and Bengal, Gujarat and the Deccan.

But Prince Hakim died on 30th July 1585, and disturbances broke out in the Kabul country. Akbar himself started from Agra on Monday, after sending an order to Kumar Man Singh, the warden of the Indus line, 'to proceed rapidly to Kabul with some troops and reassure the people, high and low, of Akbar's justice and love, and also comfort Muhammad Hakim's survivors'. The Kumar entered Peshawar at the beginning of September. Shah Beg fled from that city to Kabul and the Afghans came in tribes to make their submission. Pacifying and reassuring the peasantry on the way, and opening the Khyber pass (hitherto closed by the Raushaniya fanatics), the Kachhwa prince entered Kabul about the 11th of November. Then making the charge of the country over to his son Jagat Singh, he turned back with the dead Mirza's property and the local leaders, in order to meet Akbar at Rawal Pindi (about 5th December, 1585)[7] and then accompanied him to Attock. (*Ak.*, iii, 703-713.)

Man Singh's Campaigns Against The Yusufzai Clans

The Yusufzai clan of Afghans had, after earlier migrations, settled in the fifteenth century in the north Peshawar district or Swat and Bajaur, and 'lived there in the practice of robbery and turbulence—ousting by force the former inhabitants and robbing them of their choice lands'. Akbar was forced to suppress these incorrigible hereditary brigands. On 20th December, Kumar Man Singh 'was sent off to Kabul in order that he might civilise that country by justice'. He was instructed to halt for sometime before entering the Khyber pass and suppress the Raushaniya sect so as to make the road safe. Man Singh halted near Attock for more than a month.

Large forces under Zain Khan Koka and other officers swept the plains and drove the Yusufzai clansmen into their rocky fastnesses (January, 1586). But soon afterwards a terrible blow fell on the Mughal army which had penetrated into the hills. There were quarrels between its leaders, Zain Khan, Birbal and Abul Fath. On 16th February, (1586),[8] during a disorderly march, the Afghans attacked it in a Swat defile. Panic seized the disunited Imperial army and 8000 men lost their lives, including Rajah Birbal and many other high officers, while all their camp and equipage were plundered. The fugitives straggling in the hills were cut off.

The news of the disaster reached Akbar in two days[9] and prompt steps were taken to retrieve it. An army under Rajah Todar Mal crossed the Indus and the Kabul rivers the next day to suppress the Yusufzais. The retributive campaign was a quick, and as usual a temporary, success. 'In a short time a great clearance was made. A large number were killed and many were sold into Turan and Persia. The country of Swat, Bajaur and Buner were cleansed of evil-doers.'

Further up the mountains, at the same time, Man Singh cleared the Khyber pass which had been obstructed by the Raushaniya sect, while the Turan ambassador was coming to India from Kabul with a large caravan. From Jamrud, the Kumar detached a force under his brother Madho Singh, across the Khyber pass to join the envoy at Dhaka. Then Man Singh himself hastened with another army to Ali Masjid. The Raushaniyas invested that fort on a dark night and got to the top of it. But the imperialists made a firm stand and dislodged them, after 'performing master-pieces of valour'. The Afghan assailants then withdrew to a neighbouring height, from which they were driven out with heavy slaughter by a Mughal counter attack at dawn (c. 17 February). It was 'a glorious victory' for the Kachhwas, in Akbar's favourite historian's words, though it could not make up for the disaster to Birbal. (*Ak.*, iii, 716-734.)

Man Singh was next sent to assist Todar Mal in the work of keeping order in the Yusufzai country. He took post near Ohind (Und) the Kohi-Lungar to overawe Swat. Thus the two exits from the Yusufzai country were blocked by the imperialists, while their punitive columns entered the encircled region everyday to raid the villages. At last the people 'had recourse to entreaties and the dust of commotion was laid'. On Thursday, 29th March 1586, Todar Mal returned to Court (at Attock) after entrusting the chastisement of the hill Afghans to Man Singh. (*Ak.*, iii. 736-739.)

Bhagwant Das Assists In Conquering Kashmir

In the meantime, another force of the Kachhwas under Rajah Bhagwant Das and his son Madho Singh, had joined Mirza Shahrukh in the expedition sent by Akbar from Hasan Abdal (on 20th December 1585) for the conquest of Kashmir. They advanced by the Baramula pass. At Peliasa, some 50 miles west of Baramula, Sultan Yusuf Khan, the weak ruler of that kingdom, visited the invaders' camp and made submission to the Emperor (*c.* 14 February, 1586).[10] But the Kashmiri Muslim leaders under Yaqub (the son of Yusuf) rose and offered resistance. There was fighting everyday, but Madho Singh (with other officers) cleared the Kuarmal Pass, while many Rajputs fell in the obstinate fighting. At last the Kashmiris submitted and made peace. (*Ak.*, iii, 715, 722-725) Coins were stamped in Akbar's name and he was proclaimed sovereign from the pulpit at the capital of the country, and the administration was taken over by the imperialists. Then Bhagwant Das and other generals returned to Akbar's side at Attock with the deposed king of Kashmir towards the end of March.

Rajah Bhagwant Das, who held the office of *subahdar* of the Punjab, was immediately ordered to proceed to Afghanistan in the place of Man Singh who had now been transferred to the Yusufzai country. But there was a delay, the cause of which it is now difficult to ascertain. The contemporary Persian histories make either obscure or conflicting statements. Badayuni says that as Akbar, had broken the safe assurance that Bhagwant Das had given to the ex-Sultan of Kashmir, the Rajah was furious about this violation of his plighted word. The courtier Abul Fazl diplomatically remarks that the Rajah made impossible demands, which Akbar ascribed to madness and that for this reason his appointment was cancelled. But after a few days the Rajah begged for forgiveness. His Majesty accepted his apologies and on 2nd April the Rajah was allowed to go to Afghanistan. Two days later Akbar set out on his return to Agra.

Bhagwant Das crossed the Indus and put up in Sarai Khairabad on the west bank, where he developed signs of madness. He was brought back to Attock and placed under medical care; but one day he suddenly wounded himself with a dagger. The physician Mahadeo, kindly sent by Akbar, cured him, but after prolonged treatment.

Rajah Bhagwant Das's command of Afghanistan was transferred to Ismail Quli, whose short administration was an utter failure. He was removed from his post and sent to confront the Yusufzais, along with Madho Singh and the Kachhwa contingent of Bhagwant Das, and Man Singh was given the supreme charge of the Afghan Government once more. (*c.* 25th April, 1586) (*Ak.*, iii, 745, 774.)

Man Singh As The Viceroy Of Afghanistan

Man Singh made his way to Kabul and stayed there till the middle of September next, when, leaving his subordinates in charge of that capital, he started for India in order to escort Mirza Sulaiman to the Imperial Court. But at Pesh Bulaq, 20 miles south of Jalalabad, he was seized with a fever and was in great pain for a month and a half. The Afghans, seizing this opportunity, rose in vigorous and universal insurrection. The Afridis of Tirah made many stone redoubts dominating the entire path from Peshawar to Tirah, while the Yusufzai and other clans supported the rising from their localities.

After Man Singh had at last recovered, he turned to the suppression of the Afridis. Sending his charge Mirza Sulaiman to India under escort of his son Himmat Singh, he marched out of Pesh Bulaq with 3000 horses to subdue the Afridis, on Tuesday, 13th December. Travelling all night in the middle of an Afghan winter the Rajput veteran reached the Chahar Chobah pass in the morning and found it snowed up. 'With great difficulty Man Singh traversed the heights and hollows and arrived at Bazarak. Next day a detachment under Mr. Quli Beg attacked the Afridis and took much spoil.' Then the whole army advanced by the Chora-gully defile, climbing the hills. The rearguard had to fight a strenuous conflict with the hillmen pressing upon them from every side. But being reinforced by the watchful Man Singh, this division after much fighting beat the Afghans back. Leaving his eldest son Jagat Singh with the rearguard, Man Singh moved towards Ali Masjid; the Afghans reappeared shortly after and the position became more difficult. At first no plain for manoeuvring and no shelter could be found. The imperialists had to move on a helpless target for the arrows and stones hurled at them from the heights on both flanks. At last they reached a sort of open space, and here Man Singh made a firm stand and fought the enemy. 'Wonderful deeds were done', and finally the enemy retreated by their narrow defiles. About sunset the imperialists reached Ali Masjid by the Shadi route, and the Afghans again collected at some distance from them. The next day in the afternoon, Madho Singh brought up Bhagwant Das's contingent from the Indian side and the Raushaniyas dispersed.

Mirza Sulaiman was brought to Peshawar by the Karapa pass through the Mohamand country. From Peshawar, Jagat Singh escorted the Mirza to Agra, where they arrived on 24th February, 1587. (*Ak*., iii, 780-786.)

The next month Man Singh was replaced by Zain' Khan Koka as *subahdar* of Afghanistan. The reason is thus given in Akbar's official history: 'the Rajput clan behaved with injustice to the subjects of that country, and Kumar Man Singh did not look closely into the case of the oppressed, and he also disliked the cold country'. Man Singh's fiefs in the Punjab were now taken away and he was assigned instead, *jagirs* in Bihar.

Man Singh Represses The Raushaniya Fanatics Of The North-Western Frontier

On his return from Afghanistan, Man Singh was appointed to command the forces sent against the rebellious Raushaniya sect in the Yusufzai country. But he was worn out by this labour of Sisyphus among the bleak and barren Afghan mountains and probably shaken in body by his recent long illness there. The *Akbarnamah* described the situation thus:

> After he had fought in the defiles and won a hard-earned victory, he could not bring himself to enter the mountains again, but spent his time in Jamrud, near the Khyber pass, and indulged in futilities of speech. The Emperor censured him and appointed another general to go to the hills by way of Bangash, while Man Singh should march from Bagram. (that is, Peshawar side, and cooperate with it.)

The first army started on Monday, 17th April, 1587, ravaging the country on the way and gaining a great victory over the Raushaniyas at Dar Samand, Thursday, 27 July. But its commander Muttalib Khan, was seized with a strange insanity and had to be sent to Court. Man Singh took no part in this campaign; he arrived at Court on 8th December[11] and was sent to govern Bihar, at the other end of India, nine days later.

In 1589, when Akbar went on a visit to the pleasant land of Kashmir (May-August) and then to Kabul (September-November). Rajah Bhagwant Das, with Todar Mal, was left in Lahore to administer the province. In these royal journeys Akbar's constant companions were the Kachhwa princes Jagannath and Ramdas. On Saturday, 9th November, 1589, Rajah Todar Mal died at Lahore, of old age and weakness, after a reposeless career of unsurpassed variety and brilliance in every part of India, great in the civil administration, no less great in war. His bosom friend Bhagwant Das, after returning from his cremation, was immediately seized by a severe illness, which carried him off in five days (13th November, 1589).[12] One sentence from Abul Fazl's history tersely paints his character: 'Rajah Bhagwant Das was endowed with uprightness, weight of counsel and courage'. Man Singh received the title of Rajah and the headship of the Kachhwa clan, with the rank of a commander of 5000, which was then the highest dignity open to a subject not of royal blood, and which no other Hindu or Muslim held as yet. (*Ak.*, iii, 817-863.)

When we take a broad survey of this period of Jaipur's history, we find that the Kachhwas' long campaigns in the Afghan hills, in the course of which they watered the frontier defiles with their best blood, had neither more nor less than the success which Indian warfare in that volcanic region has always had. As the present writer has put the case in another work:

> Highway robbery was the hereditary profession of these hardy savages, as cunning as they were bold. Every year this prolific

> race multiplied, and their growing population, "more numerous than ants or locusts", and ignorant or contemptuous of peaceful industries, pined for some outlet for their martial instincts. The occasional victories of the guardians of law and order checked for a time, but could not finally remove this source of disturbance, as its economic causes remained unchanged.
>
> When the Indian Government, firmly disregarding the huge expenditure of men and money in these hills, persisted in the policy of annual invasion and chastisement, the tribes would make peace, promise tribute and obedience, and the weary Mughal troops would gladly withdraw. But such promises were forgotten as soon as the sufferings of the late war became a shadowy memory. In a few years the growth of population would more than fill the void caused by the Mughal sword; and the hungry hordes would again begin to swarm into the neighbouring districts or plunder trade-caravans. (*History of Aurangzib*, vol. iii, Ch. 33)

The accusation that Man Singh ruled the Afghan races in a harsh and unjust manner is refuted by contemporary records. In September, 1653, Bhai Khan Maral writes to this Rajah's great-grandson Jai Singh I, 'My tribe has been connected with your august family from olden times. My ancestors, through the patronage and mediation of the late Maharajah Man Singh, became *mansabdars* of the Emperor. I wish to present myself before you, enter your service and thus manifest our old devotion'. (*J.R.* No. 475)[13] One volume of my Jaipur transcripts[14] contains many letters from Afridi Khans of the Khyber pass professing long-standing devotion to the Jaipur Rajahs.

Notes

1. In the Kachhwah genealogies his name is written as Sur Singh. For his short life-sketch see *Solahwin Sadi men Rajasthan*, ed. by Manohar Sinh Ranawat. *Ed.*
2. सब ही भूमी गोपाल की या में अटक कहा ।
   जाके मन में अटक है वो ही अटक रहा ।।

3. The correct date is Thursday, July 27, 1581, *Ed.*
4. The correct date is Friday, July 28, 1581. *Ed.*
5. Obviously he is Sur Singh Kachhwah, younger brother of Man Singh Kachhwah, mentioned as Suraj Singh by Abul Fazl elsewhere in his *Akbarnamah*. *Ed.*
6. Akbar left Kabul on Tuesday, August 15, 1581, i.*e*. 2 Shahariyar (*Ak*., iii, p. 542). *Ed.*
7. The exact date is Tuesday, December 7, 1585 (= 25 Azar). *Ed.*
8. This date corresponds to Tuesday, 5 Rabi-ul-Awwal, 994 A.H., the date of this disaster mentioned in *Tabqat* (ii, pp. 609-610) and *Al. Badaoni* (ii, p. 361-362). The account given by Abul Fazl (iii, pp, 731-733) is confused and contradictory. *Ed.*
9. The dates cited by Abul Fazl (iii, pp. 732-733) are of Rabi-ul-Awwal and not of Isfandarmaz. *Ed.*
10. The exact date is Saturday, February 12, 1586. *Ed.*
11. The correct date is Saturday, November 15, 1589, which corresponds to Margashirsh *Vidi* 3, 1646 V.S. But Jaipur *Vamshavali* (p. 13) cites Margashirsha *Sudi* 7, 1646 V.S. which corresponds to Thursday, December 4, 1589 A.D. *Ed.*
12. The correct date is Sunday, December 10, 1587. *Ed.*
13. This entire letter is available in *Jaipur Records, Additional* Persian, Vol. III, pp. 1-3, in Shri Raghubir Library, Sitamau. *Ed.*
14. *Jaipur Records*, Vol. VI, of Sir Jadunath Sarkar's Collection, contains transcripts of such letters from the Afridi Khans. The transcript copy is also available in Shri Natnagar Shodh-Samsthan, Sitamau. *Ed.*

VII

Man Singh In Bengal, Bihar, Orissa And The Deccan

The Disturbed Condition Of Bihar And Bengal Before Man Singh's Viceroyalty

With the transfer of Man Singh to Bihar (1588) one scene of Kachhwa activity closed, and another, of great enduring effect, began in the opposite corner of our country, and changed completely the map of north-eastern India.

The Afghan ruling families from whom Akbar had finally wrested the throne of Delhi, found shelter in the eastern provinces. Bengal, Bihar and even Jaunpur did not pass into Mughal hands as the immediate result of the second Panipat. These princes were a standing menace to the new Emperor of India. As soon as Akbar felt himself firmly in the saddle, he turned to settle accounts with these eastern chiefs. In September, 1574, his arms had conquered Bihar, and the next year, Bengal. But for many years afterwards, victory in the field did not mean consolidation of territory. The numerous branches of the reigning Afghan or the noble families, maintained a semi-independent status in different parts of Bengal and Orissa, now nominally included in the Empire. They were always on the look-out for any chance of rising and shaking off their alien supplanters. Such an opportunity was soon presented by the discontent of Akbar's Muslim officers in the eastern provinces caused by his new rules (in 1575) about the strict muster of their contingents and the consequent curtailment of their dishonest gains. Their selfish greed soon found a respectable cloak and an instrument of popular appeal in Akbar's liberal measures which the ignorant fanatics denounced as a violation of Islam. The orthodox traitors in Bihar and Bengal made a collusion with Akbar's brother Mirza Md. Hakim, the ruler of Kabul, whom they conspired to place on the Delhi throne and use as a soft puppet, entirely in their hands. The revolt of the Afghan chiefs began in 1580 and lingered on for five years. It was aggravated by the mutiny of Akbar's own officers in that region. The work of pacification was also hampered seriously by the sudden deaths of four successive viceroys of Bengal (1575-1587)—three from the unhealthy climate and one at the hands of the victorious rebels, while a fifth governor left Bengal quickly as he hated the climate. Though by the year 1584, the tide had begun to turn in favour of Akbar, he found it necessary to make a more organized effort to stamp out the long smouldering fire of rebellion. On 26th August, 1587,[1] Said Khan was sent off to govern Bengal (*vice* Wazir Khan, who had died a month before). And on 31st December,[2] Man Singh was recalled from his post as warden of the north eastern frontier (at Jamrud) and appointed viceroy of Bihar.

This was the beginning of the longest and most glorious chapter in his life and of the records of Kachhwa achievements. He was now supreme in command and controlled both civil and military affairs: he conquered provinces and made treaties with hitherto independent sovereigns, on behalf of a distant master (the Emperor) and he lorded it over the eastern marches of India for twenty years without a break (1588-1607).

Man Singh's Conquests In Bihar

Man Singh's task in this new sphere was one of peculiar difficulty. Owing to the disloyalty, negligence or natural failure of his predecessors, Imperial prestige had almost touched the nadir in Bihar and Bengal. Everywhere scions of the former Afghan rulers and nobles, disloyal Mughal officers, and proud semi-independent zamindars were up in arms, fighting with each other, robbing the peasantry, and disavowing any higher authority. Many of the Emperor's new officers were lukewarm or defiant.

The work done by Man Singh in Bihar is admirably summed up by Akbar's official historian in one short but very eloquent sentence: 'the Rajah united ability with courage and genius with strenuous action; he administered the province excellently; the refractory became obedient'. (*Akbarnamah*, iii, 872.) His hand first fell upon Puran Mal, the Rajah of Gidhaur, who had declared independence during the recent eclipse of the Government in the province, and whose lands lay across the eastward route from Patna. Man Singh with the Kachhwa army and his Imperial contingent, marched upon Gidhaur, and easily captured its mud-fort with all the Rajah's treasure. Puran Mal then submitted and gained his pardon by offering a tribute of many noted elephants and valuable articles and betrothing his daughter to his conqueror's brother Chandra-bhan Kachhwa.[3] Sangram Singh, the Rajah of Khargpur (near Monghyr) was next cowed into submission and payment of tribute.

From the east, Man Singh returned to Patna and marched south against Anant Chero of the Gaya district, from whom much plunder was taken. During the Viceroy's absence his eldest son Jagat Singh ably guarded Patna. Taking advantage of Man Singh's preoccupation in the southern districts, two Muslim rebel leaders from Bengal made raids into Purnia and Darbhanga (in North Bihar) and penetrated to within 14 miles of Hajipur, threatening the provincial capital itself (which faces Hajipur across the Ganges). Young Jagat Singh boldly advanced at the head of the local militia, against the fleeing invaders who abandoned their collected booty to the imperialists. Man Singh sent the most valuable portion of the spoils of these wars and 54 elephants to the Emperor, who received them at Lahore on Thursday, 2nd April, 1590. (*Ak.*, iii, 872-873.)

Man Singh's First Conquest Of Orissa

After thus 'ably settling the province of Bihar and reducing the refractory to obedience', Man Singh set out in April 1590 for the conquest of Orissa, being reinforced by the Bengal artillery on the way. By the route of Bhagalpur and Burdwan, he reached Jahanabad (now in the west of the Hughli district) on the then frontier of Orissa, that is the modern Midnapur district, and encamped there in view of the early rains of Bengal. Qutlu Khan Lohani, the Afghan ruler of North Orissa, sent up a large force under Bahadur Kuruh to the fort of Raipur. The leader of the Mughal advanced division, 'the inexperienced youth' Jagat Singh, was entirely deluded by the Afghans and did not take adequate precautions, so that on 21st May, (1590), near sunset, he was suddenly surprised by the enemy in overwhelming force. The careless and disordered Imperial army broke up and dispersed after a little fighting. Bika Rathor, Mahesh Das and Naru Charan bravely sacrificed their lives, but could not change the issue. Jagat Singh was wounded and left alone, but saved by the loyal Rajah Vir Hambir who took him to his fort of Vishnupur (in the Bankura district), and a rumour even arose that the Kachhwa prince was dead.

But after ten days Qutlu died, and his young son Nasir was placed on his throne by his wazir Khwajah Isa, who wisely made terms with the Mughals, promising to read the *Khutba* and stamp coins in Akbar's name and live as his faithful vassal. He also promised to cede the temple of Jagannath (at Puri) and its surrounding district to the Emperor. On 15th August,[4] the Afghan boy-king made his bow before Man Singh, and presented his tribute of 150 elephants and many choice articles. After this success Man Singh returned to Bihar. (*Ak*., iii, 878-880.)

The Afghans are a faithless passionate race. After the death of Isa Khan, the wise regent of their boy-king, there was none who could keep their nobles in check; they broke the treaty, seized the temple of Jagannath from its Mughal custodian, and attacked Rajah Vir Hambir for his loyalty to the Delhi throne. Man Singh was therefore called upon to proceed against them again. Leaving Bihar on 3rd November 1591,[5] he marched in two divisions by land and down the Ganges, and was joined by the local landholders and the Bengal troops under their viceroy Said Khan. The Afghans met the threat by advancing to their northern frontier and encamping some miles north of Jalesar city, in the midst of a jungle with the river encircling their position.[6] Man Singh advanced to the encounter and a severe battle was fought, on Sunday, 9th April, 1592. There was a lack of real coordination between the Bengal contingent and Man Singh's troops, and at first the enemy's charges threatened to route the imperialists. But supports were pushed up from the rear in good time, and the Mughal artillery and archers spread havoc among the Afghans and the elephants on whom they chiefly relied. At last the enemy broke and fled leaving 300 dead on the field, including one divisional commander, while another commander was taken captive. Man Singh's own clansmen, especially his sons, Jagat and Durjan,[7] took a conspicuous part in charging the enemy and turning the dubious tide of the battle. (*Ak.*, iii, 934-937.)

The next day the victorious general arrived in pursuit at Jalesar, where he had the *Khutba* read and coins struck in Akbar's name. The Afghans retreated and he continued to advance further south into Orissa, 'digging up the roots of disaffection' and accepting the submission of the local zamindars. Said Khan, in a mean spirit of jealousy, gave up his partnership in the campaign and returned to Bengal, in spite of Man Singh's earnest attempts at conciliation.

At Bhadrak the Kachhwa Rajah learnt of the Afghan concentration at the fort of Saranggarh (Cuttack District). Leaving a garrison in Bhadrak, he marched to Cuttack which fell to him without a blow. This success led to further successes: the fort of Aul was peacefully surrendered. The Tila Rajah joined in near Kalkalghati, but the greatest of the Orissa rulers, the Rajah of Khurda, still held out in Sarang-garh. From Cuttack Man Singh made a pilgrimage to the famous shrine of Jagannath at Puri, and thereafter took post near Pipli (midway between Cuttack and Puri), raiding the Khurda territory. At last the Khurda Rajah, Ram Chandra Dev, submitted and sent his son Birbar with presents to the Mughal viceroy. Man Singh next moved to the neighbourhood of Sarang-garh. In the meanwhile, the dispersed Afghans rose in his rear and wrested the town of Jalesar from his lieutenant Babui Mankali, but a Mughal detachment from Cuttack recovered the post. On 30th May the fort of Sarang-garh capitulated to Man Singh.

But the Khurda Rajah continued to evade waiting on Man Singh in person. An expedition was therefore sent into his territory under Jagat Singh and other officers. Rajah Ram Chandra Dev shut himself up in Khurda, but many of his other forts and cities[8] fell rapidly to Mughal arms (1592).

Akbar disapproved of this rigour towards an ancient dynasty that had acknowledged his suzerainty. Man Singh received a censure from his master and as a consequence recalled his troops from Khurda territory. Then, at last, the Khurda Rajah personally waited on Man Singh (Tuesday, 30th January, 1593) and gave him a daughter (Akshaya Devi)[9] in marriage. The conquest of Orissa was thus completed.

But the conquest of Orissa did not bring peace to the Mughals in the eastern provinces; it only shifted the disease to another part of the body. Man Singh had seen too much of the Pathans both in Afghanistan and Bengal to trust them implicitly. He removed their surviving chiefs Sulaiman and Usman (the nephews of Qatlu Khan) and three others from the soil of Orissa altogether, and assigned them fiefs in the Faridpur (Khalifatabad) district of East Bengal. But before they could arrive there he realized that it was unwise to plant them so close to the border of Orissa where they had many adherents and a long local connection, and so he wrote cancelling their new grants and recalling them to his camp. At this they broke out in open rebellion and went plundering up to Satgaon (modern Hughly town), and on being repulsed there turned to Bhushna (Jessore district.) Here they killed their host Chand Rai (the son of the local zamindar Kedar Rai) who had tried to seize them (11th February, 1593).[10] They captured and plundered Bhushna fort and proceeded to join Isa Khan Masnad-i-ala, the greatest of Bengal zamindars, who ruled over the Dacca district. Thus the Afghan royal power, subverted in West Bengal and Orissa was established anew in East Bengal, beyond the Brahmaputra river. (*Ak*., iii, 968-969)

At this time Man Singh took the fort of Bhanpur (30 miles north of Ganjam city), situated between Orissa and Telingana, and gave it to Ram Chandra Dev. Then he returned to Rohtas (in south-Bihar) and stayed there till a summons from his master took him to Lahore. The Kachhwa Rajah, crowned with the laurels won in Bengal and Orissa, was welcomed by the Crown Prince Salim who went some miles outside Lahore to meet him (23rd February, 1594).[11] He was also introduced to the Emperor who personally invested him with a robe of condolence for the death of his father Rajah Bhagwant Das. Man Singh presented at Court three sons of Qatlu Khan and two great nobles of Orissa, namely Kashi Parija and Purushottam. (*Ak*., iii, 969, 997.)

Man Singh As The Viceroy Of Bengal—His Campaigns In East Bengal

On 17th March of the same year, Prince Salim was appointed to a nominal command of 10,000 horses, with Man Singh as his guardian. 5000 of the Prince's troops, including Jagat Singh, Durjan Singh and Sakat Singh[12] received *jagirs* in Bengal, while Himmat Singh,[13] Bhau Singh, Rajah Ram Chandra Dev (of Khurda) as well as many Bengal Pathan chiefs (of the Lohani and Sur clans) were granted fiefs in Orissa. 'Rajah Man Singh, whose ability and loyalty were conspicuous, was made *ataliq* (guardian) and his maintenance-*jagir* was allotted to him in Bengal, of which province he was now made viceroy, in the place of Said Khan, transferred to the Subahdari of Bihar.' On 4th May, 1594,[14] Akbar sent Man Singh to his new province with many wise counsels as to the administrative policy to be followed there. (*Ak.*, iii, 998-999.)

On arriving at Tanda (near Gaur, the ancient capital of Muslim Bengal), Man Singh sent detachments to subdue the various districts. One of these, led by his son Himmat Singh, conquered Bhushna fort (2nd April, 1595).

On 7th November[15] of this year, Man Singh laid the foundations of a new capital of Bengal at Rajmahal, as a place 'which could to some extent be safe from attack by boats' and named it Akbarnagar after the Emperor. Soon 'a choice city sprang up here', at a much healthier site than Gaur or Dacca, and nearer to Bihar.

From this rising capital, Man Singh set out on 7th December 1595,[16] to conquer from Isa Khan Bhati or the East Bengal delta. The Afghans retreated before him beyond the Brahmaputra, and Man Singh encamped at Sherpur Khura (in the Bogura district) for the coming monsoons, and built a mud-fort which he named Salimnagar. Much of Isa Khan's territory fell into Mughal hands. In far-off Orissa, his son Durjan Singh Kachhwa captured the fort of Kakruya, the zamindar of which had sought an alliance with the sultan of Golkonda. This young general, after much fighting, also recovered the fort of Bhushna (on Monday, 21st June, 1596), which had been wrested from its negligent Imperial commandant by Sulaiman and Kedar Rai. A gun burst inside the fort during the siege, killing Sulaiman and wounding Kedar Rai, who fled away to Isa Khan.[17]

In the rainy season of 1596 (July-September) while Man Singh was cantoning at Ghoraghat (in North Bengal), he fell so ill that the physicians began to despair of his life. This tempted Isa Khan, Masum Khan Kabuli and other half-suppressed rebels to rise again and advance to within 24 miles of the viceroy's camp in their war-boats, to which arm the imperialists had no adequate reply. But since the river-level had fallen, the rebel flotilla was forced to hurry back downstream and thus escape the fate of being stranded in the shallows and captured by the Mughal horse and artillery. Man Singh, immediately on his recovery, sent a select force under Himmat Singh, whose approach drove the rebels into the jungly interior of Mymensingh (Egara Sindur), and he plundered their territory freely.

Lakshmi Narayan, the Rajah of the newborn kingdom of Cooch Behar, begged for Akbar's protection on being attacked by his cousin Raghudev in alliance with Isa Khan. Man Singh hastened to his aid from Salimnagar to Anandpur, where Lakshmi Narayan came to welcome him on 23rd December, 1596 and to give him his sister (named Kshamadevi)[18] in marriage. The two enemies of the Cooch Rajah took flight on hearing of Man Singh's prompt advance, and Lakshmi Narayan sent his deliverer back with honours and gifts. Thus a new vassal state was created on the north-eastern frontier of Bengal. But very soon Man Singh lost two great lieutenants: his son Himmat Singh 'distinguished for courage and power of management', died of cholera in Bengal (16th March, 1597), while his eldest son (Jagat Singh) was sent on an expedition to Nagarkot in the far off north Punjab hills (April, 1597-June, 1598).

The pretender Raghudev collected a force again, seized some portion of the Cooch Behar territory and drove the mild Lakshmi Narayan into a fort for shelter. A detachment sent by Man Singh defeated Raghudev (on Monday, 2nd May, 1597), but as soon as these Mughal troops returned to Bengal, Isa Khan set out to help Raghudev. Man Singh countered this move by detaching a force by land and river, under his son Durjan Singh, to attack Katrabhu (opposite Khizrpur), the very seat of Isa Khan. A discontented kinsman of Isa Khan offered to guide the Imperialists. On 5th September, 1597,[19] 12 miles from Vikrampur (Dacca), the flotilla of Isa Khan and Masum Khan surrounded the Mughal detachment in overwhelming force, slew Durjan Singh and many of his troops, and took some prisoners. Isa Khan, however, thought it wiser to make peace; he set the prisoners free, gave up his attack on Lakshmi Narayan and offered submission to the Emperor. (*Ak*., iii, 1063-1093.)

Man Singh In Ajmer—Troubles Renewed In Bengal

No doubt saddened by the loss of two such brilliant sons and shaken by the Bengal climate, Man Singh begged permission to live in Ajmer (close to his long unvisited home) and govern Bengal by deputy (1598). Isa Khan died in September, 1599, and one great danger to the peace of the province was removed. But there was to be no rest for the war-worn viceroy. Prince Salim (Jahangir) had deeply wounded his father's heart by his addiction to wine and opium and pursuit of women. With the object of reforming his character by means of responsible work, he was appointed (16th September, 1599)[20] to conquer Mewar, now ruled by Amar Singh, the son of Maharana Pratap. Man Singh (from Ajmer) and many other officers were selected to accompany the Crown Prince. His eldest son, Jagat Singh, was ordered to Bengal to act as his father's deputy there. But the young man died near Agra on 6th October.[21] Grief prostrated Man Singh, and Maha Singh[22] (the son of Jagat Singh), though a lad in his teens, was sent to Bengal to lead the Kachhwa contingent there and serve as deputy viceroy.

Seizing this long absence of the veteran viceroy and despising his boy substitute, Usman, Sajawal and other turbulent Pathans, who had made a deceptive submission, rose in revolt. On 29th April, 1600,[23] they defeated a small Imperial force led by Maha Singh and his guardian, Pratap Singh Kachhwa (a younger brother of Rajah Man).[24] The Afghans recovered north Orissa.

Dangers thickened round the Mughal throne. While Akbar was detained in far-off Deccan by the long siege of Asir-garh, Prince Salim rebelled against his father and proclaimed himself Emperor at Allahabad (December, 1600). The Bengal rebels, finding the field vacant, inflicted defeat on several small Imperial detachments, and even captured the Inspector General (*Bakhshi*) of the provincial army, Abdur Razzaq Mamuri. (*Ak.*, iii, 1140-1174.)

Man Singh Returns To Bengal; His Vigorous Measures

These events forced the hand of Man Singh. He hastened east from Allahabad, halted for some weeks at Rohtas to make preparations, and then pushed on to face the rebels in East Bengal. Near Sherpur-Atia (in Murshidabad District), in a single field he routed them with heavy loss (12th February, 1601),[25] pursued them for eight miles and rescued his captive *Bakhshi* from threatened death at their hands. (*Ak*., iii, 1174.)

From the Mymensingh district, Man Singh marched south to Dacca, and from this base induced Kedar Rai, the zamindar of Bhushna, to submit. Then learning that Jalal Khan of Purnia was looting Malda and Akra, the Rajah sent orders to his grandson Maha Singh to march from Ghorahat against this new rebel. The young Kachhwa prince overtook the enemy (500 horse and 5000 foot) as they lay sheltered behind Kalindri river. 'Maha Singh impetuously forded the river on horse back and clambered up the steep opposite bank, though losing about a hundred men by drowning or the enemy's blows, and put the rebels to the rout like the wind.' The victor next proceeded to Purnia (Zainabad) to put down Qazi Mumin, a local rebel, who had taken post on an island protected by a dense jungle. This leader was killed. (*Ak*., iii, 1213.)

Next Usman, the nephew and successor of Qatlu Khan, crossed the Brahmaputra and drove out Baz Bahadur Qalmaq, the Mughal *thanahdar* of Mymensingh, to Bhawal. Man Singh rushed from Dacca in one day and night and attacked Usman on the bank of the Banar river. Many Pathans were slain and much booty in the form of boats and artillery obtained by the victorious Rajah. After re-establishing this outpost, Man Singh returned to Dacca (about February, 1602) and sent a detachment across the Ichhamati against Musa Khan (son of the dead Isa Khan) and Kedar, the rulers of Vikrampur and Sripur. These rulers had leagued in rebellion with Daud, the son of Qatlu Khan's late wazir, and other zamindars, and were blocking the river crossings. This obstacle held up the detachment for many days. When Man Singh heard of this, he came up from behind to Shahpur (16 miles west of Dacca and on the north bank of Dhaleshwari), and immediately on his arrival drove his elephant into the river. Many of his brave retainers followed him by swimming their horses. The river was crossed and the enemy routed and pursued up to nightfall, when Man Singh reached Burhanpur and Tarah.

Sher Ghazi, a powerful local zamindar, now waited on Man Singh, who next proceeded to Sripur and Vikrampur, but since Daud and the other Pathans had retreated to Sonargaon, he returned to his base at Dacca.[26]

A fleet of the Arracan pirates (called *Maghs* or Burmese) invaded the Dacca waters and invested the fort at Tri-mohani, the junction of two rivers. The imperial captain there, Sultan Quli Qalmaq, had a fracas with the Kashmiri garrison of this fort and was wounded. He fled at night, so that the emboldened enemy advanced, plundering many Mughal posts on the way. A force sent by Man Singh under Ibrahim Beg Ataka, Reghudas, Askarn, Dalpat Rao and other captains, chastised the invaders after a stiff fight, killing many of them. The Arracanese then withdrew from the dry land to their boats and opened a hot fire with their muskets and cannon, but the Mughals sank some of their gun-boats (*ghurabs*), about August, 1603.

Kedar Rai now joined the Maghs with his own powerful fleet and attacked the Mughal outpost of Srinagar, to which Man Singh had to send relief with artillery. Near Vikrampur a great battle was fought, in which Kedar Rai was wounded and captured. When brought before Man Singh his life ebbed out. Many Portuguese pirates and Bengal sailors in his service were killed. With the death of this active and turbulent zamindar the flames of disturbances in deltaic Bengal were quenched. After this Man Singh started from his base at Bhawal against the Magh Rajah who fled to his own country. Back at Bhawal once again, Man Singh turned his military preparations against Usman, who too fled. The Bengal viceroy then returned to Dacca, and later encamped at Nazirpur for the rainy season (July-September) of 1604. (*Ak.*, iii, 1231-1236.)

Man Singh Recalled To Court—The Death Of Akbar

Akbar's mother died on 24th August, 1604[27] His grief was intensified by the persistent misconduct and disobedience of his sole remaining son Salim (Jahangir). But at last some good sense prevailed over the infatuated prince and he came back from Allahabad to wait upon his father (15th November). Akbar put him under observation in the female apartments of the palace, censured him at length, denied him wine and prevented his evil counsellors from having access to him. After ten days Salim was released and restored to his rank and fiefs.

Akbar now felt his own end approaching and saw his venal servants going over to the rising sun, the Crown Prince. So he summoned Khan-i-Khanan, Man Singh and other trusty high officers to come quickly to his side, ostensibly to counsel him about a projected invasion of Turan. The wily Khan-i-Khanan who had been cherished by Akbar from his infancy, excused himself on the ground that the pressing affairs of the Deccan did not allow him to be absent from that province. But the ever-reliable Man Singh came at the first call of his loving master and personal friend, arriving at Agra shortly after 11th March, 1605. He was made Commander of Seven Thousand (6000 *sawar*), an unprecedented rank for anyone outside the circle of the Emperor's sons, and appointed guardian of Khusrau, the eldest son of Jahangir and Man Singh's sister, 26th August, 1605.[28] Not two months were to pass from this date before Akbar died on 15th October.[29] (*Ak.*, iii, 1250-1260.)

Akbar conferred the highest possible title on Man Singh by declaring him *Mirza Rajah*. The word Mirza is short for the Persian epithet *amir-zadah*, meaning 'born of a king, a prince'. Timur, the most famous progenitor of the Mughal Emperors of Delhi, bore the title of Amir (just as the Caliph was known under the title of Amir of the Faithful). The Timurides, including the family of Babur, were known as *Mirzas*. Akbar thus openly declared to the world that Man Singh was no less than his own kith and kin, like the nephews of Humayun, a prince of the blood royal in status, though a Hindu by creed. Bhau Singh, Jai Singh I, Jai Singh II and their descendants were similarly honoured by the suzerain power.

Akbar's Death; Recalled From Bengal By Jahangir

The last days of the great Akbar were darkened by the prospect of the future. His empire had spread over a vaster area, his power had grown more formidable and his riches more immense than any former Sultan of Delhi had dreamt of. But his 'house had been his bane'. Brother and sons alike had failed him. Two of his sons had died young from a mad addiction to drink, and the sole survivor among his progeny, Prince Salim, seemed determined to follow the same path to the grave. Worse than this, the Crown Prince had attempted to defile his father's bed, as the affair of Anar-Kali proves. Reading between the lines of a certain passage in the official account of Akbar's visit to Kashmir, we get a hint that this prince had tried to intrude into his father's harem and had to be forbidden from the Presence. His disregard of public welfare and private morality alike in the pursuit of personal vengeance had been recently illustrated by his murder of Abul Fazl, a minister of whom any empire might have been proud. Jahangir's rebellion against his loving father and his doings at the rival Court that he set up at Allahabad betrayed a character that threatened to make Akbar's successor the foe of all good men.

There were serious consultations and sad misgivings among the elder statesmen and loyal ministers gathered round the deathbed of Akbar, and we can well believe that alternatives to Jahangir as the next sovereign were considered. But there is no evidence that a conspiracy was set on foot by Man Singh to crown his own nephew Khusrau (the eldest son of Jahangir). The idea of disinheriting Jahangir must have been given up as impracticable and worse than useless, as soon as conceived. There is also the wild rumour—worthy only of the opium-eaters on whom Tod relied—that Akbar in trying to poison Man Singh, poisoned himself by mistake. Of the poison-complex of the writers of that age, in Europe no less than in India, the reader will find ample evidence in Macaulay's account of the death of King Charles II of England.

It is true that Jahangir has written in his autobiography that Man Singh had done him an ill turn in his father's reign.[30] This can only mean that Man Singh had given to Akbar, who needed no telling of it, a true character of Jahangir, instead of making a futile attempt to keep the old Emperor in a fool's paradise as to the future. The treatment of Man Singh by Jahangir after his accession shows that the Rajah could not have really opposed his right to the Crown.

A fortnight after his accession, Jahangir sent Man Singh from Agra to Bengal as *subahdar* of that province once more (*c.* 10th November, 1605). A few days later Bhau Singh, 'the most capable of Man Singh's sons' (in Jahangir's own words), was promoted to a 1500 *mansab*. On 4th August, 1606, the Emperor, then in Lahore, having pursued his rebel son Khusrau,[31] sent a special robe of honour to Man Singh in his province. About the middle of 1607,[32] Maha Singh (the grandson of Rajah Man) was appointed to command the army sent against the rebels of Bangash, with Ramdas Kachhwa[33] as his guardian (*ataliq*).

But Man Singh's third viceroyalty of Bengal was a very short one. Jahangir was disconsolate. His home was dark, because she who was destined to be the Light of his Harem, and afterwards to blaze forth as the Light of the World (*Nur Jahan*) was illuminating the humble tent of her lawful husband, Sher-Afgan Istajlu, a petty Turkish *jagirdar* of Burdwan in Bengal. The royal sorrow found a sympathetic listener in his foster-brother Qutbuddin Khan Koka, who was now (2nd September, 1606) appointed governor of Bengal, with whispered instructions about means of procuring the healing balsam for the afflicted royal heart. The service required of the new *subahdar* was too delicate for a man of honour like Man Singh. The result is history; on 20th May, 1607, husband and abductor both perished and the fair and frail Helen was sent to her royal lover.

In consequence of Qutbuddin's appointment, Man Singh was transferred to Bihar and took up his residence in the salubrious hill-fort of Rohtas, overlooking the Sone river for which he had a special liking. Though summoned to Court shortly after Qutb's murder, he delayed his coming, probably because the Emperor was away in Kabul from where he came back to Agra only at the end of the next February (1608). Man Singh waited on Jahangir near Agra on (Sunday), 28th February. The Emperor was highly exasperated at the Rajah's delay and records in his autobiography: 'Man Singh came from Rohtas and waited on me after orders had been sent to him six or seven times. He, like Khan Azam, is one of the hypocrites and old wolves of the State'.

Man Singh In The Deccan: The End

But Jahangir's own acts showed that Man Singh had not really sinned against his sovereign, for on 21st April, less than two months after the Rajah's return to Court, the Emperor presented him with one of his finest horses. It had been received as a gift from Shah Abbas I of Persia to Akbar, and the royal diary records, 'No horse like this had ever come from Iraq to Hindustan'. At the same time, the Rajah's only surviving son Bhau Singh was promoted to the rank of a Commander of 2000. This is not the treatment that a king would accord to a 'hypocrite and old wolf' among his servants.

After this recall, Man Singh spent some months in attendance at Court. His grand-daughter (i.e. a daughter of his deceased eldest son Jagat Singh) was married to Jahangir on 8th June of this year. A little later he was ordered to join the reinforcements which were being assembled for strengthening the Imperial army in the Deccan. On Sunday, 11th September, the Rajah, who had been absent from his home for many years, received permission to go to Amber and there complete his contingent by recruiting more Kachhwas. He returned about the middle of the next year, 1609, and was given a jewelled waist-band on 28th July[34] and afterwards sent to the Deccan.

In the Deccan, soon after Akbar's death, the dying kingdom of Ahmadnagar had been galvanised into a new life by the genius and energy of an Abyssinian slave named Malik Ambar, whom all the forces of the Delhi empire failed to crush so long as he lived. At this time he had driven the Mughal army into the defensive within the walls of Burhanpur (the capital of Khandesh) and besieged their garrison in Ahmadnagar, the Nizamshahi capital which Akbar had gained a few years before. Khan-i-Khanan, the Mughal viceroy of the Deccan, fell short of success, and Jahangir decided to send his son Parviz at the head of a new Deccan expedition with enormous sums of money and vast forces, for subduing Malik Ambar. The prince set out on 30th October 1609.[35] But before he could reach Burhanpur, the Deccanis burst into the Imperial dominions and raised disturbances. The Emperor, therefore, sent his favourite Afghan general Khan-i-Jahan Lodi (entitled *Amir-ul-umra)* at the head of large forces, including Man Singh's division, to support the prince. These troops left Agra on Friday, 2nd February, 1610.[36]

In the meantime, the prince, after reaching Burhanpur, had as ordered by Jahangir, immediately pushed on towards Ahmadnagar, and reached Badnera on the Berar plateau (10 miles east of Malkapur) railway station). When Khan-i-Jahan and his officers arrived near this place and were advancing to interview the prince, the Deccanis under Adam Khan Habshi, Jadu Rao Maratha and others, blocked their path two miles from the camp. A severe battle ensued, in which the Deccanis fought most bravely, and so did the Afghans of Khan-i-Jahan and the Rajputs of Man Singh, and many were slain. At last, at the approach of reliefs from the prince's camp, the enemy fled. This happened in March 1610. For lack of provisions and fodder, the prince, with Man Singh and other generals, had no help but to fall back on Burhanpur. (*Masir-i-Rahimi*, ii, 516-518. *Tuzuk.*, i, 145-162.)

Thereafter Man Singh lived at Burhanpur which was the Imperial base of operations. He was no longer Commander-in-Chief, as he had so often been with conspicuous success in Akbar's reign. He was now only one of the three divisional commanders, with a prince (Parviz) as their nominal head and a great noble (like Khan-i-Khanan or Khan-i-Jahan) as the prince's guardian and executive agent. The Mughal leaders achieved no success against Ambar, and indeed suffered one humiliating reverse—the defeat of Abdullah Khan—through their mutual jealousies, gross mismanagement, and lack of supreme control. For this Man Singh was in no way to blame; he held no responsible post or command with freedom of initiative, while the frequent changes of order by the distant and distracted Emperor did not improve matters.

In this atmosphere of stagnation Man Singh's marvellously eventful life ended in a peaceful death at Elichpur on the 6th of July, 1614. His iron constitution had successfully defied the murderous snowfall (*Khuni barf*) of the Afghan winter and the steam bath of the Bengal monsoon alike. And now a career that had attained an eminence unequalled by any Hindu before or after, closed amidst inglorious inactivity in a far off land. His portrait gives him a short thick-set dark figure, with piercing eyes, a deeply intelligent self-controlled forehead and a firm masterful chin. His last hours must have been saddened by the thought that he was leaving no son behind him, worthy to sustain the house of Amber at the high pitch to which he and Bhagwant Das had raised it. The dawn of Mirza Rajah Jai Singh was yet to be. (*Tuzuk*, i. 266)

Friends And Companions Of Emperors

In the Anglo-Saxon period of the English nation's growth, the devoted warriors who defended the king in battles and formed his personal 'war band', became the aristocracy of the land and the highest noble houses originated from these *gesiths* or royal companions-in-arms. The same services were rendered by the house of Jaipur—though of much older and royal origin—to Akbar and his successors. We have already seen Bhagwant Das's defence of Akbar at the storming of Paronkh. Some years later, in the Gujarat campaign of 1572, when Akbar with less than 200 men desperately forded the river before the city of Sarnal, Man Singh begged and obtained permission for the dangerous privilege of leading his van, so as to get an opportunity of proving 'his devotion by marching in the front and displaying life-sacrifice'. After ascending the rugged opposite bank, superior enemy forces attacked the Emperor and his handful of comrades, some of whom were swept away. But Bhupat Singh, the brother of Bhagwant Das, fell resisting numbers, and Bhagwant Das rode stirrup to stirrup with the Emperor in the dangerous street-fighting within the walls of Sarnal. These two were isolated from the rest of the party and attacked by crowds of the enemy. Bhagwant Das took on some of the assailants and thus relieved the pressure on Akbar, till at last the enemy broke away and fled. (*Ak.*, iii, 19-21.)

In Man Singh, Akbar found not only a brave general and wise administrator, but also a frank and hearty companion of his hours of repose. The Kachhwa Rajah saved Akbar not only from foreign enemies and domestic traitors, but also from his lower nature in his moments of self-forgetfulness. The courtly pen of Abul Fazl does not hesitate to record how in 1573, in his private drinking party, Akbar made a suicidal attempt to prove his own valour.

> The talk was that the heroes of Hindustan paid no regard to their lives. For instance, some Rajputs would hold a double-headed spear, and two men would run from opposite sides against the points, so that the latter would transfix them and come out at their backs. The Emperor... fastened the hilt of his own sword to a wall and placing the point near his own breast, declared that if Rajputs were wont to show their valour in that way, he would rush against this sword... Man Singh ran... and gave such a blow with his hand that the sword fell down... Those present removed the sword and His Majesty angrily flung Man Singh on the ground and squeezed him. (*Ak.*, iii, 43-44.)

The Kachhwa princes who were attracted by Akbar for the honourable reasons given earlier, were no timid sycophants or servile tools of a despot. They retained their manly freedom of speech and thought. Bhagwant Das had the courage to reject the syncretic religion *Din-i-Ilahi* which was dearest to the heart of Akbar. He did not care for its pantheistic subtleties, but bluntly replied that he could understand Hinduism, he could understand Islam, but (he asked) 'What is this new-fangled religion which is neither?' And Akbar had the wisdom not to force his faith on anybody. (*Al Bad.*, ii, 323, 375.) Man Singh carried the idols of his daily worship into the Afghan country, and when one day they lagged behind him owing to a breakdown of transport, he fasted until they arrived and the daily honour was done to the gods. The incident moved the free thinker Akbar to a smile, but not to scorn or censure.

Such was the *bon camaraderie* among the men, differing in religious belief but similar in greatness of soul, who formed the inner circle of Akbar's court. Such a king deserved and received freely the unstinted devotion and fullest possible service of his servants because they were also his friends.

The Jaipur princes can truly be called empire-builders under the Mughal sovereigns and they had to pay the necessary price for such careers. Their ashes, and even those of most of their wives and children, lie scattered all over India from the north-western frontier to the Tapti river in the Deccan. Of the six successive Rajahs from Bhagwant Das to Bishan Singh, not one died in his native land, but in far off places such as Lahore, Balapur, Burhanpur, Kohat and Darband. Man Singh's mother died near Patna in Bihar and many children of his family for several generations perished in infancy in different provinces. Such is a soldier's life. Mirza Rajah Jai Singh lost three sons and four daughters in their childhood and only two of his numerous progeny came of age.

This history has hitherto traced the careers of only the kings of the House of (Amber) Jaipur. But their gallant clansmen worthily supported them with their life-blood. It is not possible to narrate here the careers of the Kachhwa barons and 'younger brothers' who rose to eminence in the service of the Empire. We must content ourselves with mentioning only those who were granted high *mansabs* or were elevated to Rajaships elsewhere by the grateful sovereign of Delhi: Askarn[37] and his sons (under Akbar) Lonkarn Shekhawat[38] of Sambhar, Jagannath[39] and Khangar[40] (son and nephew of Bhagwant Das),[41] Ramdas[42] of Loni, Raghunath[43] Das and Ramdas.[44] Raj Singh (son of Askarn and nephew of Bihar Mal) was made a Rajah by Jahangir. Many others have already figured in this narrative.

Notes

1. Mir Murad Khan was sent on Tuesday, August 29, 1587, from the Court to escort Said Khan, then the Governor of Bihar, from Bihar to Bengal. (*Ak.*, iii, p. 801) *Ed.*
2. Man Singh arrived from Jamrud on Sunday, December 10, 1587, and was sent to Bihar on Monday, December 18, 1587. (*Ak.*, iii, p. 801) *Ed.*
3. The step-brother of Man Singh; his mother was the Bhati Rani, the daughter of Raisal. He died issueless. *Ed.*
4. The correct date is Monday, August 17, 1590. *Ed.*
5. The correct date is Friday, November 5, 1591. *Ed.*
6. The printed Persian text (111.611) reads 'the forest of Malnapur', which may be a copyist's error for Midnapur, the town of Midnapur being at that time a part of the district of Jalesar (*Ain.*, ii, 143). The battle did not take place near the town of Midnapur, but within one day's march north of Jalesar city, and the site may well have been spoken of as falling within the jungle land of Midnapur. The India Office ms. reads Benapur, which is a place 34 miles north of Jalesar, and therefore a rather unlikely alternative. *J.S.*
7. Durjan Singh was the younger brother of Bhav Singh, who succeeded Raja Man Singh. Their mother was Rani Sahodra Gaud, daughter of Raimal. (*Vamsavali*, pp. 20, 22) *Ed.*
8. *Akbarnamah*, iii, 967, names these conquests thus: Sahajpal (? Sakhi-gopal), Kharagarh, Kalupara (on the west shore of the Chilka lake, 5 miles south-east of Khurda Road Railway Junction), Kahnan (? Kannaus), Longarh and Bhunmal (? Talmal). For this long campaign, see *Akbarnamah*, iii, 940-968. *J.S.*
9. The *Vamsavali* (p. 21) gives her name as *Udani Achcha de*, an obvious regional variant of 'Akshaya Devi of Orissa'. She died issueless. *Ed.*
10. The correct date is Friday, February 9, 1593. *Ed.*
11. The correct date is Thursday, February 21, 1594. *Ed.*
12. Sakat Singh was a younger son of Raja Man Singh from Rani Sumitra, daughter of Ishwar Das Rathor. His descendants held Paharia village (Jaipur State) in *jagir*. (*Vamsavali*, pp. 20-22) *Ed.*
13. Himmat Singh was another younger son of Raja Man Singh from Rani Jamoti (Jambvanti), daughter of Ratan Singh Chauhan. His son Kushan Singh died issueless. (*Vamsavali* pp. 20-22) *Ed.*
14. The correct date is Tuesday, June 4, 1594—24 Khurdad Ilahi Year 39. This is an inadvertent mistake in noting down the month. (*Ak.*, iii, pp. 1000-1001) *Ed.*

15. The correct date is Sunday, November 9, 1595. *Ed.*
16. The correct date is Tuesday, December 9, 1595. *Ed.*
17. *Ak.*, iii, 1023, 1042-1059. Sherpur is 12 miles south of Bangura town in North Bengal. The place is usually called Sherpur Murcha (or the extended Sherpur), as in *Baharistan*, and also in the Persian text of *Akbarnamah*, which Beveridge has misread as Sherpur Hurra and located it in the Mymensingh district, an erroneous identification. Egara-sindur is 28 miles south of Mymensingh town, but on the opposite or left bank of the Brahmaputra. *J.S.*
18. In *Vamsavali* (pp. 21, 23) her name appears as 'Kochil Chhamavati, Raja Narayan Ki' i.e. Chhamavati (Kshamavati) daughter of Kochi Raja Narayan. When Maharaja Man Singh died at Ellichpur she became a *sati*. She had two sons, Keshodas and Atibal. Her descendants held the *jagir* of Dhula in Jaipur state. *History of Cooch Behar,* translated from Bengali, by Sarat Chandra Ghosal (1942) gives the name of the Kochi Rani as Prabhavati Devi (p. 172). But Maharaja Man Singh had another Rani Prabhavati Bangalan, daughter of Kishan Rai, who too became *sati*, at Amber. She had no issue. (*Vamsavali*, pp. 22, 23-24) *Ed.*
19. The correct date is Thursday, September 8, 1597. *Ed.*
20. The correct date is Wednesday, September 19, 1599. *Ed.*
21. The correct date is Tuesday, October 9, 1599 = Kartik Sudi 1, 1656 V.S. Aban 26, Ilahi year 44. *Ed.*
22. Maha Singh was born on Friday, September 10, 1585 (*Literary Heritage*, p. 360. No. 3). *Ed.*
23. The correct date is Sunday, April 27, 1600. *Ed.*
24. Pratap Singh Kachhawa was born of Rani Bhagwati, daughter of Panchayan Panwar, mother of Raja Man Singh. He died issueless. *(Vamsavali*, pp. 18-19) *Ed.*
25. The correct date is Monday, February 9, 1601 = 1 Isfandar, Ilahi year 45. *Ed.*
26. The East Bengal campaign,—*Ak.*, iii, 1213-1215. For Akra and Maldah, the Persian text (p. 808) has Agra and Malira. Akra is 12 miles west of Maldah and on the north bank of the Kalindri (misprinted Mandri in the Persian text), a river west of Malda city. Bhawal is 15 miles north of Dacca. Banar is the name of the northern portion of the Lakhya river. *J.S.*
27. *Ak.*, (iii, p. 1245), cites Monday, 19 Shahriyar, Ilahi year 49, as the date of her death. The Ilahi date corresponds to Friday, August 31, 1604 (15 Rabi-us-Sani, 1013 A.H.). But as the day of the week given in the *Ak.* is different from the corresponding Christian date, it is difficult to accept the same as the correct day and date. The date of her demise has been noted differently in various works. (See f.n. I on *Ak.*, iii, p. 1245). *Ed.*

28. The correct date is Thursday, August 29, 1605 = 19 Shahriyar, Ilahi year 50. (*Ak*., iii, p. 1257) *Ed*.
29. Sir Jadunath Sarkar records this date as Tuesday, Jamadi-us-Sani 12, 1014 A.H., cited in *Takmil*. *Tuzuk* (I, p. 148) also mentions Jamadi-us-Sani 12 as the date of Akbar's death anniversary. *Akbar Nama* (iii, p. 1260) gives the date of Akbar's death as Wednesday, 4th Aban = Thursday, October 17, 1605, i.e., 14 Jamadi-us-Sani, 1014 A.H. Vincent Smith, however conclusively fixes October 17, (October 27 Ns.) as the correct date of Akbar's death as recorded by Father Du Jarrie (*Akbar*, pp. 323-324 f.n.) *Ed*.
30. 'What they (*viz*., Man S. and Kh. Azam) have done to me, and what has happened to them from me, God the knower of Secrets knows; possibly no one could mention such another case.' (*Tuzuk-i-Jahangiri*, Roger's tr., i, 138.) And, again, 'I made Man Singh,—who was one of the greatest and most trusted noblemen of my father,... as before, ruler of Bengal. Though in consequence of certain of his acts, he had no expectation of this favour towards himself, I dignified him with a *Charqab*...' (p. 15) *J.S.*
31. Khusrau was captured on Sunday, April 27, 1606, and pro duced before Jahangir in Mirza Kamran's garden near Lahore on Thursday, May 1, 1606. Jahangir was at Lahore from Wednesday, May 7, 1606, to Thursday, March 26, 1607. (*Tuzuk*, i, pp. 67-68, 70, 90). *Ed*.
32. The exact date is Monday, January 29, 1607. (*Tuzuk*., I, p. 111). *Ed*.
33. Ram Das Kachhawa, a descendant of Patal, son of Raja Udaikarn of Amber, referred to as 'of Loni'. See foot note 44 at the end of this chapter. *Ed*.
34. The correct date is Monday, August 7, 1609 = 16 Jamadi-Awwal, 1018 A.H. (*Tuzuk*, i, p. 155). *Ed*.
35. The correct date is Tuesday, October 3, 1609 = Tuesday, 14 Rajab, 1018 A.H. *Tuzuk*, (i, p. 156) mistakenly gives the date as 4 Rajab, which falls on Saturday, September 23, 1609. *Ed*.
36. *Tuzuk*. (i, p. 161) cites Tuesday as the day of the week on this date, which is obviously wrong. *Ed*.
37. Askarn, son of Bhim and grandson of Prithviraj, who was granted Narwar by Akbar. His son Raj Singh succeeded him at Narwar. *M.U*., (E.T.), II, pp. 578-579. *Ed*.
38. Lunkaran Shekhawat of Sambhar. *M.U*., (E.T.), I, pp. 836-837. *Ed*.
39. Jagannath, Younger son of Biharmal of Amber, *M.U*., (E.T.), I, pp. 724-725. *Ed*.
40. Khangar, son of Jagmal Kachhawa, the younger brother of Biharmal of Amber. *M.U*., (E.T.), I, p. 727. *J.S.*

41. This should be Biharmal. *Ed*.

42. Raja Ram Das Kachhawa, who was 'cherished and made an *Amir*' by Akbar. *M.U.*, (E.T.), II, pp. 587-589; *Proceedings I.H.C.*, 1953, pp. 251-259; Nainsi, *Khyat*, (RPP. Ed.) I, p. 302, 331. *Ed* Luni (*var*. Boanli) was some small village in Amber region; Ram Das later shifted to Newata. *Ed*.

43. This obviously refers to Raghav Das Kachhawa, son of Khangor, whose sacrificing his life has been mentioned by Jahangir (*Tuzuk*., i, p. 43); also see *Thirty Decisive Battles of Jaipur*, by Narendra Singh, pp. 13-14). *Ed*.

44. Ram Das, son of Raja Raj Singh of Narwar, hence known as Narwari. *M.U.*, (E.T.), II, pp. 579, 586; Nainsi, *Khyat* (RPP), I, p. 303. *Ed*.

VIII

Interlude And Mirza Raja Jai Singh (First Phase): 1614–1657

Interlude: The Careers Of Maha Singh And Bhau Singh

On the death of Man Singh the headship of the Kachhwa clan and the kingdom of Amber should, by Hindu custom, have passed on to Maha Singh, son of the late Rajah's eldest son Jagat Singh, who had died in Man Singh's lifetime. But Jahangir by his royal will bestowed the succession on Bhau Singh, a younger son of Rajah Man, saying, 'Since the time when I was prince, Bhau Singh had done much service with me', and also declaring him as 'the most capable of Man Singh's sons'. So Bhau Singh was given the title of Mirza Rajah and raised to the rank of a Commander of Four Thousand; at the same time Maha Singh was consoled with promotion to the 1000 rank and the grant of the district of Garha (modern Jabalpur), and shortly afterwards raised to the dignity and title of a Rajah, with the highest insignias of honour, namely a standard and drums. Bhau Singh left Court on short leave for Amber on 25th August, 1615.[1] Two years later (20th March, 1617)[2] he was raised to the still higher rank of a Commander of Five Thousand.

Maha Singh, who had served well as leader of the expeditions against the Bangarh rebels in 1607 and Rajah Vikramajit of Rewa in 1610, was sent to the Deccan war and died of hard drinking at Balapur (in Berar) about the 20th of May, 1617.[3] His son Jai Singh, then a boy in his sixth year, came to Court at the royal call (9th August, 1617) and was given the rank of a Commander of One Thousand and an elephant by the Emperor.

In Jahangir's reign these two Kachhwa princes felt themselves under a cloud: they were sent to the endless languid war in the Deccan against Malik Ambar. Here they served as subordinate captains and not as supreme commanders such as Bhagwant Das and Man Singh had been, and even as they themselves had been in lesser North Indian campaigns of an earlier time. A deep melancholy seems to have settled on them as the effect of this inactive and inglorious life, and they tried to drown their sorrow in the wine cup and other pleasures to which an idle brain naturally leads, where the feeling of responsibility is not present to exert its steadying influence on character.

Bhau Singh returned to the Emperor's Court in March, 1619 and was sent at the end of the next October, to support the army of the Deccan. In that southern land, he too died in the same way as his nephew Maha Singh. Jahangir thus records his death in his autobiography: 'From excess of wine-drinking Bhau Singh had become very weak and low. Suddenly a faintness came over him. He did not recover his senses, but died after a night and a day.' The Emperor had a warm personal love for him and writes about the deceased Rajah, 'he was of very good disposition and sedate. From the days when I was a prince, he was constantly in my service, and by the blessings of my education he had reached the high rank of a Commander of Five Thousand'.

The news of Bhau Singh's death reached Jahangir at Hardwar at the end of the year 1621[4] and he conferred the succession to the late childless Rajah on Jai Singh (the grandson of his eldest brother Jagat Singh), with the title of Rajah and a *mansab* of two thousand. On Saturday, 29th March 1623, the boy Rajah was raised to the rank of a Commander of Three Thousand.

With the accession of Jai Singh I, the Kachhwa royal family entered a new and unrivalled stage of prosperity and fame, which will be now described in this and the following chapters.

Mirza Rajah Jai Singh I: His Character

Jai Singh I was born on 15th July, 1611, to Maha Singh (then Kumar) and Damiyanti,[5] the granddaughter of Maharana Udai Singh of Mewar. At the age of two years he was removed by his mother to the fort of Daosa, evidently as a precaution against designs on his life, and here he lived till he was nine. On succeeding to the Kachhwa throne at the end of 1621, he paid a visit to the Emperor and then came to his own capital Amber.[6]

Jai Singh's career was one of undimmed brilliance and of unapproached eminence almost from the day when he, an orphan in his eleventh year, received the throne of Amber (1621). When he came of age, he fought under the Imperial banner in every part of the empire, from Balkh in Central Asia to Bijapur in the Deccan, from Qandahar in the west to Monghyr in the east. Hardly a year passed during the long reign of Shah Jahan when this Rajput chief did not see active service somewhere and receive some promotion for conspicuous merit. His marked ability found recognition in his being given the command of the vanguard or of one of the wings in the Mughal armies led by princes of the blood in campaigns beyond the frontiers of India, or in the still independent Deccan land. Latterly he was placed in supreme command, and in the first decade of Aurangzib's reign, after Mir Jumla's death, he attained an eminence and position of importance which was really unequalled by any other noble, Hindu or Muslim.

In diplomacy he attained success surpassing even his victories in the field. Wherever there was difficult or delicate work to be done, the Emperor had only to turn to Jai Singh. A suave speaker, adept in the ceremonious courtesy of the Muslim Court, a master of the Turk and Persian languages besides Sanskrit and Hindi, he was an ideal leader for the composite army of Afghans and Mughals, Rajputs and *purbias* that followed the crescent banner of the Emperors of Delhi. His foresight and political thinking, his smoothness of tongue and cool calculating self-possession, were in striking contrast with the impulsive generosity, reckless daring, blunt straightforwardness, and impolitic chivalry which we are apt to associate with the word Rajput.

Jai Singh's Work In The Deccan Under Shah Jahan

The life of Mirza Rajah Jai Singh is practically a history of Shah Jahan's reign and that of the first decade of Aurangzib's. It is not possible here to describe all his campaigns in detail, but a fuller study of the campaigns in which he held independent commands is necessary if we are to understand his character and capacity. Some time after his appointment as a Commander of Three Thousand (1623), Jai Singh, who had just entered his teens was sent[7] by Jahangir to command the Kachhwa contingent then serving under the Imperial *subahdar* of the Deccan in the endless war with Malik Ambar. He is not mentioned among the officers present in the battle of Bhatvadi (October, 1624), in which the Mughals and their Bijapuri allies received a crushing defeat at the hands of that Abyssinian genius. Then followed years of languor and inactivity on the part of the imperialists due to the rebellion of Shah Jahan, the growing infirmity of Jahangir and the treason of his Deccan Commander-in-Chief Khan Jahan Lodi, and the record of the three years 1625-27 is blank.

Jahangir died on Sunday, 28th October, 1627. Jai Singh, who had then completed his sixteenth year, was posted under Khan Jahan at Burhanpur with the rank of a Commander of Four Thousand (2500 *sawars*.) His chief had been bribed by the Ahmadnagar prime minister with three lakhs of *hun* (12 lakhs of rupees) to sell all of Balaghat and the fort of Ahmadnagar to the enemy. But Khan Jahan's treason did not prosper. When Shah Jahan, on learning of his father's death, summoned Khan Jahan to join him as the lawful sovereign, this Afghan general openly rebelled and came to Malwa in order to seize that province for himself. Shah Jahan, on his march from the Deccan to Agra, reached Ajmer, and Jai Singh and other loyal generals who had slipped away from the traitor's camp, joined their new Emperor (*c.* 17th January, 1628.)[8] At Agra, on the next Coronation Day, Jai Singh was rewarded with a standard and kettledrums and his *mansab* was increased by 500 horses (4th February, 1628). The next month he was sent under Qasim Khan to punish the rebels of Mahavan (opposite Mathura), and he returned, successful, in June. In July he had to march to Afghanistan in the army of Mahabat Khan to defend Kabul from an Uzbak attack, but the enemy fled without fighting.

In October, 1629, Khan Jahan Lodi threw off the mask and fled from Shah Jahan's court to the south. The Imperial army sent against him under Khwajah Abul Hasan included the Kachhwa contingent. The chase was long, continuous and harassing; the rebel fled very fast, often doubling back like the hunted fox. The rebel finally joined Nizam Shah, while the imperialists, after missing him, halted for breath in Gondwana. At this point, Shah Jahan himself took charge of the campaign. He went to the Deccan and detached three divisions, under three generals, with Azam Khan as Commander-in-Chief, totalling 50,000 men against the rebels. Jai Singh was attached to the division of Abdullah Khan and his *mansab* was further increased by a thousand horses, so that he now became a *char hazari* both in rank and number of troopers (March, 1630).

One day the Afghan rebels, 12,000 strong, lured Azam Khan's army four miles away from its rearguard by a pretended flight, and then suddenly wheeling round attacked the isolated rear, where the Kachhwas (including Shekhawats) and Mughals offered a desperate resistance. Chhatra Singh (the son of Madho Singh, the brother of Rajah Man) with his two sons (Bhim and Anand), Balbhadra Shekhawat, Karmasi Rathor, and Rajah Girdhar (the son of Keshodas and grandson of Jaimal of Mairta and Chitor) were slain, and Dwarkadas, the son of Girdhar Shekhawat, was wounded. But the battle ended in victory for the imperialists after heavy slaughter on both sides. (This was in May.)

In October, 1630, the campaign was renewed, with Asaf Khan as Commander-in-Chief. Jai Singh led his van. In a great battle near Bir (some 60 miles east of Ahmadnagar), Jai Singh with his division ascended a hill and fell upon the rebel army which stood at bay. A desperate fight ensued, in which Bahadur (the nephew and right hand man of Khan Jahan) was slain and the Afghans put to flight (*Abd. Ham.*, I-A, 323-324). The pursuit was kept up, but the rebels, abandoning everything, fled to Malwa and thence to Bundelkhand, where their two leaders Darya Khan and Khan Jahan were slain. Khan Jahan fell in fight on the Ken river near Sihinda (south of Bands) on 24th January, 1631, to the spear of Madho Singh (Hada), and all his remaining kinsmen and retainers were cut to pieces. (*Ibid.*, 338-351.)

In the meantime the war against the Ahmadnagar dynasty continued. Azam Khan marched to attack Parenda (50 miles south of Bir) and sent Jai Singh to raid the village and *peth* lying at the foot of the fort. The coup was successfully carried out; the village mud-wall was battered down with the heads of Jai Singh's elephants and seven enemy elephants, besides all their property, were seized (c. February, 1631). While the siege of Parenda continued, Jai Singh, with his chief, drove away a relieving army of the Deccanis; but through the utter failure of provisions the siege had to be abandoned. The enemy followed close behind, but Jai Singh and the Rajputs kept them in check all through this dangerous movement. (*Ibid.*, 357-360.)

On Sunday, 4th December, 1631, Asaf Khan led an expedition against the Sultan of Bijapur, with Jai Singh in command of the left flank of his centre; but it was foiled by the great Deccan famine and he was compelled to return. In 1632, Jai Singh went on leave to Amber, and on his return interviewed the Emperor at Agra on 15th March, 1633. Here, two months later, he had a chance of displaying Rajput coolness and contempt for danger, reminding us of the earlier scene in which Bihar Mal had first gained Akbar's admiring notice. On 28th May, while Shah Jahan was watching from the Agra palace-balcony a combat between two elephants, and the princes were standing below, one of the two combatants broke away and rushed towards prince Aurangzib, who coolly kept his place and struck the beast with his spear, but was felled to the ground with his horse by a sweep of the brute's tusk. While other people were running about in terror and confusion, Jai Singh rode up to the right side of the elephant (his horse having refused to face it) and hit the animal with his lance. The elephant then moved away. (*Ibid.*, 489-492.)

But the Kachhwas were not meant for dancing attendance at the royal court; their proper place was the camp. Only four months after the affair of the charging elephant, a second expedition was sent forth to attack Parenda, under Prince Shuja as its nominal commander, and Mahabat Khan (Khan-i-Khanan) as his right-hand man. Jai Singh, in command of the vanguard, arrived rapidly with all the Rajputs, in the neighbourhood of Parenda (January, 1634). When Khan-i-Khanan issued on foraging expeditions, forcing his way through the enemy hordes hovering round, Jai Singh had the most dangerous post, namely his rearguard, so as to meet and defeat repeated attacks. The Court historian records how 'Rajah Jai Singh, all the way, engaged with the enemy, making brave charges, and in this way traversed the distance'. On Friday, 14th March, he took part in a night march for surprising the enemy's baggage camp. 'Jai Singh, the commander of the vanguard, galloped at the fleeing enemy, capturing many of their infantry. Then, from the Imperial centre, many came and joined him.'

We need not go into the details of this campaign. The imperialists had in the end to raise this siege also, for lack of grass and firewood. In the retreat to Burhanpur, Jai Singh again bore the chief burden. (*Abd. Ham.*, I-B, 35-46.)

In November, 1634, the Mughals resumed the offensive. Jai Singh, under Khan-i-Dauran, took part in a long chase of Shahji Bhonsla (the father of the famous Shivaji) who was out on raid near Daulatabad. This pursuit was as tirelessly waged as that of Khan Jahan Lodi. After many days' hard riding, Jai Singh surprised the enemy's baggage at the Manik-dawa pass, capturing 8000 oxen loaded with provisions, arms and rockets, besides 3000 men (January, 1635). On Sunday, 29th March, came Jai Singh's reward; he was created a Commander of Five Thousand, and later, on 17th September had his audience of the Emperor at Agra. (*Ibid.*, 63-104.)

Early next year Shah Jahan returned to the Deccan in person in order to overawe the Sultans of Golkonda and Bijapur who had been obstructing the settlement of the newly annexed Nizamshahi dominions. Khan-i-Dauran, at the head of 20,000 men, with Jai Singh and other Rajputs as his vanguard, invaded Bijapur, plundering the country and laying it waste, and making prisoners of the population. At every point in the advance to Bijapur, enemy attacks had to be met and beaten back, with Jai Singh always assisting the main army. But the Sultan of Bijapur offered desperate resistance in his capital, and at last the Mughals had to return to their own territory and patch up a peace of compromise. Thereafter, Khan-i-Dauran besieged and captured the forts of Udgir (28th September) and Ausa (19th October). (*Ibid.*, 135-220.)

Immediately afterwards, Jai Singh went with Khan-i-Dauran to invade the Gond country[9] (the modern central provinces) and exact tribute. Nagpur (belonging to the Gond Rajah Kukia) was besieged, and a breach made by mining, through which Sipahdar Khan and Jai Singh entered and took the fort by assault. On Tuesday, 17th January, 1637, Kukia came from Deogarh and made his submission to the Mughal general, who then returned to Court.

On Monday, 13th March, 1637, Jai Singh and other officers who had come with Khan-i-Dauran were presented to the Emperor at Agra. The Kachhwa Rajah was promoted to the level of five-*hazari* both in his rank and the number of his troopers. The *pargana* of Chatsu, which had hitherto been crownland (in the *subah* of Ajmer) was granted to him, and he received other marks of Imperial favour for his services, such as a *khilat* from the Emperor's own wardrobe, a jewelled dagger with a *phul-katara* and a *qipchaq*, a horse from the Emperor's own stable with a gold saddle. On Sunday, 30th April, the Rajah was given another royal robe and an elephant, and granted leave to go home and take rest for some time to recover from the fatigue of his campaigns. (*Ibid.*, 232-256.)

Jai Singh's Campaigns Beyond The North-Western Frontier

On the first of March, 1638, Jai Singh came to the Emperor at the end of his home leave. Within a week he was sent to Afghanistan along with other generals, under Prince Shuja and Khan-i-Dauran (Nusrat Jang) to take delivery of the fort and district of Qandahar, which its Persian governor Ali Mardan Khan had offered to hand over to the Emperor. A war with Perisa in consequence was feared and the Imperial forces in Kabul were greatly strengthened. However, the surrender passed off peacefully. Ali Mardan met the Prince at Butkhak, a short distance east of Kabul, and at the interview between these two, Khan-i-Dauran and Jai Singh sat on the right hand of the Prince and Ali Mardan on the left (19th July, 1638). The next year, after visits to the Emperor at Rawalpindi and Hasan Abdal and the receipt of gifts (Jai Singh's share was a pearl necklace), these officers were sent back to their posts on the frontier. Jai Singh was appointed to hold the upper and the lower Bangash country, and supply grain during Shah Jahan's march to Kabul and stay there. (*Abd. Ham.*, ii, 23-144.)

On Saturday, 20th April, 1639, the Emperor held a grand review of his troops (50,000) in the wide plain outside Naushera, viewing their movements from a hillock in the middle and then passing between the ranks on an elephant. On this day, Jai Singh was given the title of *Mirza Rajah*, like his great-grandfather Man Singh, who had received a similar honour from Akbar. (*Ibid.*, 145.)

In October the additional troops (including Jai Singh's contingent) returned from Afghanistan to Lahore and on 15th November the Mirza Rajah was given leave to go to his own State. He returned to Court on 13th February, 1641 and less than a month afterwards was ordered to Kabul in the train of Prince Murad Bakhsh. From Kabul this army marched against Mau, in the skirt of the hills north of Sialkot. Here Jagat Singh (son of Rajah Basu) had turned refractory and defaulted in his tribute. Three divisions of the Imperial forces attacked this difficult hilly terrain from three sides. Jai Singh made his way by the bank of the Chaki river and the defiles beyond to the foot of Mau fort. After a long fight the fort was stormed on Tuesday, 14th December, 1641, Jai Singh being among the first to enter it. His reward was an increase in his rank and pay, 1000 of his 5000 *sawar* being made *do aspa seh aspa*. (*Ibid.*, 163-165, 224-240, 261-273.)

The victorious troops from Mau reached the Court on 17th March, 1642, and again less than a month after this, Jai Singh was sent off on a distant expedition. On 10th April, he started with Prince Dara Shukoh for the defence of Qandahar which was threatened by Persia. Jai Singh on this occasion was presented by the Emperor with a robe of honour from the Imperial wardrobe, a jewelled dagger and *phul-katara*, and a horse and an elephant from the Emperor's personal stables, the saddle of the horse being golden. (*Ibid.*, 294.) The war cloud, however, blew away and Jai Singh with other officers returned to Court on Thursday, 6th October. A month later he was sent to Amber on long leave, as no danger seemed to threaten the Empire. (*Ibid.*, 285-293, 310-317.)

In November, 1643, Shah Jahan made a pilgrimage to Ajmer. Jai Singh waited on him with his two sons (on Saturday, 11th November) and paraded his troops, who were counted as 5000 horsemen. A week later the Mirza Rajah was permitted to return home.

On 8th October, 1644, Jai Singh, then at Amber, was asked to go to the Deccan and take charge of that province during the absence of Khan-i-Dauran (Nusrat Jang) at Court. The Khan had been murdered on 22nd June, 1645, while still on leave. Jai Singh continued to guard the Deccan till the beginning of 1647, when he was summoned to join the Emperor in Afghanistan. On his way north, Jai Singh escorted one crore and 20 lakhs of rupees and three lakhs of *mohars* from the Agra treasury to Lahore, in order to feed Shah Jahan's insane invasion of Balkh and Badakhshan. The Mirza Rajah met the Emperor in Kabul on Thursday, 20th May, 1647, at the head of 2000 of his contingent and was promoted by another thousand of his troopers being made *do aspa seh aspa*. He was given one of the Emperor's own horses with a gold saddle and an advance of two lakhs of rupees and sent (on Saturday, 5th June) to join Aurangzib in Balkh.

Prince Murad had invaded Balkh and Badakhshan in 1646, but proved an utter failure there. Though the country was easily overrun he left it in disgust and against orders. Aurangzib was sent next to take his place, and he reached Kabul on Sunday, 4th April, 1647. The prince set out from Kabul, after only four days' halt and made his way to Balkh, fighting hard against the opposition of the Uzbaks who were a nation in arms. His vanguard was composed of Rájputs, who bore the brunt of the fighting on that bleak and rugged table-land.[10] Aurangzib entered Balkh city on Tuesday, 26th May, and placed Madho Singh Hada in command of its fort. As the Prince made a further advance towards the Oxus river, there was endless fighting with the Uzbaks hovering around under the able leadership of Abdul Aziz Khan. The story of this campaign may be read in my *History of Aurangzib*, Volume 1, and need not detain us here.

Shah Jahan's invasion of Central Asia met with the same fate as did the British invasions of Afghanistan two centuries later. The invaders, though never defeated in field action, merely held the ground they encamped upon, and the whole country was up in arms against them. And there was also the reluctance of Indian soldiers to face the winter of Bukhara and the fear of their communications being cut off by the snowing up of the Hindu Kush passes. So Aurangzib decided on abandoning his conquest and began his retreat on 3rd October. Jai Singh led his right wing during this perilous movement, with the exultant Uzbaks crowding round him on three sides. The Prince himself, by rapid marches, reached Kabul on 27th October, but the rest of the army had to thread the Hindu Kush passes in small groups day after day and they suffered untold hardships from the continuous snowfall, which forced them to bivouac on the crest or the enemy's end of the pass for a week together, till the weather cleared. Much baggage and treasure were abandoned through lack of transport, and many followers perished from the cold or the knives of the Uzbaks. The tail of the invading army reached Kabul on 10th November. (*Waris*, Sarkar ms., *8a*.)

In the meantime the Emperor had left the Afghan hills for the Indian plains, ordering Aurangzib to stay in Kabul and guard the province against any Uzbak counterattack, for five months. From Kabul Jai Singh went home and then returned to Court, where on the next royal birthday (April, 1648) he received another promotion, one thousand more of his troopers being made *do aspa seh aspa*. (*Ibid.*, 18–22.)

Jai Singh At The Three Sieges Of Qandahar, 1649-1653

The fort of Qandahar, the last outpost on the frontier between Persia and Mughal Afghanistan, had been secured by Shah Jahan in 1638 by bribery. Ten years later, Shah Abbas II recovered it for Persia by a vigorous siege in February 1649. This blow to the prestige of the Delhi Empire had to be rectified and Shah Jahan fitted out a large expedition for the recovery of the fort. Prince Aurangzib and the wazir, Sadullah Khan, were sent forth at the head of 50,000 men and an inadequate part of artillery, in April, 1649. Jai Singh commanded the left wing of this army. There was fighting for three months before the walls of the beleaguered city and also in the level country west of it towards Persia. But in the end, the Mughal efforts failed. Through lack of battering artillery and bad strategy, Aurangzib lost two to three thousand fighting men and double that number of horses, camels and oxen in the siege, and his army was severely tried by scarcity of grain and fodder. (*Waris*, 28-40.)

The first siege of Qandahar had failed for want of heavy guns and material. The honour of the Mughal arms required that the attempt should be repeated. The next three years were spent in preparations on a scale worthy of the grandeur of the task. Big guns were cast, provisions accumulated at convenient depots on the route, thousands of camels assembled for transport, and money and munitions stored at the base in Kabul. Again Aurangzib was sent in command, with the help of the grand wazir, Sadullah Khan. This time Jai Singh led the vanguard. The siege began on 2nd May, 1652; in the division of the siege lines, Jai Singh (with Sadullah Khan and the artillery chief Qasim Khan) was given charge of the trenches facing south-west of the Khwajah Khizr gate of the fort. The Prince fought with dogged persistence in order to retrieve his fame; but all his efforts failed, owing to the bad gunnery of the Indians, while the Persians had the most efficient marksmen and superior artillery. Shah Jahan had strictly enjoined that there was to be no assault before breaching the walls, and a breach with the few guns and bad gunners on the Indian side was out of the question. So the Emperor ordered the siege to be abandoned. The retreat began on 9th July, 1652 and ended in Kabul early next month. Jai Singh could do nothing in this inglorious campaign. (*Waris*, 60*a*, 64-67.)

Thereafter Jai Singh was posted in Kabul to support Sulaiman Shukoh (the eldest son of the Crown Prince Dara Shukoh) who had been appointed governor of Afghanistan. The next April (1653) he again went to Qandahar with Dara Shukoh in the third and the costliest attempt to recover that fort. In the distribution of the lines of investment, Jai Singh had charge of the trenches facing the Mashuri Gate, near the south-western corner. For escalcade or breaching by artillery, the Kachhwa contingent was neither equipped nor naturally fitted; they were trained for field-action only, and of this they had no opportunity except once, at the very end of the retreat on 14th October.

Dara with 70,000 soldiers, 58 Rajput *mansabdars* and twice that number of Muslim commanders, continued operations for five months, but met with as complete a failure as the two earlier attempts. The main causes of the ill-success were the bad guns and worse gunnery of the Indian army, the natural superiority of defence over attack against such an impregnable fort,[11] and the remarkable efficiency of the Persians (learnt from fighting with the Turks of Constantinople) in the use of firearms and fire control. But Dara's personal incompetence robbed the failure of every element of redeeming heroism and covered the Indian army with contempt.

The Prince was entirely in the hands of his two favourites, Jafar Khan and Izat Khan, and wished that all the credit of the efforts to capture the fort should go to his own servants, particularly to these two. This made the other generals, who belonged to the Emperor's service, jealous of the two Khans, and there were frequent quarrels between the rival parties in the Prince's presence. Nor were the two favourites any less jealous of each other; Dara's ignorance of war, his thoughtlessness of speech and act and frequent changes of mind, and above all his utter want of tact made him insult and antagonize his highest officers. He taunted Jai Singh with the two previous failures against this fort, as if the Rajah had any initiative or responsible command in Aurangzib's sieges of it. Led by inexperienced flatterers, 'every one of whom considered himself a Rustam or Afrasiyab,' and putting faith in magicians, faqirs, astrologers and similar quacks, the darling son of Shah Jahan only led his unfortunate soldiers to unavailing death and the deserved ridicule of the Persians.[12]

A plan for surprising the Chihil Zina Tower (20 June) by Rajah Rajrup of the Kangra hills, was sadly bungled; it was countermanded by the fickle prince as soon as it was launched, and it ended in a futile loss of lives. No practicable breach had been made and the Persian artillery had not been silenced, and yet in a fit of desperation, the grand assault was launched on 23rd August. After four hours it ended in failure, with a thousand dead on the Mughal side (500 of them being Rajputs). Then followed mutual recriminations among the Imperial generals for this senseless slaughter. Feelings became so bitter that on 30th August, Jai Singh (and another divisional commander) were relieved of their trenches and detached to guard the routes by which new raiders might come from Persia. Jai Singh's new post was in the village of Shutar-garden which blocked the path from Tarin to Qandahar.

At last the siege was abandoned and the prince began his retreat to India on Thursday, 29th September, by the Pishin-Duki-Multan route. The predatory Afghan tribes prowled round the dejected Mughals and tried to overwhelm their rearguard. Jai Singh, who had the onerous duty of bringing up the last portion of the army, faced round near Duki on 14th October and defeated the Afghans, slaying about 40 of them and taking some prisoners. (*Lataif*, 175*a*.) Four marches eastward brought the army from Duki to the Indus, and then across the river to Multan, from which city the Prince arrived at Lahore on 22nd November, 1653.

Jai Singh And The Delhi Government Till 1657

In the middle of the year 1650, the Kachhwa Rajah had been rewarded for an eminent service of great difficulty. The hereditary brigand population of Mewat used to rob travellers on the way between Agra and Delhi and raid the villages of the region bound by Kho, Kama and Pahari, so that the fields were turned desolate and the *jagirdars* could realize no rent from their tenants. So in April, 1650, Shah Jahan bestowed the *parganas* of Kama-Pahari and Kho Mujahid as fief (*watan, tayul*) on Kirat Singh, the second son of Mirza Rajah Jai Singh, with the rank of a Commander of Eight Hundred (same number of troopers), and ordered Jai Singh to root out the miscreants and colonize the tract with his own men. The Mirza Rajah returned from Amber with 4000 horses and 6000 foot musketeers and a large number of pioneers, who cut the jungles of the Mewat and made roads. Many of the robber clan of Meos were slain, many enslaved and others expelled. On hearing of this feat the Emperor, on Thursday, 11th July, 1650, gave Jai Singh a promotion by making another thousand of his troopers *do aspa seh aspa* and bestowing on him the *pargana* of Chal Kalians, with a rent-toll of two lakhs of rupees a year, as salary of this addition to his command. Kirat Singh's *mansab* was increased and he was appointed *faujdar* of Mewat. (*Waris*, 42-43.)

But on his return from Qandahar, Dara pursued Jai Singh with malignant hostility, and he had the ear of his doting father. The Mirza Rajah received absolutely no recognition for his services in the siege and the retreat. On the other hand, Jaswant Singh, the head of the rival house of Marwar, though younger by 16 years and with no such achievements to his credit, was promoted to the rank of a Commander of Six Thousand with the title of *Maharajah* (6th January, 1654). A month later (9th February), Kumar Ram Singh was given a rise of 500 *zat* in his rank (now 3-*hazari*) and Jai Singh was given leave to go home without any expensive gift. (*Waris*, 83*a*-84*b*.)

But Jai Singh was not destined to enjoy any long spell of repose at home. In September he was appointed to the army of 30,000 men whom the prime minister, Sadullah Khan, was to lead into Mewar for demolishing the fortifications recently restored at Chitor by the Maharana in violation of his treaty with Jahangir in 1615. Shah Jahan himself moved to Ajmer, professedly on pilgrimage, but really in order to overawe the Maharana, should he fly to arms. Happily, better counsel prevailed at Udaipur, the Maharana submitted and appealed to Dara Shukoh to be his intercessor. (For Dara's letters to the Mirza Rajah expressing sympathy with the Maharana, see the English translations in Qanungo's *Dara Shukoh*, pp. 169 and 172.) The unauthorised structures were pulled down peacefully in a fortnight (in November) and the Imperial troops returned to their own places. (*Waris*,90*b*—93*a*.)

After the armed demonstration before Chitor at the end of 1654, Mirza Rajah Jai Singh went back to his home and continued there throughout the next year. Though he returned to the Court at Delhi on 9th January, 1656, we see clearly that he lay under a cloud of royal disfavour because of Dara Shukoh's unreasonable hostility from 1654 to 1657. It is true that his eldest son Ram Singh received a promotion (on Saturday, 19th January, 1656) making him a 3-*hazari* (2000 troopers) with the grant of kettledrums and an Iraqi horse, and his second son, Kirat Singh, was made a *hazari* in rank (with 900 troopers) and *faujdar* of the environs of the Imperial capital (February, 1657); but Jai Singh himself remained as he had been in 1653. (*Waris*, 103-124.)

Then at the end of the year 1657 came the most momentous revolution in the Delhi monarchy, which at once called up Jai Singh to the foremost place among the officers of the State and made him play a decisive part in shaping the history of the house of Timur. He defeated Shuja, captured Dara, neutralized Jaswant, and conquered the invincible Shivaji.

Notes

1. The correct date is Friday, August 4, 1615 = 22 Amardad, Ilahi year 60, (*Tuzuk.*, i, p. 297). *Ed.*
2. The correct date is Tuesday, March 25, 1617 A.D. = 15 Farwardin, Ilahi year 62. (*Tuzuk.*, i, p. 372). *Ed.*
3. The correct date is Friday, May 30, 1617 = Jyesth Sudi 6, 1674 V.S. (*Vamshavali*, p. 29). *Ed.*
4. Bhau Singh died on Thursday, December 13, 1621. (*Purohit Vamshavali*, p. 19). Jahangir received the news on Tuesday, December 18, 1621, and on that very day Jai Singh was given the succession to the Amber *gadi*. (*Tuzuk.*, ii, pp. 218-219.) *Ed.*
5. Damyanti was the daughter of Saha, the brother of Rana Sagar and Jagmal. (*Nainsi*, i, p. 25; *Vamshavali*, p. 30). *Ed.*
6. Sometime after the death of his father Maha Singh, Jai Singh was summoned to the Court by Jahangir. He arrived there on Friday, August 9, 1617, and on Thursday, August 28, 1617, he received his first *mansab* of 1000 *zat* — 1000 *sawars*. Later on Tuesday, December 18, 1621, he succeeded to the *gadi* of Amber, and received a *mansab* of 2000 *zat* — 1000 sawars. (*Tuzuk.*, i, pp. 386, 389; ii, pp. 218-219). *Tuzuk.*, does not mention the date of his departure, but does mention his return on Tuesday, March 11, 1623. (II, p. 253.) *Ed.*
7. Jai Singh was ordered on Monday, May 5, 1623, to accompany the Imperial forces under Mahabat Khan to the Deccan. (*Maasir-i-Jahangiri*, p. 369.) *Ed.*

8. The definite date is Tuesday, January 15, 1628 – 17 Jamadi-ul-Awwal 103 A.H. (*P.N.* I-A, p. 76.) *Ed*.
9. Gondwana is now divided; the Hindi speaking region is included in the reconstituted Madhya Pradesh, while the Maratha speaking region now forms a part of Maharashtra. *Ed*.
10. Among the Rajputs are mentioned Rajah Rai Singh (son of Maharajah Bhim Sisodia), Rao Chhatra Sal, Rao Rup Singh Chandrawat, Rajah Amar Singh Kachhawa, Balaram Hada and Indra Sal (Hada). Under Jai Singh went Ratan Singh Rathor (son of Mahesh Das of Jalor), Hamir Singh Sisodia, Ballavi Chauhan, Jaswant Singh (brother of Mahesh Das) and others. (*Ibid.*, 672, 684.) *J.S.*
11. This *old* fort of Qandahar was afterwards demolished by Nadir Shah in 1738, who built modern Qandahar in the plain two miles east of it. 'The ramparts of the old town were built of dried clay, strengthened by a mixture of chopped straw and stones. An English officer in 1878 wrote of these walls as about the stiffest things of the kind he had seen. Such walls according to him, might have stood modern battering guns for a length of time. Beyond the triple walls, on the side of the plain was a wide and deep ditch full of water.' (Sarkar, *History of Aurangzib*, i, ch. VII.) *J.S.*
12. The full history of this siege is given in Persian, in Waris's *Padishahnamah* (Sarkar ms. 70-81) and *Lataif-ul-akhbar* (Sarkar ms., entire volume.) English readers will find details in Dr. K.R. Qanungo's *Dara Shukhoh*, ch. IV. *J.S.*

IX

Jai Singh In The War Of Mughal Succession

The Hour And The Man

It was the hour of danger that made Shah Jahan—who was now sunk in dotage and entirely led by his favourite son Dara Shukoh—do justice to Jai Singh after the last four years of unmerited neglect.

On 6th September, 1657, Shah Jahan became seriously ill. For some time his life was despaired of. His eldest son Dara, who attended on him daily, stopped the courtiers on the roads and prevented his three brothers—Shuja in Bengal, Aurangzib in the Deccan, and Murad in Gujarat—from getting accurate news of Court affairs. This only aggravated the evil: the wildest rumours prevailed all over the country. The Emperor was believed to be already dead and that fact concealed by Dara for paving his way to the throne. Then began the inevitable war of succession. Shuja and Murad crowned themselves as Emperors in their provincial seats and began to march towards Delhi with their available troops. Aurangzib decided to play a subtler game; he denounced Dara as an apostate from Islam and declared his own design to merely to march to Delhi in order to free his father from that apostate's mischievous influence. He made an alliance with his neighbour Murad and promised to join their forces together in the march to the capital.

When Shah Jahan recovered and was removed to Agra, he learnt of the rebellious conduct of his three sons. As they had refused to obey his previous command to march back to their respective provinces, he was easily persuaded by Dara to send armies against them, with orders to induce them to return to their headquarters by persuasion or threat and to resort to fight only if this show of force failed. The two armies sent against Aurangzib and Murad were placed in charge of Maharaja Jaswant Singh and Qasim Khan respectively and they left Agra on 18th[1] and 26th December,[2] while the force against Shuja was placed nominally under Dara's eldest son Sulaiman Shukoh with Jai Singh as his guardian and man-of-work (*ataliq wa kar-guzar*). The Rajah was promoted to the rank of 6-*hazari* (with 5000 troopers *do aspa seh aspa*), given one lakh in cash and many presents and sent from Agra on 30th November, at the head of 22,000 men. We are not concerned here with the first two armies, which combined on the way and were defeated by Aurangzib and Murad at Dharmat (now Fatihabad,[3] a railway junction south-west of Ujjain) on Friday, 16th April, 1658, after which Jaswant fled to his own home.

The Battle Of Bahadurpur

Jai Singh, leading Prince Sulaiman, came in touch with Shuja's army at Bahadurpur, 5 miles north-east of Benares and two miles east of the modern Mughal Serai end of the Dufferin Bridge,[4] about 25th January, 1658.[5] Here on the high bank of the Ganges, Shuja had formed an entrenched camp, with his flotilla moored close at hand. Sulaiman's army halted three miles away. For some days there was a distant artillery duel, and now and then skirmishes between the scouts of the two armies; but the Bengal army refused to come out into the open and fight a pitched battle. So Sulaiman made his own preparations. Early in the morning of 14th February, 1658, he marched his troops out on the pretence of changing their ground, and suddenly fell upon Shuja's camp, convulsing it. Shuja took an elephant and hurried out to retrieve the day, but the battle had already been lost. The enemy had swarmed into his camp and were looting it. 'All his captains from their respective quarters had fled, without caring to ask what became of their master.' The enemy pressed closer still, and tried to capture Shuja's elephant, but it broke through the enemy's cordon and reached the bank where Shuja quickly dismounted and sought safety among his boats. Sulaiman's men now plundered the entire camp. Shuja's own losses were estimated at 50 lakhs of rupees; his chief minister, Mirza Jan Beg, lost property worth six lakhs in addition to horses and elephants.[6] The fugitive prince immediately weighed anchor and sped down the river. Shuja reached Patna on 19th February, and then retreated to Mungir (Monghyr), where he stopped to arrange for making a stand against the pursuers. By great efforts and daily supervision he built a wall two miles long from the hill to the river, across the plain outside the city. This unforeseen obstacle brought Sulaiman to a sharp halt. He wavered, halted at Jaitpur for several days in order to find a safe path of advance with the help of the local *zamindars*, and then marching 14 miles further east, encamped at Surajgarh, 15 miles south-west of Mungir, and took time to make new plans.

Here, on 4th May, alarming news reached him from the Court. His father wrote urging him to patch up a truce with Shuja and hasten back to Agra to meet a new danger coming up from the south. Aurangzib and Murad had advanced from the Deccan, joined their forces on the way, crushed the Imperial army which barred their way at Dharmat (Friday, 16th April), and were now in full march on the capital.

Terms were quickly arranged between Shuja's wazir, Mirza Jan Beg, and Rajah Jai Singh, and confirmed by the principals. It was agreed that Bengal, Orissa and Bihar to the east of Mungir should be left to Shuja, but his seat should be Rajmahal, as his presence at Mungir, his western frontier, would be a menace to the ruler of Delhi. As soon as the treaty was signed (about 7th May, 1658), Sulaiman set out on his return towards Agra, but, alas, too late to save either his father or himself.

After his victory at Dharmat, Aurangzib had pushed on steadily and defeated Dara at Samugarh (Sunday, 30th May), got possession of Agra fort (Tuesday, 8th June), deposed his father, treacherously imprisoned Murad Bakhsh at a banquet, and made himself supreme ruler of Hindustan.

When Sulaiman Shukoh, in his attempt to return to his father, reached Kora (105 miles west of Allahabad), he received news of Dara Shukoh's crushing defeat at Samugarh and flight from Agra. The news produced the greatest alarm and distraction among his soldiers, who trembled for the vengeance of Aurangzib on their families and estates;

there was no other sovereign under whom they could seek shelter, because Shah Jahan was known to be a helpless dotard. So they decided to submit to the new Emperor as their legitimate master. Jai Singh, Dilir Khan and most other generals of Sulaiman's army left him for Delhi with this object. With a daily dwindling army the prince fell back to Allahabad, and thence after many adventures took refuge in Garhwal. Here in December, 1660 he was surrendered to Aurangzib's agents, to be doomed to lifelong imprisonment in the fortress of Gwalior.

The Final Defeat Of Dara At Deorai

Dara Shukoh, who had fled to Multan and Sind after his defeat at Samugarh, made a fresh bid for the throne by crossing the Rann of Cutch into Gujarat, and thence advancing to Ajmer, enroute to Delhi, at the invitation of Jaswant Singh (February, 1659), because Aurangzib had been called away to the province of Allahabad by a new invasion of Shuja. But Shuja was signally defeated (at Khajwa) on Tuesday, 4th January, 1659. Aurangzib, hastening back to meet Dara, arrived at Deorai, four miles south of Ajmer (11th March), where Dara stood at bay behind an almost impregnable line of trenches across the narrow valley between the Bithli and Gokla hills, strengthened with redoubts and a formidable display of big guns. Jai Singh commanded the Imperial vanguard and faced the enemy trenches near the Gokla hill.

After the battle of Khajwa, the Emperor, justly angry with Jaswant for his treachery on that day, wanted to make an example of him. He despatched an army of 10,000 men and guns under Muhammad Amin Khan to invade Marwar and expel Jaswant. For a time Jaswant meditated resistance, but he soon realized his own impotence. He lost heart and fled to the hill-fort of Siwana.[7] Meanwhile Aurangzib had seen the wisdom of not driving Jaswant into his enemy's arms. In the impending conflict with Dara, Jaswant was the decisive factor. So Aurangzib made Jai Singh write a friendly letter to Jaswant, professing true friendship for him and a natural reluctance to see such a great Hindu prince meet with utter ruin. As a friend, Jai Singh pointed out the folly of defying Aurangzib and the certainty of utter destruction as its result. He therefore tendered his own good offices as a mediator with the Emperor, to secure for Jaswant a full pardon and restoration to his title and *mansab*, as well as a high post under the Crown, if he gave up Dara and returned to the path of loyalty. The letter reached the Rathor chief at a critical time,[8] when the future looked darkest to him. He at once closed with the offer, decided to side with Aurangzib, and began to retreat to Jodhpur, instead of going to Dara's camp.

At Deorai for three days there was an almost continuous artillery duel between the two sides, in which Dara had an overwhelming superiority of calibre and weight of metal. Aurangzib's men could make no impression to the defence lines, ever after heavy sacrifice of lives. In the evening of the third day (14th March), new tactics were adopted and they brought victory.

Rajah Rajrup of the Jammu hills was serving under Aurangzib with a body of his Rajput clansmen, expert in mountaineering. His followers had discovered a path by which the back of the Gokla hill could be scaled. Aurangzib ordered the ascent to be made and lent a party of musketeers from his own army to support the attempt. Towards evening when the gunners on both sides were tired with the day's fighting, Rajrup sent his infantry up the back of the Gokla hill, while he appeared with his cavalry in front of it to divert the enemy's attention. A body of 1000 troopers sallied out of Shah Nawaz Khan's trenches and encountered Rajrup. The other Imperial generals had been smarting under the Emperor's reprimand in the morning, and now the sight of the enemy within easy reach of their weapons roused their martial ardour. Dilir Khan with his Afghans galloped into the fray from the right side of the artillery; Shaikh Mir from behind the guns turned to the right and came up to the front line alongside of Dilir Khan. Shaista Khan with the right wing, the artillery men from the middle, and Jai Singh with the Van, all flocked to this point to support the attack. The left wing also made a forward movement against Dara's extreme right. The fight now became general. The bulk of the Imperial army was massed in front of the enemy's left, where the assault was delivered. The hardest fight raged in this part of the field. Dara's men obstinately defended their lines, and the rival generals freely exposed themselves to encourage their men. The slaughter in Aurangzib's ranks was heavy at this point. The attack persisted for over an hour with undiminished vigour. Wave after wave of imperialists swarmed up to the charge; and at last they pushed the enemy out of the field and won the ground on the edge of the trenches.

By this time Rajrup's men had toiled up the back of the Gokla hill, while the enemy were absorbed in the severe contest in their front. They planted their banners on the top and raised a shout. Dara's left wing was seized with despair at its rear being turned. The struggle in Shah Nawaz Khan's trenches was most terrible: 'the firing was severe, the enemy resisted to the utmost. Dilir Khan's Afghans carried the day. The Imperial banners were planted in the trenches. Jai Singh entered with the Van and brought fresh strength to the assailants.' 'The enemy totally lost heart and firmness. The resistance in the third section of the lines was at last over-powered.' When Shah Nawaz Khan's redoubt was carried and the victors pressed on towards Dara's position, the luckless prince fled in headlong haste towards Gujarat by the first road he could reach.

Jai Singh's Pursuit Of Dara Shukoh

A strong force under Jai Singh and Bahadur Khan was detached in pursuit of Dara. Only 2000 troopers accompanied Dara when he left Mairta. At Mairta the pursuers were six days behind; but the rumour of their coming preceded him everywhere, and at every halting place robbed the unhappy prince and his followers of their sorely needed rest, and lent wings to their flight. Covering 30 miles or even more a day, they fled southwards to Gujarat. Their misery was extreme. The baggage and tents had been abandoned in the wild rush to escape from the battle-field, and now all along the route various essential articles and even treasure had to be sacrificed for want of porters. The pursuing force under Jai Singh and Bahadur Khan reached Mairta on 20th March. Jai Singh sent letters to the princes and *zamindars* in every direction to bar Dara's path, to Sirohi and Palanpur in the south, Daiwara in the south-east, to the princes of northern Kathiawar and Cutch and the *zamindars* of Lower Sindh, and to the officers of Gujarat. Thus it was that everywhere Dara found enemies warned of his coming and ready to seize him. At Mairta, Jai Singh learnt of the true route of Dara's flight and immediately set out southwards after him by way of Jalor and Sirohi. On the way, one march before Sirohi, he was joined by Jaswant Singh and his Rathor army (31st March),[9] and then, 'in order not to allow Dara time to gain composure at Ahmadabad,' the imperialists pushed on, marching from 16 to 20 miles a day, 'in spite of scarcity of water, want of fodder, and exhaustation of the horses and transport-cattle'. Reaching Sidhpur on 5th April, they learnt that Dara had been refused entrance into Ahmadabad and had turned aside towards Cutch. The pursuing army marched on to Ahmadabad to refit. Their misery was hardly less than that of Dara. The year was one of drought in Gujarat; and this vast army of 20,000 men moving together exhausted the scanty water-supply and fodder in their path. It was summer and the forced march broke down the horses and cattle; grass was very scarce and grain so dear that even six seers of *bajra* (spiked millet) could be had for a rupee with difficulty. They reached Ahmadabad about 11th April. Halting there for probably one day only, Jai Singh distributed two and a half lakhs of rupees from the treasury to his troops to enable them to provide themselves with enough water and fodder for the journey, and on the 12th set out again. Turning his face to the west, he arrived (22nd) in the Pathri district, west of Viramgaon, and getting further news of Dara's movements, advanced towards Halwad, enroute to Cutch. On 3rd May, he reached a place six miles from Halwad and there learnt that Dara had crossed the Rann and entered Sindh again.

On the 13th the pursuers reached the capital of Cutch. As Jai Singh approached Bhuj, the Rao sent his son in advance to welcome the Imperial general and then personally received him with due honours outside his capital (13th May), and gave him a bond solemnly asserting that Dara was not in his territory. Jai Singh halted there to learn the truth, and soon got news from the Mughal officer of Badin that Dara had reached Lower Sindh.

In crossing the Greater Rann, Jai Singh's army suffered frightful privations. It was 70 miles in breadth, in the whole extent of which not a drop of drinking water could be found, nor for ten miles beyond its northern shore. The army plunged into this dreary wilderness at sunset. Up to midnight the moon lit up their path, and when it set, torches were kindled at every mile's interval to guide the soldiers on. No trooper or follower was lost in this trackless plain.

Jai Singh had thus achieved a most remarkable military feat; but he had to pay a heavy price for it. His soldiers were dead beat; and his camels, horses, and other transport animals had been almost exterminated. On the 11th June, he struck the Indus near 'the river of

Siwistan'. Here he learnt that Dara had crossed over to the right bank of the Indus and entered Siwistan, intending to go to Qandahar with the help of the Maghasi tribe.

Jai Singh's task was done; the enemy was no longer on Indian soil. So he wrote to the Emperor asking to be recalled to Court. With the object of returning to Northern India, Jai Singh was slowly moving up the Indus towards Bhakkar, when about the middle of June he received the startling news that Dara had been captured on Friday, the tenth of that month, and that the Imperial generals must hurry on to take charge of the prisoner.

A Baluch chief named Malik Jiwan of Dadar (near the Indian end of the Bolan pass), had invited Dara to his house, and treacherously made him prisoner with his second son Sipihr Shukoh (10th June), and offered to hand them over to the Imperial generals in hope of reward.

The Years At Court: September 1659-September 1664

After sending the captive Dara Shukoh to Delhi in charge of Bahadur Khan, Jai Singh returned from Sind by slow marches in order to give relief to his troops who were utterly worn out by their long and strenuous chase through appalling difficulties of country and climate. Many of the horses and elephants with him perished under privation, heat and incessant forced marches and the Emperor had afterwards to give him 200 horses from his own stables to make the loss good in part at least.

Thus Jai Singh arrived at Delhi on Friday, 2nd September, 1659, and had the good fortune of not being present at the humiliating public parade of the vanquished Crown Prince through the street and the debates at the royal Court which ended in the decree for his murder (in the night of 30th-31st August). At his audience the veteran Kachhwa prince received a robe of honour made for the Emperor, a jewelled fishtail ornament (*punchhi*), an elephant from the royal stables adorned with a silver *howda* and gold-embroidered housing, a female elephant and 200 good horses. He had already attained the rank of a Commander of Seven Thousand (with seven thousand troopers), which could not then be exceeded in the case of any officer, whether Hindu or Muslim, who was not of the royal blood. (See the explanation of Aurangzib's official historian in *Alamgirnamah*, 618.) Therefore, the only rewards which he could henceforth receive were the robes of honour bestowed in the winter and rainy seasons and the solar and lunar birthdays and Coronation Day of the Emperor. On 22nd May, 1661, he was given another *jagir* consisting of *mahals* with a revenue of two and a half lakhs of rupees, making a total of five lakhs of rupees received from Aurangzib.

He continued to live with the Emperor (with occasional visits to Amber) till his deputation to the Deccan in September, 1664.

During these five years, his eldest son Ram Singh led an expedition to the foot of the Kumaun hills, and less by this demonstration of force than by the persuasive appeals of Jai Singh to the local Rajah and internal troubles in the State, secured the surrender of the fugitive prince Sulaiman Shukoh who had taken asylum there (December, 1660).

The 4000 strong Kachhwa contingent, under Kumar Kirat Singh, which had been accompanying in the pursuit of Shuja after the battle of Khajwa, was alarmed by false rumours, and suddenly left that army amidst the jungles of Birbhum (in Bengal) on 26th March, 1659, and returned home. The offence, due to ignorance and panic rather than disloyalty, was forgiven by the Emperor, and Kirat Singh was sent back to his *faujdari* of Kama in November.

Early in 1661, Jai Singh lost his wife, for which the Emperor gave him a robe of condolence, while Ram Singh received a jewelled *sarpech* and a pair of pearl earrings.[10]

On 10th November 1659, Jai Singh received a reward of one lakh of rupees in cash, and by his intercession, Jaswant Singh was restored to his Command of Six Thousand and title of *Maharajah* of which he had been deprived after his desertion at the battle of Khajwa.

When in May, 1663, Aurangzib, after recovering from a severe fever went to Kashmir for a change of air, Jai Singh who had accompanied the Court to Lahore, was left behind on the bank of the Chinab river near the city of Gujarat, in order to guard the Emperor's rear and line of communication with Hindustan. And on the Emperor's return, he followed the Court to Delhi (where they arrived on Tuesday, 19th January, 1664).

Notes

1. The correct date of Jaswant Singh's departure is Thursday, December 17, 1657 (Paus Vidi 7, 1714 V.S.) in the evening; hence Friday, Rabiul-Awwal 22, 1068 A.H. (*Hukumat Bahi*, p. 15; *A.N.*, pp. 32-33). *Ed.*
2. Dec. 26, 1657 corresponds to 30 Rabi-ul-Awwal 1068 A.H. But the correct date of Qasim Khan's appointment is Tuesday, February 23, 1658, which corresponds to Jamadi-ul-Awwal 30, 1068 A.H. (*Kambu.*, 3, p. 285; *Ahmadi*, E.T., I, p. 210). *Ed.*
3. Dharmat is situated on the west bank of the Gambhir river, is two and a half m. south of Fatehabad, which is two and a half m. east of the Gambhir river. Before it was thus renamed it was known as Chornarayana. The Imperial army under Maharaja Jaswant Singh had encamped at Chornarayana. (*Hukumat Bahi*, p.16). *Ed.*
4. Now renamed Malviya Bridge. *Ed.*
5. The Imperial forces arrived at Banaras on Thursday, January 14, 1658, and crossed over the Ganges on Saturday, January 16, 1658 (*Jai. Hindi*, I, pp. 175, 178). *Ed.*
6. When the news of the victory over Shuja reached the Emperor, he promoted Jai Singh on 21st March to the rank of a Commander of Seven Thousand—the highest *mansab* open to any noble not of the royal blood. His troopers were also increased by one thousand. (*Kambu.*, III, 279). *J.S.*
7. According to *Hukumat Bahi* (p. 35) Jaswant Singh had gone to Siwana to inspect its fortifications. He was there for a day only and returned to Jodhpur on Thursday, February 8, 1659. *Ed.*
8. This letter from Jai Singh reached Jaswant Singh at Rabriawas on Monday, March 7, 1659, and the following day Jaswant Singh began his retreat. (*Hukumat Bahi*, p. 37.) *J.S.*
9. According to *Hukumat Bahi* (p. 39-40) Maharaja Jaswant Singh joined the Imperial army at Sena, a *kasba* 14 m. south of Jalor on Wednesday, March 30, 1659, and went along with him up to Ud (9 m. north-west of Sirohi) the following day. Later on when Jai Singh and the Imperial army continued their pursuit of Dara, Jaswant Singh stayed behind to celebrate his marriage at Sirohi on Thursday, April 14, 1659 (*Akshaya-Tritya*, 1716 V.S.). *Ed.*
10. The date of the award was Wednesday, January 16, 1616 = 24 Jamadi-ul-Awwal, 1071 A.H. (*A.N.*, p. 603.) *Ed.*

X

Jai Singh And Shivaji

The Genius Of Jai Singh Fully Unfolded In The Purandar Campaign

The defeat of Shivaji was the crowning achievement of a long life crowded with feats of arms and diplomacy in almost every part of India and even beyond the north-western frontier of our land. This opportunity came to Jai Singh when, on 30th September, 1664, he was appointed to lead an army, 14,000 strong, against the Maratha hero Shivaji, who had remained unsubdued by every Mughal or Adilshahi general hitherto sent against him. Nay, more, the intrepid young hero of the Deccan land had surprised and wounded Aurangzib's maternal uncle Shaista Khan, killed one of his sons and several inmates of his harem (1663), and for four days sacked with impunity the rich city of Surat (1664). After making the necessary preparations, and collecting his subordinates, Jai Singh left Upper India and crossed the Narmada at Handia on 9th January, 1665. He pushed on rapidly never wasting a day by halting, except when strong necessity compelled him, arrived at Puna on 3rd March, and took charge from Maharajah Jaswant Singh, who immediately afterwards (7th) started for Delhi.

And now this veteran of a hundred fights donned his armour at the age of 55 to crush a petty chieftain, who in less than ten years had grown great enough to baffle all the resources of Bijapur and to challenge the prestige of the empire of Delhi. The full correspondence between Jai Singh and Aurangzib during this campaign has come down to us.[1] We can learn from Jai Singh's letter how he employed every possible device for dealing with an enemy, how wide awake and full of many-sided activity he was, how he looked far ahead, and how he handled his force so as to cause distraction to the enemy or deal a concentrated blow at a vital point.

It was, however, with no light heart that Jai Singh set himself to the task of subduing Shivaji, against whom Bijapuris and rival Maratha chiefs, Shaista Khan and Jaswant Singh, had toiled in vain. The Deccan had been the grave of many a reputation, and he had the failures of his predecessors before him. Shivaji had already established a name for stratagem, and his *maules* had measured swords with the best regular troops on more than equal terms. Then, again, there was the likelihood that the arrival of a large Mughal force in the Deccan would alarm Bijapur and Golkonda and throw them into the arms of Shivaji to make a common cause against the invader from the north. Jai Singh, therefore, could not give his undivided attention to the Marathas; he had to keep an eye on Bijapur too. The problem before him was no easy one. As he wrote to the Emperor, 'not for a moment, in day or night, do I seek rest or ease from being busy about the task on which I have been sent'.

In Western Maharashtra with its heavy rainfall, campaigning is impossible during the monsoons. It was already 3rd March, when Jai Singh reached Puna, and if he was to effect anything it had be done in the next three months. From his despatches we learn how he utilized every day, how he struck swiftly and hard, and how he followed up every success to the utmost. The mariner does not scan the sky for the storm-cloud with more anxiety than did this general for the herald of the monsoons which would interrupt his work in the middle and drive him into the forced inactivity of cantonments.

Jai Singh very wisely decided to take up a position between both of his enemies, that is, in the eastern part of Shivaji's dominion, whence he could also easily threaten Bijapur. He knew that if he could strike fatally at the heart of the Maratha kingdom, the distant limbs would drop down of themselves. Secondly, he played skilfully upon the hopes and fears of the Sultan of Bijapur. He held forth the chance of a reduction of his tribute and removal of the Emperor's displeasure, if Adil Shah aided the Mughals and thus clearly proved his want of connection with Shivaji. Thirdly, he arranged to combine against

Shivaji all his enemies and distract his attention by attacks from all possible quarters. As early as January he had sent two Europeans named Francisco de Mello and Diogo de Mello to the western coast with letters to the chief of the Portuguese settlement of Goa inviting him to help the imperialists by attacking Shivaji, who had collected a fleet of his own. In January he had sent his *brahman* emissaries to various Deccani chieftains, to stir them up against Shivaji. Above all, Jai Singh concentrated all authority in his own hands, as an indispensible condition of success in war. He rightly insisted that in war there should be only one head, and that 'the man on the spot' should be given full authority, or else the work would suffer. The Emperor yielded to the argument and Jai Singh gained absolute civil and military authority alike.

Purandar Fort Described: The Siege Begins

With a true general's eye for the ground, Jai Singh made Saswad his base. After arriving at Puna which was strongly garrisoned, he spent some days in settling the country and establishing outposts, which he regarded as the 'first of the pillars supporting the work of this expedition'. Deciding to take up his position at Saswad and besiege Purandar, Jai Singh marched out of Puna on Wednesday, 15th March. On 31st March, he carefully escorted his baggage to a permanent camp serving as a base, between Saswad and Purandar, only four miles from the latter place.

The stupendous mountain mass of Purandar, the highest point of which towers 4564 feet above sea level and more than 2500 feet above the plain at its foot, is really a double fort, with an independent and very strong sister enclosure, named Vajragarh on a ridge running out east of it. Purandar consists of an upper fort or citadel with precipitous sides all around and a lower fort or *machi*, 300 feet or more below it. The high spur named Bhairav Khind, starts from the base of the steep overhanging north-eastern tower (called *Khad-kala* or the skyscraper) of the upper fort, and runs for about a mile eastwards in a narrow ridge, ending in a small tableland (3618 feet above sea-level), crowned with the fort of Rudramal (now called Vajragarh). This Vajragarh commands the *machi* or lower fort of Purandar on its northern and most important face, as the garrison has to live here. Jai Singh decided to attack Vajragarh first.

Dilir Khan entrenched between Purandar and Rudramal. In front of him were the chief of the artillery, Turktaz Khan, and the party sent by Jai Singh. Kirat Singh, with 3000 troopers of the Kachhwa Rajah and a few other *mansabdars*, made a stockade opposite the north gate of Purandar. Jai Singh visited the trenches every day, encouraged his men, and supervised the progress of the siege. At first all his efforts were directed to dragging guns up to the top of the steep and difficult hill.

The incessant bombardment of the Mughals demolished the bases of the tower in front, and pioneers were sent to its foot to dig a hole underneath. At midnight, 13th April, Dilir Khan's division stormed the tower and drove the enemy into an enclosure behind it. Jai Singh reinforced Dilir Khan with a party of his own Rajputs. The next day, the victorious Mughals pushed on to the inner enclosure. The garrison, oppressed by their fire, capitulated in the evening (14th April), left the fort, and were disarmed. The possession of Vajragarh was the stepping-stone to the capture of Purandar. Dilir Khan now turned to the latter fort, while Jai Singh organized raids into the Maratha country. There was a secret reason for thus sending away certain generals from the siege-camp. He had some disloyal officers under him, whose presence was worse than useless.

Meantime the Maratha captains had not been idle, but tried hard to harass the Mughals and raise the siege. But Mughal detachments hastened in pursuit, and the Maratha host melted away. The hill of Lohgarh was scaled, and a body of Marathas on the top slain or routed. Daud Khan returned with 300 captives and nearly 3000 cattle.

After the capture of Vajragarh in the middle of April, Dilir Khan advanced along the connecting ridge and laid siege to the *machi* or lower fort of Purandar. At first, the garrison made sorties to drive back the besiegers. One night they attacked Kirat Singh, who was quite prepared and repulsed them with slaughter.

When, in the course of May, the Mughal trenches reached the foot of the two White Towers, which had been dismantled by bombardment, the garrison began to throw down lighted naphtha oil, leather bags full of gunpowder, bombs and heavy stones which effectually stopped the further advance of the Mughals. Jai Singh ordered a high wooden platform of logs and planks to be made, on which guns were to be mounted and parties of gunners and musketeers placed to command the enemy's position. On Wednesday, 31st May, some Ruhela soldiers, tried to storm the White Tower without informing Dilir Khan. The enemy crowded on the wall in large numbers and checked them. But reinforcements rapidly arrived: the men of the trenches on both hands scaled the wall with ladders, and ran towards the enemy. Jai Singh's officer Bhupat Singh Puar, a commander of 500, was slain on the right side of the smaller White Tower, with several other Rajputs. Just then the line of supports, under Achal Singh and Kirat Singh, arrived on the scene of battle from their shelter behind the wooden structure. After an obstinate struggle at close quarters, the Marathas lost heavily and retreated. Jai Singh remained content with the capture of the three bastions made that day.

In the course of the next two days the wooden structure was completed and two small pieces of cannon were mounted on it. The enemy, unable to reply to this fire from a superior height, evacuated the Black Tower and another bastion near it. Purandar now seemed doomed.

Shivaji Forced To Sue Personally For Terms

At last the steady pressure of Jai Singh bore fruit. Shivaji found it futile to prolong the resistance. He resolved to interview Jai Singh and offer terms for peace with the imperialists. Shivaji next demanded and secured from Jai Singh an assurance, confirmed with solemn oaths, that he would be allowed to visit Jai Singh and return home in safety, whether his terms were accepted or not.

On the 11th of June, at nine o' clock in the morning, while Jai Singh was holding court in his tent at the foot of Purandar, *the brahman* agent Raghunath[2] came in and reported that Shivaji had arrived at hand in a *palki* accompanied by only six *brahmans*. Jai Singh immediately sent his secretary Udairaj and Ugrasen Kachhwa to meet him on the way and tell him that if he agreed to surrender all his forts he might come, otherwise he should turn back from the place. Shivaji agreed to the terms in general and proceeded to the tent with the two officers. The Rajah advanced a few steps, embraced Shivaji, and seated him by his side.

Up to midnight the two sides higgled for the terms of a permanent peace. But Jai Singh knew the strength of his position. As he wrote in his despatches to the Emperor, 'I declined to abate a single fort. Gradually, after much discussion, we came to this agreement: (*a*) that 23 of his forts,[3] the lands of which yield four lakhs of *hun* as annual revenue, should be annexed to the Empire; and (*b*) that 12 of his forts,[4] including Raigarh, with an annual revenue of one lakh of *hun*, should be left to Shivaji, on condition of service and loyalty to the Imperial throne'.

Shivaji, however, begged to be excused from attending the Emperor's Court like other nobles and Rajahs, and proposed to send his son, as his representative, with a contingent of 5000 horses, (to be paid by means of a *jagir*), for regular attendance and service under the Emperor or the Mughal governor of the Deccan. This was exactly the favour shown to the Maharana of Udaipur.

Next day (12th June), according to the agreement, 7000 men and women (of whom 4000 were combatants), left Purandar, and the Mughals entered into possession of it; all the stores, weapons, artillery, and other property found within were attached by the Government. Mughal officers were sent with Shivaji's men to take charge of five other forts to be surrendered by the Marathas. On the 14th, Shivaji was presented by Jai Singh with an elephant and two horses, and sent away to Raigarh with Kirat Singh, after paying a ceremonial visit to Daud Khan.

Thus, in less than three months from the date when he opened the campaign, Jai Singh had succeeded in bringing Shivaji down on his knees; he had made this haughty chief cede a large part of his dominions and consent to serve as a dependent vassal of the Emperor. It was a splendid victory. Shivaji loyally carried out his promises.

On 23rd June, 1665, when the news of the conquest of Purandar and the submission of Shivaji reached the Emperor, he rewarded Jai Singh with a royal robe of honour, a sword from his personal armoury with enamelled decoration, an elephant with a silver *howda* and cover of cloth of gold, and made 2000 more of his troopers *do aspa seh aspa*, so that the Mirza Rajah now became a Commander of Seven Thousand troopers, all of whom were *do aspa seh aspa*, which was the highest possible class in the highest grade of the nobility, open to a person other than the princes of the Imperial family. Kumar Ram Singh, who was his father's deputy at Court, received many gifts, and his younger brother Kirat Singh, who was in the

Deccan, received a lift in his rank, making him a Commander of 2500, with 2000 troopers. (*A.N.* 907.)

A Marathi poet has boasted with legitimate pride,

> Thou canst not weigh the water of the Ocean,
> Thou canst not gaze at the noonday Sun,
> Thou canst not grasp fire in thy hand,
> So thou canst not conquer King Shiva.[5]

The Kachhwa king could reply to him, with perfect truth, 'Yes, I have done it.' Jai Singh had gained the war with the Maratha hero, and if Aurangzib lost the peace, the Mirza Rajah cannot share the blame; it was done in his absence from Court and against his advice.

Shivaji's Visit To Aurangzib At Agra

At the end of the first stage of his Bijapur campaign (January, 1666) the Mirza Rajah had undertaken to send Shivaji to the Imperial Court. He plied Shivaji with hopes of high reward and the enlistment of his splendid talents in the service of the Empire, in order to induce him to go to Aurangzib's presence. The country-bred Maratha hero hesitated for a long time, as he and his friends were afraid of the Mughals. But Jai Singh took the most solemn oaths possible for a Hindu that Shivaji would not be harmed during his visit, and made his own son Kumar Ram Singh the caretaker and patron of Shivaji at the Imperial Court. So the Maratha Rajah started on his journey with Jai Singh's noble Tej Singh as his guide, on (Tuesday) 6th March, 1666, and arrived at Muluk Chand's Sarai, near Agra where the Emperor was then in residence, on Friday, 11th May. The fullest and most authentic details of what happened to him at this Imperial city were written by the officers of Ram Singh every evening, and these accounts have recently come to light among the Jaipur archives[7] and these records must sweep aside all accounts that have hitherto been current, insofar as they differ from them.

Shivaji, who had never seen a polished Court or capital city before, naturally had no correct idea of his own relative status and importance. Moreover, the vague hopes held forth by Jai Singh had inflated his ambition and sense of dignity. Thus, the materials of a *contre temps* were ready on one side. On the other side, it cannot be denied that there was unjustifiable neglect of him by Aurangzib's Court Marshal and even by Ram Singh, due to carelessness and not to deliberate slight. These two causes combined to produce the unforeseen result of tumbling down the diplomatic edifice so patiently and tactfully built up by Jai Singh and ultimately revolutionizing the course of Indian history. The Mughal Emperor succeeded in making the Father of Maratha Nationalism his bitterest enemy, and lived to regret his error to the end of his days, as he has admitted in his last will and testament. (See Sarkar's *Anecdotes of Aurangzib*, No. 8.)

In the Audience Hall itself, the Court Marshal placed Shivaji among the third grade nobles, without consulting the Emperor about the Rajah's proper position. Aurangzib too, after the introduction of Shivaji and the short formal exchange of words, turned to other business and evidently forgot all about the Maratha hero's existence. Then the fire burst forth, which ended by consuming the Empire though half a century after Shivaji's death and in a manner undreamt of by any one present at this memorable scene.

In the morning of 12th May, Kumar Ram Singh was on patrol duty round the palace fort, and after posting his men, he went to receive Shivaji, who had already started from Muluk Chand's Sarai, so that they met together in a garden in the suburb of Agra city. A little while after bringing his guest to the tents set up for him near his own camp, the Kumar conducted him to the royal Court. By this time, the Emperor had left the Diwan-I-Am and gone to the Diwan-I-Khas. Shivaji was taken there and introduced to the Emperor by Asad Khan Bakhshi, and he and his son Shambhuji offered their presents and propitiatory gifts (*nisar*) to the throne, after making three *salams*. Aurangzib spoke a few conventional words and thereafter Shivaji was led back to a place in the row of Commanders of Five Thousand, i.*e*. third-grade nobles, behind Jaswant Singh (a six-*hazari*) and in front of Rai Singh (five-*hazari*) and kept standing like all the rest. Then the work of the darbar proceeded, and Shivaji seemed to have been forgotten.

It was the Emperor's birthday, and the betel-leaf of the ceremony was distributed to the nobles and also to Shivaji. Then robes of honour were presented to the Princes, Jafar Khan and Jaswant Singh, but not to Shivaji. By this time he was inwardly fretting and fuming. He inquired and learnt that his rank was that of a five-*hazari-mansabdar*.

'What!' he exclaimed, 'My little son of seven years of age was created a five-*hazari in absentia;* my servant Netaji Palker is a five-*hazari*. And am I, after rendering all these services, to get the same low rank?' When he found that Jaswant Singh was placed one grade higher than himself, he cried out, 'Jaswant, whose back my soldiers have seen; I to stand behind him! What does it mean?' This remark was overheard in the Darbar, and Jaswant Singh did not soon forget or forgive it.

The presentation of the robe of honour to Jaswant and his own exclusion, made Shivaji's rage boil over. His angry voice and gestures were noticed by the Emperor from his throne, who sent Ram Singh to inquire into the cause. When the Kumar came to Shivaji's side, the latter said, 'You have seen, your father has seen, your Padishah has seen what a man I am; and yet you have kept me standing so long! I cast off your *mansab*. Don't make me stand up.' Saying this he began to walk away violently from his place in the line. The Kumar tried to detain him, but Shivaji wrenched away his hand, came to a corner and sat down. Ram Singh followed him there and tried to reason with him, but all in vain. 'Kill me if you like, but I am not going back to the Emperor's presence,' was his reply. He kept up the same obstinate attitude, when three other nobles were sent by the Emperor to pacify him. Aurangzib then asked Ram Singh to take Shivaji back to his quarters and reason with him.

For the next three years, there was a hope that Ram Singh would succeed in pacifying Shivaji and bring him to Court again, as the Kumar promised to the Emperor day after day. But when the Maratha hero proved irreconcilable, the Court nobles hostile to him and his patron Jai Singh, urged the Emperor to punish Shivaji's open act of insolence and contumacy. Otherwise (as they said) the report of it would spread far and wide and damage the royal prestige, and every petty landholder would be emboldened to insult the Emperor. The shrill voice of Roshanara Begum cried out for vengeance on Shivaji for that attack on Shaista Khan, her grand-uncle. Then, at last, the Emperor decided upon killing or at least imprisoning Shivaji.

The news startled Ram Singh. His father's word had been pledged for Shivaji's safety at Agra and his return home. He went to Amir Khan and through him sent a prayer to the Emperor to slay him (Ram Singh) before a hair of the Maratha's head was touched. The Emperor agreed to keep Shivaji in Ram Singh's hands, if the latter signed a bond taking full responsibility for his escape or mischievous action. This was done on 15th May.

The Captivity And Escape Of Shivaji From Agra

Thereafter Shivaji continued in his own tents, close to Ram Singh's camp, but under surveillance of a large body of the Delhi police prefect's troops and also bands of Ram Singh's Rajput followers, who patrolled round him day and night. In the meantime the Emperor wrote to Jai Singh asking to be informed exactly what promises he had made to the Maratha king on behalf of the Emperor. The Mirza Rajah's reply came after a long delay, and in it he explained the clauses of the Treaty of Purandar and solemnly asserted that nothing beyond them had been promised. Jai Singh was placed in a dilemma and harassing anxiety by this unexpected result of Shivaji's visit to the Court, which he had brought about. He tried to persuade the Emperor that nothing would be gained but much harm done to the Imperial cause in the Deccan by killing or even imprisoning Shivaji; and at the same time he wrote repeatedly urging Ram Singh to see that his own word of safety to the Maratha chief when at Court remained inviolate.

All this while Shivaji kept bribing the highest nobles to use their influence with the Emperor for securing his release. He promised to cede all his remaining forts if he were allowed to return home in safety. The Emperor's reply was, 'There is no reason why he should not do it by writing from here to his officers'. Then in despair Shivaji asked permission to turn a *sannyasi* and pass his remaining days in the holy city of Allahabad. To this the Emperor grimly replied, 'Yes, let him live within the fort of Allahabad, where my governor will take good care of him!' And on one occasion an order was issued to send Shivaji to Kabul on military service!

At last in despair, the Maratha hero turned to his own resources for effecting his release. First of all, with a noble consideration for the Mirza Rajah, he made Ram Singh take back the bail-bond he had signed for Shivaji and get rid of all responsibility for him in future. Then he sent away all his servants (7th June),[8] to the Deccan, so as to have no encumbrance with him except his son and a few ministers. Being thus freed from anxiety about his followers, Shivaji set about devising plans for his own escape. He feigned illness and began to send out of his house every evening sweetmeats for *brahmans*, religious mendicants and influential courtiers. The guards searched the baskets for some days and then allowed them to pass out unchallenged. This was the opportunity for which Shivaji had been waiting. In the afternoon of 19th August,[9] he sent word to his guards that he was very ill and had taken to his bed and that they should not disturb him. His half brother Hirji Farzand, who looked somewhat like him, lay down on his cot, with a quilt covering all his body except the outstretched right arm adorned with Shivaji's gold wristlet, while Shivaji and his son crouched down in two baskets which were safely sent out shortly after sunset through the line of unsuspecting guards, being preceded and followed by baskets of real sweets.

The baskets were deposited at a lonely spot outside the city; the porters were dismissed; and then Shivaji and his son issued forth and made their way to a village six miles from Agra, where they smeared themselves with ashes like Hindu ascetics and hastened towards Mathura, while the others of his party took their own way homewards.

The next day about four hours after dawn, at his Agra residence, the guards' suspicion was aroused; the house seemed strangely deserted; no crowd of visitors came to see Shivaji as usual; and there was no sound, no stir in the house. They entered his room and found that the bird had flown! A hue and cry was immediately raised and fast couriers and sergeants-at-arms were sent to watch the road to the Deccan through Berar and Khandesh, and to warn local officers to look out for the fugitives.

The Emperor's suspicion fell upon Ram Singh. The Kumar was unjustly punished by being forbidden the Court and reduced in his rank by one thousand (both *zat* and *sawar*). It took the Emperor's wrath seven months to cool, and then only at the intercession of Jaswant Singh, who on the eve of the departure for the Deccan with Prince Muazzam (to supersede Jai Singh) secured from the Emperor permission for Ram Singh to come to Court again (Sunday, 24th March, 1667).[10]

Notes

1. This correspondence was put together in *Insha-i-Haft Arjuman* by Hemat Yar, son of Udairaj Munshi alias Taleyar Khan, (*House of Shivaji*, by Jadunath Sarkar, 3rd edn., 1955, chap. IX; *The*

Military Despatches of a XVIIth Century Indian General, by Jagdish Narayan Sarkar, 1969). *Ed.*

2. Raghunath Ballal Atre, Shivaji's minister as well as *guru*, *J.S.*
3. The following 23 forts were to be surrendered:

   (a) in the Deccan— (1) Rudramal or Vajragarh (2) Purandar 3) Kondana (4) Rohira (5) Lohgarh (6) Isagarh (7) Tanki (8) Khadkala near Kondana, and (9) Tikona;

   (b) in Kokan — (10) Mahuli (11) Muranjan (12) Khirdurg (13) Bhandardurg (14) Tulsikhul (15) Nardurg (16) Khaigarh or Ankola (17) Marg-garh or Atra (18) Kohaj (19) Basant (20) Nang (21) Karnala (22) Songarh and (23) Mangarh (Sarkar, *Shivaji*, 1952, p. 126.) *Ed.*
4. The following 12 forts were to be retained:

   (1) Raigarh (2) Torna (3) Rairi (4) Linganagarh, (5) Mahargarh (6) Paligarh (7) Ghosala (8) Asheri (9) Palgarh (10) Bhorap (11) Kumari and (12) Udaidurg (Sarkar, *House of Shivaji*, 1955, p. 149.) *J.S.*
5. सरित्य तीचें जल मोजवेना

   माध्यान्हिचा मास्कर पाहवेना ।

   मुष्टीत वैश्वानर बांधवेना ।

   तैसा शिवाजी नृप जिंकवेना ।।

   Quoted in Sane's *Sabhasad Bhaskar*,[6] with Sardesai's emendation of the first word. *J.S.*
6. *Shiv Chhatrapati Chen Charitra*, by Krishnaji Anant Sabhasad, ed. by K.N. Sane, 4th edn., 1923, pp. 76-77, f.n. 58.

   The original reading 'समुद्र याचे' has been amended 'सरित्पती चें' *Ed.*
7. All the important contemporary Rajasthani letters now in the Rajasthan State Archives, Bikaner, dealing with this historic episode have been published in *Shivaji's Visit to Aurangzib at Agra*, ed. by Sir Jadunath Sarkar and Raghubir Sinh, 1963, Calcutta. *Ed.*
8. *Agra Visit* (Let. No. 41, p. 42) gives the date as *Ashad Vidi* 1, Friday. Friday was on June 8. According to *I.A.*, *Ashad Vidi* 1 fell on Thursday, June 7. *Ed.*
9. This should be Friday, August 17, 1666, as Shivaji's escape was discovered in the forenoon of Saturday, August 18, 1666. (*Agra Visit*, Let. No. 29, p. 53). *Ed.*
10. Though originally Ram Singh was scheduled to be brought to the Imperial presence in the evening of Sunday, March 24, 1667, he was actually presented in the evening of Sunday, March 31, 1667. (*Agra Visit*, Letters No. 66-67, pp. 113-114). *Ed.*

XI

The Last Campaign And Death Of Jai Singh

Jai Singh Invades Bijapur

When appointing Jai Singh to the Deccan, Aurangzib had instructed him to punish both Shivaji and the Bijapur king. But the Rajput general had pleaded, 'It would not be wise to attack both these fools at the same time.' He had at first directed all his forces against Shivaji alone (*H.A.*, *68a*). By the treaty of Purandar (June, 1665), the Maratha chief was shorn of two-thirds of his dominions and reduced to the rank of an obedient vassal. It was now the turn of Adil Shah to feel the weight of the Mughal arm.

The truth of the matter is that never since the reign of Akbar did the Mughal Government once abandon the ambition of annexing the Deccan, and the Sultans of Bijapur and Golkonda could never forget this cardinal fact of seventeenth century Indian politics. They naturally looked round for allies, and after 1663 found in Shivaji their only efficient bulwark against the Mughals.

Jai Singh also intrigued with many officers and vassals of Bijapur and sent to them letters to seduce them from loyalty to their sovereign, and offered them service under the Mughal Emperor. As he wrote to prepare his master for the financial drain of the war,

> As soon as our army enters this kingdom, many Deccanis will have to be enlisted in our service and every one of them will have to be supplied with money according to his rank, to enable him to arm and equip (his followers). Expenditure of money will be necessary till the conquest of Bijapur, when our costs will be recovered, as I hope. (*H.A.*, 74*b*.)

His diplomatic web having thus been subtly woven, Jai Singh collected the sinews of war. The Imperial forces under his banners numbered about 40,000 troopers, to which must be added local auxiliaries. Shivaji sent him 2000 troopers whom his son as a five-*hazari* was bound by the regulations to supply, and 7000 expert infantry of his own. The Maratha contingent was commanded by Netaji Palkar, reputed in the Deccan as 'a second Shivaji'. Jai Singh thought that Shivaji could be more usefully employed in capturing forts and making diversions in other parts of the Bijapur territory than in accompanying the Imperial army.

During the first month of the campaign against Bijapur, Jai Singh's march was an uninterrupted triumph. From Purandar to Mangalvide, a fort 52 miles north of Bijapur, the invaders advanced without meeting with any opposition. The Bijapuri forts on the way were either evacuated in terror or surrendered. The invaders marched on, and then on 24th December had their first contact with the enemy, because the Bijapuri king had wisely concentrated all his forces near his capital and suffered the Mughals to penetrate unmolested, far from their own frontier.

The next day (25th December), a detachment under Dilir Khan and Shivaji marched ten miles from the Imperial camp and fought a Bijapuri army of 12,000 men under the famous generals Sharza Khan and Khawas Khan, and their Maratha-allies Jadav Rao of Kalian and Vyankaji, the half-brother of Shivaji. The Deccanis evaded the charges of the heavy cavalry of Delhi, but harassed them by their 'Cossack' tactics, forming four divisions and fighting loosely. After a long contest, Dilir Khan's tireless energy and courage broke the enemy by repeated charges, and they retired in the evening leaving one general and 15 captains dead on the field, and many flags, horses and weapons in the Mughal hands. But as soon as the victors began their return march, the elusive enemy reappeared and galled them severely from the two wings and rear.

After two days, Jai Singh resumed his march on 27th December, and two days later arrived within 12 miles of Bijapur. This was destined to be the furthest point of his advance, for here the first stage of the war ended and the second stage began, in which the Mughals were outnumbered and outmanoeuvred by the Bijapuris, totally lost the initiative, and lived like a besieged camp as long as they continued in hostile territory. By this time the fort of Bijapur had been put in a strong posture of defence. Its walls had been repaired, and large quantities of provisions and material laid in, and its regular garrison strengthened by 30,000 Karnataki infantry, renowned for their fighting quality. In addition to this, the country around, for a radius of six miles, had been remorselessly laid waste; the two large tanks of Nauraspur and Shahpur, each of which could have supplied the needs of an entire army, had been drained dry. All the wells in the environs had been filled up with earth; every building had been razed to the ground and every tree cut down, so that 'not a green branch or shade-giving wall was left standing' to afford shelter to the invaders. At the same time a select force under the noted generals Sharza Khan and Siddi Masaud had been sent to invade the Imperial dominions and create a diversion in Jai Singh's rear, while the main Bijapuri army hovered round the general's camp.

Jai Singh Begins To Retreat From Bijapur

Jai Singh at once recognized that the chance of taking Bijapur by a *coup de main* was gone; his position was now critical. Therefore, when within 12 miles of Bijapur, he decided to turn back in order to expel the enemy's raiding parties from the Imperial territory. After a seven days' halt, which was marked by another running fight between the patrols on the two sides, the Mughal general began his retreat on 5th January, 1666, the Bijapuris hanging on his rear. He reached Sultanpur (on the Sina), 16 miles south of Parenda, on the 27th and halted there for 24 days. The news of his return march had an immediate effect: the Bijapuri division under Sharza Khan evacuated the Imperial territory and joined the army under Abdul Muhammad (the *wazir*) which was following Jai Singh. But in this month of January, four great misfortunes befell the Mughals. First, about the 12th, a brave Afghan captain named Sikandar (the brother of Fath Jang Khan), convoying provisions material and munitions to the army of Jai Singh, was wounded and taken prisoner to Sholapur, and all his rich convoy was plundered.

Then on the 16th (January, 1666), Shivaji who had at his own request been detached to make a diversion in the west by attacking Fort Panhala, met with a dismal failure in trying to escalade it. The garrison were on the alert and a thousand Marathas fell down, killed or wounded, when the rising sun lit up the scene. Shivaji found it madness to continue the struggle, and retired baffled. About the 20th came the evil news that Netaji, Shivaji's chief officer, had deserted to Bijapur for a bribe of four lakhs of *hun* and was leading raiding parties into Mughal territory. Jai Singh could not afford to lose such a man, and so he lured him back (Wednesday, 21st March) with many persuasive letters and the acceptance of all his high demands—the rank of a five-*hazari*, and *jagir* in the settled and lucrative old territory of the empire.

The fourth misfortune of the Mughals was the sending of 12,000 cavalry and 40,000 infantry by the Sultan of Golkonda under his trusty eunuch Raza Quli (surnamed Neknam Khan) to assist Adil Shah. Jai Singh's position now became extremely dangerous. The Battle of Lohri, 22nd January, was very sanguinary, the imperialists losing 190 men slain and 250 wounded, besides many horses, while the enemy's casualties exceeded 400 slain and 1000 wounded. (*Cf. KK*. ii, 197.) The enemy seized this opportunity to make an onset on the Rajah's person. But his Rajputs, under Harnath Chauhan and other leading officers of his own contingent who formed his van, gallantly dashed into the enemy's ranks after saluting him, and desperately resisted them at close quarters. Harnath fell after receiving 21 wounds; and so also did most of his comrades. Several other Rajputs were wounded. 'The dead formed heaps on the field of the encounter.' The battle raged for six hours from 3 p.m. 'The Deccanis tried their utmost, but at last fled with heavy loss.'

After fighting five such battles in less than a month (25th December-22nd January), Jai Singh's army was clearly no longer fit for further exertions. So he rested his men at Sultanpur for 24 days (27th January-19th February).

The raiding parties of Bijapur, under Bahlol Khan and Netaji, in the lately annexed Bidar-Kaliani districts (at the north-east corner of the old Bijapur Kingdom) could no longer be ignored. On 20th February, Jai Singh issued from his camp at Sultanpur and marched due east into the disturbed area.

Jai Singh's Campaign In The Bhima-Manjira Region, February-June, 1666

The third stage of the war now began, which was to end with his retreat to Bhum, 18 miles north-east of Parenda, early in June next. During these three months and a half Jai Singh moved about in the small quadrilateral formed by the Bhima on the west and the Manjira on the east, and the cities of Dharur in the north and Tuljapur in the south. In the course of this campaign, he fought four more bloody but fruitless battles like those described before. Each time the Bijapuris were repulsed in the field and driven some distance, but they were not crushed and continued as before to hover round the Mughal camp, cut off stragglers and weak foraging parties, and stop the arrival of supplies. During this period, the forts of Dhoki (44 miles east of Parenda), Gunjoti (20 miles east of Naldurg), and Nilang (23 miles further north) were captured by the Mughals—not very important gains—and Netaji returned to the Mughal side. A new plan of war was adopted in the middle of May:

> As the elusive enemy could not be caught in one body, nor crushed once for all, but they scattered like quicksilver, and the imperialists who were encumbered with a camp and heavy baggage could not pursue them for any long distance—therefore, Jai Singh decided to make his army more light and mobile, so as to be capable of following the enemy till a crushing blow could be inflicted. He took with himself only small tents and light kit and urged his officers to do the same and send all the baggage of the soldiers and camp-followers to Dharur (31 miles n. of Dhoki), where a strong garrison was left to guard them. (*A.N.*, 1018).

But at this point the Imperial army completely broke down and the campaign had to be abandoned.

> The soldiers were exhausted by privation, long marches, and heavy loss of horses and transport animals. The rainy season was near and the Emperor wrote to Jai Singh to return to Aurangabad, canton there for the monsoons, and send a part of his army to the *jagirs* of his officers, where they could live in (greater) comfort. (*A.N.*, 1020)

So a retreat was decided upon.

Mangalvide was too far from the Mughal frontier and too isolated a post to be held easily. Jai Singh, therefore, detached Dilir Khan to remove the guns and material from the fort (Friday, 25th May), distribute the grain and other property, burn whatever could not be carried away, and dismantle the fortifications. This was done, and the party rejoined him on Thursday, 31st May.

Phaltan had been deemed untenable and its Mughal garrison withdrawn as early as February last. It was then presented to Mahadaji Nimbalkar, a son-in-law of Shivaji, and an officer of the imperialists.

The return march northwards began on Friday, 1st June. Reaching Bhum (about 10th June), Jai Singh halted there for three and a half months, and then, on 28th September, started for the environs of Bir (37 miles north of Bhum) where he stayed till 17th November, finally reaching Aurangabad on the 26th of that month. By the end of May when the Mughals began this final retreat, the Bijapuris too were exhausted. The Sultan of Golkonda recalled his troops. Both the combatants were sick of war, and longed for peace; and negotiations were opened. The Bijapuris retired within their own frontiers when the Mughals did the same.

Jai Singh's invasion of Bijapur was a military failure. Not an inch of territory, not a stone of a fortress, not a piece of indemnity was gained by it. As a financial speculation it was even more disastrous. Only the most complete success could have justified such a costly adventure immediately after the war with Shivaji had thrown the pay of the Mughal army into arrears for six months. In addition to the thirty lakhs of rupees advanced to him from the Imperial treasury, Jai Singh had spent more than a *krore* out of his own pocket. (*Dil.* 56.)

The Emperor's Displeasure With Jai Singh For His Failure

As early as the beginning of January, 1666, when Jai Singh retreated for the first time, Aurangzib had censured him for his failure and asked him to show what he had gained with the vast army and treasure given to him. When Jai Singh's second campaign produced no better result, he felt that he had fallen under his master's wrath, and that if this failure were not retrieved, his lifelong devotion to the Mughal throne would be forgotten and he would be dismissed with every mark of ignominy. The unhappy general tried hard to retain the command of the Deccan Army, so as to get another chance of retrieving his fame. He was troubled by Court news of the Emperor's angry remarks about him, and of talk about sending Prince Muazzam to the south to supersede him in the viceroyalty. He then besought his son and friends at Court to exert themselves to save him; he offered the prime minister a bribe of Rs 30,000 for inducing the Emperor to let him continue as *subahdar*. But it was all in vain.

The escape of Shivaji from Agra (August 18, 1666) added to Jai Singh's troubles. He was held to be in some way responsible for the conduct of his son Ram Singh, who was more than suspected of having connived at Shivaji's flight. After Jai Singh's final retirement to Bir (October), he received orders to return to Aurangabad and on the 23rd March following (1667) he was recalled to Court and the viceroyalty of the Deccan was given to Prince Muazzam, assisted by Jaswant Singh. (*A.N.*, 1037.)

Mirza Rajah Jai Singh's innermost feelings during the dismal year between Shivaji's flight and his own death are clearly laid bare in his private letters, included in the *Haft Anjuman* of his confidential secretary, Udairaj. Extracts from a few of them are given below.

Jai Singh wrote to Kumar Ram Singh at Delhi (1666) after urging him to see the Emperor and induce him not to remove Jai Singh from the Deccan command as he had done the difficult preliminary work and borne all the cost of it, while the noble who would replace him would cheaply take all the credit of success without having to exert himself for it; and Jai Singh would be unjustly branded before the public as a failure, after his lifelong distinguished service.

> The greater part of my life is over, and little remains, and that little has now almost reached its terminus. I seek refuge with my *pir* and *murshid* (i.e., the Emperor) to escape from shame in my old age. At the end of my days I am suffering disgrace. (Folio 195)

Jai Singh to Kumar Ram Singh (a letter in cypher):

> In whatever action, great or small, I do, I, keeping your interest in view, bring you in (as my intermediary at the Imperial Court). And yet, your attitude is such that at the time when my urgent

> requests in connection with the Emperor's work are written to you, you go out to hunt and do not send any reply; and when your reply comes, which is very late, you do not touch all the points of my letter. If you are forgetful of my relationship as your father, at least the duty of acting as my Court agent is incumbent on you. If our master asks, "When did this letter from Jai Singh arrive? And on what date have you placed it before me?" you will have to answer. If you do not care for either of these two things, do as you please; Shri Ramji is over my head too (*Bar sar-i-ma ham Shri Ramji-st*). (Folio 196)

Jai Singh to Giridhari Lal, his wakil:

> Strange times have become my lot. Every man labours so much only for his sons, and yet he (i.e. Kumar Ram Singh) does not write anything to me, and the only thing that he writes is, 'I have got no information on this point.' In four ways losses have fallen upon me—First, my *mujra* is gone; Secondly, the *parganas* of my home (*watan*) are gone; Thirdly, what I have spent (out of my own pocket) in the Deccan wars is gone; and fourthly—what is worst of all—my son's affairs have been ruined. Although these considerations do not reach his mind from my writing, yet I cannot help apprehending these misfortunes.

The Misery And Death Of Jai Singh, 1667

The Rajput veteran of a hundred fights made over charge to his successor at Aurangabad in May, 1667, and bent his way towards northern India in humiliation and disappointment. His brilliant career which had unfolded under three Emperors, and in which he had won laurels from Qandahar to Mungir and Balkh to Maharashtra, was clouded by a single ill-success at its close. Not a pice of the *krore* of rupees of his own money that he had spent in the Bijapur war would be repaid by his master. Broken-hearted from disgrace and disappointment, and labouring under disease and old age, Jai Singh sank in death at Burhanpur, on 28th August, 1667. Like Walsingham of Elizabeth's Court, he died bankrupt after serving too faithfully an exacting but thankless master.

Jai Singh's death was due to an accident. When he was mounting his huge elephant outside Burhanpur, the wooden ladder slipped and crushed his leg as he fell down, and within two days he died in great pain.[1]

Aurangzib refused to forgive Jai Singh the one failure of his life. But the Rajah never had a fair chance in this war. His army was hopelessly inadequate for the conquest of so large and rich a kingdom; his war material and food supply were sufficient for a month or two only, and he had no siege-guns. At the same time the power of Bijapur State was unimpaired in contrast with its exhausted condition when Aurangzib himself captured its capital 20 years later. Not only was Jai Singh's army relatively small for the task laid upon it; he was also badly served by his subordinates. In the Mughal camp itself they acted as the enemy's spies. Many of his officers were unreliable and refused or delayed in carrying out orders. Success under these conditions was not humanly possible. Jai Singh died, overwhelmed with loss and disappointment and public disgrace. But the best defence of his reputation as a general and diplomatist is the 18 months' siege and the employment of the entire resources of the empire under the very eyes of Aurangzib by which alone was Bijapur captured in 1686.

Immediately after the death of Jai Singh, his secretary and favourite manager, Udairaj—to whom we owe the invaluable letter-book, *Haft Anjuman*—went to the governor of Burhanpur and turned Muhammadan, to save himself from the persecution of the Rajah's followers. From this they suspected that he had brought about Jai Singh's death by poison.[3] Kumar Kirat Singh wished to avenge his father's death by dragging the renegade out of the governor's house and killing him with insult, but he found it impossible to molest a Muslim. (*Dil.*, 63-64.)

Notes

1. This fact is proved by the recently discovered contemporary *official* records preserved among the Jaipur archives,[2] and these completely exonerate the house of Kama from the false charge popularly made against its founder. *J.S.*

2. *Jai. Akh. Aurangzib*, Year 10-Pt. II, p. 381. *Ed.*
3. Manucci recounts the bazar gossip that Aurangzib caused poison to be given to Jai Singh on the road (ii. 152), while Tod makes Kirat Singh the murderer of his father at the instigation of Aurangzib, according to one of the fabling 'chronicles' on which he invariably relies: 'The tyrannical Aurangzib determined to destroy him (Jai Singh)... He promised the succession to the *gadi* of Amber to Kirat Singh if he effected the horrid deed. The wretch, having perpetrated the crime by mixing poison with his father's opium, returned to claim the investiture; but the king only gave him the district of Kama.' (*Annals*, ii, Amber, ch. I.)

   The absurdity of the allegation is proved by the fact that according to the authoritative official history of Shah Jahan, Kama had been bestowed on Kirat Singh by that monarch (and not by Aurangzib), and the grant had been made *17 years before* the death of Jai Singh! *J.S.*

XII

Ram Singh And Bishan Singh, 1667–1700

Ram Singh's Succession To The Throne

Aurangzib's wrath against Kumar Ram Singh for his supposed complicity in the escape of Shivaji from Agra (on Saturday, 18th August, 1666) had been somewhat softened at the entreaty of Jaswant Singh seven months later (Saturday, 23rd March, 1667).

On 7th September of the latter year news arrived of the death of Mirza Raja Jai Singh at Burhanpur, and the Emperor, on 10th September, granted full pardon to the Kumar with succession to the throne of Amber and the title of Rajah. He put the *tika* mark of kingship on his forehead with his own hand. The Rajah's rank was that of a Commander of Four Thousand (3000 troopers) while his younger brother Kirat Singh, the lord of Kama, was made a Commander of Three Thousand (2500 troopers, including 700 *do aspa seh aspa*—*AN*. 1051, 1061; and *J.R.*). On September 10, Ram Singh received an elephant (price Rs 12,000) a horse (Rs 5000), a jewelled sword (Rs 3000), another sword (Rs 2000) and a royal robe of honour. (*J.R.* No. 333).[1]

At the end of March 1667, when Ram Singh first came out of the cloud of royal disfavour, an order was issued by the Emperor restoring to him 20 *parganas* which had been attached after Shivaji's flight. They are—

(a) Audi, Songar-Songri, and Bari, in Agra district;
(b) Bawal, in Rewari district;
(c) Baroda (Rana), Kotputli, and Chal Kaliana, in Narnol district;
(d) Biwani (probably Pangwan of *Ain-i-Akbari*), in Tijara district;
(e) Malarna, Nawai and Barwara,[2] in Ranthambhor district (Batwara is evidently a copyist's error);
(f) Jalalpur, Balhar (variant Bairohar), Patan, Bharkol, Khohri, Malakhera, Mandawar, Thana (Ghazi) and Ismailpur, in Alwar province (*J.R.* No. 332).[3]

The revenue of 18 of these in 1595, when the *Ain-i-Akbari* was compiled, amounted to a total of nearly ten and a half lakhs and if we can assume a safe average from this, the other two *parganas* which are not noticed in the *Ain* would yield an additional lakh and one-eighth—or approximately Rs 11,60,000 in all. But the statistics of Imperial revenue which we possess for the year 1660 show that in some places Akbar's assessment had been doubled and in a few others quadrupled on Aurangzib's accession. Hence, the Amber Rajah's *jagirs* in this quarter probably yielded 25 lakhs of rupees as standard or theoretical revenue. In addition we learn from a contemporary record that the Mirza Rajah had been granted the *pargana* of Tonk as his reward for the Purandar campaign, but that the Toda *pargana* did not as yet belong to him. (*J.R.* No. 325.)[4]

Ram Singh In Assam, 1667-1676

At this time the imperialists in Bengal had suffered a great disaster, and lost the fort of Gauhati on the Assam frontier to the new Rajah of Assam. The Emperor, on hearing of the loss of Gauhati, had appointed Rajah Ram Singh, on 27 December, 1667, to recover the Imperial prestige in Assam. The Rajah was accompanied by 4000 troopers in his own pay, besides 1500 gentlemen-troopers (*ahadis*) and 500 artillery-men of the Imperial service. Auxiliaries from Kuch Bihar, numbering 15,000 archers, also joined him, but their fighting value was little. The Bengal viceroy was ordered to reinforce him out of his own contingent. On the way through Patna the Rajah took with himself the Sikh *guru* Tegh Bahadur.

Ram Singh reached the frontier post of Rangamati in February, 1669. But from the first his task was hopeless. Service in Assam was extremely unpopular, and no soldier would go there unless compelled. Indeed, there is reason to believe that Ram Singh was sent to Assam as a punishment for his having secretly helped Shivaji to escape from his captivity at Agra. He had only 8000 troopers round his standards, and his losses were seldom replenished. The Ahoms, being a nation in arms, mustered 100,000 when mobilized. Unlike the time of Mir Jumla's invasion, the mastery of the water now belonged to the Ahoms, and the Mughals could do little with their 40 war-vessels on the Brahmaputra river.

The situation was rendered worse by the insubordination and disloyalty of Rashid Khan, the *faujdar* of Gauhati. Instead of obeyir.g Ram Singh, as he had been ordered to do, this man foolishly set up a claim to equality of rank with him. Having lived at Gauhati with viceregal splendour and been all in all in the eyes of the Ahoms, he could not bear to take his orders from Ram Singh. He was even suspected, probably with truth, of being in secret correspondence with the enemy; at all events they found a friend in him. At last Ram Singh had to expel Rashid Khan from his camp after cutting his tent ropes.

From his base at Rangamati, the Rajah advanced along the north Brahmaputra valley. The Ahoms fell back before him, and he reached the Bar Nadi. The Mughals gained a few victories, but no decisive success; and soon the tide of war began to turn against them and they had to fall back westwards to Hajo (Kamrup). Then he laid siege to Gauhati, but all his attempts to take it failed; after wasting four months he had to retire with heavy loss. A detachment which had advanced into Darang was cut off by the local Rani. The Ahoms bought the aid of the Nagas, and these wild warriors proved a new danger to the Mughals.

In the second half of 1670 the Imperial forces suffered three severe defeats. Ram Singh now begged for peace, on condition of a return to the ancient boundary. Both sides were weary of the war. But the death of the Ahom King Chakradhwaj and other causes greatly protracted the negotiations, during which, however, there was a lull in the fighting.

The attempts at peace failed. The Ahoms renewed their attacks, and the fresh troops that now joined Ram Singh (especially the Bengal *zamindar* Munawwar Khan), bore down his apathy to war. A long course of desultory fighting followed, the general result of which was the success of the Ahoms. So in March 1671 Ram Singh retired to Rangamati, foiled in his purpose and heartily sick of the war. Here on the Assam border he stayed for some years, but was too weak to attempt to advance again. Finally in 1676 he received permission to leave Bengal, and reached the Imperial Court in June.

Ram Singh In Afghanistan

After his nine years' exile in the pestilential climate of Assam and under constant threat of the black magic for which the Assamese were dreaded throughout India, Ram Singh was allowed to return to Delhi in June, 1676, and was raised to the rank of a five-hazari (5000 troopers, out of whom 1000, were *do aspa seh aspa*). By this time the storm cloud threatening the Empire had moved from the north-east to the north-west frontier in an even more menacing form. In 1672 there was a general rising of the Afghan tribes (Afridis and Khataks) along the Khyber pass, against the Delhi Government, and after the disastrous defeat of the Imperial general Muhammad Amin Khan, the revolt of the exultant Pathans spread from Qandahar to Attock; and two years later came the defeat and death of another great noble Shujaet Khan. So, Aurangzib himself took post at Hasan Abdal, between Rawalpindi and Peshawar, in order to guide the operations against the frontier tribes. Ram Singh's son, Kumar Kishan Singh, along with a Kachhwa contingent, served in Afghanistan from September, 1674 to April, 1677, after which he was sent home to recoup. Ram Singh too was given leave for Amber after his ten years' absence in Agra and Assam. The next two years, 1677 and 1678, were spent by father and son in well-earned repose at home. But at the end of the second year arose a storm which was destined to overthrow the Mughal Empire.

Maharajah Jaswant Singh, when serving as a guardian of the Khyber pass, died at Jamrud[5] on Wednesday, 11th December, 1678;[6] his posthumous son Ajit Singh (born at Lahore in February[7] next) was forcibly detained at Delhi by order of Aurangzib and his kingdom of Marwar was seized. But Durgadas Rathor cut off the infant prince through the opposition of the Imperial forces and conveyed him to Marwar (23 July, 1679).[8] Aurangzib hastened in pursuit and took post at Ajmer on 25th September and the Rajput war began. This detained him there for the next two years, and continued to inflame Marwar to the end of his life. Meanwhile, seizing the opportunity presented by the death of the foremost Rajput ruler of that time, Aurangzib had imposed the punitive poll tax on the Hindus (*jizya*) on 2 April, and issued orders for vigorously enforcing everywhere his decree of 1669 to destroy 'all the temples and places of religious instruction of the Hindus.' (*M.A.*, 81 and 174.)

The conflagration spread through the country. There was opposition to the iconoclasm in Rajputana and Malwa, though in some places the superior forces of the Delhi Government carried out its object against the unorganized local Hindus. But in the end, the Rathor leaders induced Aurangzib's son, Prince Muhammad Akbar, to undertake the task of saving his ancestral empire from disruption through the old Emperor's bigotry. Akbar crowned himself (January 1, 1681) and advanced to attack his father near Ajmer. How the attempt failed and the young pretender to the throne had to take asylum with the Maratha King Shambhuji (June) is a well known tale. Aurangzib patched up a peace with the Maharana of Udaipur (June 14) and himself took the road to the Deccan (September 8) to oppose Akbar and his protector.

Ram Singh was now the most prominent of the Rajput kings and he could not be safely left in the rear in such a troubled time. So, the Emperor posted him to Afghanistan, to be guardian of the Khyber pass, under Amir Khan, the highly gifted and tactful *subahdar* of that province. The appointment was made in the middle of this year (1681). His only son and heir Kumar Kishan Singh was sent to the Deccan, to serve in the army for invading Bijapur.

Ram Singh's headquarters were at Jamrud and he had charge of the Khyber route from the Indian end up to Haft Chah. He had to keep the road open, send escorts for treasure convoys, distribute the annual subsidy (six lakhs in all) among the Afghan tribes on the border in order to keep them friendly, and enlist in the Imperial army suitable headmen and warriors who seemed likely to be loyal. A large number of letters (in Persian) from the Afridi, Khatak and other tribesmen, and despatches from Kabul addressed to the Rajah during this period have been preserved in the Jaipur archives.[9] Amir Khan was extremely friendly with Ram Singh and sought to convenience him in every way. He gave Ram Singh timely information and advice for guarding his outposts (*thanahs*) in that pass—Jamrud, Ali Masjid and the Kotal of Gharibkhanah.

But shortly afterwards, things took the saddest turn for Ram Singh. On Tuesday, 11th April 1682,[10] his only son Kishan Singh, then posted at Parenda fort in the Deccan, died of wounds inflicted by an Afghan soldier in the course of a private quarrel. (*M.A.*, 217; *Dilkasha*, I, 174.) The stricken father was prostrated by the shock, and fell severely ill, from which he recovered in September next. A year later, as difficulties thickened round the Rajah, Darya Khan Afridi rose in the Khyber district. Amir Khan wisely forbade the use of the route the imperialists took and directed the traffic from India to the Karapa pass. Ram Singh had been given a promotion in rank and pay (December 6, 1681) on the condition of guarding the Khyber and keeping that route open. Now that it was closed, the Rajah was deprived of the honour and emolument, 1500 troopers *do aspa seh aspa*, and the *jagirs* covering the cost of these troops (November 29, 1685). Worse than this, Aurangzib demanded that the Rajah's grandson Bishan—the sole heir and prop of his house—should go and serve in the army of the Deccan as his murdered father had been doing, for immediately after the death of Kishan Singh, the boy Bishan Singh had been created a Commander of One Thousand (400 troopers) 'in his father's place'. (*M.A.*, 217; *J.T.*, II, p. 213) Ram Singh could never consent to it. It was the universal belief among the Rajputs that Aurangzib had caused poison to be given to Mirza Rajah Jai Singh, and also to Maharajah Jaswant Singh's only son Pirthi Singh, when out with the Imperial armies; and also that he had recently contrived the death of Kishan Singh. The suspicion of political murder under which Aurangzib laboured among the public has been well illustrated by the Venetian traveller Niccolas Manucci. Ram Singh therefore delayed sending his grandson to such a fatal post for over a year. At last the Emperor lost all patience, (December 28, 1686), complained bitterly against Ram Singh to his chief ministers and rejected the recommendation of Amir Khan to give Ram Singh the *faujdari* of Upper and Lower Bangash and a promotion of *mansab*. He took away Jamrud from the Rajah and posted him to Kohat, where he died in April, 1688, in unspeakable sorrow. (*J.R.*, Nos. 352,[11] 10 and 354.)

Bishan Singh's Jat Wars

On his grandfather's death, Bishan Singh (born in 1672), who had been deprived of his *mansab* and *jagir* (Malarna) for absence from the Deccan at the beginning of the preceding year, was, on 30th April, 1688, given the title of Rajah, a *farman, khilat* and kettledrums, with the rank of a Commander of 2500 (2000 troopers—*do aspa*), and a cash reward of Rs 1,25,000 for these 2000 horsemen, and a further sum of Rs 75,000 on the condition of suppressing Rajaram the Jat rebel, whose stronghold was Sansani (now in Bharatpur State). He held the office of *faujdar* of the Mathura district, and his duty was to establish outposts on the line of communication with the Imperial army campaigning against the Jats and to suppress the rebels of the Mathura district (especially in Mahaban, east of the Jamuna).[12] Both these tasks he performed capably, often engaging in bloody fights with the Jats who tried to cut off grain convoys, or menaced the isolated Mughal posts on the line. Against the other rebels also he gained striking successes. But the siege of Sansani by Prince Bidar Bakht (grandson of the Emperor) dragged on, and the campaign in the jungles of the Jat country severely taxed the invading army. The Mughals before Sansani had to undergo great hardship from scarcity of provisions and water, as the enemy by frequent attacks cut off their grain-convoys and watering parties. Incessant night-attacks kept the siege-camp in perpetual alarm. 'The men were prostrated by hunger, and the animals perished in large numbers through weakness.' But the besiegers held on tenaciously and in four months carried their trenches to the gate of the fort, mounted guns on raised platforms and laid mines. The jungle round the fort was cleared. One mine under the gate was fired; but the Jats had detected it and blocked its further side with stones, and the charge was driven backwards, destroying many of the artillerymen and supervising officers of the Mughal army. A second mine was then laid and carried under the wall in a month's time. It was successfully fired (end of January, 1690), the wall was breached, the Jat defenders lining it were blown up, and the Mughals stormed the fort after three hours of stubborn opposition. The Jats disputed every inch of the ground and were dispersed only after losing 1500 of their men. On the Imperial side, 200 Mughals fell and 700 Rajputs were slain or wounded. The remnant of the garrison was put to the sword. (*Ishwar*, 136 *b*-137 *a*; *M.A.*, 334; Hamid-ud-din's *Akham* No. 26; *Jaipur Records*.)

Next year (21st May, 1691) Rajah Bishan Singh surprised the other Jat stronghold of Soghar.

> The Rajah hastened there with the Imperial army. By chance, as the gate of this little fort was kept open at the time for admitting grain, the invaders entered it at the gallop, slaying all who raised their hands and taking 500 of the rebels prisoner. (*Ishwar*, 137 *a* and *b*; *M.A.*, 340; *J.R.*)

The Last Days of Bishan Singh

Bishan Singh's military jurisdiction spread over the Mathura district westwards across the modern state of Bharatpur to Kama and the frontier of the kingdom of Jaipur, and eastwards across the Jamuna to the Mahaban *pargana* along the edge of the Doab. Much of this country was occupied by the sturdy belicose Jat peasantry living in villages defended by mud walls and belts of dense jungle outside. No Jat kingdom of Bharatpur had as yet arisen, and the Agra and Mathura districts west of the Jamuna as well as the opposite bank of that river northwards up to Dankaur almost facing Delhi, were dotted with numerous Jat villages, each under its headman, who occasionally combined together in a common resistance to the Imperial Government. The Hindu reaction brought on by Aurangzib's iconoclastic policy was favoured by the Emperor's long absence in the Deccan, the decay and corruption of the local administration, and the constant reports of the failure of Imperial arms in the Maratha war which invariably swallowed up the treasures and soldiery sent out from Agra and Delhi in a ceaseless stream.

The first successful Jat leader Rajaram (*not* entitled Rajah) had been slain in a private feud between two local clans (1688), and the revolt against the Delhi Government was continued in a more secret and spasmodic manner by his brother Churaman and son[13] Rupa. But each village headman among the Jats fought for his own hand, without recognizing any common leader of their clan, and hence they were defeated by Bishan Singh during the years 1690-1694. The

Rajah had also to send out detachments for collecting the revenue from defaulting villagers in the manner painfully familiar in the history of Oudh under its effete Nawabs. 50 such mud forts were taken and demolished by his son Jai Singh II.

After the capture of Sansani and Soghor (1690 and 1691), the ostensible head of the Jat rising was crushed, but the country was so wild and the people so stubborn that the orderly administration or even peaceful occupation of the district was beyond Bishan Singh's resources. Gradually the Jat leaders came out of hiding and reoccupied their lost homes, like Sansani and Soghor, because Bishan Singh had neither the men nor the money to hold the entire district in awe. Hence, after 1694, we find frequent complaints to the Emperor, and censure by him of Bishan Singh on the allegation that the Rajah had neglectfully let the rebel Jats recover their fortified villages. Aurangzib's mind now turned completely against the Amber chief, and in March 1696 he removed Bishan Singh from the *faujdari* of Mathura, conferring that post on Itiqad Khan, who had served actively under the Rajah during the last few years.

Dangers thickened round the Rajah. The disaster to Mughal arms at the end of 1695, when two great generals, Qasim Khan and Himmat Khan, perished after defeat by the Marathas, made the Emperor summon Bishan Singh to the Deccan with his brave clansmen. The Rajah pleaded and bribed, both at the darbar of Prince Shah Alam, who had come to Agra as governor in July, 1695 and under whom Bishan Singh was now posted; and also at the Imperial Court in the Deccan to get this order cancelled.[14] The royal ministers, the Emperor's beloved daughter Zinat-un-nisa, and her eunuch were appealed to (with the customary *douceurs*), and at last this summons to the Deccan was changed into a demand for the sending of the Rajah's son Jai Singh II to the Emperor's camp with half the family contingent, while Bishan Singh was allowed to stay at Agra in Shah Alam's service.

But remembering the tragic end of Kumar Kishan Singh in 1682, the Rajah was alarmed at the prospect of deputing his little boy to the Deccan. He interceded with every minister and delayed as long as he could, till at last the Emperor lost all patience. Now Jai Singh was sent to Aurangzib (early in 1698). The friendly Mir Bakhshi, however, contrived to secure for the prince speedy permission to return home (July 4, 1698) on eight months' leave for the purpose of marrying a Bikaner princess.[15] But as Jai Singh long outstayed his leave and no preparations for his marriage were reported from Amber, the Emperor was naturally enraged, and his anger was fanned by Prince Azam Shah under whose son (Bidar Bakht) the heir of Amber had been ordered to serve (March, 1699).

Meanwhile, Bishan Singh, with his younger son Chimaji (literally 'the Infant') and half his family contingent, had joined Prince Shah Alam, who had been appointed *subahdar* of Afghanistan after the death of Amir Khan in April, 1698. This prince used to spend the winter in Peshawar (then included in the province of Kabul and not part of the *subah* of Lahore) and the summer at Jalalabad or Kabul. Bishan Singh, like his grandfather, was posted at the rugged north-western gateway of India. Like his father, he died there, as *faujdar* of Derbend in the depth of the Afghan winter, on 19th December, 1699.[16] His second son Chimaji continued to attend Shah Alam's son Refi-ul-qadr at Peshawar[17] and Jalalabad, till the death of Aurangzib in 1707.

Notes

1. *Jai. Hindi,* IV, p. 158. *Ed.*
2. 'Batwara' in the text has been corrected here by Sarkar to Barwada, as this name appears in the list of parganas in Sarkar Ranthambhor in the first edition of Jarrett's English translation of *Ain.*, II (p. 275), though in its second edition (p. 280) he has himself corrected it to 'Jarwara'. Moreover, at that time Barwada was in the possession of Sher Singh Rotla Rathor, son of Ram Singh Rotla, who had been killed in the Battle of Shamugarh (May 30, 1658). (*Thirty Decisive Battles of Jaipur,* by Narendra Singh, 1939, p. 189.) *Ed.*
3. *Jai. Rec., Addl. Pers.*, III, pp. 8-9. *Ed.*
4. *Jai. Hindi,* I, pp. 12-15. *Ed.*
5. Should be Peshawar. He was then camping in the garden of Puranmal Bundela. *Bahi.*, pp. 75-76. *Ed.*
6. The correct date is Thursday, Paush Vidi 10, 1735 V.S. i.e. November 28, 1678 A.D. = 23 Shawwal, Julusi Yr. 22. *Bahi.*,

pp. 75-76. The date of Jaswant Singh's death given in *Maasir-i-Alamgiri* (E.T., p. 106) 6 Zilqad (Wednesday, December 11, 1678) is obviously wrong. *Ed.*

7. The exact date of Ajit Singh's birth is Chaitra Vidi 4, 1735 V.S. after midnight, i.e. Thursday, February 19, 1679 A.D. *Bahi.*, p. 94. *Ed.*
8. The correct date of this Battle of Delhi is Wednesday, July 16, 1679, i.e. 16 Jamadi-us-Sani, Julusi Yr. 22, = *Shrawan* Vidi 3, 1736 V.S., which is confirmed by *M.A.* (Pers. Text, p. 177; *E.T.*, p. 109. The Christian date is incorrect); as well as all Rajasthani sources. *Ed.*
9. Transcripts of these letters to the Amber Rajas from the Afridis, etc., from 1684-1693 A.D., are to be found in Vol. VI of the Sarkar Collection of the Jaipur Records, transcript of which is also preserved in the Shri Raghubir Library, Sitamau. *Ed.*
10. The date given in *M.A.*, is incorrect. He died sometime during the later half of March, 1682. His death was reported to Aurangzib on 5 Rabi-us-Sani, Julus Saneh 25 = Tuesday, April 4, 1682. (*Jai. Akh. Aur.* 25, pp. 185-186.) *Ed.*
11. *J.R.* No. 352. *Jai Rec.*, *Add. Pers.*, III, pp. 68-76. *Ed.*
12. *Jai. Hindi*, I, pp. 30-34; *Jai. Rec.*, VII, pp. 314-315, 318-320. *Ed.*
13. Rupa was the younger son of Bhav Singh, the step-brother of Churaman. *Ed.*
14. *Jai. Hindi*, II, pp. 141-142. *Ed.*
15. *J.R.* No. 483 and 487. *Jai. Records; Additional Pers.*, III, pp. 140-141, 151. *Ed.*
16. The correct date of Raja Bishan Singh's death is Sunday, December 31, 1699 = Rajab 19, *Julusi* Yr. 43. (*Akh. Aurangzib*, London, ff. 189*b*-190*a*) *Ed.*
17. When in April 1700 Rafi-ul-qadr, carrying Chimaji with him, crossed the Indus and marched into Afghanistan, the now leaderless Kachhawa troops refused to go into the highlands which had proved fatal to two of their successive kings. But Chimaji continued at Shah Alam's Court and came back to Hindustan in 1707 when that Prince contested and won the Delhi throne.[18] *J.S.*
18. *Jai. Hindi*, I, pp. 59-65. *Ed.*

XIII

Sawai Jai Singh's Early Career

The Situation On Jai Singh's Accession

With the accession of Jai Singh II the history of Jaipur enters a new stage. The 32 years before him had been a very dark period for the Kachhwa race. Three generations of their ruling dynasty had been crowded into this span of a single human lifetime and had perished in distant fields far from home; the family fortunes and prestige had sunk very low; and the future looked hardly more promising, with a boy of twelve[1] on the throne and its army reduced to a thousand men engaged in very minor services. But the glory of the Kachhwa royalty was retrieved by the genius and opportunism of Sawai Jai Singh II and raised to an even loftier pitch than under the great Man Singh or Mirza Rajah Jai Singh I.

If the lifework of Sawai Jai Singh did not benefit the Empire as Man Singh's did or the first Jai Singh's had done, it was not his fault. His masters got only what they deserved; the hopeless moral decay of the later Mughals and their nobility defeated the attempts of Sawai Jai Singh, as it had done the equally sincere efforts of Nizamul-mulk Asaf Jah, to arrest the fall of the Delhi monarchy. Jai Singh's active life entirely covers the eventful period from the death of Aurangzib to the sacking of Delhi by Nadir Shah and even overlaps it at both ends by several years. The tragic story of this age is well known in general outline, and the historian of the Kachhwas need concern himself only with the doings of Jai Singh, for which an enormous number of contemporary records, state papers and newsletters have been preserved at Jaipur[2] and are being utilised in the following pages for the first time.

Since his return from the Deccan (in July, 1698) Jai Singh had been staying at home in spite of the Emperor's angry summons. On 18th February, 1700, the news of Bishan Singh's death reached the Imperial camp in Maharashtra, and two days later Aurangzib conferred the throne of Amber on the late Rajah's elder son, changing his name from Bijay Singh to Jai Singh, while his younger brother, customarily called Chimaji or 'the infant', was ordered to be henceforth named Bijay Singh.[3]

Six months after his accession, Jai Singh received the Emperor's call to the Deccan with his troops. But there was nearly a year's delay in his responding to the call. One reason for this was that he had been instructed to recruit a large force of his clansmen, in excess of the contingent required by his *mansab*, in order to fill up the ever-gaping void the Mughal manpower caused by the Maratha wars. This meant money, of which nothing could come forth from his sovereign, whose own soldiers' pay was three years in arrear! Besides this, Jai Singh could not leave his home territory denuded of troops, as the Naruka and other local rebels were constantly rising against this child on the throne of Amber. He had also to conclude the affair of his marriage (with the daughter of Udit Singh, the nephew of Rajah Uttam Ram Gaur of Sheopur) in March, 1701.

As early as 17th November, 1700 the Emperor had sent mace-bearers from his camp to fetch Jai Singh to the Deccan. After much delay the young Rajah made a start and reached Burhanpur on 3rd August, 1701, but here he was brought to a month's halt by the heavy rains which made marching impossible over the black cotton soil of Khandesh. By this time Aurangzib's patience was exhausted; he had now embarked on his ruinous sieges of the Maratha hill forts and required every man that the Rajahs and officers in the North could supply. On 13th September, he reduced Jai Singh's rank by 500 and turned his agent out of the Imperial camp. The Rajah now quickened his pace and in October joined the army of his commander, Prince Bidar Bakht, who was under orders to guard the environs of the newly conquered fort of Panhala, when the Emperor advanced to lay siege to Khelna in Konkan, west of the Ambaghat pass.

Jai Singh Under Bidar Bakht

The siege of Khelna dragged on for five months (January-June, 1702), the Mughal army and camp followers suffering indescribable hardship and loss from the rugged barren nature of the country and the cyclonic weather of the Western Ghats. Success was long delayed, partly by the impregnable character of this rock-fortress, but more by the mutual jealousies of the leading Muslim generals. The Mughal artillery beat in vain against the solid rock of the walls; on the other hand, the catapults of the garrison showered huge stones upon the advancing siege-works; they also raided the trenches at night.

Bidar Bakht was given charge of the Imperial trenches opposite the Konkani or western gate of the fort, and with Jai Singh took his post on a fortified hillock facing that gate. The Kachhwa contingent's work before Khelna was strenuous and eminently successful, and naturally a heavy price in human lives had to be paid for it. On 14th February, 1702, Jai Singh detached a force under one of his generals to take the Maratha post outside the postern-gate *(khirki)*. After clearing a path through the rock and scrub, the Rajputs engaged the enemy, and at the cost of many losses in slain and wounded, expelled the defenders and established themselves at that post, which was only 15 *jaribs* from the gate. Eleven days later several Kachhwas were rewarded with *mansabs*.

On 17th March, Bhojraj Chauhan (an Amber captain) beat back a sortie of the Maratha garrison upon Jai Singh's trenches. On 11th May, Jai Singh delivered an assault upon the *fausse braye (rauni* or outer earth-work) of the Konkani gate, and scaled it in spite of heavy loss from the bombs flung from the walls. The charge was headed by his diwan, Budh Singh, who fell, but the Barli Burj was captured and the five-coloured banner of Amber was the first to be planted on the conquered bastion. Jai Singh thus earned his restoration to his original *mansab*; on 13th May he became once more a Commander of 2000 (with 1000 troopers *do aspa)* and Rs 1,25,000 as allowance.

After the fall of Khelna on Friday, 5th June, the Imperial army withdrew from it. Bidar Bakht was appointed in September next, *subahdar* of Aurangabad in addition to which the deputy governorship of Khandesh on behalf of his absentee father Prince Muhammad Azam Shah was conferred on him. The prince arrived at Aurangabad on Monday, 23rd November, and sent Jai Singh and other officers to guard Khandesh against Maratha incursions. This was a physically impossible task; with his small contingent, neither Jai Singh nor any other Imperial general could completely block the paths of the myriads of Maratha light horses out on raid, or catch them up by pursuit. In February, 1703, Nima Sindhia entered Khandesh, and looted many places including the suburbs of that province's capital and also the city of Khargon (then included in Malwa). Jai Singh was visited with the Emperor's wrath for his supposed negligence and his *mansab* was again reduced by 500 *zat*. But soon afterwards he redeemed his credit: in May, he was detached by Bidar Bakht to assist the Mughal *thanahdar* Kuchak Khan, who had been invested by Nima Sindhia at the village of Anwa near Deulghat. The Kachhwas drove away the besiegers, after slaying and wounding several men. From this duty Jai Singh returned to his station at Aurangabad, but soon after was called upon to rescue his chief Bidar Bakht, who was threatened by a Maratha band when hunting near the Fardapur pass (Ajanta), on Friday, October first.

With the return of winter, Nima Sindhia burst into Berar and Malwa, and at first carried everything before him. But in the end he was foiled and expelled after a long and active chase by Firuz Jang, the governor of Berar. Bidar Bakht co-operated by sending a detachment from Aurangabad to the scene of this war. For Jai Singh's activity in this campaign, he was rewarded by the reduction of 500 in his *mansab* being restored (28th January, 1704). The gross cowardice and incompetence displayed by Shaista Khan II, the Malwa governor, during this Maratha raid induced the Emperor to remove him and place that province in charge at Bidar Bakht (3rd August, 1704). The prince sent Jai Singh as his deputy *(naib subahdar)* to govern Malwa. The Rajah safely escorted the Bengal revenue on the way to the Deccan, from Sironj to Ujjain (arriving at Ujjain on 16 December), whence other officers took it to the Emperor.

Bidar Bakht was so pleased with Jai Singh's ability and devotion that he nominated him his deputy governor for Malwa, where he could not attend in person. But the pious Aurangzib vetoed the appointment as opposed to Islam (*Jaiz nist*) and ordered it to be given to a Muhammadan, for in his bigotry he had now made a rule that no *subahdari*, not even the minor post of a *faujdar* should be given to a Rajput. (Inayetullah's *Ahkam-i-Alamgiri*, ff. 68 *a* and 72 *b*.) The contrast with Akbar's full and frank rewarding of talent is here obvious—and no less obvious is the effect of such narrow sectarianism and suspiciousness on the fate of an Empire which had now come to have such a sovereign as its helmsman. To insult the greatest Hindu Rajah then under his banners, Aurangzib ordered that Jai Singh must not hold office sitting on a cushion (*masnad*) but should squat on a printed cloth (*suzani*) spread on the floor. (*Ibid*. 72 *b*.)

Aurangzib pursued Jai Singh with a malignity which looked like a personal feud. The Rajah, after his great deeds at Khelna (1702) had begged the Emperor (through his mother) for the grant of kettle-drums. Now Bidar Bakht repeated the same prayer and also recommended that he should be given the *parganas* of Chatsu, Dausa, Muizzabad and Rewari, to enable him with this additional revenue to raise and keep a large efficient contingent for the Imperial service in the Deccan. Aurangzib's reply was, 'No; he is too young and led by others'. Bidar Bakht made a second appeal for the Kachhwa Rajah, pointing out how impoverished and scantily supplied with troops he was. The Emperor angrily replied, 'His father in the Sansani campaign brought to the muster ten or twelve thousand horsemen. This Rajah (Jai Singh) is the master of treasures and territory and the head of a clan. He can get together such a large contingent.' A later appeal from the same prince to increase Jai Singh's trooper rank from 1000 *do aspa* to 2000 (*barawardi*) and to grand him kettldrums, was rejected by the Emperor who caustically wrote on the petition, 'this proposal is crude, crude, *kham kham* ast'. (Inayetullah, 29 *a*, 75 *b*, 106 *b*.)

Thus we find Jai Singh, at the end of Aurangzib's reign after six years of strenuous service, still a *two hazari* in rank (with 1000 troopers *do aspa)*, just as he was at the time of his succession to Amber, and still attached to the army of Bidar Bakht wherever he went. One good, however, had been done to him; two Imperial *faujdars* with local assistance captured the fort of Jhilai from Khush-hal Singh and other rebel Rajputs, and established Jai Singh's rule over it (13th November, 1704), and next forced the rebels to vacate Isarda also. The Imperial collector of Ajmer having reported that no revenue was being yielded by the *pargana* of Malarna (with a nominal rent-roll of one and a half lakhs of rupees), then under the crown administration, Aurangzib was pleased to pass it on as a bad bargain, to Jai Singh, to be held as *ijara*.

Jai Singh In Bahadur Shah's Reign

The scene suddenly changed on Friday, 21st February, 1707, when the nonagenarian Emperor Aurangzib died and the usual wars of succession among his sons began. Jai Singh followed his commander Bidar Bakht from Gujarat where this prince was last posted, to Jajau, 20 miles south of Agra, where Bidar Bakht, his father Azam Shah and many chiefs of his party perished (8th June). In this battle the Kachhwa prince, who was not yet out of his teens, with probably 1000 retainers (after deducting the wastage of the long Deccan warfare) could not have turned the tide, when over a lakh of men were ranged on the opposite side. He shared the flight of the highest Muslim generals from the hopelessly lost field, and paid his homage to the victor, who was now the lawful sovereign of Delhi.

This change of sovereigns took place in June, 1707, and towards the end of that year Bahadur Shah I, the new Emperor, started with his army for Rajputana, where the 30 years' war provoked by Aurangzib's seizure of Marwar after Maharajah Jaswant Singh's death, had reached a decisive turning point in the recovery of Jodhpur and the expulsion of its Mughal garrison by Jaswant's heir Ajit Singh immediately after the death of the oppressor of Rajputana.

Jai Singh had so long been the follower and favourite of Bidar Bakht, the son of the new Emperor's fallen rival, and fought on the same side at Jajau. His younger brother Bijay Singh ('Chimaji'), on the other hand, had during these years been a refugee at the court of Bahadur Shah and a protege of that Emperor's son. So, when Bahadur Shah arrived at Amber (c. 10th January, 1708)[4] on his way to Marwar, he gave the Kachhwa kingdom to Bijay Singh, with costly gifts and other marks of Imperial favour, and thus Jai Singh was deposed and relegated to the rank of a mere *mansabdar* out of employ. Ajit Singh submitted to this display of Imperial arms and waited on the Emperor on Monday, 16th February. On Wednesday, 24th March, Bahadur Shah was called away to the Deccan to fight the pretensions of his youngest brother Kam Bakhsh, who had crowned himself Emperor at Haidarabad. During this southward march, Jai Singh and Ajit Singh, who had been dragged in his train, fled away from his camp at the halting place of Mandleshwar,[5] on Wednesday, 21st April, 1708. The Emperor's reply was to confer on Bijay Singh the title of Mirza Rajah; but this boy had no energy or capacity, and everywhere in Amber territory the local Mughal officers were successfully resisted by Jai Singh's partisans. Untaught by the disastrous result of Aurangzib's grabbing at Marwar through a subservient Rathor prince Indra Singh, Bahadur Shah repeated his father's mistake and was even more quickly discomfited.

Bahadur Shah was absent from the scene from Wednesday, 24th March, 1708 (when he left Ajmer) to 12th June, 1710 (when he returned to that holy city after the death of Kam Bakhsh). During this interval the flames of war spread over all of Rajputana. Mewar, Amber and Marwar were united in opposing 'the Turks', and Jai Singh and Durgadas Rathor were the national leaders. Asad Khan, the Regent of the Empire, who had been left behind in Agra, wisely tried to patch up some kind of peace by coming to terms with the Rajput chiefs. Ajit and Jai Singh recovered their respective capitals from their Mughal garrisons in July, 1708. Sayyid Hussain Barha, *faujdar* of Mewat, at the head of a large force of imperialists and Churaman with his Jat troops, advanced from Narnol to attempt the reconquest of Amber (early in October), but near the town of Sambhar he was shot dead with his two brothers (the *faujdars* of Bairat-Singhana and Narnol) and his army routed.

The news of this last disaster induced Bahadur Shah, then about to encounter Kam Bakhsh, to conciliate the Rajputs by restoring Jai Singh and Ajit to their *mansabs*. But there could be no real peace unless all of Marwar and Amber were evacuated by the Mughals and the state of things before Aurangzib's usurpation of 1679 restored. The Emperor and his advisers had not the wisdom to see this. So the fighting continued; Mughal *faujdars* went marching through the unhappy land pillaging the crops and sacking the helpless villages; but every fort and fortalice defied them. Mir Khan, the new *faujdar* of Narnol, who had come with his own 7000 troops and Churaman's 6000 Jat horses, was effectively checked by Gaj Singh Naruka, who held Javli on behalf of Jai Singh (January, 1710). Muhammad Khan, the qiladar of Tonk, was driven out on 24th March, 1710.

Soon afterwards Bahadur Shah returned towards Rajputana. He bowed to necessity and sent conciliatory letters and gifts to the two rebel Rajahs (May). The matter was clinched in the Imperial council chamber by the news of the rising of the Sikhs under Banda, who had killed the *faujdar* of Sarhind. On 11th June, 1710, Jai Singh and Ajit Singh were again presented to the Emperor and were sent home with robes of honour and valuable presents.

Jai Singh's First Viceroyalty of Malwa, 1714-1717

This truce in Rajputana continued during the remainder of Bahadur Shah's life and the year of Jahandar Shah's reign (1712). Farrukhsiyar, after defeating his rival, entered Delhi on 2nd February, 1713, and on Friday the 16th of the following October he appointed Jai Singh viceroy of the great province of Malwa. The Kachhwa Rajah had been under a cloud for the long years since the death of his patron Bidar Bakht, and he now at last got a high appointment which enabled his merits, so long kept depressed by the bigotry of Aurangzib and the suspicion of Bahadur Shah, to find full scope for display. This recognition was forced out of the hands of the new Emperor by the annual Maratha raids into Malwa, since it was felt that no general other than one of Jai Singh's calibre had the capacity to prevent.

It was two months before Jai Singh's preparations for his onerous task were completed, and he started from Amber about the end of December. By way of Bundi (where he made a long halt for intervening in the dispute between his protege Budh Singh and his cousin Bhim Singh of Kotah), he arrived near Ujjain, the capital of Malwa, at the end of February, 1714. Besides the Marathas, the disruptors of the province's peace were the Afghan soldiers of fortune settled at many places whose only profession was fighting for hire or gang robbery. The petty princes of the country, in their insane passion for usurping their neighbour's lands or defying the Imperial Government, used to call these local Afghans and also the Marathas from beyond the Narmada to their aid. And whenever the Imperial peace suffered a temporary eclipse, petty robbers called *Girasias* appeared in arms to exact blackmail. Malwa lay directly across the path of Maratha advance into Hindustan; on the west it adjoined the broken savage border country and Gujarat, the home of many turbulent races; and the trade between Delhi and the Deccan as well as the western ports of India flowed through Malwa now that the Rajputana route had been closed for half a century by Aurangzib's war of usurpation there.

Jai Singh's task, therefore, was an extremely difficult one. If he had only the Marathas on his hands, with a loyal and peaceful people behind him, he could have easily kept the intruders out and maintained the regular administration in the province. His first year's work showed what he could achieve so long as he was not attacked from before and behind at the same time. The Rajah had a force of

10,000 good soldiers, including a large body of musketeers with artillery and a copious supply of munitions and money. His own reputation as a vigorous general trained in Aurangzib's wars, had preceded him: and he had around him veterans like Chhatrasal Bundela and Budh Singh Hada with their reputable clansmen. The result was that during 1714 he succeeded in suppressing disorder in Malwa; the Marathas (probably owing to internecine wars in their royal family in the homeland) abstained from any noticeable raid in the ensuing winter: and the local rebels, after receiving one or two swift sharp lessons were cowed into submission or went into hiding. It was, therefore, only natural that on 13th August the Emperor should send him a robe of honour with a royal letter of appreciation, praising Jai Singh's successful administration in these terms: 'You have not left any trace of the robbers; travellers can now pass in peace.'

This result was achieved only by tireless movement and prompt demonstration of force on his part. A week after his arrival at Ujjain, Jai Singh left the town for suppressing an Afghan chief named Inayet, who was plundering near Ujjain [at Kanasia and Mahigarh (Mahidpur?)] with a horde of 7000 troopers. The Rajah detached Nandlal Choudhuri against him and at the approach of the Imperial force the Afghans withdrew towards Shajahanpur. Next Dilir Afghan was defeated near Kashigaon (*c.* 25 March, 1714), and Mohan Singh (Umat Rajput) of Rajgarh, who had rebelled in concert with Ruhela mercenaries was slain on 14th April. Early next month Jai Singh sent a Bundela contingent under Chhatrasal's son to Khimlasa and Bhorasa, and at their approach the Maratha camp south of the Narmada gave up the idea of crossing over that river into Malwa. After personally marching about and chastising rebels, the Viceroy returned to Ujjain on Wednesday, 12th May.

But the peace thus imposed could not be either universal or enduring in a province with the racial composition of Malwa. Robbery on the highways was reported near Narwar, where a military post had to be set up in August. The Ahir country was up in arms under Puranmal Ahir, who closed the road from Sironj to Kalabagh, and from his strongholds of Ranod and Ondhera (Indar?)[6] continued to trouble the Government for many months.

Rampura (west of Bhanpura) on the Mewar frontier was the next scene of Jai Singh's activity. Here a succession dispute had been raging since Aurangzib's days. On Monday, 24th January 1715, the lawful chief Gopal Singh Chandrawat recovered possession of it by ousting Badan Singh, the son of his apostate son and supplanter Ratan Singh who had been baptized by Aurangzib as 'Islam Khan'. Jai Singh supported the cause of Gopal Singh and soon afterwards arranged a compromise between the old chief and his grandson, especially as the Afghan mercenaries called into this family-feud were destroying the small principality.

With the commencement of March, 1715, just when the first and happy year of Jai Singh's viceroyalty of Malwa had been completed, trouble began to reappear on many sides. He first set out from Ujjain towards Chaukigarh (32 miles north-east of Hoshangabad) in order to expel a Maratha raider named Ganga. Then he turned north towards Dhamuni to chastise the Ahirs and Afghans and reached Sironj near the Bundelkhand border. Here a Maratha host was reported to be coming at the call of the irrepressible Dilir Afghan. Jai Singh struck his blow promptly. In a battle fought about the 2nd of April, he defeated the Afghan army of 12,000 killing 2000 of them with a loss of 500 on his side. Six elephants, a banner and a palki were captured from the defeated rebel chief. Then he turned south to Bhilsa to devastate the Afghan colony of that district, while his lieutenant Azam Quli Khan was detached on the heels of the fugitives.

But the scene suddenly changed. Reports arrived in quick succession that two vast Maratha armies had entered Malwa. One, 30,000 strong, under Kanhoji Bhonsle and Khande Rao Dhabade, crossed the Narmada at Akbarpur on the 1st and 2nd of April, and established their base at Tilwara, pillaging the country to within four miles of the provincial capital; the large town of Dipalpur was looted and set on fire. The other band, consisting of 12,000 light horses, crossed the same river at Barwah (5th April) and roved about in the country south of Indore, demanding three years *chauth* from the Kampel *pargana* (15 miles south-east of Indore). In terror of them the Imperial revenue collectors and local magistrates fled from their posts and crowded into Ujjain for shelter within its walls.

Confronted with this sudden development, Jai Singh hurried back from Bhilsa to Ujjain, sending his deputy Rupram Dhabhai[7] ahead to ensure the safety of his capital. From Ujjain the Rajah reached Kampel on 8th May, to come closer to the invaders. On learning that the Marathas under Kanho and Ganga were planning to go back across the Narmada near Palsud (19 miles east of Maheswar) with their enormous accumulations of booty, Jai Singh made a forced march of 38 miles and arrived within sight of the Maratha camp an hour before sunset on the 10th of May. The Marathas, proud of their superior numbers, advanced to bar his path. Nothing daunted, the travel-worn Rajput army took up the challenge. Budh Singh Hada led the van. Chhatra Sal Bundela and Dhiraj Singh Khichi (of Bajrang-garh) as well as many local zamindars who had joined on the way, fought under Jai Singh. After four hours of struggle in darkness, the Marathas broke and fled, losing heavily in men and horses and abandoning many weapons. Jai Singh bivouacked on the blood-stained field, men and horses, officers and privates, all going without food for the night after their long strenuous march and fight. But there is no rest for an active general. Three hours before dawn he roused his troops and resumed the march on the Maratha base at the Palsud ferry, some six miles south of the battlefield. The enemy had not expected such vigorous pursuit. Confident of the broken terrain and rocks of Palsud they had been passing the night in fancied security. At the sight of Jai Singh's approaching banners, they fled across the Narmada (11th May) in a panic, abandoning all their wounded, and droves of lifted cattle and much other booty acquired during months of raiding in Khandesh and Malwa.

The Imperial army which had so gallantly responded to their commander's call, were rewarded by every man being allowed to keep for himself whatever spoils he could lay his hands on, and 'every one gained booty enough to feed him for years'. 'The Zamindars of the neighbourhood confessed that ever since the first coming of the Marathas into Malwa, this kind of chastisement and expulsion had not been inflicted, on them by any royal officer before.' The Emperor praised Jai Singh highly.

A Setback In Malwa Administration During Jai Singh's Absence

Two resounding victories had been won by Jai Singh, over the Afghan and the Maratha, and the province knew an unwonted peace for some time after. But neither of them had been crushed, and at the approach of the campaigning season in autumn, the political situation in Malwa grew worse. This was partly due to Jai Singh's absence from the province from October, 1715 onwards. Its main cause was the character of Farrukhsiyar, a weak vacillating man entirely swayed by any strong or smooth-tongued man who happened to possess his ears at the time, and unable to take a bold plunge. Into the ceaseless intrigues of the Court factions against the all powerful ministers, the two Sayyid brothers Husain Ali and Abdullah, Jai Singh wisely refused to be drawn, for he knew full well the worthlessness of the Emperor who solicited him. At the same time his neutrality failed to please the Sayyids, because they felt that he was the only vassal prince capable of making a combination against them successful. Hence they distrusted him and tried to weaken his power. The Emperor had invited Jai Singh to Court (on 25th September, 1715) for the secret purpose of heading a plot against his regents. Torn between a spineless master and that master's hostile keepers, Jai Singh deemed it best to retire to his own realm, avoiding Malwa and Delhi alike.

This withdrawal took place in October, 1715, and when seven months later he did go to Court, at the urgent call of the Emperor (26 May, 1716), he was sent (on 15th September) to lead the war against Churaman Jat. This kept him busy till the month of March, 1718. His viceroyalty of Malwa ended in November, 1717, and out of his nominal tenure of four years (November, 1713-October, 1717) in Malwa, Jai Singh actually spent only 20 months in that province. In his absence his authority devolved on his deputy Rupram Dhabhai, who naturally could not pretend to his master's prestige and power of command. Moreover, half the Kachhwa contingent, or more of it, was withdrawn by the Rajah to remain round his person.

This was the opportunity the enemies of the Government were waiting for. Prithvi Singh, the *zamindar* of Garh Banera (near Dhamuni) who had built a fort and coined money as a sign of independence, was driven out of his stronghold by Jai Singh, but he joined Dilir Afghan to loot Imperial territory. In November Puranmal Ahir renewed his depredations in Malpur. In March of the next year (1716) troubles thickened in the province. Dost Muhammad Ruhela roving near Mandsaur, killed Kesari Singh, the Rathor Rajah of Ratlam, placed his younger brother Pratap Singh on the throne, and then exacted his promised fee of six lakhs by squeezing the Imperial villages (early March). About the same time, Maratha raids were renewed in force, and people began to flee to Ujjain from all sides. The Emperor urged the absentee *subahdar* Jai Singh to send 3000 packed troops from his side to reinforce his deputy in Malwa, in order to enable him to meet this threat, or go there in person if necessary (27th April,

1716).[8] Ruhelas, other Afghans, Girasias, Bhils, Ahirs and other Hindu princelings rose up on all sides, and Rupram could not cope with so many dangers at the same time.

Early in 1717, Rupram the *naib subahdar* and Himmat Rai the collector *(mutasaddi)* of Ujjain, went south towards the Narmada to face a Maratha horde led by Santa (the son of Bapuji Bhonsle), but were defeated. According to rumour they were released only on promise of a ransom of two lakhs. Ujjain was put in a strong posture of defence and every preparation made for standing a siege by the Marathas. The utmost alarm prevailed in the province. The Marathas remained encamped near Kalibhit throughout the monsoon, and renewed their raid in October next. Handia *pargana* passed into their hands. But in this month Mohammad Amin Khan was officially nominated to relieve the absentee Jai Singh of the Malwa viceroyalty.

Jai Singh Against Churaman Jat

Churaman, the Jat leader against whom Rajah Bishan Singh had fought in the last decade of the seventeenth century, was again plaguing the empire with his gang robberies, blackmailing road traffic and seizing the *jagirdars'* lands in the Agra-Mathura district, though in Bahadur Shah's reign he had helped the Imperial generals, with his own troops, in the war on Kachhwa territory. Sansani and Soghor having fallen, he had constructed a new stronghold at Thun, and become a great menace on the flank of the main royal road of Hindustan.

Jai Singh, when a boy, had taken part in his father's Jat campaigns, and he now approached Farrukhsiyar with an offer to conduct the war against Churaman. Making a formal start on Dussehra day (15 September, 1716), he spent sometime getting his army together and sending orders to Amber to recruit more men. With him were Bhim Singh Hada of Kota, Budh Singh Hada of Bundi and Gaj Singh Kachhwa of Narwar. Operations began on 9th November. But the fort of Thun was protected by lofty walls, a deep wet ditch and a thick thorny jungle around it, and well stocked with provisions and munitions. While Churaman himself led the defence from within, a

Jat field army under his son Muhakam and his nephew Rupa, harassed the imperialists outside and attacked their long line of supplies.

Jai Singh proceeded methodically, cutting down all the trees around the fort and setting up block-houses along the route eastwards to Agra. But his progress was necessarily very slow. He was fighting against the same race and the same terrain which were destined to baffle Lord Lake in the nineteenth century. All the roads could not be effectually patrolled, because the Jats were a nation in arms, sturdy hardy peasants familiar with the use of arms from their childhood and practised in highway robbery, ambuscade and night attacks. The outbreak of this war prompted them to carry their gang-raids as far north as half the way from Agra to Delhi, inflicting severe losses on the Government and the loyal people.

In January, 1717 the Emperor sent to his army a very large cannon (come from L.M.I.P., 325). For a long time, the siege trenches could not be carried within range of the walls. On Sunday, 10th February, Jai Singh left Budh Singh in charge of his camp and went out with Bhim Singh to plant an outpost at Sonkh, a *garhi* ten miles south-west of Mathura. During his return at night, as his troops were marching without order or caution, they fell into a Jat ambush lying hidden in a *nala* overgrown with jungle near Thun. The enemy fired volleys of musketry which struck down many men, horses and camels on the Rajput side, and some of their bullets even reached the elephants ridden by the Imperial generals. Happily the mischief went no further. The Emperor wrote censuring Jai Singh for a conduct which was 'a little remote from a general trained by Aurangzib', and ordered him to punish the head of his intelligence service for his neglect in discovering the enemy's trap. Reinforcements were ordered under some Muhammadan generals, particularly Sayyid Muzaffar Khan (entitled Khan Jahan Bahadur), a kinsman of the wazir, in June.

The rainy season put an end to operations for the time and added to the sufferings of the besieged. The rains that year were very late in coming, and prices rose very high, driving the Mughal army into great privation. The wazir (Sayyid Abdullah, Qutb-ul-mulk) was secretly hostile to Jai Singh. His kinsman, Khan Jahan introduced in the siege camp a division of authority and a policy of underhand intrigue with Churaman which destroyed the chances of Jai Singh's success. At last in January, 1718 the Rajah wrote to the Emperor in despair about how his internal enemies had neutralized the effect of his feats of arms. Khan Jahan, under secret orders of the Wazir, favoured Churaman and arranged for his nominal submission and visit to the Emperor (March), and the Emperor wrote to Jai Singh ordering peace to be made and the Jat people saved from molestation. On Thursday, 10th April, Churaman and Rupa were presented to the Emperor at Delhi through Khan Jahan; and thus the credit of victory was snatched away from Jai Singh's hands, though he received a highly flattering letter of praise and some gifts from the Emperor. On Tuesday, 20th May, he returned to Delhi with his forces.[9]

For the sake of continuity, we may here narrate the story of Jai Singh's final war against the Jats in 1722, when he enjoyed undivided authority and quickly crushed the nascent Jat power. The peace patched up by Wazir Abdullah with Churaman in 1718, solely in order to spite Jai Singh, bore the fruit to be expected from such a truce. The dissensions in the Court of Delhi which followed from the clash between the two Sayyid king-makers and the Emperor Farrukhsiyar and Muhammad Shah, and the risings of local governors and pretenders, distracted and paralyzed the Imperial administration. But with the fall of the last Sayyid, Abdullah Qutb-ul-mulk, on 4th November, 1720, peace and stability of some sort returned to the Delhi Government. The new Emperor Muhammad Shah became his own master, at least as far as his indolent pleasure loving character allowed him to be. And next year it was decided to suppress the rebel nearest the capital.

Churaman had broken every promise he had made to that throne in 1718, and actually fought against the Emperor in his battle with Sayyid Abdullah, besides sending his troops to aid rebels like Ajit Singh and Chhatrasal. The Jat chief's eldest son Muhakam had slain (16th September, 1721) the deputy *subhadar* of Agra and plundered the Imperial army. Soon afterwards Churaman died (? October). Sadat Khan, the viceroy of the Agra province, having totally failed against the Jats, was dismissed, and Jai Singh was appointed on Thursday, 23rd August, 1722 *subahdar* of Agra, with instructions to suppress the Jats and capture their new capital Thun.

Jai Singh started with an army 14,000 strong, plenty of munitions and a copious war-chest. They reached Thun and operations begun in the middle of October. Churaman's successor, Muhakam, was driven into Thun, around which daily skirmishes took place. Jai Singh approached closer after clearing the jungle and then set up his batteries for bombardment. The Jats used to make night attacks on the Imperial camp after creeping through the intervening trees, and inflicting as well as suffering casualities. Within three weeks the rigour of the siege began to be felt by the defenders. Badan Singh (the son of Churaman's brother Bhau Singh), on being denied his share of their common grandfather's heritage when Muhakam seized the headship of the clan after Churaman's death, had begun to intrigue with the Imperial generals. He now came over to Jai Singh's side, pointed out the weak places in the defences, and thus helped in two outlying forts being taken. The besieged then lost heart. At midnight between 7th and 8th November, 1722, Muhakam set fire to the houses, blew up his powder magazines, and evacuated Thun, carrying off as much cash, jewels and portable property as he could. Next day Jai Singh entered Thun, but the fabulous treasure accumulated by Churaman by a full lifetime of robbery could not be discovered.

The success was most timely, because a Jodhpur army under Bijairaj Bhandari, hired by the Jats for three lakhs of rupees down and future expenses, had reached Jobner, on the way to Thun by the 23rd of October. It was now too late. Soghor and Sansani had fallen, and now Thun the last stronghold of the Jat leader shared the same fate. Many smaller forts *(garhis)* were also dismantled by the victor. So bitter was the feeling excited in the Delhi Government by the persistent lawlessness of the Jats since the days of Aurangzib, that under orders of the Emperor, the site of Thun was ploughed by asses, to mark it publicly as an accursed soil unfit to serve again as a seat of royalty. Churaman was dead; his sons Muhakam and Zulkarn were driven into exile, and the leadership of the Jats in the heart of the present kingdom of Bharatpur was given to Badan Singh, a son of Churaman's brother Bhau Singh. But neither then, nor ever up to the time of his death, was Badan Singh a *Rajah*; he lived and died the headman of group of villages and called himself *Thakur* (like a laird in Scotland), and even this humble position he owed to Jai Singh's patronage.

Through the Ajmer province Muhakam fled to Jodhpur for refuge, outpacing the detachment sent to pursue him. In reward for his services, Jai Singh received (on 2nd June, 1723) the titles of *Raj Rajeshwar, Shri Rajadhiraj, Maharajah Sawai*. This was an addition to the title of *Saramad-i-Rajahhae Hind* conferred on him on 21st April, 1721.

Jai Singh's Statesmanly Policy Towards The Jats

Two prominent Hindu royal houses of today owe their origin to the kings of Amber, Bharatpur by friendly protection, and Alwar by succession.

The Jat policy followed by Jai Singh's wise statesmanship after the decisive victory of 1722 is finely described by Father F.X. Wendel, a Belgian Jesuit of Agra, who supplied a history of the Jats, the result of his inquiries at Bharatpur, to his patrons, the English Government in Calcutta. It is preserved in a French manuscript of the India Office Library London. This highly capable observer writes:

> First of all, Badan Singh followed the path of suppleness in getting into the good graces of Sawai Jai Singh and securing him as a protector. His manners were so humble and submissive and his conduct so obliging, that Jai Singh was quite won over and began to take a special delight in favouring this man, whom he had raised from the dust and whose greatness, he felt, would shed reflected lustre on his patron. Jai Singh bestowed on Badan the *tika*, the *nishan*, the kettledrum, the five-coloured flag, and the title of *Braj-raj* (or Lord of the holy land of Mathura), so as to give him authority among the Jats at home and to entitle him to greater respect abroad. But Badan Singh very astutely abstained from assuming the title of *Rajah*, and throughout life represented himself publicly as a mere *Thakur* or baron of the Rajah of Jaipur. He did homage solely to the Rajah of Jaipur, acknowledging himself as that Rajah's vassal and attending his Dasahara *darbar* every year till old age curtailed his movements. Outside Jaipur he built a mansion, a garden and other houses for himself at a village assigned to him by Sawai Jai Singh and named Badanpura.

Having thus neutralized the most troublesome enemy within the province in his charge, and sick of the sordid intrigues of the Court nobles around the spineless Emperor Muhammad Shah, which were soon to drive away the Nizam from Delhi in disgust—the conqueror of Thun retired to his own dominions. He spent the next seven years there (1723-1729) in cultivating the arts and science dear to his heart and laying out a new capital which was to be the finest city in India and the worthiest monument to his name for all time to come. The rich harvest of these fruitful years of peace will be described later.

Notes

1. Sawai Jai Singh's birth date is Margshirsha bidi 7, v.s. 1745 = (Sunday), 4th November, 1688. *Ed.*
2. The State Archives of the former Jaipur State are now preserved in the Rajasthan State Archives, Bikaner. Many more important and valuable records and papers are preserved in the *Kapad-Dwara* Collection of the Kachhawa House of Amber-Jaipur. *Ed.*
3. In order to avoid confusion, I have named Bishun Singh's elder son *Jai* Singh from his first mention in this history and restricted the name Bijay Singh to his younger brother. The new Rajah also gained the title of *Sawai*, which means 'one and a quarter', because Aurangzib was so pleased with this youthful prince's feats before Khelna that he cried out 'You are more than a man; you are sawa.'—i.e., *a hundred and twenty-five per cent hero!* This high title has since then been borne by every sovereign of Jaipur. *J.S.*
4. According to *Akhabarat*, Bahadur Shah arrived in the vicinity of Amber on Wednesday, January 7, 1708, and on Friday, January 9, 1708, Bahadur Shah prayed in the mosque in Amber. *Ed.*
5. Mandleshwar is on the bank of the Narmada. Jai Singh, Ajit Singh and Durga Das fled from Mandsaur, the headquarters of Mandsaur sarkar in suba Malwa. (*Kamwar* ed. by Muzaffar Alam, p. 27). *J.S.*
6. The small village Andora Kalitor Pahadi is about 22 miles east of Narwar. *Ed.*
7. Dhabhai means wet-nurse's son, or foster brother, corresponding to the Turki title of *Kokaltash*, shortened into *Kokah*. These men were loved and trusted by their kings and have often played an important part in Jaipur History. *J.S.*
8. This should be Sunday, 22nd April, because *Hasbul hukm*, is dated 10th Jamadi-ul-Awwal Saneh 5. *Ed.*
9. *Kamwar* (p. 240) records that on his visit to the Imperial Court, along with other costly presents Maharaja Sawai Jai Singh was granted the insignia of *Mahi* and *Maratib*. But the grant of this unique honour to him is recorded in the *Akhabar-i-Darbar-i-Mualla* of that day. (29 Jamadi-us-Sani, Julus Saneh 7) and *(Jai. Akh. Farrukh.*, year 6-8, p. 71). Similarly *M.U.* (E.T., I, p. 735) too does not take note of the grant of this unique honour. But on the basis of an entry about the grant of *Mahi* and *Maratib* in *Dastur Qaumwar* (Vol. 18), only in the Jaipur State Archives, Dr. V.S. Bhatnagar has recorded this grant in his book, *Life and Time of Sawai Jai Singh*, (p. 128), possibly on the basis of lack of any other confirmation about *Mahi* and *Maratib* to Maharaja Sawai Jai Singh. Sir Jadunath Sarkar has not mentioned it in his account above. *Ed.*

XIV

Sawai Jai Singh's Dealings With The Marathas

The Changed Situation Of Malwa During Jai Singh's Second Viceroyalty, 1729-1730

In October, 1729, Jai Singh was again appointed governor of Malwa, but this second viceroyalty lasted barely ten months, after which followed a two-year-interval during which Muhammad Khan Bangash tried his hand at the work involved. Finally on 28th September, 1732, Jai Singh was appointed *subahdar* of that province for the third time and held the office till Thursday, 4th August, 1737. He was practically the last Imperial *subahdar* of Malwa, because Nizam-ul-Mulk Asaf Jah who replaced him in 1737 met with the most ignominious failure at the hands of the Peshwa and in five months ended by formally ceding the province to the Marathas.

When Jai Singh came to Malwa for the second time early in 1730, he found that a complete change had taken place in the political situation there during the twelve years that had passed since his first viceroyalty. While the Imperial power had been crippled by the rebellion of the Nizam and the Maratha occupation of Gujarat, the strength of the Marathas had increased immensely. In 1717 there was in truth no organized Government in Maharashtra; the two branches of the royal house, Rajah Shahu and Tara Bai, were fighting each other. The hereditary ministers and generals were ranged under the two hostile banners and frequently changed sides. Everything was in a fluid state in their homeland, and their raids into Malwa were not backed by the resources and authority of a regular Government but often formed purely personal and uncoordinated enterprises. Any Maratha general then foraying in Malwa might be suddenly recalled home by the news of an attack on Shahu by some partisan of his rival.

This state of things was ended by the first Peshwa, Balaji Vishwanath, who imposed Shahu's authority over a good deal of the distracted country of Shivaji and by his treaty with the Mughal Government, concluded through Sayyid Husain Ali in 1718, secured Imperial recognition for Shahu's position, which legitimised his authority.

But with the year 1728 came a turning point in the fortunes of the Maratha race. The Nizam of Haidarabad, after successfully overthrowing the yoke of his Imperial master in 1724, had tried for three years to neutralize the Maratha power by favouring Shahu's rival and seducing as many of the hereditary officers from Shahu's side as his money could buy. Thus the Maratha State remained weak because of internal dissension. He frankly confessed this policy in a letter to Jai Singh preserved in the Jaipur archives. But he was foiled by the genius and enterprise of Baji Rao, the second Peshwa. This heaven-born cavalry leader by his Palkhed campaign (1727) led the Nizam through a devil's dance for three months from Ahmadnagar to Gujarat, and at last manoeuvred him into an utterly untenable position at Palkhed, where the new lord of Mughal Deccan was forced to make a complete surrender (Treaty of Sheogaon, February, 1728). The Nizam agreed to allow the Marathas a free hand in Hindustan and a free passage through Berar and Khandesh in their northward march, while Baji Rao promised to spare the Nizam's own domains in return for a stipulated *chauth*. Thus the way was cleared for Baji Rao up to the Narmada and a permanent Maratha camp was planted just beyond the southern frontier of Malwa.

The effect was seen at once. The Peshwa's brother Chimaji Appa invaded Malwa in overwhelming force, slew the provincial viceroy Girdhar Bahadur and his cousin and general Daya Bahadur (surnamed Rajah Anandram) at Amjhera on 29th November, 1728 and convulsed the whole country. The next Imperial *subahdar*, Bhawaniram (surnamed Rajah Chimna Bahadur) had much ado to defend his capital. He, however, struggled on for a year in spite of his limited family resources, lack of support from the Imperial Court, the constant ravaging of his villages and towns by the jealous selfish

Imperial collectors and petty princes ever bent on family feuds, the chronic lawlessness of the local Ruhelas, and the mutiny of his own troops for their overdue salaries. These evils, even more than the Maratha incursion of 1728, totally convulsed the province and shattered its orderly administration. In the adjoining province of Bundelkhand, the rebel Chhatra Sal finally shook off the yoke of Delhi with the help of Baji Rao (March, 1729) and expelled the Delhi Governor Muhammad Khan Bangash. The Imperial authority had now collapsed not only south of the Narmada but even north of it, within easy reach of the Chambal and the Jamuna.

Jai Singh Advocates Compromise With Rajah Shahu To Stop The Maratha Incursions

This was the perilous situation which confronted Jai Singh when the Emperor sent him to Malwa for the second time. As a true statesman and experienced man of action—who had personally tested Maratha toughness and tenacity in Aurangzib's days, Jai Singh advocated the only practical policy that could succeed. It was exactly the policy towards the Marathas which the equally sagacious Asaf Jah I pursued throughout his life and which he recommended to his sons on his death bed,[1] the policy of coming to terms with the Marathas by mutual concessions and living amicably by their side, the policy of trying diplomatic appeasement as long as possible and of going to war only as the last resort. Jai Singh advised the Emperor to appeal directly to Rajah Shahu, who had not yet become a puppet in the hands of his ministers and who gratefully remembered the Mirza Rajah's kindness to his grandfather Shivaji in the dark days of 1616. A satisfied Shahu would keep the Maratha generals in check and thus prevent raids into Malwa. For this immunity a price would have to be paid, namely ten lakhs of rupees a year, to be granted in *jagir* in favour of Shahu's adopted son Kushal Singh.[2] In return for it a general of Shahu would render service in Malwa under the Imperial *subahdar's* banners and also collect the revenue of the *jagirs* assigned. When we consider the natural richness of the province and the immense loss which every Maratha raid inflicted, directly by their own ravage stirring up all the local law-breakers and bandit leaders, this amount worked out a cheap price for the peace and prosperity which its regular payment would have ensured. (It was only ten per cent of the normal revenue of that province.)

But Jai Singh had to take his orders from a master incapable of right thinking or asserting his own will. A faction at the Imperial court, jealous of Jai Singh and his friend Khan-i-Dauran (Samsam-ud-daulah) contrived to pique the Emperor's pride. They cried out that Imperial prestige would suffer if the Maratha claim to tribute from Malwa were peacefully conceded, and that it was more honourable to spend the royal treasures in fitting out a large army for keeping the Marathas out of the province by force. And yet not one of these counsellors would undertake to lead such an expedition. The only fighter among the Muslim grandees was Muhammad Khan Bangash, and he had failed hopelessly against the Marathas in Malwa and Bundelkhand alike; all the rest were carpet knights who would not venture out of Delhi. To the arguments of this faction Jai Singh replied with calm reason:

> Your Majesty has appointed me to chastise the Marathas in Malwa and I shall engage in the work. But these people have been testing this *subah* for a long time past. If this year, by reason of our heavy concentration of troops, they are unable to enter the *subah* or are chastised (after they have broken in), you know what heavy expenditure would be necessary for this object every year in future. I, therefore, suggest that as Rajah Shahu has been ranked as an Imperial *mansabdar* since the day of Aurangzib, your Majesty should give him *jagirs* worth ten lakhs a year in the name of his (adopted) son Kushal Singh, on condition that he would prevent any disturbance in Malwa and an auxiliary contingent of his troops should attend the *subahdar* of that province. This will give peace to the land and save us the expenses of campaigning (eternally).

Shahu's agent, Dado Bhimsen, gave written undertakings to this effect on behalf of his master (26th February and 27th September, 1730).

Muhammad Shah at first approved of this policy and wrote on Jai Singh's letter 'Agreed'. But he was swayed by the men close to his ears and was induced in a few months to reverse Jai Singh's policy, charge him with slothfulness and treachery, and replace him as governor with Muhammad Khan Bangash, whose utter failure in two years proved how correct the Kachhwa statesman-king's prediction was.

It will be tiresome to go through the details of Jai Singh's campaigns in Malwa, all abortive in their ultimate result in spite of occasional victories. A brief summary of the doings of the Marathas in the North during these years 1732-1737 will be adequate here. In the year of his retirement from this viceroyalty, the unopposed dash of Baji Rao to the very gates of Delhi (30th March, 1737) and his crushing defeat of Nizam-ul-mulk Asaf Jah at Bhopal (December, 1737) conclusively proved that Jai Singh was right and that force against the Maratha myriads would fail under the weak Muhammad Shah as surely as it had done under the incomparably mightier Aurangzib. The humiliating treaty of Duraha, signed on Saturday, 7th January, 1738 by the greatest Muslim servant of the Crown, is the complete vindication of Jai Singh from the charge of collusion with the Maratha enemies of the State.

Jai Singh's Third Viceroyalty In Malwa, 1732-1737

Jai Singh's stay in Malwa in 1729-1730 was very short. He arrived at the provincial capital Ujjain in December and made an attempt to recover by force the great fortress of Mandu which had been taken by the Marathas a few weeks earlier. The task was beyond his power, but his strong appeal to Rajah Shahu in the name of the old friendship between their royal ancestors induced the Maratha king to restore Mandu to the imperialists (order dated Thursday, 19th March, 1730). Early in May, Jai Singh was recalled to Rajputana by more pressing business there.

Then followed his two years' dissociation from Malwa. On 6th September, 1732[3] the Emperor conferred that province on him for the third time. The conditions were that he must maintain 30,000 troops (equal numbers of horse and foot) and take two-thirds of the total provincial revenue from land, tribute customs etc.[4] Jai Singh's deputy, his foster-brother Nagraj, was to remain in the province for at least six months in the year during the Rajah's absence from it. The Imperial diwan of Malwa, whose office, according to the traditional policy of all Muslim States, was to serve as an independent check and spy on the *subahdar*, was to maintain 18,000 soldiers and get one-third of the total collection, and post his agents and collectors side by side with Jai Singh's (*J.R.* 98 and 99).

On getting an advance intimation of his being made the Viceroy of Malwa for the third time, Sawai Jai Singh began to think of ways and means of restoring peace and order in Malwa. He deemed it advisable to ensure involvement of the Mewar State too, in the management and defence of his new charge against the invading Marathas. Hence a plan of joint management and combined command of Jaipur and Mewar forces under Sawai Jai Singh's directions was prepared.

Dhabai Rao Nagraj was deputed to Jaipur by Maharana Sangram Singh to finalise the details of the proposed plan. Its terms, mutually agreed upon, were incorporated in two letters, both dated Asoj bidi 13, s. 1789 (6th September, 1732), one written by Raja Ayamal on behalf of Sawai Jai Singh (916), and the other written by Dhabai Rao Nagraj on behalf of Maharana Sangram Singh of Mewar.

Their terms were:

1. Out of 24,000 horse and an equal number of foot, 9000 horse and 9000 foot were to be of Mewar. The remaining 15,000 horse and the same number of foot would be from Amber.
2. In the respect of revenues of *subah* Malwa, one part of the income from land and *peshkash* will be of Mewar, and two parts of Amber.
3. Besides the *subah*, both of them were to take the *parganas* of the *mansabdars* on *ijara* and after paying the *ijara* amount, distribute the savings in the ratio of 1:2 to Mewar and Amber respectively.
4. Dhabhai Rao Nagraj was to be with Maharana for the seven months of s. 1798 (1732-1733), and after that year, he would be with Sawai Jai Singh and Maharana for six months respectively.
5. The Bakhshis, the Naibs and the Mutsaddis of both the darbars were to work jointly. The agricultural produce collected by the officials of both the states were to be shared according to the agreed ratio 1:2).
6. In case more troops were needed for opposing the Marathas, then both the states were to furnish them in the same proportions; for raising them, the Maharana and the Maharaja will levy *peshkash* from the areas under their respective controls.
7. Along with the Maharaja's forces, Mewar-forces would also collect grass and fuel and in that operation if any damage is caused to the standing crops, the necessary action will be taken for the same.[5]

The new *subahdar* left his new city of Jaipur on Saturday, 21st October and arrived at Ujjain in December, 1732. Early next month, Malhar Holkar and Ranoji Sindhia entered Malwa from the Gujarat side; Anand Rao Pawar and Vithoji Bule were already there with their troops, and Udaji Pawar soon afterwards joined them. The unified Maratha generals, leaving their camp and baggage behind, advanced with a light force and hemmed Jai Singh round at Mandsaur (February). Reduced to the utmost distress by the countless Maratha light horse completely cutting off his grain and water supply, the Rajah had to sue for peace, offering six lakhs of rupees, but Holkar held out for more While negotiations were thus protracted, the Rajput captains, encouraged by the news that the Emperor had issued from Delhi to support them, came forth to battle. The commander of Jai Singh's rearguard was slain. On Holkar's side fifteen high officers were killed and he fell back 30 miles. Next Jai Singh advanced 16 miles in pursuit, but Holkar rapidly doubled back to Jai Singh's position and thus compelled him to make peace promising six lakhs in cash and ceding 28 *parganas* in lieu of *chauth* (end of February). Then the Marathas evacuated the province (Sunday, 18th March). Thereafter Jai Singh was too involved in the affairs of Rajputana to pay any personal attention to Malwa, though that province continued in his charge for four years longer. During the campaigning season of 1733-1734, the main Maratha forces were deeply engaged elsewhere and Malwa enjoyed a comparative respite from their inroads.

In the cold weather of 1734-1735, a vast Imperial army under the Wazir Qamruddin marched into Malwa, and after a few skirmishes, the rovers under Pilaji Jadav received a bribe of five lakhs and vacated the province (March, 1735). A second Imperial force led by the Mir Bakhshi Khan-i-Dauran, had set out from Delhi at the same time (10th November, 1734) in order to expel the Marathas from Rajputana. On the way to Ajmer the Khan was joined by Jai Singh, Abhai Singh and Rao Durjan Sal of Kota, and the combined force became a vast mass of men with 'artillery and the munition-carts beyond count'. Crossing the Mukund-dara pass, it reached Rampura territory, where Holkar and Sindhia were sighted early in February. The Imperial army, because of its unwieldly size, composite character, slack organization and the cowardice and incapacity of Khan-i-Dauran, was doomed to failure against the Deccan light horse led by born cavalry leaders such as Malhar and Ranoji. For eight days the Marathas circled round Khan-i-Dauran, absolutely immobilising his army, cutting off his provisions and capturing his horses and camels. Then they made a lightning raid. Leaving the Mughals there, they crossed the Mukund-dara pass, went to Bundi-Kota and thence into the now defenceless Jaipur and Jodhpur kingdoms. The imperialists, completely outwitted by the Maratha strategy, tried to toil up painfully behind them. Finding the field clear, Malhar raided many places in these two regions. The loot of the rich city of Sambhar (28th February, 1735) yielded him a rich harvest. Its Imperial *faujdar* was robbed of everything he possessed (worth three lakhs of rupees) and let off with only the clothes he stood in; its *qazi* slew his women and fell down wounded. Early in March the position of the two sides was this: Khan-i-Dauran was at Kota, Jai Singh was near his own capital, and Ranoji and Malhar were some twenty miles from the latter city. Khan-i-Dauran, after wasting many days in utter inaction, at last listened to Jai Singh's advice and induced the Marathas to retire beyond the Narmada by promising them on behalf of the Emperor 22 lakhs of rupees as the *chauth* to Malwa. This understanding was effected on 22nd March at a meeting between the two sides arranged by Jai Singh near Kota. Then Jai Singh and his friend returned to Delhi (end of April, 1735).

Rival Nobles Set The Emperor Against Jai Singh

When the vast armaments and heavy expenditure of the two Imperial campaigns in the first quarter of 1735 not only failed to crush the Marathas, but in addition saddled the Government with a promise to pay them 22 lakhs of rupees, the court faction opposed to Jai Singh and his constant supporter Khan-i-Dauran were loud in charging the Rajah with treason. The Persian braggart Sadat Khan (the first Nawab of Oudh) told the Emperor,

> Jai Singh has ruined the entire empire by secretly supporting the Marathas. Give me only the governorship of Agra and Malwa, I ask not for any money aid, but I shall keep Malwa free from the Marathas, while the Nizam who is my friend will hinder them from crossing the Narmada.

Sarbuland Khan joined in the same outcry. The volatile Muhammad Shah censured Jai Singh and Khan-i-Dauran, who again pleaded that the surest way of ensuring peace in Malwa was to win the Peshwa over by friendly negotiations, convert him into an Imperial officer by the grant of a *jagir*, and induce him (or at least his brother Chimaji Appa) to visit the Emperor, as 'the Marathas could not be effectually subdued by fighting'. This was the wise policy which had succeeded with so many Hindu rebels in the days of Akbar. But the ignorant clamour of the war party drowned the voice of reason and statesmanship at Delhi.

This talk of taking away his two provincial viceroyalties, which the Emperor had promised in writing to continue for life, reached Jai Singh's ears, and he immediately took measures to protect himself from the mean selfish carpet knights who now ruled over a Court utterly wanting in courage and wisdom alike. Calling the Maratha envoy to his Court, he told him, 'I cannot trust the Turks. If they triumph over the Deccani forces, they will set us aside. Therefore in every matter I shall act as the Peshwa wishes' (August 1735). He sent a proposal to Baji Rao to come to Jaipur at the head of only 5000 horse, taking care not to plunder any place on the way. Jai Singh promised to supply his daily expenses (Rs 5000) and ensure for him the long promised *chauth* of Malwa and the rent of Pilaji Jadav's *jagir*, after discussing the situation with him and taking him to the Emperor's presence under due assurances of safe conduct. If this plan of conciliation failed, Jai Singh undertook to send the Peshwa back from Jaipur in safety.

The agreement of 22nd March, 1735 not having been ratified by the Emperor and the anti-Jai Singh party at Court, Baji Rao planned a grand campaign in Hindustan under his own command in the coming winter. His real object was to visit the Rajput courts personally and impose *chauth* on them by peaceful persuasion if possible.

Baji Rao Peshwa's Visit To Rajputana, 1736

Leaving Puna on 9th October, Baji Rao arrived, via Lunawada and Dungarpur at the southern frontier of Mewar, about the 15th of January, 1736. After a most artfully courteous interview with the Maharana, he secured a written promise for Rs 1,60,000 a year and to cover this, the Banhada *pargana* was ceded to the Marathas (*c* 4th February).

While Baji Rao was still at Udaipur, his agent Mahadev Bhat Hingane went to Jaipur and was introduced to Jai Singh by his minister Aya Mal (popularly known as Rajah Mal and Malji). Jai Singh agreed to present the Peshwa with five lakhs in cash and kind, and sent a message inviting him to his dominions and promising to introduce him to the Emperor and secure a lasting peace between the Imperial Government and the Marathas, in return for a cash grant and *jagirs* in Malwa. Aya Mal personally conveyed this offer to Baji Rao and conducted him to Jaipur territory. A settled peace being thus in prospect, Baji Rao immediately sent orders to his generals everywhere in North India to suspend hostilities and to vacate Rajputana.

From Udaipur, Baji Rao moved north *via* the holy city of Nathdwara towards Jaipur. At the village of Bhamola 30 miles east of Ajmer, he met Jai Singh, who had hastened southwards to welcome his august guest. A pavilion was erected as the meeting place between the two camps, while the Rajput and Maratha escorts stood fully armed on the two sides (*c.* 15th February). The two chiefs descended from their elephants, exchanged embraces and sat down on the same cushion. Baji Rao, in spite of his being a priest by caste and the prime minister of the leading Hindu Rajah of India, had the manners of a moss-trooper, which had been anything but improved by his consorting with Mastani, a Muslim dancing-girl devoted to the wine-cup. He puffed at his *huqqa*, blowing the smoke into the face of his host. The Jaipur Rajah had the perfect courtesy and self-control to be expected from a first-class grandee of the polished Court of Delhi, and bore the rough manners of the Deccani without turning a muscle of his face.

The meeting being over, Jai Singh went back to his capital, telling Baji Rao that it was better for him to return to the Deccan, as the time was not favourable for his intended march on Delhi. In the meantime, he promised to use his influence at the Imperial Court to secure for Rajah Shahu the grant of the *chauth* and the cession of Malwa from the Emperor. The Peshwa accordingly came back to Puna.

Baji Rao, Alienated By The Emperor, Makes A Raid On Delhi And Crushes The Nizam, 1737

At Jai Singh's recommendation, the Emperor had (in May, 1736) agreed to appoint Baji Rao the deputy Governor and *de facto* master of Malwa, while Jai Singh was to continue as the nominal *subahdar*, but the other demands of the Deccanis were rejected. Convinced of the utter weakness and incompetence of the Delhi Court, Baji Rao determined to exact the utmost from it. He no doubt occupied Malwa by his troops as deputy *subahdar* during the middle of the year 1736, but as soon as the rainy season was over, he sent exorbitant fresh demands to Delhi, which the Emperor naturally declined (29th September, 1736).

Baji Rao now launched on the most spectacular campaign of his career. Leaving Puna on November 12, 1736 (it is said after receiving a secret invitation from Jai Singh), he swept through Malwa, Bundelkhand and the Gangetic Doab with his myriads of irresistible light horsemen, and reached the very gates of the Imperial capital, sacking Kalka Devi (six miles south of the Turkman gate of Delhi) on 30th March, 1737), routing the Imperial army at Tal Katora (about 6 miles south west of the city) and then suddenly retreating to Rajputana. Nizam-ul-mulk Asaf Jah I, who had at last come to his master's rescue, was hemmed round by Baji Rao near Bhopal (December), utterly defeated, and forced to sign the humiliating treaty of Duraha (Saturday, 7th January, 1738), by which the Peshwa gained the whole of Malwa, the complete sovereignty of the territory between the Narmada and the Chambal, and a promise of 50 lakhs as war idemnity payable by the Imperial Government. Thus the total loss of Malwa which Jai Singh had tried to prevent by his far-sighted policy of peace with Shahu and timely appeasement of the Peshwa, was effected by 'the Regulator of the Realm', the last prop of the tottering throne of Delhi.

That throne was finally shattered to pieces by Nadir Shah, whose victory at Karnal (13th February, 1739) and massacre of Delhi (11th March) put an end to any organised government of an Indian empire from Delhi. The entire Indian world remained in a sort of stupor and dumb terror during the seven months of the terrible Persian's stay on

Indian soil and for nearly a year afterwards. In 1740 Baji Rao died and was succeeded by his eldest son Balaji Rao to the regency of the Maratha State.

Jai Singh Befriends Peshwa Balaji Rao

The new Peshwa set out for the North in March, 1741 and reached Gwalior. Between him and Delhi lay Jai Singh, the *subahdar* of Agra. This Rajah reported to the Emperor that the captains under him were quite inexperienced in Deccani warfare and would therefore fail in an armed contest. He then sent envoys to open peace negotiations with Balaji, telling him to remain content with the *subahs* of Gujarat and Malwa, and not to disturb any other province of the Empire. The Peshwa agreed on condition of his receiving an Imperial *farman* which would legally confer these two provinces on him. At the same time, to save the Emperor's face, a petition was submitted by Balaji, professing loyalty to the Delhi throne and declaring himself a devoted servant of the Emperor. Following Jai Singh's advice, Muhammad Shah issued the required *farman* on 4th July, 1741,[6] bestowing the deputy governorship of Malwa on the Peshwa. This was another device for disguising the fullness of the Imperial surrender and keeping up *on paper* the pretence of continued Imperial right to Malwa.

Balaji Rao visited Jai Singh near Dholpur on 12th May, and three days later the Kacchwa Rajah returned the visit. Then each went back to his home. Malwa henceforth ceased to be a part of the Empire of Delhi.

Notes

1. See his last will and testament in Appendices. *Ed.*
2. *Jaipur Records Additional Persian Vol. II*, p. 120, (Shri Raghubir Library, Sitamau). It is not known who this adopted son of Shahu, Kushal Singh was, for whom the jagir was required. Possibly he was a younger scion of the Sisodia House of Mewar. It is known, however, that Raja Shahu once thought of adopting Nathji, the younger son of Maharana Sangram Singh of Mewar. *Vir Vinod*, II, 1595, *Ed.*
3. This should be Thursday, 28th September, 1732, because the *farman* granting him the *subahdari* of Malwa is dated 19th Rabi-us-Sani, Julus Saneh 15. (Sarkar, *Fall* I, First Edition, p. 246.) *Ed.*
4. Omit the following sentences beginning with 'Jai Singh's deputy...side by side with Jai Singh's,' because they do not correctly sum up the contents of the two Rajasthani letters referred to here. Sir Jadunath Sarkar seems to have missed the fact that in Rajasthani correspondence the Maharana of Mewar is usually referred to as "Sri Diwanji" (of Sri Eklingji). Dhabai Rao Nagraj, the foster brother of Maharana Sangram Singh of Mewar, was a trusted noteworthy minister of the Mewar State. A correct summary within brackets containing details of these two letters are included in the main text to give an idea of his assuming the Viceroyalty of Malwa for the third time. *Ed.*
5. But the plan proved abortive at the very outset and could not possibly be implemented. *Ed.*
6. This should be Wednesday, 15th July, 1741, because the *farman* is dated 12 Jamadi-ul-Awwal, Julus Saneh 24. (S.P.D., XI p. 86). *Ed.*

XV

Sawai Jai Singh And Rajputana

The Hopeless Disintegration Of The Mughal Empire Under Muhammad Shah

To understand the true cause and meaning of Sawai Jai Singh's policy in Rajputana we must bear in mind the condition of the Delhi Empire in Muhammad Shah's reign after the Sayyid brothers had been killed and Nizam-ul-mulk had declared his independence (1724).

Mughal civilization was now a spent bullet. The great work of Akbar had been undone in a century and a half; Imperial peace, orderly administration, security of life, property and female honour had disappeared from the Empire. The political dissolution was evident on every side, and nothing could conceal the moral canker which was the root cause of it all. Whenever any particularly serious invasion, tumult or crime was reported to the Court of Delhi, Muhammad Shah and his wazir, the smooth-spoken topper Qamruddin Khan, used to withdraw from the capital to some lonely park or lake and forget their duty in the enjoyment of Nature's beauty and peace. A serious problem was therefore pricking every thinking mind in India. What of the future? How was this intolerable collapse of Government to be remedied?

With a mere cypher on the throne, the people of the provinces became the helpless prey of local governors, who did their best to make money out of their province during their brief uncertain period of office. Witness the heartless plunder of Malwa by its *official* protectors Muhammad Khan Bangash and Sayyid Najmuddin Ali Khan, of which we get sickening details among the Jaipur records. The Imperial connection therefore became merely a means of draining the *subahs* of their wealth, without giving them security from internal disorder, growth of property or fair justice in return. The unifying and life-giving centre having become really dead, the parts began to fall off. the provinces farthest from the capital were the first to be lost, either by declaring their independence under some dynasty of their own, or by being conquered by a foreign power.

But the rise of an independent provincial dynasty was preceded and rendered easier by some local governor during the declining days of the Empire ruling over the province continuously for a long time, at first as an avowed servant of the Central Government. Such founders of local dynasties have always been men of exceptional capacity and vigour, and have won an abiding place in the hearts of their subjects by promoting their safety and welfare amidst the dissolution of political order around them; it was their personal interest to protect and encourage trade and manufacture, banking, literature and the fine arts within their jurisdiction. One source of their strength and efficacy, in addition to their extraordinary personal capacity, was their union of several *subahs* in their charge, thus forming a compact block of territory like a full province of British India. Murshid Quli Khan's house ruled over Bengal, Bihar and Orissa, Nizam-ul-mulk over six *subahs* in Mughal Deccan. Sadat Khan's house ruled over Oudh, Allahabad and later Rohilkhand and parts of the Doab, and Zakariya Khan's over the entire Panjab. These founder-viceroys worked for the immense benefit of the people whose happy lot it was to be governed by them. The people really gained by thus securing a permanent local master instead of a rapidly changing succession of blood-suckers sent out from the Imperial Court. In short, such a local or limited hegemony was the only possible salvation of the people in that age of the decline and fall of the Mughal Empire.

Jai Singh Plans A Local Hegemony For Peace In Rajputana

Such local hegemony for the good of Rajputana and the holy land of Braja became the aim of Sawai Jai Singh, after he had scanned the political horizon of North India for many years. He was incomparably the highest Hindu vassal of the Crown and, after the retirement of Nizam-ul-mulk, its most powerful general. He had long been the medium[1] through whom all the petitions of the Rajput States had to be submittted to the Emperor and royal orders communicated to them, and the Emperor had assured him in writing that he would do nothing concerning those countries except at Jai Singh's recommendation. Many letters from the rulers of Jodhpur, Bundi, Kota and even Mewar are extant in which Sawai Jai Singh is appealed to as their protector and mediator.

In carrying out this plan Jai Singh wisely left the Maharana untouched, because the latter had isolated himself for a century and maintained only the barest connection with the Court of Delhi and the world outside. Jodhpur and Bundi were neutralized by being held by two of his sons-in-law, and he had no territorial ambition westward of the Sambhar Lake at the expense of the Rathors. His policy, in the ultimate analysis, was reduced to the formation of a compact dominion from the Sambhar lake to the Jamuna at Agra and Mathura in the east and if feasible to the Narmada in the south. It would include the *subahs* of Agra and Malwa and the lesser Rajput States that lay on the route from Jaipur to Malwa. He sought also to give political unity to the Dhundher country by acquiring through formal Imperial rescripts, sometimes in return for services, at others for money payments, possession of many small units of territory *(parganas)* hitherto held by others directly under the Emperor, which diversified and puzzled the political map of that region. The territories gained and fully annexed to his own kingdom under this last category will be described in detail in another chapter.

The Affairs Of Rampura

The larger political units, i.e., States as distinct from mere *parganas* or revenue areas, with which he was involved, were three: Rampura, Bundi-Kota and (for a different reason) Jodhpur.

The little State of Rampura, on the north-western border of Malwa and wedged in between that province and Mewar, was ruled over by a Chandrawat branch of the Sisodia clan. Late in the seventeenth century, its Rao Gopal Singh when serving under Aurangzib in the

Deccan, was dispossessed by his son Ratan Singh, who turned Muslim under the name of Islam Khan, and thus secured recognition from the pious Aurangzib! The father, thus turned adrift, returned home and tried force to recover his own from his unnatural son, but all his attempts failed. In despair he at last joined the Marathas in their raids into Gujarat (1705). Ratan Singh fell in a battle in 1712 and Gopal Singh at last reoccupied Rampura (1714) with the help of the Maharana's forces,[2] who gave only a portion of the whole district to him and annexed the rest to Mewar. In August, 1717, Gopal Singh and his grandson Sangram Singh signed an agreement by which they became tribute-paying *zamindars* under the Maharana renouncing their independent status. In 1718,[3] at Jai Singh's request, the Emperor Farrukhsiyar confirmed this change. In December, 1728, a son was born to Jai Singh by his Udaipuri queen and the Maharana was induced by Jai Singh (Tuesday, 25th March, 1729), to grant Rampura as a fief to this infant, Madho Singh, who was to remain a loyal vassal of Mewar. Soon afterwards Jaipur agents took charge of Rampura. The ousted Sangram Singh went to Delhi to intrigue at the Imperial Court, but unsuccessfully, and on his way back he was killed in a fray. We may conclude this story by saying that Madho Singh, on succeeding to the throne of Jaipur in 1750, attached Rampura to the Kachhwa dominions, though nominally as a fief belonging to Mewar, and from his house it passed on to Holkar in 1757.

Bundi Under Rao Rajah Budh Singh

We next turn to the history of the Haras, who now live divided between the two States of Kota and Bundi. This clan first became a separate political body when its chief Rao Surjan of Bundi overthrew his hereditary overlord the Maharana of Udaipur, gave Ranthambhor fort to Akbar (1569) and entered the Mughal service.[4] A second split occurred in 1623 when Jahangir gave Kota to the second son of Rao Ratan to be held direct of the Mughal Crown. A century later, at the battle of Jajau (1707) Budh Singh of Bundi fought for Bahadur Shah while Ram Singh of Kota fell in the ranks of his defeated rival Prince Azam Shah. The grateful new Emperor conferred on Budh Singh the title of *Rao Rajah*, with 54 forts of Harawati, including Kota, which capital had been confiscated for its late ruler's treason. But this city remained in the hands of Bhim Singh (the son of Ram Singh) who later secured the patronage of the Sayyid brothers. As Budh Singh, sunk in pleasure, did not come to Court after repeated summons, Farrukhsiyar transferred Bundi to Bhim Singh, but in 1716 at Jai Singh's entreaty Bundi was restored to Budh Singh, the Kota Rajah retaining the *parganas* of Baran and Mau. Both these Hara chiefs served under Jai Singh in his wars with Churaman Jat, and Budh Singh especially distinguished himself by his reckless valour in Jai Singh's great victory over the Marathas at Palsud (1717).

Budh Singh remained true to Farrukhsiyar during the plots of the Sayyids against that Emperor, and in 1719 he had to cut his way through the troops of Bhim Singh who tried to entrap him at Delhi. During the short dictatorship of the Sayyid brothers after Muhammad Shah's accession, Bhim stormed Bundi (2nd March, 1720), only to be killed three months later in the defeat of the Sayyid partisan Dilawar Ali at the hands of the Nizam at Khandwa (19th June, 1720). Bundi now reverted to Budh Singh. With Bhim begins the title of *Maha Rao*, borne by his family, as a fruit of his adhesion to the Sayyid king-makers. His youngest son Durjan Sal succeeded in 1724 and reigned till 1756.

After the capture of Thun (1722) followed a period of idleness in which Budh Singh sank deeper and deeper into slothfulness and vice, totally neglecting the administration of Bundi, in spite of Jai Singh's friendly counsels. He lived at various places in Jaipur territory, such as Basai, Kanikho and Amber, hospitably entertained by his brother-in-law Jai Singh. But everywhere he lay in the stupor of wine and opium, while his unruly followers plundered the shops and abducted women from their husband's houses, in the Kacchwa cities which harboured them. He and his entourage rioted in the same manner even in the Maharana's territory when he fled there for refuge in 1730. Out of regard for his sister's husband, Jai Singh could do nothing to protect his subjects from such gross outrages. This is admitted by Suraj Mal Mishran, the official eulogist of the Court of Bundi.[5]

Things moved to a crisis in 1728. Budh Singh had three queens, the chief of them being Jai Singh's step-sister, a female fury from whose tempestuous outbursts her poor henpecked husband found consolation in the bosom of his second wife, a Chundawat princes of Begham (in Mewar territory) who bore him many pledges of her affection.

About 1720, the principal Rani who was childless, smuggled an infant into the palace and declared him to be her son by Budh Singh. In 1728 when she proposed to have this boy, named Bhawani Singh, married to a daughter of the Maharana, Budh Singh forbade the match on the ground that Bhawani was no son of his. A furious storm now raged in the family. Jai Singh protested against this aspersion on his sister's virtue and rightly asked Budh why he had not killed this infant when first produced if he was really a bastard. He taxed Budh Singh with repudiating the paternity of Bhawani in order to keep the succession open for a son of his favourite Chundawati queen. The Bundi chief disavowed any such intention and in proof of his sincerity gave Jai Singh a written undertaking to kill Bhawani Singh, and to exclude from the throne of Bundi any of his issues by his other two queens. He authorized Jai Singh to choose a successor for him by adoption. This curious document was attested by a number of his nobles and also verified the next year in the presence of the Maharana.

Bundi Raj Transferred From Budh Singh To Dalel Singh

On Jai Singh's return from Udaipur, at the beginning of 1729, his sister, maddened by the failure of her projected match between Bhawani Singh and the Maharana's daughter, abused Jai Singh and ran at him with a dagger. After this, Budh Singh carried out his promise. The bogus heir-apparent of Bundi was handed over to Jai Singh and put to death in a hill fort. The Kachhwai Rani of Bundi, Jai Singh's step-sister, thereafter pursued him with the fury of a tigress robbed of her whelp.

The Kachhwa Rajah now unfolded to the Emperor how Budh Singh was an incurable drug addict, incapable of rendering the armed service on condition of which he held his Imperial *mansab* and *jagir;* or even of governing Bundi properly. There was now no male issue left to him, as his only legitimate son Padam Singh had died of disease some years before. In fact, Bundi had so long been practically under the Court of Wards, its administration being looked after by an agent of Jai Singh. So, Muhammad Shah granted the State to Dalel Singh, the second son of Salim Singh Hada of Karwar as recommended by Jai Singh.

The matter was further complicated by the birth (on 14th June, 1729) of a son to Budh Singh by his Chundawati queen (who was destined to raise his house to the height of glory), the heroic Ummed Singh Hada. Jai Singh demanded the surrender of this infant, in the terms of Budh Singh's written engagement of two years back. The father refused, and though living on Jai Singh's hospitality for several years past, he did not scruple to plan a surprise attack on Amber fort. Here Bijai Singh the rebellious half-brother of Jai Singh was confined, with a view to releasing and crowning him king of Jaipur, while Jai Singh would be absent in Malwa, where he was ordered to go as viceroy. The loving brother-in-law's plot leaked out and Jai Singh assured his rear by putting Bijai Singh to death before starting from his own dominions.

On 23rd October, 1729 Jai Singh set out from his capital for Malwa. Three weeks later Budh Singh left his asylum at Kanikho (in Jaipur territory) and marched to recover Bundi. Friends gathered around him from many places. Jai Singh's agent Salim Singh, who was governing Bundi for the new king Dalel Singh, issued from that city to meet the invaders. At Kusathal Pancholas, on the border between the two States, the rival armies came into contact. Jai Singh pushed up strong reinforcements to Salim Singh. In fear of the all-powerful Kachhwa Rajah many of Budh Singh's adherents left him, and that Hada chief himself urged his remaining troops not to seek battle. But Devi Singh and a few other die-hard partisans of the house of Bundi could not be held back. They delivered an attack on 6th April, 1730, when after a most obstinate hand to hand fight such as only the insane fury of civil war between men of the same blood can provoke—the Hada (legitimists) were defeated, but only after exacting a terrible price from the Kachhwas. On Jai Singh's side fell five great vassal chieftains, Fath Mal (of Sarsop), Kojuram (of Isarda), Shyamaldas (of Suhad), Bahadur Singh (of Buddhani), Ghasiram (of Rasor), besides many others, including Khande Rao the celebrated regent of Narwar. The poet Suraj Mal gives the Hada casualties as 1200 slain and 1000 wounded; the abnormally small proportion of the wounded best illustrates the sanguinary nature of this fratricidal contest. (*Vam. Bh.* iv, 3147 *et seq.*)

The unworthy lord of the Hada desperadoes, unnerved by opium, had kept out of the fight and at last took refuge in Mewar. Here he died, a derelict in body and mind, at Begham, the home of his father-in-law, in 1730. But his legacy of war with Jaipur passed on to Ummed Singh, a son worthy of a nobler father.

Jai Singh who had now hurried back from Ujjain, reached Bundi, crowned his *protege* Dalel Singh as Rajah (on 19th May, 1730) and married him to one of his daughters. Then, after visiting the fatal field of Kusathal pancholas, and ordering temple cenotaphs to be erected for the five vassal chiefs who had fallen there, and gardens laid out around them (at a cost of Rs 5000), he returned to his own capital.

But this injustice to the legitimate heir of Bundi began a course fraught with the greatest evil to Rajputana for nearly a century to come. It first brought the Marathas in as an invited party in a domestic feud of the Rajputs. Pratap Singh Hada (the eldest son of the regent Salim Singh), on seeing his younger brother Dalel raised to the royal throne of Bundi, came over to Budh Singh's side out of wounded pride. He was now sent to the Deccan by Budh Singh's senior Rani (the vindictive sister of the murdered Raja Bijai Singh Kachhwa) with her own money for hiring Maratha aid. The price was settled at six lakhs of rupees. On 22nd April, Malhar Holkar and Ranuji Sindhia, guided by Pratap, attacked Bundi, captured the fort and carried away Salim as prisoner. But as soon as the Maratha army had withdrawn, a Jaipur force, 20,000 strong, drove out Budh Singh's partisans and restored Dalel Singh at Bundi.

This first Maratha penetration into Rajputana had opened the eyes of the more thoughtful among the princes to their perilous condition. The terror of it continued to be remembered for long afterwards. In the second half of October, 1734, Jai Singh called a Congress of all the Rajahs of Rajasthan at Hurda, near Agaunch in Mewar, in order to concert measures for keeping the Deccani spoilers out of their fatherland. That end could be reached only by the closest cooperation among the princes themselves and also with the forces of the Emperor. The draft conditions of the princes' alliance can be read in Tod, and the original is still preserved in the Jaipur archives. But nothing came of the meeting and Tod says, 'no public or general benefit ever resulted from these alliances, which were obstructed by the multitude of petty jealousies inseparable from clanship'. Besides, the moral decay of the Mughal nobility made any policy of defence against the Marathas marked by the necessary degree of union and vigour, impossible.

The Murder Of Ajit Singh, Maharajah Of Jodhpur

Maharajah Ajit Singh of Marwar had been allied to Jai Singh in putting an end to the Imperial encroachments on Rajputana after the death of Aurangzib. Since then their ways had lain apart. Jai Singh gained the *subahdari* of Malwa and Ajit Singh that of Gujarat, but the Rathor chief proved habitually refractory to his suzerain. Two expeditions in full force had to be sent out against him from Delhi—one in 1713 (under Sayyid Husain Ali Khan) and the other in 1722-1723 (under Iradatmand Khan). In 1721-1722, he had seized Sambhar salt lake from its Imperial collector and many neighbouring *parganas*, and harried Narnol and the Mewat district up to within 16 miles of the Mughal capital. In January, 1723 he slew the Diwan of the province of Ajmer, beheaded 25 of his officers and looted all their camp and baggage. But a strong army from Delhi pressed Ajit so hard that he was glad to make his submission by returning Ajmer and 13 *parganas* and sending his eldest son Abhai Singh with several elephants and a large sum of money as propitiatory gifts to the Emperor (November, 1723). The terms of his pardon were arranged by the mediation of Jai Singh who was eager to save a brother prince from ruin, as the Mirza Rajah had saved Jaswant from Aurangzib's wrath in 1659.

Abhai Singh lived at Delhi as the representative of his father at Court, because Ajit Singh had begged for a year's delay in attending on the Emperor. The next incident in Marwar history was the murder of Ajit by his second son Bakht Singh, when he was asleep in bed in the depth of night on 23rd June, 1724. The Jodhpur historians try to explain away this horrible crime by ascribing it to political expediency. They say that when Abhai Singh came to Delhi with the old family minister Raghunath Bhandari on his peace mission, he found the Emperor and the Nazir implacable towards his father for his lifelong contumacy, and bent on annexing Marwar. In order to save his 'home' from being lost to his family, the heir of Jodhpur decided to remove his father from the world, because it is the Rajput practice to regard his patrimony as his mother, who is a nearer and dearer relative than the natural father. Jai Singh, who was then at Delhi, and who acted as intermediary in Abhai Singh's negotiations with the Mughal Government, is said in Jodhpur tradition and the Bundi Court epic *Vamsha-Bhaskar*, to have induced the Emperor to confer the Jodhpur throne on Abhai if the incorrigible Ajit was put out of the way.

A more natural and probable cause of the murder—which was committed not by Abhai who was to benefit by it, but by his younger brother Bakht Singh—is given in the contemporary Persian history *Tazkirat-us-Salatin-i-Chaghtaia* of Kamwar Khan, and need not be related here. (See W. Irvine's *Later Mughals*, ii, 115, with an attempt at refutation in *Indian Antiquary*, vol. 58, pp. 47-51.)

The Rathor bardic fabricators have embroidered this tale in order to throw the blame of the patricide on Sawai Jai Singh, the head of the rival clan of Kachhwa. In the latest history of Marwar, issued by the Archaeological Department of the State, it is asserted:

> The Emperor seduced the Bhandari through Jai Singh. These two forged a letter which they contrived to get signed unawares by Abhai Singh [*Query:* Is it suggested that this young man was already a habitual drunkard like his father?], and which was secretly sent to Bakht Singh urging him to murder their aged father for the sake of preserving the raj...
>
> Bakht was startled and bewildered; but he at last bowed to the necessity of averting the coming disaster to his (elder) brother and country; accordingly in the last quarter of the night of 23rd June, 1724, Ajit Singh when asleep took his departure out of this world. (Bishweshwarnath Reu's *Marwar ka Itihas*, i, 327.)

No such forged letter has been preserved, and no historian has admitted to have seen it since the day when the legend originated. It is surprising that such opium eaters' tales are circulated in print even in the twentieth century.

Abhai Singh Succeeds In Supressing Jodhpur Rebellions

The Emperor conferred the throne of Marwar on Abhai Singh who was then at Delhi (17th July, 1724), together with the lordship of Nagor, which had previously been granted to Indra Singh. Next month, the new Rajah went to Mathura and married Jai Singh's daughter. By this match Abhai Singh hoped to secure as his patron the most influential noble at the Imperial Court. But this very step raised a sea of troubles against him. Its swift sequence to the murder of his father seemed to verify the wild rumour that murder had been concerted by Jai Singh and Abhai Singh as a prelude to a family pact which would be sealed with such a marriage tie. But a glance at Rajput history will show that the Kachhwa and Rathor royal houses had most frequently married together, and that sons-in-law have seldom proved tame vassals to their royal fathers-in-law, and Abhai Singh's later relations with Jai Singh only confirmed this.

The Rathor nobles, eternally bent on faction and refractory to the throne except under a strong dominating Rajah like Jaswant Singh, at once left Abhai Singh's side. Two of his younger brothers, Anand and Raj Singh, declared their independence with the support of the rebels, and a third seized Jalor for himself. In addition, feudal anarchy was let loose all over Marwar. Utterly helpless, Abhai Singh appealed to the Emperor, who earnestly besought Jai Singh to go to that distracted country, end the rebellion by force or seduction and support the tottering throne of Abhai Singh. He was also to wrest Nagor from Indra Singh's hands.

Abhai Singh took leave of the Emperor and coming home tried to put the rebels down. Merta was saved to him and then he laid siege to Nagor. After an obstinate resistance Indra Singh capitulated and Nagor was given as an appanage to Bakht Singh (4th July, 1726). The two rebel brothers then hired Maratha aid in their domestic feud; they invited Kanthaji Kadam and Pilaji Gaikwad to come from Gujarat and raid the Jalor district. Finally, in 1728 the two princes occupied Idar, and Abhai Singh after some delay had to recognise their usurpation as the only means of pacifying them. In this civil war in Marwar, a strong Jaipur contingent under some Kachhwa generals ably backed Abhai Singh, as urged by the Emperor (*J.R.* 76 189). But Jai Singh could not go there in person, having been pressed by the Emperor to march to Malwa 'with all the Rajahs of Hindustan for punishing the Marathas thoroughly' (*J.R.* 438).

Then followed about twelve years during which Abhai Singh was kept busy in Gujarat and Jai Singh with his new planned capital and astronomical research and the ever-clouded politics of his *subah* of Malwa. By the year 1740 they could turn again to Rajputana.

The Rupture Between Jaipur And Jodhpur

Bakht Singh had loyally supported his elder brother Maharajah Abhai Singh in the early troubles of his reign and also in his thorny governorship of Gujarat (1730-1737). But in the course of years the two brothers drifted apart. While Abhai Singh, after returning from Gujarat, sank deeper and deeper into indolence and wine, Bakht Singh's insatiable ambition and consciousness of superior capacity and spirit looked around for new ways of aggrandising himself, if necessary at the expense of his unworthy tribal head. As lord of Nagor, he had boundary disputes with his neighbour in the north, the Rathor Rajah of Bikaner. One such quarrel had ended in March, 1734, when Abhai Singh took up his brother's cause and wrung some concessions from Bikaner. Again, in the autumn of 1739, Abhai Singh was induced by Bakht to invade Bikaner. The capital was besieged, one ward of it was looted and the garrison hard pressed. Its Rajah Zorawar Singh appealed to Jai Singh to save him. The Jaipur Rajah wrote to Abhai Singh urging him to have pity on Zorawar. But the Marwar Maharajah sent back a defiant answer, saying that it was a purely domestic quarrel between two branches of the Rathor clan and the Kachhwa chieftain had no business to intervene in it.

Jai Singh was fully provoked and led a well-equipped force of 20,000 men to attack Jodhpur. Abhai raised the siege of Bikaner and hastened to the defence of his capital. He clearly realized his own military weakness and without fighting decided to buy Jai Singh off, as his nobles and ministers wisely advised him to do.

As a condition for inducing the Jaipur army to withdraw, five of the highest barons of Marwar submitted the following memorial to Jai Singh on 25th July, 1740, and it was signed and ratified by their accredited representatives Maha Singh and Sher Singh on Monday, 11th August: (1) the State of Marwar would present to the Emperor one lakh rupees in cash, Rs 25,000 in jewels and three elephants. (2) It would pay twenty lakhs of rupees to Jai Singh as the pay of his additional levies, and if his expenditure under this head calculated at the rate of Rs 20,000 daily was found to exceed 20 lakhs, the extra amount also would be paid. (3) In four days bankers' orders for all the above amounts would be handed to Jai Singh, and the five barons and Bhandari Raghunath were to remain hostages for it. (4) Abhai Singh would give up the Bikaner territory that he had seized.

(5) He would give Merta to Bakht Singh. (6) He would not obstruct Jai Singh in his possessions of the Ajmer *subah* (*parganas* held by him both in *ijara* and *mansab* named). (7) No prince or baron of Marwar would serve the Emperor in independence of the Jaipur Rajah, nor maintain their own agents at the Imperial Court, nor seek private audience, but be presented only through the mediation of the Jaipur Rajah. (8) Similarly, the foreign relations of Marwar with Marathas were subordinated to Jaipur. (9) Abhai Singh's counsellers in future must be men selected by these (pro-Jaipur) barons, all others being denied access to him.

Abhai Singh wrote on this document, 'I agree to the terms. I shall not cherish ill feeling towards any of the five *Thakurs* for this' (*J.R.* 107 and 108).

This treaty turned Marwar into a mediatised State entirely subject to the suzerainty of Jaipur in its external relations. It was a most humiliating surrender for a first-rate power. The Rathor nobles complained with good reason that 'their noses had been cut off by the Kachhwas'. There was bitter discontent among the barons (*thakurs*) of Jodhpur and they cried out for a war of revenge against Jaipur. The blame of all this loss and dishonour was laid on Bakht Singh, who had gone over to Jai Singh's side against his own native land and profited by his tribal head's recent troubles to get possession of Merta. After this treaty with Marwar, Jai Singh returned to Agra in August, 1740, but early next year reports of active war preparations in Jodhpur roused him to fresh exertions. Ordering a *levee en masse* of his vassals and allies (including the Jadav Rajah of Karauli and some of Chhatra Sal Bundela's progeny) and joined by three Muslim generals in the Emperor's service who had been ordered to follow him in driving the Marathas out of the north, Sawai Jai Singh left Agra and marched towards Ajmer in order to meet the challenge to his realm. Meanwhile Bakht Singh had awoken to a full sense of his clan loyalty and come back from Jai Singh's side to that of Abhai Singh. When the brothers with the tribal army reached Merta, there was a stormy scene at the Rajah's durbar. Everyone donounced Bakht Singh for having been false to his brethren and lord. Then Bakht said penitently that as all this harm was the result of his having previously joined Jai Singh, he would now make amends for it by going forth alone with his own personal contingent of 5000 horse, and oppose the coming Kachhwa invaders. Maharajah Abhai Singh and all his other vassals stayed behind at Merta.

The Battle Of Gangwana, 1741

Then followed the astonishing battle of Gangwana (11th June, 1741),[6] which so fully illustrates the Rajput spirit and mode of war. With a vast but disjointed host, numbered variously from 40,000 to one lakh of men, Jai Singh took post at Kunchgaon, near Gangwana, *eleven miles north-east* of the Pushkar lake, and encamped, planting a long line of guns in front. The Rathors were hopelessly outnumbered. But Bakht Singh at the head of a thousand horsemen desperate like himself, charged the enemy, swept through the line of guns, and fell upon Jai Singh's own selection of the battle front, 'like tigers among a flock of sheep'. Nothing could stand their onset; they convulsed the Jaipur army galloping from this end to that; many thousands on the Kachhwa side were slain and wounded, and the rest fled; and within four hours the vast field of battle was entirely cleared, as by magic, of all save the dead and the wounded. Jai Singh's tents were set on fire and his baggage plundered, including his family idol Sitaramji, which was carried into battle on an elephant. Ummed Singh Sisodia of Shapura's brother and Bhairo Singh Chauhan were chief among those who fell in the Jaipur ranks.

His army shattered by the wild bear rush of Bakht Singh, the Rajah of Jaipur at first fell back two miles and stood for some time almost alone and in perplexity. The three Muslim generals, who had joined him at Agra by order of the Emperor, had not been attacked by the Rathors in their section of the battle line. They coolly kept their places in the field, near Pahari, though their followers had panicked and fled, leaving barely a hundred men out of their ten thousand behind their elephants. By this time Bakht Singh's gallant band had been reduced from a thousand to seventy and he himself was wounded with a bullet and an arrow. His fight was magnificent, but it was not war.

Just then, the three Imperial generals, who had formed a rallying centre for more of their men after the momentary panic was over, opened fire with their rockets on Bakht Singh and his men. This unexpected renewal of attack on a field where he could see no enemy before him, was more than the Rathor remnant could bear. So he turned the reins for his brother's camp at Merta. Jai Singh (after this unexpected and pyrrhic victory), advanced to Gangwana and encamped, to receive congratulations for his victory. Arriving at Ajmer

(13th June) he offered condolences to the kinsmen of the fallen on his side and rewards and horses to all who had fought well.[7]

A charming story, characteristic of Rajput piety and chivalry, is told about this battle. During the heat and confusion of the Rathor charge, the elephant carrying Bhakt Singh's tutelary good Girdharji had stampeded and been seized by the Kachhwas. As the pious Bakht never ate cooked food without first viewing and adoring the idol, he sent his diwan to Jai Singh, saying, 'For the last two days I have not taken a solid meal. [i.e., he had lived on fruits only.] If the god Girdharji comes here from your camp, I can eat cooked food.' Jai Singh at once sent the idol and its elephant back after praising highly Bhakt Singh's valour. On the other side too, the Jaipur idol Sitaramji and some jewellery which had been made prize of by the Rathors during the battle, were sent back to Jai Singh by Abhai Singh on 8th July. The Maharana of Udaipur now intervened and made peace between the two sides.

This was the last battle fought by Sawai Jai Singh, whose military career had begun forty years earlier, under the eyes of the veteran Aurangzib. He died at his new capital two years later (21st September, 1743) after a long and painful illness. His policy of ensuring peace in Rajputana by establishing a regional hegemony there was foredoomed to failure when his sceptre passed into weaker hands, because it ran against the grain of the Rajput character. Absolute local autonomy was the life breath of every Rajput State and sub-clan, however small, as it was of every petty city-republic of ancient Greece. No more than the Hellenese who fell through disunion before the Imperial advance of Macedon and Rome, could the noblest Hindu martial race forget their petty feuds and merge their local independence in a great political federation for the sake of mutual defence and mutual progress in the arts and culture of peace. Rajputana became again a mere 'geographical expression', a bundle of warring atoms, less than ten years after Jai Singh's death. And this brought the Marathas on the scene, and then the rapacious Pathan Amir Khan, and this 'land of princes' had to pass through seventy years of agony before Pax Britannica spread its healing hand over the tortured people.

The Death Of Kumar Shiv Singh, 1724

Following the popular gossip *(khyat)* the author of the *Vamsha Bhaskar* ascribes the death of Jai Singh's eldest son, Kumar Shiv Singh, to poison given by his father at the instigation of his second son Ishwari Singh, and adds that the unhappy prince's mother shared his foul end. Let us examine this story in the light of common sense and *known* facts.

Shiv Singh died at Mathura in July-August, 1724, the terrible cholera season of upper India. The fact that his mother died at the same time and place strengthens the inference that it was an epidemic, the infection of which spread to the family, especially to the patient's nursing mother. An exact parallel is supplied by the death of Bakht Singh Rajah of Jodhpur in September, 1752, which the *contemporary Persian* histories record as due to cholera, but the *Vir Vinod*, written in the late nineteenth century, ascribes to poison, given by Jai Singh's son Madho Singh.

Shiv Singh was at this time over 22 years of age, as he was the father of two sons and had been *faujdar* of Mathura for some years before, and the Emperor had chosen him to deputise for his father (as governor of Agra province) during Jai Singh's campaign at a distant place. Therefore, his mother, now an elderly matron, could hardly have raised any suspicion of infidelity, the usual ground on which Oriental Othellos kill their wives in jealous fury. As for the alleged crime having been suggested by Ishwari Singh to pliant Jai Singh, we should remember that Ishwari Singh was probably four or five years old at this time. In the Jaipur records there is an entry that he was born at Delhi. Now, when did Jai Singh II live at Delhi? Not once from 1700 to 1716. On his return from Malwa in May, 1716 he visited Delhi and passed three months at the Imperial Court, after which he went away to fight Churaman Jat. During the plots against the Emperor Farrukhsiyar, 1718-1719, the Rajah kept at home. It was only after the fall of the Sayyid brothers that he lived at Delhi for a considerable time, from May 1721 to 1723 (after the last named year he removed to Mathura). Ishwari Singh, therefore, was probably born late in 1721; the year 1717 is possible, but not likely.

We are asked to believe that the veteran soldier statesman killed his own grown-up and worthy son in order to please an infant of three years (or at the utmost seven); though Ishwari Singh neither had the blue blood of a Maharana's daughter nor was ever remarkable for intelligence and spirit. Such is the basis of bardic tradition! Sixty years later, when Mahadji Sindhia during the summer of 1789 suffered at this very Mathura from obstinate 'şummer boils' (which are still dreaded in that season at Agra and Mathura), it was ascribed to black magic practised by his enemies.

Such is the 'poison complex' of the Bundi Court poet, who also tells us (*Vamsha Bhaskar*, IV, p. 3033) that Bahadur Shah I was stabbed to death at Lahore by a male music-master who had been smuggled into his harem. This is an absolutely original discovery in the history of the later Mughals. No reason was assigned, no evidence has ever been produced, but suspicion was enough for these retailers of bardic gossip. The death of Shiv Singh, if it was a murder at all, must remain one of the unsolved mysteries of history, like the death of Don Carlos in prison imputed to his father, Philip II of Spain, or that of Tsarevitch Alexis for which his father Peter the Great is blamed.

Notes

1. 'La Cour de Jaipur... a eut la preseance et la mediation sur toutes les autres cours Indiennes aupres de l' Empereur Mogol.' (J. Pillet to John Murray, June, 1794). (The Court of Jaipur... had the authority and mediation on all the other Indian Courts according to the Mughal Emperor.) *J.S.*
2. Omit 'with the help of the Maharana forces', and read: 'by defeating his grandson Badan Singh, the ruler then of Rampura fled. In response to Maharana Sangram Singh's repeated request, ultimately on (Sunday), 16th September, 1716, Emperor Farrukhsiyar granted the *pargana* of Rampura to Maharana ...' (*Jaipur Records*, Sitamau Collection, Misc. Vol. III, p. 11-12. Copy of *parwana* from Sayyed Abdullah Khan, wazir, of 10 shawwal, Jalus Saneh 5. Kapad-Dwara No. 656.) *Ed.*
3. Omit the sentence 'In 1718, at Jai Singh's ... this change.' *Ed.*
4. Omit 'A second split ... Jahangir.', and read 'On Thursday, 1st December, 1631, Shahjehan,' (Lahori, *Padshahnamah*, vol. I-A, p. 401.) *Ed.*

5. Budh Singh's vices were incorrigible. Even the bardic eulogist of his son calls him 'a beast in a human form'. (*Vamsha Bhaskar*, IV, p. 3203.) *J.S.*

6. This date corresponds to Thursday, Ashadha Sudi 9, 1798 V.S., while in '*Fall* I, (IInd ed.) p. 157-8, Sir Jadunath Sarkar himself has dated the battle at 28th May, 1741, corresponding to Thursday, Ashadha vidi 9, 1798 V.S. and 23 Rabi-ul-Awwal, 1154 H. *Jodhpur Rajya ki Khyat* (Vol, II, p. 249) corroborates the date given in *Fall* I. *Ed.*

7. The events leading up to the battle are described from the Browne ms. (Br. Museum Or, 1271) and *Vamsha Bhaskar*, pp. 3297-3305, supported by Jaipur ms. records. The confused and erroneous narrative of Tod (which may have been partly due to mistranslations of *Khyats* made by his clerks or his own careless habit of writing) has been rejected. The best account of the battle is given in the Persian history *Chahar Gulzar-i-Shujai* of Harcharandas, who was present in the battle by the side of one of the three Muslim generals from Agra, though he wrote 45 years afterwards (hence the inaccuracy of his numbers). He gives a horrid picture of the battle-field as it looked when he walked among the dead the next day. Compare the futile charge of the Rathor cavalry on De Boigne's artillery at Merta on 11 September, 1790, the date of the Gangwana battle in the Jaipur records. (Hindi, Sitamau Collection, Vol. 3, p. 58-59.) *Ed.*

XVI

Sawai Jai Singh's City And Observatories

Jaipur City, Its Foundation And Growth

The name of Sawai Jai Singh has been perpetuated by the new capital which he founded. It was originally called Jai-nagar and afterwards Sawai Jaipur, which has been shortened into Jaipur in the popular mouth. After his return from the capture of Thun (1723), Jai Singh lived for four years at Delhi and Mathura, making pilgrimages to the Ganges and the religious ambulation of the holy land of Mathura (*Braja Mandal parikrama*). In 1725 he was busy erecting his Astronomical Observatory in the Jaisinghpura suburb west of Shah Jahan's city. He now issued orders to his officers in Amber to build a palace (Jai Niwas) on the site of his future capital, on the plain below, according to the plans sent.

The nucleus of Jaipur was the palace and garden at Jai Niwas, the foundations of which were laid in 1725. The building of the city and its surrounding walls and gates was started with due propitiatory rites (*sankalpa*) on 18th November, 1727;[1] the astrologer-priest who conducted these ceremonies was granted eight *bighas* of rent free land in Hathroli village (Or. 1271 and J.R.No. 101). Its chief want was water, as the city stands in the midst of a wide belt of sand. But a canal was dug which brought water to it. For this purpose Anandram was commissioned to survey the neighbourhood. His report, written on 16th July, 1726, is still preserved. The source selected was the Jhotwada river four miles north-west of the new city.

Jaipur was built with perfect symmetry; its artery roads are wide; absolutely straight avenues cross broad straight streets at right angles, and the house-facades along the roads are so designed as to produce a uniform artistic effect. The plans were drawn up by a Bengal *brahman* named Vidyadhar Bhattacharya, who was deeply read in the ancient Sanskrit books on architecture and town-building (*silpa-sutra*).[2]

The city of Jaipur stands in a crescent-shaped valley embosomed among hills on three sides of it, which are strongly fortified both by nature and art, while the fourth or southern side has no defence except the city wall. This wall, rising 20 to 25 feet in height, is of stone, with a brick facing unprotected by either ditch or rampart. It is crenellated with towers at intervals and bastions and lofty screen walls before the gateways. These gates are double, with a space between.

The city stretches about two miles from east to west, between the Gates of the Sun and Moon (the Suraj Pol and the Chand Pol), and is laid out in rectangular blocks. The central avenue, a hundred and twenty feet in breadth, runs throughout its entire length, and is crossed by three wide roads, which thus divide the city into eight equal portions. These again are intersected at regular intervals, and this subdivision is carried on until the thoroughfares become merely small lanes. Its breadth, south to north, from the Ajmer Gate to the foot of the citadel Nahargarh, is one mile.

The central block, called the Sarhad, is set apart for the palace, which occupies about one-seventh of the whole town area. Here the personal establishments of the sovereign are situated, and several of the departmental offices of the State. The most noticeable of the buildings here, besides the residences of the Maharajah and the Ranis, are the Diwan-i-Khas, the Diwan-i-Am, the Astronomical Observatory, and the temples of Brajanandji and Anand Krishnaji.

The Streets And Their Appearance

The principal avenue, called the Grand Chawk, is 120 feet broad, and down the centre of it runs an aqueduct, which affords, by means of wells placed at every 10 or 12 paces, a plentiful supply of water.

In the centre of this street is the principal entrance to the Royal Palace, and another road leading from it in which the Hawa Mahal (Wind Palace) is situated.

All the main streets are bordered with stone edifices. The houses are generally two storeys high, but some rise to three or even four, with ornamented windows and balconies, most of which are finely carved. They are interspersed with handsome temples in the same style as those of Benares. In the centre of the town adjoining the palace is a very noble tower about 200 feet high. All the houses in the principal streets are coloured pink. (To produce the illusion of Akbar's favourite red sandstone city of Fathepur and fort of Agra?) The square in the centre of the town where four main roads meet, serves as a marketplace. Here there is also a reservoir of water constructed of freestone, with twelve or more steps leading to the water's edge.

Sawai Jai Singh, after the completion of his palace and the city wall and gates, devoted his treasure to 'building the *pucca* shops and bazar with every splendour, and summoning traders and bankers, and artisans from Udaipur, Delhi and other places, at a cost of thousands of rupees, colonised Jaipur... Ishwari Singh ordered upper rooms to be built on these shops with stone lattices; whoever pleaded poverty was given money for their construction out of Government funds'. (Or. 1271, pp. 80 and 88.)

The first European account of the city is by the Tyroless Jesuit Father Jose Tieffenthaler, who came to India in 1729 and lived for many years at Narwar. He used to visit Agra often in order to meet Father Andre Strobl, one of the learned astronomers brought by Sawai Jai Singh from Germany. His description of Jaipur may have come from personal observation or from Father Strobl's report. He writes,

> The view of Jaipur city from the hill behind it is ravishing... The city, while it is new, is assuredly the most beautiful among the ancient cities of India, because in the latter everything is old, the streets are unequal and narrow. This, on the contrary, has the splendour of the modern with equal wide and long streets. The principal road, which begins at the Sanganer Gate, and goes on to the South Gate, is so broad that six or seven carriages can drive abreast without difficulty and without having to touch each other or turn aside... There are many temples of idols in the city, of which one is dedicated to *Na-Kalank* or Vishnu, who took the figure of a man without sin at the end of the world...[3]

Such was Jaipur in its pristine beauty. But even in 1820, when the city had fallen into neglect and decay, a British military visitor could remark of it, 'I am disposed to think that, in point of neatness and beauty, the Grand Chawk would scarcely be surpassed by more than half a dozen streets in England,' and he rightly calls it 'the most beautiful city in India'. Bishop Heber who passed through Jaipur four years later, gives it the same high praise, and notes a curious similarity: 'The fortifications of the city... are so like those of the Kremlin that I could almost have fancied myself at Moscow.' (Journal, ii, 397).

Victor Jacquemont's Impressions Of Jaipur And Amber In 1832

But the finest early European account of Jaipur is by a refined French scholar, the personal friend and honoured guest of the Governor-General (1832). He describes the scene thus:

> The main streets are the principal bazars; on each side, under the arcades of the palaces, temples and houses, are the shops of the artisans, who are seen working almost in the open air at their trades, the tailors, shoemakers, goldsmiths, armourers, pastry-cooks, confectioners, copper-smiths etc. The grain-merchants occupy very spacious huts of thatch, constructed in a sort of coarse lattice work,... in the midst of the main streets. The stalls are removed whenever the Rajah issued from his palace. Delhi has only one similar road, namely the Chandni Chawk: but at Jaipur all the roads resemble it and bear that name.
>
> The ordinary houses have been built with the stone of the hillocks around. The houses of a higher rank, built of the same materials, are plastered with a lime cement of brilliant whiteness. The cement is sometimes polished like stucco... Most of the temples and palaces have facings of white marble. There is no hut, no ruined building, no rubbish heap. The city has the look of what it really is, an entirely new town, which has not yet been subjected to the horrors of war. In general, the architecture of Jaipur is of a very elegant style.[4]

The highly sensitive heart of this young French writer could not fail to vibrate at the contrast between the new capital favoured by royalty and Amber, the discarded aged mistress of her Rajahs. He writes:

Amber, which has the melancholy charm of a ruin, is indeed such. It is not more than a hundred years since it ceased to be the residence of the Rajahs of Jaipur, and since the foundation of the new city it has been constantly kept up and at intervals resided in, by the descendants of Jai Singh, who are justly proud of this magnificent monument of the ancient splendour of their house. It is not one palace, it is rather a city of palaces, united to one another in order to form one system of common defence...

The palace of Amber, built by Rajah Man Singh,... is of a purely Indian architecture. Everything here is more grand, more massive, more solid than in the modern constructions of the princes of the house of Timur and in the buildings of the pupils who have followed the taste introduced by them. What struck me first was the resemblance of a multitude of details in the architecture of the palace to the remains of Hindu ruins in the valley of Kashmir. Almost all the columns are, like those of the palace of Shahi-bag, prisms with twelve faces; their socles and their capitals are of the same (pattern), and their friezes are decorated with the same ornaments.

In the palace are courts or square gardens, which are covered with a large awning or *sayaban*, surrounded on four sides by halls which open on the porticoes. Every one of these courts has its basin and, frequently, its jet of water too.

White marble is the stone most lavishly used at Amber. All the columns are cut out of single pieces. The red sandstone of Agra is likewise employed, in the same way as the compact reddish quartz forming the hillock on the steep slope of which the palace is built. It is this great slope of its base that renders its prospect so magnificent, by spreading out all its parts like an amphitheatre...

The terraces of all the edifices of the Amber palace form, as it were, immense steps on the slope of the mountain and overtop its summit. From here we see the ancient city of Amber, which occupies the bottom of many valleys all abutting on the hollow which the lake embellishes. In the west, on the crest of a hillock, still higher than that of Amber and separated from the latter by a valley, towers the fort of Jaigarh, celebrated for its strength and antiquity.

The winter has turned the country-side brown, and framed round by these wild hillocks the lake, with its white marble kiosks and the magnificent verdure of its gardens, forms a ravishing tableau. The gardens deserve the pretty name they bear; they are called *Dil-aram* or peace of the soul.

The city of Amber has fallen into ruin. We can call it a city, marked by a fatal providence, visited by a desolating plague, without an inhabitant, without one voice except the monotonous murmur of the prayer of a *brahman* who has remained faithful to one of its old temples.

The aesthetic soul of Bishop Heber also responded to the spirit of the place, when he visited Amber eight years before the Frenchman. He writes,

> I have seen many royal palaces containing larger and more stately rooms,... but for varied and picturesque effect, for the richness of carving, for wild beauty of situation, for the number and romantic singularity of the apartments, and the strangeness of finding such a building in such a place and country, I am able to compare nothing with Amber... I could not help thinking what magnificent use Ariosto or Sir Walter Scott would have made of such a building.

Palaces In Jaipur City

The Chandra Mahal or principal palace is a massive building of two storeys, from which a magnificent view is obtained of the surrounding hills, forts, and extensive gardens. The ground and other floors of the palace comprise apartments richly decorated with floral designs, embellished with quaint and beautiful paintings, adorned with mirrors, and sumptuously furnished and fitted in the most elegant style.

The Hawa Mahal or 'Palace of the Winds' is a remarkable structure of the Saracenic order of architecture, and has been finely described by Sir Edwin Arnold as

> a vision of daring and dainty loveliness, of storeys of rosy masonry and delicate overhanging balconies and latticed windows. Soaring with tier after tier of fanciful architecture in a pyramidal form, a very mountain of airy and audacious beauty, through the thousand pierced screens and gilded arches of which the Indian air blows cool over the flat roofs of the very highest house. Aladdin's magician could have called into existence no more marvellous abode.

The Diwan-i-am or Hall of Public Audience, is a large stately massive building, open on all sides and supported by marble pillars. Wisely kept free of rich ornamentation, it presents by its simplicity a remarkable contrast to the highly decorated interior of the palace. Bishop Heber calls it 'a noble open pavilion, with marble pillars richly carved, rather inferior in size, but in other respects fully equal to the Hall of Audience in the castle of Delhi. The interior contains an oblong vaulted hall, surrounded by a very spacious verandah.' (ii. 406.)

The Rani's State apartments are extremely beautiful, immediately above the palace gardens, which are laid out in the most tasteful and elegant manner. The rooms are spacious, and decorated with pictures and mosaic work of a superior kind; the ceilings are most exquisitely adorned. (*Asiatic Journal*, 1820.)

Why Jai Singh Built His Observatories

Col. James Tod, not a very friendly critic of Sawai Jai Singh, has admitted that 'he erected monuments which irradiate this dark period of the history of India'. And indeed, no history of Jai Singh would be complete without an account of his astronomical studies and observatories, which are the greatest contribution of the House of Jaipur to the enrichment of India's cultural life.

> Jaipur became the refuge and sanctuary of Hindu learning, and it was from thence that Colonel Polier procured in 1779, the first complete copy of the Vedas, which he afterwards presented to the British Museum. (an English officer writing in the *Calcutta Govt. Gazette*)

Five of the astronomical observatories built by him still survive, at Delhi, Jaipur, Ujjain, Mathura and Benares. Their genesis is thus given in his own words in the preface to his Table of Stars named Zij-i-Muhammad Shahi, in which he speaks of himself in the third person:

> This admiring spectator of the theatre of infinite wisdom... was, from the first dawning of reason in his mind and during his progress towards maturity, entirely devoted to the study of mathematical science,... and by the aid of the Supreme Artificer he obtained a thorough knowledge of its principles and rules. He found that the calculation of the places of the stars, as obtained from the tables in common use (Sanskrit, Arabic and European) in many cases give them widely different positions from those determined by observation, especially in the

appearance of the new moons. Seeing that very important affairs, both regarding religion and the administration of the Empire, depend upon these,... he represented the matter to the Emperor Muhammad Shah, who was pleased to reply:
'Since you, who are learned in the mysteries of science, have a perfect knowledge of this matter, having assembled the astronomers and geometricians of the faith of Islam, and the *Brahmans* and Pandits and the astronomers of Europe, and having prepared all the apparatus of an observatory—do you so labour for the ascertaining of the point in question, that the disagreement between the calculated times of those phenomena and the times which they are observed to happen, may be rectified.

So he (Jai Singh) constructed at Delhi several instruments for astronomical observation... But finding that brass instruments did not come up to ideas which he had formed of accuracy, because of the smallness of their size, the want of division into minutes, the shaking and wearing of their axes, the shifting of the planes of the instruments etc.,... he constructed in Delhi instruments of his own invention, of stone and lime of perfect stability,... such as Jai Prakash, Ram Yantra and Samrat Yantra... And, in order to verify the truth of these observations, he constructed instruments of the same kind in Sawai Jaipur, Mathura, Benares and Ujjain,... so that every person who is devoted to these studies, whenever he wished to ascertain the place of a star—might observe the phenomena.

But seeing that in many cases it is necessary to determine past or future phenomena, and also that... the opportunity of access to an Observatory may be wanting—he deemed it necessary that a table be constructed by means of which the daily places of the stars being calculated every year and disposed in a calendar, may always be in readiness.

After having constructed these instruments, the places of the stars were daily observed. After seven years had been spent in this employment, information was received that observatories had been constructed in Europe and that the learned of that country were employed in the prosecution of this important work... For this reason, having sent to that country several skilful persons along with Padre Manoel de Figueiredo he procured the new tables of stars which had been published there thirty years before under the name of Pere de la Hire (*Tabulae Astronomicae*, completed in 1702) as well as the European tables anterior to these (especially Flamsteed's *Historia Coelestis Britannica*, 1712-1725)... On comparing these tables with actual observations, it appeared that there was an error of half a degree in the former in assigning the moon's place, and there were also errors in the other planets, although not so great—especially in the times of the eclipses... Hence he concluded that,

> since in Europe astronomical instruments have not been constructed of such a size and such large diameters, the motions which have been observed with them may have deviated a little from the truth.

Hence, on the basis of his own long researches, he constructed and published his own astronomical tables, named after his suzerain *Zij-i-Muhammed Shahi*, in 1733.

Jai Singh Gathers Scientific Knowledge From Europeans And All The World

With no less catholicity of mind than wisdom, Sawai Jai Singh called to his aid the best scholarship of the Hindu, Muslim and European worlds. He took his first lessons in Hindu astronomy from Jagannath Pandit, who later translated on his command the ancient Greek scientist Ptolemy's *Syntaxis*, from its Arabic version *Almagest*, into Sanskrit under the name of *Siddhanta Samrat* (also known as *Siddhanta Sar Kaustuva*).

'Jai Singh collected and studied all the available astronomical works.' (G.R. Kaye) For the purpose of acquiring manuscripts of the great medieval Muslim astronomers and apparatus, and also for making observations, he deputed Muhammad Sharif and Md. Mahdi abroad.

> Several European works were translated into Sanskrit under his orders, particularly Euclid's *Elements*, with a treatise on plane and spherical trigonometry; and on the construction and use of logarithms,... and also a treatise on conic sections... maps and globes of the Feringhis were obtained from Surat (Kaye).

But he would not be content unless he could quench his thirst for knowledge at the very fountain-head of European science. For this purpose he made an application to the King of Portugal, through the Viceroy of Goa, for a learned European scientist and also a physician to be sent to Jaipur, whose expenses he would pay. The scholar chosen was Pere Manoel de Figueiredo, the Superior of the 'Mogor Mission' at Agra. He left Goa about 6th November, 1730 for Jaipur, whence he was afterwards sent to Europe with money for buying books and instruments. The doctor who accompanied him to Jaipur was Pedro da Silva Leitao, who settled at the Kachhwa capital and whose son or grandson, known as 'Hakim Shewair', was an influential courtier in 1799. But in the twentieth century his descendants have sunk very low owing to ignorance and economic decay.

Next came, by the Rajah's invitation, two French Jesuits, Claude Boudier and another, who left Chandernagore on 6th January, 1734 and reached Jaipur after taking astronomical observations on the way, at Benares, Mathura and Delhi. Andre Strobl, a Bavarian Jesuit, arrived by ship at Goa on 30th September, 1737, reached Jaipur on 4th March, 1740, and after passing some years at Jaipur, went away to mission work at Narwar in 1749. (He died at Agra in 1758).[5] Another Bavarian Jesuit, Antonne Gabelsperger, accompanied him to Jaipur but died next year. Jai Singh's observatories thus had the benefit of the latest state of scientific knowledge in Europe.

His Chief Astronomical Instruments Described

Technical details and a precise appraisal of the scientific value of each instrument in these observatories would be out of place in a history such as this. For them the reader is referred to A.H. Garrett and C. Guleri's *The Jaipur Observatory and its Builder* (1902), G.R. Kaye's memoirs in volume 40 of the new Imperial series of the Archaeological Survey of India, and the last named writer's short but useful *Guide to the Old Observatories at Delhi*, Jaipur (1920). These works supersede earlier descriptions like those of Tieffenthaler (*c.* 1745) and Dr. W. Hunter (1793). Only the most important instruments will be described here, and briefly, on the authority of Kaye.

> Jai Singh claims to have devised the *Samrat Yantra*, the *Jai Prakash*, and the *Ram Yantra*. These three instruments are indeed peculiar to his Observatories, and must be to some extent attributed to his personal ingenuity.

The *Samrat Yantra* is a huge equinoctial dial, consisting of a triangular gnomon with the hypotenuse parallel to the earth's axis, and on either side of the gnomon is a quadrant of a circle parallel to the plane of the equator. Each edge of the quadrants is graduated in hours and minutes as well as in degrees, and each edge of the gnomon has two seales of tangents. At Jaipur it is 90 feet high, 147 feet long, and the radius of each quadrant is nearly 50 feet. At Delhi it is 68 feet high, 125 feet from east to west and 113.5 feet from north to south.

The *Jai Prakash* is a hemisphere on the concave side of which are mapped out certain coordinates. Cross wires are stretched north to south and east to west, and the shadow of the intersection of the wires falling on the surface of the hemisphere indicates the position of the Sun in the heavens; other heavenly bodies can be observed directly by placing the eye at the proper graduated point and observing the passage of the body across the point of intersection of the wires. For this purpose the instrument is duplicated. At Delhi it has a diameter of 27 feet, five inches, and at Jaipur ten feet less.

The *Ram Yantra* is a cylindrical instrument open at the top and with a pillar at its centre. The floor and the inside of the circular wall are graduated for altitude and azimuth observations. To facilitate observation the floor is broken up into sectors—30 at Delhi, 12 at Jaipur. The walls are also broken up and one section of the wall corresponds to one sector. On each side of the wall sections are notches in which sighting bars can be placed horizontally.

The *Digamsha Yantra* or azimuth instrument, is a small and useful device, consisting of a pillar surrounded by two circular walls. Cross wires are stretched from the cardinal points on the outer wall, and both walls are graduated.

The *Narivalaya Yantra* is a cylindrical dial, the axis of the cylinder being horizontal and pointing north and south, and the northern and southern faces being parallel to the plane of the equator. There are also two 'meridian circles' of different designs.

The final appreciation of his scientific achievement can be best given in the words of a specialist like G.R. Kaye.

> The Hindus had no instrument of precision before Jai Singh's time; neither were they interested in making practical observations of the heavenly bodies; their rules and the elements given in their approved works sufficed for them... But the work of Jai Singh was exactly of that nature which differentiates between the two schools, Hindu and Muslim astronomy. What the Muslim astronomers had, and what the Hindu lacked, attracted Jai Singh.

That Jai Singh made no new astronomical discoveries is hardly a fair criterion of the value of his work; for, indeed, a great deal of the most valuable astronomical work is not concerned with new discoveries. His avowed object was the rectification of the calendar, the prediction of eclipses, and so on... Considering the state of the country in which Jai Singh lived, the political anarchy of his time, the ignorance of his contemporaries, and the difficulties in the way of transmission of knowledge, his scheme of astronomical work was a notable one, and his observatories still form noble monuments of a remarkable personality.

Notes

1. *Jaipur Records*, Hindi, Sitamau Collection, vol. III, p. 53. *Ed.*
2. An absurd story was told to the British military officers who visited Jaipur in 1820; that 'the plan of the city was laid out by an Italian, who had gone thither in his early youth, and who was specially sent by the Rajah to Europe, to be instructed in the knowledge of the arts and sciences necessary for the completion of his plans. The Italian was amply supplied with the means of obtaining every sort of information, and after several years returned to Jaipur, it is added, to his honour, that he brought back with him a very considerable portion of the money that has been advanced to him, and that he died in the city which his talents and ingenuity had principally formed. It is probable that this story may not be correct in every particular, but it is certain that the arrangement of the building and streets of Jaipur is superior to the genius of a Rajput or any other native of India.' (*Calcutta Government Gazette*, 1820).

   Yes, a black man can do nothing good. That is why some Europeans have started the canard that the Taj Mahal was designed by an Italian named Austin de Bourdeaux. The above story confounds the Jesuit Fathers sent by Jai Singh to Europe with money for buying astronomical books and instruments with a mythical Italian city-planner. The honest European who died at Jaipur was the Jesuit Father Gabelsperger, no Italian.

   Vidyadhar, the true designer, occupies a proved position in the Jaipur Government service, as the State records show. He was promoted to be a *Desh Diwan* in 1729 and rewarded in 1734 for the speedy construction of a seven-storeyed palace and in 1735 for bringing the Dravayavati river to Jaipur city. Many more rewards to him are on record, including an elephant on 23 February, 1751. On the last date he was a bed-ridden invalid, and he died in April next. His father was named Santoshram, his son Murlidhar was a *Desh Diwan* and held a *jagir* worth Rs 5000 a year. Murlidhar's son named Lakshmidhar drew Rs 800 annually.. A street in the middle of Jaipur city is named after Vidyadhar and a garden two miles south-east of the city, at Ghat, is named *Vidyadhar-ka-bagh*. *J.S.*

3. *Description Geographique...De l'Inde,* tr. par Bernouli, i. 314-317. *J.S.*
4. V. Jacquemont, *Etat Politique et... de l'Inde du Sud,* 33-37 (including Amber). *J.S.*
5. Tod's wish, 'It would be worth ascertaining whether the archives of Lisbon refer to this circumstance' *viz.*, the sending of Portuguese scientists to Jai Singh, has been gratified in our own days by the research of Chevalier Panduranga Pissurlencer, in his *Ultimas Embaixadas Portuguesas a Corte Mogol*. I have based this section on that work, as well as Tieffenthaler's *Description... de l'Inde*, French version by Bernoulli, and Kaye's well-known guide, with a date from Br. Mus Or. 1271. *J.S.*

XVII

Sawai Jai Singh's Achievement And Character

The Expansion Of The Jaipur Kingdom

When Sawai Jai Singh, then just entering into his teens, succeeded to the throne of Amber, his heritage had been greatly curtailed by Aurangzib's vindictive pursuit of Ram Singh and Ram Singh's progeny. The new Rajah held the low rank of a Commander of 1500 (nominal), and for years after even a well-deserved promotion by 500, though recommended by his superior general of conspicuous service, was delayed in the giving by that jealous old Emperor. We shall here see how, step by step, this Kachhwa prince raised his kingdom to the richest position in Rajasthan while he himself became for all practical purposes the supreme counsellor at Court in the last fifteen years of his life.

A mass of contemporary letters, Imperial rescripts, orders and other State papers of the highest value, dating from 1620, have come to light during the exploration of the ancient State archives of Jaipur, conducted recently under a historical expert's guidance, as preparatory to the writing of this history. These original documents enable us to reconstruct the growth of this kingdom stage by stage with the greatest accuracy and minuteness of detail. Such an authentic account must henceforth replace the ignorant or prejudiced outpourings of bardic traditionalists and the short perfunctory and unfair narrative which Lt.

Col. Tod has vouchsafed to the annals of the most illustrious dynasty of Rajasthan.

First, the territorial expansion of the Kachhwa State. In 1594 or Bhagwant Das's time,[1] and later under Man Singh, the Jaipur Rajahs held extensive *jagirs* in the Panjab and Bihar, besides suburban villages (*puras*) with extra-territorial jurisdiction near many provincial capitals where they served, such as Patna, Aurangabad, etc. But we are not concerned with them because they never formed integral parts of the *kingdom* of Jaipur and many of them have now been lost to this royal house. We shall confine our attention to the growth of their dominions in Rajputana alone.

In the geography of the Mughal Empire, the largest territorial unit was a *subah* or province, which term then represented an area smaller than a province of British India, and was roughly equal to two or three Commissioner's Divisions as known today. Next below came the *sarkar*, being equal to a modern district or often rather smaller than that. Still lower units were called *mahals* or *parganas*, which roughly corresponded to the sub-divisions of a district.

We know that the standard or theoretical revenue of the Rajahs of Jaipur in the middle of the eighteenth century was one *kror* of rupees[2] though during the dark days of the Maratha and Pindhari ravages it shrank to one-third of that amount or even less. The only addition to the area of the State after Jai Singh II, was made by Madho Singh who gained (1753) the fort and sub-district of Ranthambhor, the revenue of which in 1590 was about Rs 40,000 (after correcting the printed text of the *Ain-i-Akbari*).

In Akbar's reign Amber was a *pargana* under the headquarters district (*sadr sarkar*) of the *subah* of Ajmer, and its estimated revenue was a little over three lakhs (3,06,407). This was the kernel of the kingdom of Jaipur. We have seen that Shah Jahan gave Kama to Mirza Rajah Jai Singh's son Kirat Singh, the revenue of which, under Akbar, was Rs 48,000. Other acquisitions of the same Rajah were Chalkaliana (two lakhs a year) and Tonk (worth Rs 1,87,500 a year, as the reward of his subjugation of Shivaji in 1665, but not Toda as yet). No further additions were made to the family possessions from this time, namely Shivaji's flight from Agra, to the death of Jahandar Shah (1666-1713), as the Kachhwa Rajahs during the intervening years lay under the wrath of successive Emperors. But the accession of Farrukhsiyar brought about a complete change in Sawai Jai Singh's fortunes and he rapidly extended his possessions by Imperial grants.

These are detailed below with the serial numbers of the supporting documents.[3]

Ram Singh's *jagir* in 1666 yielded about 20 lakhs of rupees a year, as we have seen in Chapter XII where the names of the 20 *parganas* constituting it are given. It should be borne in mind that these were held on service tenure and were therefore liable to resumption at the Emperor's will. They therefore belonged to a different category from his ancestral heritage, Amber (worth probably five lakhs at the time).

On Friday, 28th May, 1714, a grant of Rs 48,350 on the revenue of *pargana* Bhangarh (also known as Khara) was made to Jai Singh II and some other officers collectively. The language suggests that it was a confirmation or renewal and not an altogether new gift (No. 38).

On 10th September, 1716, *pargana* Malarna,[5] then worth Rs 3,33,273 a year, was granted in *jagir* to Jai Singh *vice* Rajah Bahadur (No. 46). On 5th April, 1717, Rs 80,000 in *pargana* Amarsar was granted to him *vice* Khan Jahan Bahadur (No. 52). On 9th October, 1717, *jagirs* yielding two and a half lakhs of rupees were granted to Jai Singh's contingent; this grant, as arranged to Jagjivandas at the Imperial Court, included Jhilai, Uniara and Barwara (No. 40). On Saturday, 19th July, 1718, Rs 80,413 in *pargana* Naraina, *sarkar* Amarsar or Muminabad, was transferred to Jai Singh *vice* Ali Khan and other Turki slaves (*qular*) (No. 57, also 50). This grant covered a little over one-fifth of the total revenue of Amarsar; Jai Singh's possessions included the village of Hasthira, 12 miles north of Amarsar town (Nos. 64, 69, 77). On 27th October, 1725, *pargana* Manoharpur, ·yielding Rs 27,525 was transferred from Inayet Khan to Jai Singh (No. 75).

On 31st January, 1727, the total *jagirs* of Jai Singh in these three *parganas*—Amarsar, Naraina and Manoharpur were officially estimated to yield Rs 2,30,030 (No. 88). A further transfer of Rs 12,500 worth of land in Amarsar *pargana* was made to him, *vice* Muharram Khan on (Tuesday), 20th August, 1728 (No. 94).

The History Of The Shekhawati Subdivision

In the following decade 51 *parganas* wrested from Qaim Khan of Jhunjhuno, were granted in *ijara* to Jai Singh for a quitrent of Rs 25 lakhs annually payable by him to the Emperor. These were therefore not held on service tenure. 16 out of these 51 are named in the British Museum Persian manuscript Or. 1271 (compiled for Major James Browne in 1785) and also in Muna Lal's contemporary *History of Shah Alam II* (written at the Delhi Court in Persian). They were Narnaul and Kanud (15 miles north of Narnaul, now belonging to the Patiala Rajah); *Kanti* (12 miles east of Narnaul city), now belonging to Nabha State; Ajabgarh, Bhangarh, Bagar Meo, Narhar, Thanah Ghazi etc.—since then annexed by Alwar State. The *parganas* that still belonged to Jaipur State are, Kot-Putli, Bairat, Sanghana, Fatehpur (29 miles north of Jaipur city) and many others.

The other story of the acquisition of these 51 *parganas* is thus given by the two contemporary Persian authorities (1784-1790) mentioned above:

Daulat Khan Qaimkhani, an Imperial captain of Fatehpur, when returning from Delhi was treacherously murdered by his own brother Abdullah Khan at Rewari. On hearing of it Daulat Khan's widow complained against the usurper. A Jaipur army conquered the district and it was annexed to the Kachhwa Kingdom, and five villages out of it were given to the widow for her maintenance.

Qaim Khan of Jhunjhuno was an Imperial *mansabdar*. He engaged in battles with the Shekhawats, slaying 80 of their sardars. Only one named Sardul Singh remained alive, whom Qaim Khan engaged as his servant and made his chief man of work. Qaim Khan and the Afghans of Bagad held *mansabs* under the Emperor, but were very proud and disobedient, refusing to go where ordered on service. So Muhammad Shah wrote to Sawai Jai Singh to expel them from their *mahals* and appropriate those lands. By order of the Emperor, Jai Singh wrote to Sardul Singh to fight Qaim Khan and take possession of Jhunjhuno. It was done. *Parganas* Narnaul, Kotputli, etc. were in the *jagir* of the Imperial wazir Qamr-ud-dim Khan Itimad-ud-daulah. At the request of Jai Singh the wazir gave him these *parganas* in *ijara* in return for 25 lakhs of rupees a year and sent a *sanad* to this effect to the Rajah. Jai Singh used to pay the amount year by year, and since then these 51 *parganas* have remained in the possession of the Jaipur Government.

With regard to Manoharpur, the Browne ms. gives the following account: Rao Sakat Singh of Manoharpur died and was succeeded by his son Jaswant Singh. Sawai Jai Singh wrote to the Emperor asking for Manoharpur to be given to him in return for a *nazarana* of two lakhs of rupees. It was accepted and Jai Singh took possession of that place. Rao Jaswant went to Delhi to make an appeal, but no one paid any heed to him.

At the request of the Shekhawats, Jai Singh granted Amarsar with 12 villages to Kumar Nathu Singh. 'Nobody asked for an explanation of this matter.' (pp. 85-87.)

In the reign of Madho Singh, not only was Ranthambhor gained, but Uniara fort was wrested from its refractory chief Sardar Singh after a four month investment. Madho Singh established his own rule there, and Sardar Singh took refuge in Dig, where he lived on a daily allowance (p. 103). Another refractory vassal of Jaipur, the Naruka Pratap Singh (founder of Alwar State), was similarly attacked by Madho Singh in punishment for his disobedience to his leige-lord's orders, and Madho Singh's direct rule was established over Macheri (old name of Alwar), Rajgarh and other places in that district (p. 104). This baron was afterwards pardoned and reinstated for his loyalty in the war with Jawahir Singh Jat.

Jai Singh Praised By The Bundi Poet

An estimate of Jai Singh's character and achievements given by the Court-poet of his mortal enemy, the house of Bundi, cannot be said to err on the side of flattery. It is therefore translated below:

> In cleverness, in statesmanship, in counsel the *Kurm* (i.e., Kachhwa Rajah) was foremost, and all the Hindu and Muslim nobles were below him. The lord of Delhi did everything as the Kachhwa told him...
>
> Jai Singh, the upholder of religion, performed the Vedic rites, mastered the scriptures (*smriti*), assembled the *brahmans*, followed the rules of the *Dharma Shastras* and thus unfolded the path for the good of the four castes and the four stages of

ordered life (*ashram*). Having studied the 14 branches of knowledge, he mastered the rules of moral conduct (*niti shastra*), and set himself to learn the 54 arts (*kala*). Strong in the strength of all the seven departments (*amsha*) of his kingdom, he kept down his peers among the Rajahs. The kings of Aryavarta used to look up to his face, the Delhi ministers could not reach the speed of his wisdom. The Emperor used to regard the Glory of Amber as his strongest supporter, despising all other Rajahs.

He performed the fire sacrifice (*agni-hotra*) yajna daily; he alone performed the Horse Sacrifice; he adored God through the suppression of sin. The son of Vishnu Singh became manifest to all as the Sun reigning alone in the sky at day. Protected by the God Vishnu, Jai Singh went forth to the lord of Delhi, and through the blessings of the *brahmans*, by his policy aimed at spiritual and material prosperity, he ruled like King Bhoja of yore. (*Vamsha Bhaskar*, IV, 3089-3102. The poet here rose to the sublime of Sanskrit versification, the vernacular tongue being deemed unworthy of such a lofty theme.)

The Military Strength And Prestige Of Jai Singh

We have seen the wealth and territory of Jai Singh II. His army was similarly powerful in northern India. We know that in 1732 he undertook, as governor of Malwa, to maintain 30,000 soldiers, in equal proportion of horsemen and foot-musketeers. These did not include his contingents in the *subahs* of Agra and Ajmer and in his own dominions and fort garrisons. The French captain J. Pillet, who wrote from Jaipur in 1794, asserts that this Rajah maintained 'more than 75,000 cavalry, mostly of his own clan'. This must be considered a popular exaggeration, because a body of only one thousand *regular* cavalry cost three lakhs of rupees a year, and Pillet's number would have consumed two and a quarter *krores*. Similarly we must discount the Persian historian Warid Teharani's figure of '30,000 horse and a still larger number of matchlockmen'. Such inflated numbers were probably formed by counting the occasional tribal levies or rustic militiamen who were called to the colours for a few months or even a few weeks only and for purely local defence.

Therefore Jai Singh's *regular* army did not exceed 40,000 men, which would have cost about 60 lakhs a year. But its strength lay in the large number of artillery and copious supply of munitions which he was careful to maintain and his rule of arming his foot with matchlocks instead of the traditional Rajput sword and shield. From a letter of the Emperor to him we can infer that *every* Rajput serving under Jai Singh in his campaigns fought with a musket. He had the wisdom to recognize early the change which firearms had introduced in Indian warfare and to prepare himself for the new war by raising the fire-power of his army to the maximum. Here he anticipated the great Delhi generalissimo Mirza Najaf Khan (who died in 1782), though he did not engage any drilled sepoy regiments, the time for which class of warriors came after his death.

This armed strength made him the most formidable prince in northern India, and all the other Rajahs looked up to him for protection and the promotion of their interests at the Imperial Court. The Jaipur records still preserve many letters addressed to him by the Maharanas of Udaipur, the Rajahs of Marwar, Chhatra Sal Bundela of Mahoba, Maharao Arjun Singh and Durjan Sal Hada of Kota, and Khande Rao, the Regent of Narwar, all of whom appeal to Sawai Jai Singh for protection, and flatter him as 'the head and crown of all Hindustan', 'the great one, a god', 'the protector of all Hindustan', 'the saviour of the honour of this house' etc.[6]

Jai Singh Relieves The Hindus Of The Empire From Oppressive Taxes

The power and position at Court which Jai Singh II had justly acquired was generously employed by him in removing the grievances and promoting the interests of the Hindus all over the Mughal empire, and we possess acknowledgments of sincere gratitude from his brother Rajahs for the success of his mediation in these matters. The best illustration is supplied by the abolition of the *jizya* tax through his efforts, seconded at one stage by Girdhar Bahadur Nagar.

The *jizya* or poll-tax on non-Muslims is as old as the origin of the Muhammadan religion. Conquered populations were called upon to embrace Islam or pay a money-tax (in three grades according to income) every year as the 'price of protection' of life and property which was granted to them. The 'faithful' who did not serve in the army or in any other public capacity had not however to pay anything for the protection which *they* enjoyed from the State. This tax, based solely on a man's relations with his maker, was invidious in its nature and oppressive in its collection, as Manucci and the *Vamsha Bhaskar* have shown. The wise Akbar abolished it in 1564, and the 'pious' Aurangzib reimposed it in 1679. In January, 1713, the new Emperor Farrukhsiyar abolished it; but on Wednesday, April 3, 1717 he was coerced by his new diwan Inayet-ullah (an ex-Secretary and blind admirer of Aurangzib) to enforce it again. When doing so, the Emperor sent an apologetic letter to Jai Singh to the effect, 'Inayetullah has placed before me a letter from the Sherif of Mecca urging that the collection of *jizya* is obligatory according to our Holy Book. In a matter of faith, I am powerless (to interfere).' (*J.R.* Add, II, p. 4.)

After the fall of Farrukhsiyar (19 February, 1719) the Sayyid king-makers, at the prayer of Ajit Singh, Bhim Singh (of Kota) and Rajah Ratan Chand, abolished the tax, but owing to the political turmoil, the order was not carried out. At the end of 1720, after the fall of the two Sayyid brothers, the Hindu traders of Delhi, owing to the famine and high price of grain, closed their shops as a protest against the *jizya* which imposed an unjustifiable burden on the starving population. Jai Singh took the matter in hand and laid their case before the Emperor Muhammad Shah. He pointed out that the Hindus were the ancient inhabitants of the country, that His Majesty was Emperor of Hind, that men of both religions were equally loyal. When Sayyid Abdullah Khan's rebellion had broken out (1720), he, Jai Singh, had called on all the Hindus to pray for Muhammad Shah's success. If their prayers should be heard, he had bound himself to ask first of all for the abolition of the poll-tax. Yielding to Jai Singh's appeal, the Emperor Muhammad Shah abolished the *jizya* permanently. (*Later Mughals*, ii. 103.) Thanks poured upon Jai Singh from all quarters of the Hindu world.

In June 1728, he secured from the Emperor a *parwana* abolishing the tax on pilgrims at Gaya, which used then to yield Rs 57,500 a year. (*J.R.* No. 489.) About 1730, the Emperor at this Rajah's request withdrew the long standing tax levied on Hindus for bathing at certain holy places. (*J.R.* 507.)

Yet another example of his eagerness to remove the unjustifiable grievances of the Hindus occurred on 4th June, 1721, when Muhammad Shah was induced to issue the following order:

> It has been represented to his Majesty by Sawai Jai Singh that Bairagis, Mahants, Sannyasis and other faqirs, both Hindu and Muslim, build houses and temples in the Imperial dominions, and live on the food bestowed by God. When they die the clerks of the royal Escheat Department (*Bait-ul-mal*) attach all their property to the State and do not allow to their successors access to the houses and goods left behind by the deceased, though intended for charity and the supply of food to faqirs and beggars. For this reason their dead bodies lie neglected for two or three days. Though orders were issued against this practice in the reign of the late Emperor and in the present reign also, the officers have not obeyed them. This fresh prohibition is issued by the wazir. (*J.R.* No. 65).

Jai Singh's Social Reforms And Public Charity

These do not exhaust the list of Jai Singh's acts of public charity for general benefit. He built many *caravan-serais* for the comfort of travellers, and set up rest-houses with free kitchens at Ajodhya, Mathura and some other holy cities. (*J.R.* 59.) He performed the *vajpeya* sacrifice (commencing on 28th July, 1734, and lasting over a month) and also the Aswamedh sacrifice, 1734, an account of which may be read in Tod. These are noticeable for the encouragement of Sanskrit scholarship and extensive charity which resulted from them, and must not be dismissed as instances of personal vanity.

The best proof of Jai Singh's liberal mind and spirit being ahead of his time is afforded by his attempts at social reform, no less than by his astronomical researches and perfect planning of cities. He tried to induce the various sub-sections of the *brahman* caste to dine together as a preliminary of their union, but he succeeded only in part. In order to save the Rajputs from the crushing load of extravagance (ordained by primeval custom) at the marriage of their children, he framed some useful sumptuary laws, but could not enforce them in that backward self-willed society. To remedy the immorality prevalent among the wandering Hindu friars (bairagis and sadhus), who had nominally vowed to celibacy, he tried to introduce the practice of lawful marriage among them, and endowed a village near Mathura, which they were financially helped to settle in as householders. (G.H. Ojha)

So many, so great, and so many-sided were the achievements

which Jai Singh II crowded into a short life of 56 years. He was no mere selfish aggrandiser of his own kingdom, but a general benefactor of the people all over Hindustan, as well as the most farsighted statesman and the most scholarly and intelligent prince in the Delhi empire in his age. From this long survey of his life and deeds we can understand why a hostile critic of his like the poet Suraj Mal Mishran is forced to admit that 'this Kachhwa Rajah was great-souled and the favourite of the Gods'.

Notes

1. Bhagwant Das had died on Margsirsa sudi 7, 1646. v.s. i.e., 4th December, 1589. At the time of his death, a *mansabdar* of 5000, and the same *mansab* was conferred on his son and successor Raja Man Singh. *Ed.*
2. J. Pillet wrote in 1794: 'See (de Sawai Jai S.) demaines excedoint un corol, et it en avoit bien advantage tant a ferme, que pour l' entretien des troupes qu'il avaoit constamment au service due Roi (Mogol.)' (India Office ms.) Also V. Jacquement, writing in 1832.
[See (de Sawai Jai S.). A vast property, and a good means to maintain the troops that he had preserved for the service of the king, (Mogol).] *J.S.*
3. When the *Ain-i-Akbari* was compiled (c. 1590), the assessed revenue of Amarsar *Pargana* was Rs 1,75,000; but when Jai Singh II gained it (in 1718) the records of the Imperial Revenue Department returned an assessment of Rs 3,80,000 or an increase of more than two-fold (to be exact, 217 per cent). This proportion may be taken as a rough measure of the revenue expansion during the intervening century and a quarter of orderly government and natural growth of prosperity. *J.S.*
4. Some of these *parganas* are recorded to have been freshly granted to Sawai Jai Singh about 1727, proving that they had been lost to his family after Ram Singh's time. *J.S.*
5. Document No. 46, of 4 Shawwal Julus Saneh 5, (Monday, 10th September, 1716) mentions the grant of Malpura instead of

Malarna. (Jaipur Records, Sitamau Collection. Additional Persian Vol. II, p. 1 & 2.) Malarna had already been granted previously by Aurangzib to Sawai Jai Singh. *Ed.*

6. J.R. Nos. 424, 442, 445, 449, 448, 79, 80, 82, etc.—*Maharajah sara Hindustan ka sir-posh. Raj thakur ho, bara ho, het maya rakho hoti,... J.S.*

XVIII

Ishwari Singh, 1743-1750

The Problems Facing Ishwari Singh On His Accession

Sawai Jai Singh's active career had been even longer and more eventful than that of the Mirza Rajah his namesake or of Man Singh, once the premier peer of the Delhi throne. He left to his successor an Imperial legacy and a fatal curse. By the treaty of Udaipur (1708), he had promised to give his throne to any son he might have by the Udaipuri princess he was then marrying and set aside the claims of all elder sons borne to him by his other queens. On this condition alone would the Maharana consent to mingle his blood with that of a family which had, 'given daughters to the Turk'. Jai Singh's only son by this Mewar princess was Madho Singh, born in December, 1738, who had two step-brothers older than himself, namely Shiv Singh and Ishwari Singh. Shiv Singh had served as his father's deputy in the office of *faujdar* of Mathura, and died suddenly about 1724.

Ishwari Singh, as the eldest surviving son of Sawai Jai Singh, assumed the crown of Jaipur, and his succession was recognized by the Emperor Muhammad Shah. But it was a crown of thorns that he placed on his head, and he had not a day of peace during his reign of seven years. Bundi, Jodhpur and the Maharana were all up against him and they could always buy the help of some selfish faction among the Kachhwa baronage. We shall deal with his rival half-brother first.

Madho Singh's Early Attempts To Oust Ishwari Singh

After his accession, Ishwari Singh stayed at home for a year, and then visited Delhi, where the Emperor put the mark of investiture (*tika*) with his own hand on the new Rajah's forehead. Taking advantage of his absence from his realm, Maharana Jagat Singh took the field to wrest the throne of Jaipur for his nephew Madho Singh, and advanced to Jamoli, five miles west of Jahajpur, and halted for 40 days, a Jaipur force facing him. Hemraj Bakhshi, the Kachhwa commander guarding this frontier, pretended to go over to Madho Singh after receiving a sum of money as the pay of his troops, but secretly wrote to Ishwari Singh to come to the defence of his kingdom. Ishwari Singh quickly returned from Delhi to Jaipur, and secured Maratha aid by the promise of a subsidy. But no battle took place; the sardars on the two sides arranged for a peace, on condition that Ishwari Singh should give Madho Singh an appanage of five lakhs of rupees a year (namely *parganas* Tonk and Toda and three others, with the city of Tonk) where the latter prince must construct a home and live in peace. This paper, dated 19th December, 1744, is signed by Baba Bakht Singh, Baba Nathji, Kaka Bhagat Singh and Thakur Sardar Singh (*J.R.*, 120,[1] *Vamsha Bhaskar*, 3328, but the Maratha letters put the revenue at 24 lakhs and *J.R.* 119[2] at 23 lakhs, referring probably to a late demand).

Ishwari Singh paid the Marathas 20 lakhs of rupees, but as the Maharana would not (or really could not) pay his moiety of the war-indemnity to the Deccanis, early in 1745 the Maratha partisans of Ishwari Singh surprised the Mewar camp at midnight, fired rockets into it and put the troops to flight. Madho Singh and his uncle escaped to Udaipur and Ishwari Singh repudiated his first agreement. Then the Marathas went back to their southern homes and Ishwari Singh to his capital.

The Deccanis were made arbiters of the throne of Jaipur, as the result of this fratricidal war. While the Peshwa had been hired by Ishwari Singh, the Maharana sent an agent (Kaniram) to Malhar Holkar, promising to pay the Marathas 20 lakhs if they could secure for Madho Singh a *jagir* of 24 lakhs a year from his brother, and thus Holkar became Madho Singh's partisan in the council of the Peshwa.

In 1747 an unprecedentedly severe famine raged throughout Rajputana and Gujarat. There was a total failure of the seasonal rains, the water-courses dried up, men and cattle perished by tens of thousands for lack of food and water. (And yet the two sides kept up their armies on a war footing in this war of brother against brother.) On 4th October, 1746, Ummed Singh (the dispossessed heir of Bundi) and Madho Singh (the pretender to the Jaipur throne) met Maharana Jagat Singh at Nathdwara and formed plans for avenging their late defeats at the hands of Ishwari Singh. They sent agents to Kalpi to hire a Maratha brigade, offering Holkar two lakhs of rupees. Malhar Rao, against the advice of his colleagues Ranoji Sindhia and Ramchandra Baba Shenvi, sent his young son Khande Rao at the head of a thousand horse to support these three Rajput chiefs in order to compel Ishwari Singh to cede four *parganas* to Madho, restore Bundi to Ummed, and allow the three *parganas* of Nenve, Samidhi and Karwar to be held by Rao Rajah Durjan Sal of Kota and Pratap Singh of Karwar (both supporters of Ummed's cause).

The Battle Of Rajmahal, March, 1747

From Kalpi, by way of Udaipur, Khande Rao crossed the southern frontier of Jaipur and reached Rajmahal on the Banas river (ten miles north of Deoli cantonment). He was joined on the way by the contingents of Udaipur and Kota. The allied army, swollen to vast numbers, was faced by the Jaipur general Narayandas, who was averse to war. Efforts at peace were made both from Delhi and Jaipur. But Ishwari Singh decided to hasten to the scene and crush the invaders before they could be reinforced by the Maharana who was coming up from behind with the rest of his troops. He transferred the command of his advanced division to Haragovind Natani, a tradesman by caste but an exceptionally brave and able general, and himself arrived with the reserve, one day's march behind the fighting front.

The battle began at noon on Sunday, the first of March, 1747, and ended at sunset the next day. The allies were completely defeated, though both sides suffered heavily. Each contingent of the ill knit invading army was successively attacked and routed through the skilful planning and personal leadership of Haragovind. The only stand made was that of a Kota vassal, the laird of Koilapur-Patan. Madho Singh's standard-bearing elephant and band, all his artillery and camp-baggage, were captured by the Jaipur troops. At night the victors slept in the deserted tents of the Mewar army. During the fighting, Khande Rao Holkar, who in the usual Maratha manner, had stood apart, fell upon the Jaipur camp in conjunction with Bhopatram Charan, the Hada general; but was repulsed by the Shekhawat guards, after some amount of looting. From the lost field Durjan Sal fled to Kota and young Holkar retired to Bundelkhand. The Maharana, who was coming up in support, turned back from the way and sought refuge in his capital.

Rajmahal was a great victory. It was also a pure Kachhwa victory unaided by a single foreign sword. Ishwari Singh arrived on the field the day after the fight and took up the pursuit. Mewar now felt the heavy hand of the victor; its rich trade-centre at Bhilwara was captured and a large ransom exacted. Continuation of the war was impossible; grain was selling at famine prices, and even a bundle of grass cost a rupee. The Maharana's war expenses had run up to Rs 12,000 a day. He then begged for peace, which was granted on his promising a large war-indemnity. A tribute was also exacted from Kota. Ishwari Singh now returned to Jaipur in triumph (April, 1747).

The Fight With Ummed Singh For Bundi

We shall now turn to the ever-fluctuating tides of the contest for the throne of Bundi between Dalel Singh (supported by his brother-in-law Ishwari Singh) and Ummed Singh Hada who secured Maratha aid, besides being joined by Ishwari Singh's rival Madho Singh. Budh Singh, the dispossessed Lord of Bundi, had died in exile in 1739. Jai Singh's death in 1743 broke the terror under which his enemies lay. Ummed, joined by Durjan Sal Hada, the Maharao of Kota, laid siege to Bundi on 10th July, 1744. Fakhr-ud-daula, the incoming *subahdar* of Gujarat, on his way to Ajmer, was hired by Durjan Sal's agent for one lakh of rupees and lent the aid of his troops in the attack of Bundi. That fort was stormed on 28th July. The defeated Dalel Singh fell back on Taragarh, from which he continued to offer a stubborn resistance. Ishwari Singh had hurriedly sent up an army to his support, but the campaign went against the Kachhwas. Ummed Singh occupied all the Bundi territory, because Ishwari Singh had soon afterwards to leave for Delhi (*c.* October, 1744). The Jaipur cause in Bundi was left in the hands of his minister Rajah Aya Mal Khatri and Maratha aid was secured for money, out of the copious treasury amassed by Sawai Jai Singh. Ummed found friends in Abhai Singh of Jodhpur and Rana Jagat Singh of Mewar. The last-named ruler promised Malhar 20 lakhs for wresting the Kachhwa crown for his nephew Madho. The Mewar envoy exchanged turbans with Jayappa Sindhia in token of brotherhood.

But the astute diplomacy of Aya Mal dissolved the alliance, and evidently by bidding higher secured for his master the support of all the Maratha generals except Malhar. The Jaipur minister on his way back bombarded Kota and plundered much of its territory (*c.* January, 1745). Meanwhile, a Mewar army had crossed the Jaipur frontier and was halting at Toda, waiting for Holkar's arrival. Here Aya Mal's Maratha associates surprised the Maharana's camp at midnight and put his troops to flight. Jagat Singh escaped by promising to pay 22 lakhs. Ishwari Singh now marched on Bundi, which was surrendered by its Kota qiladar. A large Maratha army guided by a Jaipur baron, then bombarded Kota for two months. At last Durjan Sal saved his capital by ceding the district of Kaprani to the Marathas, to be shared between Holkar, Sindhia and the Peshwa (early April, 1745).

Then the satisfied Maratha generals retired and immediately afterwards Ummed, with a gift of 16 lakhs from Durjan Sal, raised a fresh army and advanced upon Bundi. Its Jaipuri Governor Nandram Khatri advanced to oppose him at Bichodi, but was forced to retire and surrender Bundi to Ummed. The victor, however, held his ancestral capital for 16 days only, because on 16th August, a superior Jaipur army defeated him at Devpur and reoccupied Bundi. Ummed Singh wandered for some time after as a homeless fugitive; the attempt of his allies to renew the war with Jaipur failed at Rajmahal on first March, 1747, where Ummed was present in the fight and the flight. The second half of this year saw a drawn battle between Jaipur and the Hadas, after which Ishwari Singh went to Bundi (17th August) and passed some months there in pleasure.

The Battle With Ahmad Shah Durrani At Manupur (Saturday, 12th March, 1748)

Towards the end of this year, the political sky of India was darkened by the threat of an invasion from Afghanistan under Ahmad Shah Durrani, the new master of Nadir Shah's eastern territories and heir to his military genius and ambition.

Near the end of November, 1747 came the news that the Afghan invaders had crossed the frontier passes and taken Peshawar. The Emperor immediately summoned Ishwari Singh to come to his aid with his army and guns. At first the danger was strangely underestimated by the worthless court circle of Delhi. The Emperor delayed his start from Delhi for a full three weeks. Irresolution, conflict of counsel, procrastination and inertia now marked the measures of the Delhi Government to an even more shameful extent than nine years ago when Nadir was threatening it. Seasoned captains told His Majesty that unless he led the army in person, the ease-loving soldiers of Hindustan would not face the veterans of Iran. The wazir seconded this counsel. The Emperor in speech agreed, but he could never resolve on such action and constantly put off the date fixed for his departure. At last, after the Durrani invader was actually threatening Lahore, the Imperial army, headed by the Wazir Qamruddin Khan started from Delhi on Thursday, 14th January, 1748. Lahore had fallen the day before. The nominal head, the Crown Prince Ahmad, began even later, and joined the Delhi army on the way on the last day of the month.

Ishwari Singh, in response to the Emperor's call, had made certain demands as a condition of his armed assistance.[3] At Muhammad Shah's court the anti-Jaipur faction was still strong, and these terms were refused or, in some points, vague general promises were given. Ishwari Singh's zeal for service naturally cooled in proportion. He could not, also, hurry to Delhi, as he had to make elaborate arrangements for the defence of his own territory against the ring of Rajput enemies around it and their Maratha allies, before he could safely set out on this long and dangerous expedition. He, however, reached Delhi on 24th December, 1747, and marched out of it on 12th January,[4] in charge of one of the wings of the wazir's army.

The Imperial army reached Sirhind on 25th February, and leaving its women, heavy baggage, treasure, and surplus stores and carts in that small fort, advanced towards Machhiwara on the Satlaj (88 miles above Ludhiana), *en route* to Lahore. But the entire campaign was mismanaged by 'that aged drunkard and smooth-tongued advocate of utter inaction, the Wazir Qamruddin, its supreme commander' and the lazy pleasure-loving rank and file. The virile alert Afghan invader, slipped round one side of it and captured Sirhind (2nd March), thus cutting into the rear of the imperialists and depriving them of all bases, Lahore in front lost already and Delhi behind now rendered inaccessible. So the Mughal prince beat a hurried retreat and arrived at Manupur, ten miles north-west of Sirhind, where the enemy was sighted, and both parties entrenched. The Afghan patrols on their superb horses, effectually cut off the food supply of the huge unwieldy Mughal camp, consisting of over a lakh of men, and famine appeared imminent.

The Imperial wazir was at last forced to seek a decision by battle, on 11th March. Utter terror ranged in the Delhi ranks, among whom the memory of Persian valour and Persian ruthlessness was still green, and here before them stood the very soldiers of the same Persian conqueror under his best lieutenant.[5] Their position was rendered almost hopeless by the death of their supreme commander in his prayer-tent by the first shot fired by the Afghans, before the ranks could join. The wazir's eldest son Muin-ul-Mulk saved the situation by concealing the death and himself riding out to battle at the head of his father's contingent. We are not here concerned with the course of this battle; the Mughals were saved by the accidental blowing up of a munition tumbril in the Afghan ranks and by Safdar Jang's quick eye for the ground and fine opportunism in the changing phases of the tide of battle. At the end of the day the Afghans were defeated and forced to retreat.

In this glorious though utterly unforeseen result Ishwari Singh had no share. In spite of Muin-ul-Mulk's precaution the news of the wazir's death had reached the Jaipur Rajah as he stood in his own sector of the battle-line. To redouble the mischief, early on that day he had received a courtier from Jaipur, reporting that, taking advantage of his absence in far-off Punjab, his brother Madho Singh had arrived near Jaipur with a larger body of hired Maratha cavalry, and that the Rajah must return home soon if he wished to save his realm. When Narayandas Khatri, his old minister, pressed him to stay for a day and see the battle through (Shambhu Bari and Khanu mahut, whom the Rajah trusted, remarked, 'But, by that time the house and the kingdom would go out of your hands.') Ishwari Singh saw the wisdom of a prompt return: as his rear had been already cut by the Afghan seizure of Sirhind, he could expect to escape unmolested only while the entire Afghan force was absorbed in the life and death struggle on the field of Manupur and no raiding party or patrol of theirs remained to bar the road to Delhi. From his position at the head of the left wing of the Imperial army, he made a hurried retreat during the heat and confusion of the battle, throwing his kettledrums and light artillery into wells and abandoning his baggage to be looted by the ruffianly camp-followers.

But his flight, however, much as it covered him with disgrace and wiped off the glory gained at Rajmahal, had the effect he wished for. At the news of his approach to Jaipur, without a single exchange of blows, Madho Singh fled back to Udaipur and his Maratha allies to Malwa (third week of March, 1748). On the way, the great minister and general Narayandas had died at Rewari, probably from hardship and fatigue. (Or. 1271. Sarkar's *Fall of the Mughal Emprie*, vol. i, ch. v for details.)

The Peshwa Interferes On Behalf Of Madho Singh: The Battle Of Bagru, August, 1748

After his signal defeat at Rajmahal, the Maharana of Udaipur sent an envoy to Puna to entreat the Maratha Court to compel Ishwari Singh to give his brother an appanage worth 24 lakhs a year—or a fourth of the total revenue of his kingdom. In return for it, a contribution of ten lakhs was promised to Rajah Shahu. The Peshwa had hitherto supported Ishwari Singh, out of consideration for Shivaji's friendship with Mirza Rajah and Sawai Jai Singh's assistance to Baji Rao and Balaji Rao. But he was overwhelmed with debt, a legacy from his father which he saw no honest way of paying off. A bankrupt cannot afford to have a conscience. So now (March, 1747) the Peshwa instructed Ramchandra Baba Shenvi to press Ishwari Singh to cede the wished for territory to his brother, if the latter prince paid him 15 lakhs. Malhar Holkar had been won over by Ishwari Singh's enemies earlier. The Peshwa instructed his agents in the north to secure this division of territory by peaceful persuasion if possible.

When this demand for alienating a quarter of his kingdom was placed before Ishwari Singh, he was rightly indignant at the Peshwa's partisanship of his rival, and wrote in reply,

> This question is one of inheritance of ancestral property. We are Rajahs and must follow our hereditary usage. The question relates to territory; how can I oblige the Peshwa in this matter? I had previously given Madho what Malhar had pressed me to grant on the ground of service to the state. He now asks for more. How can I give him that without fighting? How can I bring down upon myself the name of a coward and an unworthy son by dividing my entire kingdom with a younger brother?

In May, 1748, the Peshwa Balaji Rao entered the Kachhwa Kingdom and was joined by Madho and other Rajput chiefs. Ishwari Singh lay crushed under the disgrace of his flight from the field of Manupur; he had not a single friend anywhere. His country was utterly devastated by the Deccani hordes. So he sent his minister Keshavdas to the Peshwa to beg for peace. But the proud Marathas made impossibly high demands, and the negotiations broke down.

In July, a Maratha army under Malhar Holkar and Gangadhar Tatya entered Jaipur territory near Uniara, wrested Tonk Toda and Malpura, and gave these *mahals* to Madho Singh. As they advanced by way of Piplod, Fagi and Ladana, some Kachhwa vassals waited on Madho Singh and did him homage, and several other petty Rajput chiefs joined him, besides the two Hadas Ummed Singh and Durjan Sal. When they reached Bagru, 23 miles east of the Sambhar town, Ishwari Singh, with sadly inferior forces, faced them.

The battle began on first August with an artillery duel, after which the soldiers grappled together at close quarters, but a heavy shower of rain put an end to the fighting for that day. The next morning the battle was renewed with heavy slaughter, but with no decisive result. On the third day Gangadhar Tatya fell upon the guns of the Jaipur rearguard and drove nails into their port-holes. But Suraj Mal Jat, an ally of Ishwari Singh, drove the Marathas back with a counter-attack. In the vanguard the Jats maintained a bloody drawn battle with Holkar's division. The battle raged for six days, often amidst showers of rain. But a convoy of provisions coming to the Jaipur army was intercepted by the Marathas, while 5000 horse under Tatya blocked the road to Jaipur in the rear of Ishwari Singh and raided the country up to the Sambhar lake.

Ishwari Singh, driven into Bagru fort, had at last to make terms, through Keshavdas, who bribed Gangadhar Tatya to soften the obduracy of Malhar Holkar. The Rajah agreed to give five *parganas* to his brother and to restore Bundi to Ummed Singh (9th August). The next day the Marathas began their retreat and a day later Ishwari Singh set out for his capital. Bundi was given up by its Jaipuri *qiladar* on 16th October, and Ummed Singh was formally enthroned five days later. Thus one act of Sawai Jai Singh was at last undone.

The Delhi Invasion Of Marwar: The Battle Of Raona (Pipar), 1750

The year 1749 passed uneventfully for Jaipur. But early in April, 1750, Salabat Khan, the Imperial generalissimo (Mir Bakhshi) invaded Marwar for enthroning Bakht Singh by ousting his nephew Ram Singh (the son and successor of Abhai Singh, who had died on 21st June, 1749). Ram Singh appealed for help to Ishwari Singh, who met him at Jodhpur and decided on war. Their united forces, 30,000 strong with an abundance of artillery, marched from Jaipur and arrived at Pipar, south of Merta, on 4th April. Salabat Khan encamped at the village of Raona, seven miles east of Pipar, on the road to Merta.

But for eight days there was only higgling, bragging and intense suffering on both sides. At last on 14th April, Salabat Khan in desperation ordered a direct attack on Ram Singh's front lines, which were protected by all his big guns. A deadly volley forced the Mughal attack back, and then after a four hours' waste of munition in futile cannonade, the soldiers dispersed in uncontrollable thirst and the battle ceased of itself. On the two sides taken together only 70 or 80 men were killed! After much bombasting and bragging on both sides, peace was made through Ishwari Singh's influence on the 16th, as 'neither side desired war' (the Maratha vakil's report)[6] and the Mughals to a man refused to face the Marwar sun again.

Ishwari Singh promised a tribute of 27 lakhs on condition of the Imperial army withdrawing from Rajputana and the Mir Bakhshi transferring the actual government (*Naib nazimi*) of Agra to him. Ram Singh paid three lakhs down and promised four lakhs more in instalments. Bakht Singh was cast off without pity by his patron. Then all parties went back to their homes.

Shortly afterwards, in September, Ishwari Singh was besought by Samant Singh,[7] the chief of Rupnagar (a staunch ally of Sawai Jai Singh), to help him in recovering his capital from his usurping brother Bahadur Singh. The two allies went to Rupnagar, but as Samant was unable to pay the war expenses, the Jaipur Rajah returned to his capital, leaving only two or three hundred horsemen under Kriparam with Samant, to conduct a languid ineffectual siege of the place.

The Maratha Invasion Of Jaipur: The Suicide Of Ishwari Singh, 1750

It cannot be denied that Ishwari Singh was no fit heir of Sawai Jai Singh. He was too indolent, too fond of pleasure and repose, and too little trained in war, to manage his father's splendid legacy worthily. As a prince he had been denied the experience of campaigning under his father's eyes, the way in which Bishan Singh and Sawai Jai Singh had been shaped into warriors. And now, after the disaster of Bagru (August, 1748) he became a sort of imbecile, buried within his harem. In consequence, confusion seized the internal administration of this noble realm. The able ministers who had so long maintained the power and prosperity of the State were gone, one by one. Rajah Aya Mal Khatri, a master of Persian prose (writing under the pen-name of *Agahi*) and the ablest of Jaipur diplomats and administrators, died on 9th February, 1747. 'All Hindustan mourned for him' reported the Maratha envoy. His son Keshavdas succeeded him as minister, but on a false charge of holding treasonable correspondence which was said to have been fabricated by his rival Haragovind Natani, he was poisoned by command of his master (*c.* August, 1750). The other elder statesman, Vidyadhar, was now a bedridden invalid. The old chief of artillery, Shivnath Bhaya, was thrown into prison with his entire family. (Ishwari Singh's only confidants were a barber[8] (Shambhu Bari) and an elephant-driver (Khanu mahut). Evidently, in disgust with the intrigues of his Rajput barons on behalf of his rival, and constant fear of being poisoned at meals or stabbed in the back when riding out, he had given his trust to these low-born men whose fidelity he had tested and who could gain nothing by deserting to Madho Singh.

The vast sums he had promised to the Marathas, either in hiring their swords in his contests with his brother or as war-indemnity after Bagru, fell into arrears, and as the Maratha collector complained, his dunning produced no effect. At last the Peshwa, himself hard pressed by his creditors, in despair of getting his dues from Jaipur by peaceful methods, had ordered his generals to visit that State after settling the affairs of Malwa. The tragic death of Keshavdas, the last honest and pro-Maratha minister, precipitated the attack from the south, as an appeal from his persecuted widow and orphans reached the Peshwa.

Malhar Holkar and Gangadhar Tatya, by way of the Mukunddara pass, reached Nenve on 28th November, and took it after a three days' siege. After a halt of ten days here, they marched towards Jaipur, and when they were still two or three marches from that city, Ishwari Singh's envoys met them with two lakhs of rupees. Holkar flew into a rage at the smallness of the amount, and ordered the advance to be resumed.

The Jaipur envoys returned and in alarm reported to their master that Malhar was coming to avenge the murder of Keshavdas. The old discarded minister Vidyadhar and Haragovind went to Ishwari Singh and advised him to assemble his troops and fight Holkar. This counsel was not to the taste of a man in his nerveless condition. He called his trusted favourites, the barber[9] and the elephant-driver, and ordered them to go to the Maratha camp, appease the wrath of Holkar with four or five lakhs, and turn him back from the way. They flatly refused to go, saying that they would be killed by Holkar in retaliation for Keshavdas's death, and that their master might slay them there if he wished, but should not send them to face the Maratha's fury. The Rajah remained silent and brooded over his fate, a youth not yet thirty, but deserted by all the world.

It was the 12th of December, 1750. Evening came and with it the news that Holkar had arrived within twenty miles of the city. Ishwari Singh ordered his servant to bring a live cobra and some poison required for preparing a medicine. It was done. At midnight he swallowed the poison and caused the cobra to sting him. Three of his queens and one favourite concubine took poison along with him, and all five of them died in the silence and seclusion of the palace chamber. None in the city, not even the ministers of State, heard of the tragedy. Only one valet held the secret of it, while the corpses lay unburnt and unattended to for 18 hours.

Next day, three hours after dawn, Khande Rao Holkar and Gangadhar Tatya with the Maratha vanguard appeared before the walls of Jaipur, while Malhar with the rest of the army encamped at Jhalane-kund, six miles away. Hours passed without any sign of activity, friendly or hostile, from the defenders of the capital. At last at noon the ministers went to the palace and sent word to the Maharajah. Then the valet disclosed that the Maharajah was no more.[10]

Notes

1. This document is in the Kapad-Dwara, No. 879 (National Register of Private Records No. 1, p. 67, Sr. No. 720). *Ed.*
2. This document is in the Kapad-Dwara, No. 872 (National Register of Private Records No. 1, p. 66, Sr. No. 719). *Ed.*
3. These are detailed in *J.R.* No. 220, and include some key offices at Court which would give him control over the Emperor's council and render impossible that constant thwarting of his policy by a hostile faction close to the Emperor's person which had nullified the devotion and ability of Sawai Jai Singh, the forts of Ranthambhor and Alwar, the police prefecture of Delhi city, and the conversion of the *ijara parganas* of his father into *jagir* lands. *J.S.*
4. This should be Thursday, January 14, 1748, as Wazir Qumruddin Khan's army started from Delhi on 23 Muharram, 1161 (*Ahmad Shah Durrani* by Ganda Singh, p. 55). *Ed.*
5. The historian Gulistani in his *Mujmil-ul-tawarikh bad Nadiriyya* (ed. by Dr. Oskar Mann, Leiden) waxes merry over the extreme terror and cowardice of Wazir Qamruddin, whom death sought out in his hole of hiding. *J.S.*
6. Given in SPD., XXI, letters No. 27-35. *Ed.*
7. Raja Samant Singh of Rupnagar (Kishangarh), is better known as Maharaja Nagri Das, the saint poet of Rajasthan. *Ed.*
8. This should be 'bari'; a person belonging to the bari community is distinctly different from a barber (*nai*) and perform only one kind of service rendered by barbers, viz. serving food, cleaning food utensils etc. and disposing of left over food. *Ed.*
9. This should be *bari*. *Ed.*
10. After sunset the corpses were cremated in the palace garden, Holkar bearing the necessary expenses. Twenty-one more wives became *satis*. *J.S.*

XIX

Sawai Madho Singh, 1751-1768

Madho Singh's Accession And The Problems Facing Him; The Marathas Leave Rajputana

Ishwari Singh had been a tragic failure. His reign had ended in the ruin of his country and of himself. His younger brother Madho Singh was of a superior character. The French captain J. Pillet, who had been in Jaipur for six years, wrote in 1794, contrasting the two brothers thus: 'Issery Singh ne indolent, n'ayant pas scu entretenir l' armonie qui regnoit parmi ses sujets. Mado Singh, son frere, plus integre et plus equitable, lui succeds.' (Issery Singh was idle, not being able to maintain the harmony that prevailed among his subjects; his brother Madho Singh, being more upright and impartial, succeeded him.) Tod holds the same opinion:

> Ishwari Singh was not calculated for the times, being totally deficient in that nervous energy of character, without which a Rajput prince can enforce no respect... Madho Singh inherited no small portion of his father's love of science, which continued to make Jaipur the resort of learned men, so as to eclipse even the sacred Benares.

But two circumstances prevented the full fruition of the bright promises of his accession: the heavy load of subsidy which the Rajput princes in their fratricidal contests had promised to the Marathas and the impact of the resurgent Jat power under the meteoric Jawahir Singh. But for these, the new king could have continued and confirmed the national prosperity and strength which his father had created after an exceptionally successful career.

When the suicide of Ishwari Singh became known, the ministers and Malhar Holkar himself wrote to Madho Singh to come away from Udaipur and take the vacant throne. He arrived in the Maratha camp on 29th December, 1750, and was conducted to his place by Holkar himself after four days during which his contribution to the invaders was discussed and settled at ten lakhs of rupees. Jayappa Sindhia arrived on 6th January, 1751, and immediately set to overthrow Holkar's arrangements by making exorbitant new demands on Jaipur. This alienated the Rajah from the Marathas, who had hitherto befriended him in his contests for the throne. While the renewed higgling for subsidy was going on, the Maratha chiefs feared that they would be treacherously poisoned or shot dead by the Rajputs during some friendly interview or feast. With feelings thus strained between the two sides, an explosion was only natural.

On 10th January, some 4000 Marathas entered Jaipur on a visit to see the temples and other sights of this newly built city, unique in India for the regularity and artistic beauty of its design, and to buy horses, camels and saddlery for which the Kachhwa capital was famous. The Marathas, despising the helpless condition of a king propped up by their arms, seemed to have behaved towards Jaipur as a city taken by storm. Suddenly the pent-up hatred of the Rajputs burst forth; a riot broke out at noon, and the citizens attacked the unsuspecting Marathas. For nine hours slaughter and pillage raged from one ward to another of the city. Some 1500 (or more probably 500 to 600) Marathas were slain and many wounded. Among the victims were several high officers and servants of Holkar and Sindhia, a hundred *brahmans*, slave girls, and even children. The horses, golden bracelets, pearl necklaces, money and accoutrements of the visitors were snatched away by the Rajputs.

The shock of this blow spread outside the capital. The Rajputs rose in the villages and killed the couriers of the Marathas wherever they could catch them, so that the roads were closed to them. After eight days Madho Singh opened negotiations and explained that the massacre was a spontaneous popular outburst, unsupported by him. The Marathas, knowing that Jaipur City was impregnable to assault, at last agreed to forgive and forget on condition of the restitution of their looted property and the payment of two lakhs by way of compensation to the dead and the wounded, besides the subsidy (ten lakhs) previously agreed upon. In the meantime agents arrived from Safdar Jang, the Delhi wazir, to hire the Marathas for aiding him in a war of revenge on the Afghans of Farrukhabad, and Malhar Holkar left the environs of Jaipur about 5th February, to join Safdar Jang in the Doab. Madho Singh, who had put off payment from day to day with smooth promises thus saved himself for the time being, but prepared the ground for future justifiable incursions into his territory.

For nearly a year and a half after this, Rajputana escaped the visitation of the locust hordes of the South, but not from her own internal troubles. Of the three States whose succession disputes had disturbed the last 20 years, Bundi was now under its lawful sovereign Ummed Singh (but crushed under a load of debt to the Peshwa). Jaipur had been gained by Madho Singh, but in Marwar, Ram Singh, who had succeeded his father Abhai Singh on 21st June, 1749,[1] was defeated by his uncle Bakht at Luniawas (27th November, 1750); robbed of his capital (8th July, 1751), and driven to seek refuge in Jaipur. Bakht Singh enjoyed his blood-stained throne for a year only, dying on 23rd September, 1752,[2] when his son Bijai Singh succeeded. Ram Singh often disturbed his cousin, but could not dislodge him, and at last died in exile at Jaipur in 1773.[3]

This history is not concerned with the Maratha invasions of Marwar in the interests of Ram Singh, except when Jaipur forces participated in the context as allies.

Madho Singh Makes Peace Between The Emperor And Safdar Jang, 1753

For two years and a half after his accession, Madho Singh did not pay the customary visit to the Emperor, who had his own troubles from the Bangash rebellion, the Durrani incursions, and above all intrigues and fights between the Persian and Turki Parties at his court. These last culminated in the Wazir Safdar Jang's rebellion in March, 1753. Safdar Jang was dismissed from the wazirship and by occupying the country south of Delhi fought his master and his rivals locked up within that walled city. Much mischief, loss and suffering was inflicted in the course of this civil war, which dragged on for seven months, Safdar Jang's strength being greatly increased by the adhesion of Suraj Mal Jat and his splendid troops.

The weak young Emperor Ahmad Shah (son of Muhammad Shah) was utterly helpless, with the rebels outside and his domineering new ministers within. He appealed to Madho Singh, as the greatest of his loyal feudatories, to come and save him. The Rajah left Jaipur with a large army, on the way took bonds from the *zamindars* of Rewari for four lakhs as subsistence money for his troops, and arriving at Delhi interviewed the Emperor during a ride on 15th October, 1753. On the 18th he and his officers were formally presented to the Emperor in the Diwan-i-Khas of Delhi fort, the Emperor advancing on foot to the door of the hall to welcome him. He made the customary presents to his sovereign and received official condolences for the death of his elder brother Ishwari Singh (three years before), investiture by the Emperor and the highest insignia of rank, namely a *palki* with a fringed cover, and the *mahi maratib* standards. At a business meeting five days later, the Emperor appealed to the Rajah, 'In view of the loyal services of your fore-fathers, it is the duty of an old hereditary servant like you to save the empire in such a crisis; otherwise, nothing but dust would remain on earth as its name and mark.' (*Br. Mus. Or.* 2005, f. 80).

Madho Singh set himself to making peace. Safdar Jang's strength lay in the Jat army under Suraj Mal. But the Jat chiefs had been proteges of the house of Jaipur, and as yet possessed no independent status among the nobility of Delhi. So, Madho Singh, as the overlord of the Bharatpur Rajah, warned him to retire from this fight against the Emperor. Suraj Mal was willing to do this if only his late usurpations of territory were recognized by the Emperor. This was one obstacle to the treaty, the other was the mutual jealousy between the two highest ministers, the new wazir and the new Bakhshi, and their aversion to Madho Singh taking the credit of ending the war. However, after long negotiations and in spite of cross-intrigues, a peace was arranged (5th November). Safdar Jang withdrew to his own province of Oudh, and Madho Singh hastened back to Jaipur on hearing that a vast Maratha army under the Peshwa's brother Raghunath Dada had crossed the Mukund-dara pass and was on the way to Rajputana. His reward was an Imperial grant of the fort and district of

Ranthambhor which his father and elder brother had coveted but failed to obtain. (*Br. Mus. Or.* 2005, f. 83*a*).

When he arrived home he learnt that the Marathas were raiding round that fort and that there was no hope of a relief force being sent from Delhi. So Madho Singh made terms with the despairing *qiladar*, Barket Ali Khan, discharged from his own treasury the arrear salary of the garrison, and received possession of Ranthambhor. (*Br. Mus. Or.* 1271, p. 102).

The Marathas In Jaipur, 1753-1756

The Maratha army under Raghunath Dada and Madhav Holkar crossed the Mukund-dara pass on 30th October, 1753, and by way of Kota-Bundi entered the Kachhwa kingdom. Madho Singh averted the devastation of his realm by sending his diwan Haragovind Natani to their camp (16th December), and agreeing to a contribution of sixteen and a half lakhs of rupees, namely fifteen and one fourth lakhs as outstanding tribute and one and one fourth lakhs as a present to Raghunath for the honour of his visit. Out of this sum Rs 7,35,074 was paid in cash and three lakhs in orders on bankers, by Jago Pandit the Jaipur Minister to Jayappa Sindhia in April 1755, leaving a balance of Rs 5,14,926 still due. The Maratha host next passed on to the Jat Country and Delhi, and one detachment from their army, under Jayappa Sindhia, invaded Marwar to restore Ram Singh to the throne (September, 1754). After the murder of Jayappa before the walls of Nagor (Friday, 25th July, 1755), Bijai Singh tried to build up a confederacy with Madho Singh, the Delhi Emperor, Suraj Mal and the Ruhela leaders, to drive the Marathas out of North India altogether. The invitation was declined everywhere except at Jaipur. Madho Singh heartily entered into the plan of liberating his country from Deccani domination, began to recruit new troops in Malwa, and treated Govind Timaji, the Maratha tribute collector quartered in his capital so harshly, that the man took poison to avoid dishonour (September).

Attacks were now delivered on the Maratha posts throughout Marwar. But by this time young Dattaji Sindhia had made himself master of the situation and he made prompt and effective arrangements for defence. While the Maratha siege of Jodhpur was continued by a detaining force, a strong detachment from Dattaji's own camp before Nagor advanced against a Rathor army coming from Jalor to the relief of Jodhpur. At Godawas, 32 miles north-east of Jalor, the Rathors were defeated and driven into the fort behind them.

Then a Jaipur force under Anurudh Singh Khangarot and Jagannath Shah with allies from Shahpura, Rupnagar, Karauli and the Hada country, making a total of 25,000 men and heavy guns, advanced to the relief of Nagor. Arriving at Ramgarh (38 miles east of Didwana), it was confronted by a strong Maratha force of 6000 men, which included many Rathor partisans of Ram Singh. On Thursday, 16th October, 1755, Anurudh tried to break out towards Nagor. The next day, he crossed the frontier from Datia and entered Marwar territory. But a light force of the enemy, under Ranoji Bhoite, Nar Singh Sindhia and Khanaji Jadav, came up by a forced night march and attacked the rear of the Jaipur army three hours after dawn. The Deccani moss-troopers galloped upon the cumbrous artillery of the Kachhwas, cut down the gunners and after a bloody fight for four hours, gained a complete victory. Anurudh lost 700 to 800 men, and a thousand horses, 50 camels, two guns, and six munition carts. But a still greater disgrace befell him: his dead were not allowed to be removed for cremation.

Severely shaken by this defeat, the Jaipur general turned his face towards Didwana, moving in regular marches, his baggage placed in the centre of the column and his guns in front. Constantly harassed and robbed of horses and transport cattle by the Maratha bands roving round him and worn out by thirst, he could advance only five miles a day, and reached Didwana on Tuesday, 21st October. On the last day of this journey he had to spend twelve hours absolutely without water, and lost 300 men, 125 horses and three guns. A Marwar force had been cooped up at Daulatpur (five miles east of Didwana) and reduced to starvation. So Anurudh and Bijai Singh alike begged for terms of peace (early November).

In the meantime, hearing of Jayappa's murder, the Peshwa had ordered reinforcements into Marwar in order to retrieve the situation. The first to arrive was Antaji Mankeshwar, who entered Jaipur territory near Newai, by way of the Lakheri pass. He first ravaged Kachhwa territory and then joined the Maratha detachment before Didwana (Wednesday, 5th November). The year had been marked by drought and even in the open Maratha camp, grain was selling at five seers a rupee, while fodder was so scarce that a rupee's worth of grass did not suffice for one horse. The water level in the wells had sunk to 225 feet below the surface. So, on 20th November, Bijai Singh slipped out of Nagor and fled to Bikaner, where matters were equally bad.

At last he bowed to the inevitable and made peace with Sindhia (end of February, 1756) agreeing to partition the kingdom of Marwar equally with Ram Singh, cede Ajmer fort and district to the Marathas and pay a war-indemnity of 50 lakhs. In May Dattaji evacuated Rajputana for Malwa.

Raghunath Dada Ravages Kachhwa Country, 1757

At the end of this year, 1756, Malhar Holkar and Raghunath Dada were again ordered by the Peshwa to invade Rajputana for exacting the promised tributes. But the insolvent Poona Government could not send an adequate army for the purpose. Raghunath came with 4000 men and Holkar with 2000, while the Maratha detachments scattered throughout northern India probably did not amount to another 10,000. But the leader had no money nor any prospect of getting money, because the Rajput States were themselves impoverished and merely negotiated to gain time.

From Indore, by way of Mewar, Raghunath reached Jaipur territory, and while dunning Madho Singh for payment, laid siege to Barwada (16 miles north-west of Sawai Madhopur). But he had no siege guns and was long held up by this *garhi* (fortalice). The Jaipur minister Kaniram offered to buy him off by paying the same tribute as agreed upon in the past, but the Peshwa's brother would not listen; he demanded 40 or 50 lakhs in cash and large cessions of territory (worth 40 or 50 lakhs annually). Madho Singh put his capital and other forts in a vigilant and active posture of defence; he called his vassals one by one and made them swear on the sacred *bel* leaf to resist the southern invaders to the death. Raghunath at last listened to the very strong argument of an empty stomach, and about 10th July, 1757, agreed to be content with 11 lakhs from Jaipur, six of which were paid down and shared between him and Holkar in the proportion of two to one. His condition had become desperate; as he wrote to the Peshwa, 'I have no money. My soldiers are in debt. Prices here are very high. I am daily getting my food only by sacking villages.' He left Rajputana at the end of this month.

The impossible indemnity promised by Bijai Singh could not be paid by his desert territory. In August, 1758, Sindhia and Holkar met together at Kota, and came to a settlement about sharing the Maratha acquisitions and claims in Rajputana and Malwa. Jankoji Sindhia then passed into Jaipur territory by way of Malpura. Rajah Madho Singh had entered into every anti-Maratha coalition since 1754 and he was now coerced into promising 36 lakhs, payable in four years, *plus* an additional three lakhs in the first year (September). Jankoji halted during the next two months on the eastern side of the Jaipur kingdom, and after being joined by his uncle Dattaji started for Delhi in the third week of December.

Holkar In Jaipur Territory, 1759

The visitation of 1759 was conducted by Malhar Holkar. In July he had received orders from the Peshwa to go to Rajputana and put pressure on its Rajahs for their promised money. His main duty was to realise 12 lakhs for 1758 and nine lakhs for 1759 from Jaipur, the most solvent of these States. But this was no easy task: Jaipur was now the strongest power in Rajputana, and its master from the safe shelter of his strongly fortified capital could laugh at an invasion with scorn. Moreover, as Raghunath Dada had found in 1757, most of the villages in this kingdom had protective walls and a martial population against whom the southern light horse could do nothing. But in November the Rajputs came out in body 4000 strong, led by Jot Singh Nathawat, to attack the Marathas. Malhar had been praying for such an opportunity of fighting in the open. With his superior numbers and artillery, he enveloped the Kachhwas at Lakhori and completely crushed them, slaying 20 of their captains. Malhar next laid siege to Barwara, defended by Vikaramjit Rajawat, and some Shekhawat captains. Calling up his big guns from Rampura, he forced the garrison to capitulate for their bare lives (middle of December).[4] Soon afterwards he had to abandon Rajputana in a hurry in order to reinforce Dattaji at Delhi against the attack of Ahmed Shah Abdali. He set off from the neighbourhood of Barwara, on 2nd January 1760, too late to save Dattaji Sindhia.

Thus the Maratha interest in Rajputana remained unsettled and uncared for during the eventful year 1760 and for six months after the fatal battle of Panipat (14th January, 1761).

The battle of Panipat saw the annihilation of the Maratha armies in the north and of their dream of a North Indian overlordship. The repercussion was a revolt against Deccani domination everywhere in Hindustan. Everywhere the dispossessed or humbled chieftains and even petty landowners, raised their heads and talked of shutting the southern spoilers out in future. But it all ended in talk; so many tribes and castes could not be united and no magnetic personality arose to lead the war of liberation. As a Maratha agent in Rajputana reported to the Peshwa in May 1761, 'all the Rajahs and *Rajwadas* have turned against us'. But within less than a year of the Panipat debacle, the tables were completely turned against the Rajputs. This was the achievement of Malhar Rao Holkar, the sole 'elder general' left of Baji Rao's time.

Holkar's Victory At Mangrol-Bhatwara

All this time Madho Singh had been intriguing at the Delhi Court to overthrow Maratha predominance in Rajasthan. Then, under the advice of his favourite minister Shyamram Trivedi, he sent two forces under Raj Singh Chauhan and Diwan Nandlal to raid the villages of his refractory vassal Sardar Singh Naruka of Uniara. After marrying at[5] Ratlam (on Wednesday, 15th May, 1761) the Rajah went towards Uniara to compel his vassal to pay his due tribute. Here many other chiefs offered to join him and he took up an attitude of open defiance to the Marathas. The rainy season now intervened to prevent military operations.

Late in October 1761, Madho Singh assumed the offensive by sending a force, 10,000 strong, to besiege Nenve (held by a Maratha garrison under Sadashiv Gopal), while another detachment under Keshav Rai crossed the Chambal and penetrated to Patan, 12 miles north-east of Kota city (early November). Malhar, hearing of it, marched from Indore with 6000 men. At Bariya in the Kota territory, he was joined by 3000 Rajput allies under Akheram Pancholi (the diwan of Kota), the youthful Zalim Singh, and the Kota Rajah's foster-brother. The Kachhwa army besieging Nenve fell back upon their main body at Patan, which thus numbered 10,000 with an abundant supply of artillery, rockets and camel-swivels. The Jaipur leaders were Raj Singh Ghorchara, the two diwans Kaniram and Nandlal, and Surat Singh Shiva-Brahma-pota.

Malhar promptly marched up and offered battle between Mangrol and Bhatwara. The two armies met in the afternoon of Sunday, 29th November, and immediately began an exchange of fire which lasted till three hours after sunset. After a night spent in watchfulness, the battle began in the morning and ended before nightfall with the total destruction of the Jaipur army. Most of their high officers, including the supreme commander, fled wounded. Saligram Shah fell dead, and all their guns, two elephants, many horses and camels, and their entire camp and baggage were abandoned to plunder. Large numbers were taken prisoners. Malhar's skin was grazed by a bullet.

The victory was decisive; this one blow destroyed all chances of forming an anti-Maratha coalition, and restored the Maratha prestige which had been eclipsed as the result of Panipat, throughout Hindustan. Madho Singh, who was at Ranthambhor during the battle, hurried back to his capital, whose defences were earnestly improved by Trivedi. The garrison of Amber fort was strengthened. Block-houses were set up in both the cities with strong bands of musketeers; outlying detachments were hurriedly called in; the royal family was removed to Amber for safety. The wise old Diwan Kaniram reopened negotiations with Holkar, who had now reached Manoharpur 40 miles north of Jaipur. Here envoys from Jodhpur, Kota and Bundi also met him. While these negotiations were being slowly spun as usual, Malhar was suddenly recalled from Rajputana by the invasion of Bundelkhand by the Emperor Shah Alam II and his wazir Shuja-ud-daulah of Oudh, and the uprising of all the Bundela princelings against Deccani rule. Malhar left Jaipur territory about 10th February, 1762, and the land had respite for three years (1762-1765).

The Kachhwa Kingdom Free Of The Marathas

Throughout 1762 and 1763 the Maratha power in the north was paralysed by the events at home—Nizam Ali's invasion of Maharashtra and sacking of Puna, Raghunath Dada's desertion to the enemies of his house during the civil war between him and the new Peshwa. It was only after the decisive defeat of the Nizam at Rakshasbhuwan (10th August, 1763) that the Puna Government gained security.

Early in October, 1764 we find Malhar Holkar revisiting Rajputana and encamped at Jobner (13 miles east of Sambhar) in order to put pressure on Madho Singh for payment. But soon afterwards he went to join Jawahir Singh Jat in his attack on Najib-ud-daulah, the Regent of Delhi, in return for a very large subsidy paid to the Peshwa. Thereafter Malhar continued outside Rajputana till his death on 26th May, 1766.[6]

Madho Singh, realizing that he could not succeed in arms against the myriads from the Deccan, and being faced with the new danger of Jawahir Singh's ambition and insolence, very wisely set himself to conciliating the Marathas as his only protectors. He made friends with Holkar and consented to make a reasonable settlement of his long-standing arrears of subsidy through Malhar's friendly mediation at the Peshwa's Court. As the Puna agent wrote in September, 1765, 'at Malhar's instance we are treating the Jaipur Rajah with every tenderness and consideration, but Mahadji Sindhia has been dunning him for the arrears... This court moves very slowly and protracts business'. However, before the end of the year the Rajah paid the current instalment of five lakhs and proposed to issue orders on the bankers for the balance.

The Jat Kingdom's Attitude Towards Jaipur Changed By Jawahar Singh

Just when the Maratha menace to Jaipur had been removed, even though for a time only, the greatest danger to Madho Singh's state came from a hitherto obscure corner with the suddenness and fury of a tropical tempest, and subsided as suddenly in less than four years. This was entirely due to the personality of Jawahir Singh Jat and naturally ended with his death.

The Jat State, as a political unit, was the nursling of the Kachhwa royal house and had been brought into being by Sawai Jai Singh and fostered by him and his two sons. Badan Singh had laid its foundation by his crushing out or winning over all the rival village-headmen of his race and accumulating an immense treasure by successful and long continued brigandage. To the last day of his life, he lay low, always calling himself a *thakur* (baron) or even *chaudhuri* (village headman) and refusing to visit the Emperor's Court when invited, on the grounds that he was a mere cultivator and not a noble (*umra*) and therefore unworthy to have the audience of an Emperor. Till age and failure of eyesight prevented him, he used to visit the Jaipur Rajah's court every year on the Dussehra day and present his humble offerings as a tenant to his lord. His son Suraj Mal was equally loyal and humble to the Kachhwa house, and whenever a Jaipur Rajah passed by Dig or Bharatpur, he would wait on him like a vassal, feed him and his troops, and lay down before him the keys of his famous forts, saying that they were the property of his overlord. Sawai Jai Singh had secured for Badan Singh *mahals* worth five and one fourth lakhs of rupees a year in *ijara* (*J.R.* 515).

These relations continued till the death of Suraj Mal in a battle with Najib-ud-daulah Ruhela on 25th December, 1763. His son and successor Jawahir Singh was a man of a different mould. Apart from his fiery reckless character and blind obstinacy, he could never forget that he was the son of a king and not of a Jat peasant, because Suraj Mal had been dignified with the title of *Rajah Brajendra Bahadur* by Safdar Jang when wazir of Delhi. Moreover, the expansion of this Jat State was a real threat to the eastern border of Jaipur. For example, the Jat Rajah coveted Kama, which fort and district was dear to the Kachhwas as a gift from the Emperor Shah Jahan and the home of the junior branch of the great Mirza Rajah's family.

Proud of the fabulous accumulated hoards of his father and grandfather, proud of his army, the finest in India, consisting of 15,000 cavalry, 25,000 infantry (apart from garrisons in forts), 300 pieces of cannon, and vast quantities of munitions, and an annual income of one and three quarter *krores* of rupees, Jawahir Singh found it galling to own allegiance to the house of Jaipur.

His first task after his accession was to wreak vengeance on Najib-ud-daulah for the death of his father. This kept him busy till the end of February, 1766, and ended in complete failure in spite of his lavishing lakhs and lakhs of rupees in hiring Sikh and Maratha mercenaries. There was a strong party among the Jat nobles and headmen opposed to Jawahir, and in order to be independent of his tribal army, he began to entertain European-drilled Sepoy brigades, especially under Walter Reinhard (popularly called Samru) and Rene Madec. This made him invincible against any indigenous force in northern India, and the greatest terror to his neighbours.

His step-brother Nahar Singh was his disappointed rival for the throne, and held Dholpur as his appanage. He had a most beautiful wife whom the licentious Jawahir coveted. In a contest between the two brothers, in which Marathas, Sikhs and the Rana of Gohad took part, Nahar was defeated, and driven for refuge into Jaipur territory, and finally at Shahpura he took poison in despair (*c*. December 6, 1766). Jawahir demanded the surrender of his widow and legacy, as his lawful sovereign and heir, and while the Jaipur Rajah was hesitating, the widow relieved him by killing herself. (*orme ms. I.O.L.* and *Br. Mus. Or.* 1271). Jawahir became furious at being baulked of his prey and meditated revenge on Madho Singh.

Madho Singh had been genuinely alarmed by Jawahir Singh's manifest design to wrest the Narnol district from him, and outraged by the incursions of the Jat Rajah and his Sikh allies into Jaipur territory in 1765. He had intrigued, though in vain, with every enemy of the Bharatpur State. Anyhow Jawahir, intoxicated with his recent sweeping victory over the Marathas in Bundelkhand (July-August, 1767), determined to beard the Jaipur Rajah in his own home. He marched with a full supply of artillery and Samru and Madec's trained battalions besides his Jat horse, to Pushkar through Jaipur territory, and invited Bijai Singh of Marwar to meet him there and form a pact for expelling the Marathas from the North.

The Battle Of Maonda, 14th December, 1767

On 6th November, 1767, the Rathor and Jat Rajahs met together on the bank of the sacred lake, exchanged turbans and sat down side by side on the same carpet like full brothers, and sent an invitation to Madho Singh to come and join them. The proud Kachhwa, long the foremost Rajput feudatory of the Delhi Empire, was provoked beyond endurance by this insult. He sharply reprimanded Bijai Singh for having degraded his Rathor ancestry by admitting a peasant's son and a mere servant of the Jaipur state as his brother and political equal. The letter roused Jawahir to fury. He set out on his return wantonly looting the Jaipur villages on his way and molesting their inhabitants.

The Jat Rajah with his immense force and ponderous artillery and baggage train had almost reached his own country, when at Maonda, only 23 miles south-west of Narnol, the last Jaipur station near the Jat frontier, the Kachhwa army which had been following him, delivered their attack (14th December). Here a narrow defile lay before the Jats; they sent their baggage ahead, covering it with the troops in the rear. The first attack of the Rajput horse in the open was repulsed by the Jats making a counter march towards them, as the Kachhwa artillery and infantry were still lagging behind. The Jats took advantage of this initial success to enter the defile, hoping thus to escape. But the Jaipur cavalry overtook them in the middle of the pass; the Jats made a half-turn and offered battle. The Kachhwa horsemen, after firmly standing a devastating fire from Jawahir's guns for some time, at last threw themselves sword in hand on the enemy, who fled at the first shock, crying out that all was lost and abandoning their artillery, baggage, and king himself.

The Rajputs immediately dispersed for plunder, and an indescribable scene of confusion followed, during which the French-led trained sepoys of Samru and Madec kept their heads, and with equal coolness and daring maintained the battle, fighting with their backs to the rocky walls till nightfall. They saved Jawahir and enabled him to make an unmolested retreat, though the rest of his army had dispersed in flight long before. But all his artillery train — 70 pieces of different calibres, tents and baggage including his royal umbrella, had to be abandoned on the field. The total loss on the two sides together was about 5000 men. The Rajputs lost 2000 to 3000 'mostly by artillery fire, before which they stood with astonishing firmness' (as the French general admits in his autobiography); but most of their principal chiefs fell on the field; there was hardly a noble family in Jaipur that did not sacrifice a son or two on that day. 'Dalil Singh, the Commander-in-Chief of the Jaipur army, fell in the fight with three generations of his descendants, and none but boys of ten remained to represent the baronical houses of Jaipur.'

Jawahir Singh claimed his escape as a victory. If so, it was a most pyrrhic victory.

> The fortune of the Jats has been shaken and the result has been fatal to them. They have returned home pillaged, stupefied and overthrown. The lands beyond the Chambal (recently conquered by Jawahir) rose at the first report of that rout... His own country is the prey of the enemy, who have followed him close. (Father F. Kavier Wendel's contemporary French ms.)

Madho Singh followed up his victory by invading the Jat country at the head of 16,000 men, and on arrival near Kama halted. Here he defeated Jawahir again, on 29th February, 1768, with a loss of 400 men killed on the Jat side and their greatest general Dan Shah wounded; they fled with their hired Sikh allies. On the arrival of a fresh army of 20,000 Sikhs engaged by Jawahir for seven lakhs a month, the Rajputs retreated to their own country.

This was the last battle fought by Madho Singh. He died on 5th March, 1768, no doubt on account of sickness from the hardships of the campaign, and Jawahir Singh perished at the hand of an assassin of his own service four months later.

Exact casualty returns for the Jaipur Rajah's own regular troops (as distinct from the tribal militia and the contingents of his vassals and allies like the rulers of Kerauli and Kota) in the battle of Maonda have been preserved, which show that in a force of 2803 men, as many as 986 were slain and 651 wounded or sixty per cent of their total strength. 929 horses were killed and 227 wounded, besides some elephants and camels. These figures clearly illustrate the sanguinary nature of the conflict. Among the chiefs slain, the following thirteen are mentioned by name—Dalel Singh Rajawat (of Dhula) and his son Lakshman S., Jaswant S. Khangarot (of Chhir), Sangram S. Khangarot (Bashi Jobner), Malam S. Madhani (Rajorgarh) Nawal S. Rajawat (Lisadni), Ummed S. Dhirawat (Gudarni), Guman S. Sheobrahmapota (Macheri), Bhopal S. Rathor (Gobalya), Sanwaldas Rajawat (Magalwada), Diwan Gur Sahai Khatri, Rajah Har Sahai Khatri, and Ummed S. Panchanwat (Jaipur City). One recovery from wounding is recorded, that of Jhujhar S. Chatrabhujwat of Bagru.

An Estimate Of Madho Singh's Reign

With Madho Singh departed, for a time, the military glory of the House of Jaipur. Then followed minority after minority, faction fights among the nobility, and inroads by Marathas and Afghans, which brought the home of Man Singh and Jai Singh to the lowest depth of misery and humiliation.

His name is perpetuated by Sawai Madhopur, the new city which he founded, by an order issued on 19th January, 1763. It has now risen to importance from the railway junction near it, and forms the headquarters of a district or revenue division of the kingdom of Jaipur. Though not pretending to the size and dignity of Jai Singh's new capital, the city of his son was built amidst far more romantic surroundings and its palaces have an indescribable charm for the visitor's eye. This can be seen in the tinted prints of the buildings and sights of Sawai Madhopur exhibited in the Jaipur Museum.

Maharajah Sawai Madho Singh had some good qualities no doubt, but he lacked the firmness of decision and far-sighted diplomatic sagacity of his father. His greatest political blunder was his active backing of the exiled Ram Singh for the throne of Jodhpur. It revived in an acute form the Kachhwa-Rathor rivalry which had begun at the Imperial Court as early as the days of Jaswant Singh and Mirza Rajah Jai Singh, and whose latest outburst had clouded the last years of Sawai Jai Singh II. By thus antagonizing the ruler of Jodhpur, Madho Singh rendered impossible that coalition of the only two first-rate powers then left in Rajputana which could have kept the Deccanis out of their country. The political emancipation of Rajasthan became more and more an empty dream in the fifty years following Madho Singh's death. In no corner could a ray of hope be seen. The Maharana of Udaipur, the acknowledged head of Rajput *society*, had long ceased to count in Indian *politics*. The Sisodia in the eighteenth century had become a phantom of his former self, whom the name of Pratap and Haldighat failed to vivify. The defence of Rajasthan could now be achieved only by the Rathors and Kachhwas in union or not at all.

Notes

1. This is the date on which the news of Abhai Singh's death was received in Jodhpur. Abhai Singh had died at Ajmer on Ashadha Sudi 15, Monday, 19th June, 1749. *Ed.*
2. This should be Thursday, 21st September, 1752, i.e. Bhadrapada Sudi 13, V.S. 1809, on which Bakht Singh died at Sindholi. *Jodhpur Rajya ki Khyat*, II, p. 314, Sitamau Collection, Shri Raghubir Library; Reu, *Marwar I*, p. 368. *Ed.*
3. In some *Marwar Khyats* Ram Singh is said to have died in September, 1772; Reu, *Marwar I*, p. 366. Ed.
4. Malhar wrested the fort of Barwara from the usurper Ratan Singh Kachhwa (the son of Fath Mal of Kusathal), and restored it to its original owner Jagat Singh Rathor, who had bought Maratha help. *J.S.*
5. Omit 'at' and read 'After marrying in Jaipur the daughter of Raja Fateh Singh of...'
   This Raja Fateh Singh was third in succession to Berisal, the son of Hate Singh, the eldest son of Chhatrasal later of Ratlam. Berisal having been dispossessed of his share in the Ratlam State by his elderly uncles was patronised by Sawai Jai Singh and he finally settled down as a grandee of the Amber State. His successors in Jaipur State continued to be called the Rajahs of Ratlam. *Ed.*
6. This should be Tuesday, 20th May, 1766 = Vaisakha Sudi II, V.S. 1823. *Holkarshahichya Itihasachi Sadhane* Vol. I, No. 253, p. 151. *Ed.*

XX

The Jaipur State And The Imperial Delhi Government, 1778-1785

Jaipur History Under Rajah Prithvi Singh, 1768-1778

The reign of Sawai Madho Singh which had commenced in December, 1750 after the tragic death of his predecessor ended 18 years later (6th March, 1768) amidst a blaze of glory caused by his defeat of the Jat Rajah Jawahir Singh. His throne passed on to his elder son, Prithvi Singh, a boy of five, and the regency was held by his widowed queen, a daughter of Jaswant Singh Chundawat, the baron of Deogarh in Mewar.

Immediately after Madho Singh's death, his father-in-law Jaswant came over to Jaipur and began to wield the regency on behalf of his grandson in concert with the three ministers, Khushali Ram Bohra, Raj Singh Kachhwa and Firuz.

A minority is a perilous time among a proud and intractable race like the Rajputs, who cannot tolerate a woman's rule. The Kachhwa nobles chafed under the new administration of their country in which none of them had any lot or part. They conspired to overthrow it and established their own control over the boy king and his state. These nobles formed two clan-groups; one was that of the Nathawats, ranged round the barons of Chomu (the premier peer of the realm) and Samod; while the second was formed by the Rajawats under the barons of Jhalai and some other places, these being the king's blood relations and therefore standing nearest in the line of succession to the throne. During the ten years of Prithvi Singh's reign (7th March, 1768-16th April, 1778), the Kachhwa kingdom was free from Maratha incursions and Mughal interference alike, as these two enemies were kept busy by their own troubles; but for all that this decade was a period of tumult and disruption in the mournful annals of that land.

The Rise Of Pratap Singh Naruka; His Doings At Jaipur

Rao Pratap Singh, of the Naruka branch of the Kachhwas, was originally a petty vassal of Jaipur State, owning only two and a half villages, for one of which he was known as the Macheriwala. But his sleepless ambition and unscrupulous opportunism succeeded so well that before his death (in November, 1790), he was recognized by the Imperial Government as a Rajah fully independent of his tribal overlord, and he built up a kingdom which today embraces 3158 square miles of territory. This Pratap Singh attracted notice with his intelligence and energy. Using the Bohra's party as his tool, he controlled the administration and gained everything that he desired without bearing the responsibility of any office in the State. His smooth tongue and ready power of deception beguiled everyone at the capital, while he continued filching the border lands of the State.

Pratap Singh Naruka used his power to oust the dowager queen's father and brother from the administration, got Firuz arrested, squeezed seven lakhs of rupees out of him as the price of his liberation, and confined Khushhali Ram Bohra with the consent of the bewildered and helpless queen-mother. But these acts set everyone in the capital against him, and the Naruka, in danger of assassination, secretly fled Jaipur one night (the second half of 1717).

The next year Rao Pratap Singh was called upon to meet an invasion of his eastern frontier by Najaf Khan, who was bent on recovering the places in Mewat lately usurped by the Naruka. His relations with Najaf, alternating between war, submission and war again throughout the year 1778, need not be described here.

The Jaipur Rajah Prithvi Singh died on 16th[1] April, 1778. He was succeeded by his brother Sawai Pratap Singh, a boy of thirteen. When at the close of the year 1778 the Emperor marched into Jaipur in person, the Kachhwa Court sent Firuz with rich presents and some tribute to Najaf Khan's camp to make peace. The faithless Naruka chief, then in attendance on the Mir Bakhshi, volunteered to promote his overlord's interests and introduced Firuz to Najaf Khan, but afterwards lured the envoy to Agra and there got him murdered, after which he seized all the wealth and other belongings of his victim.

Minority Of Sawai Pratap Singh; The Rivalry Of The Bohra And Haldia Ministers; The Wars Against Macheri Rao

Prithvi Singh died on 15th April[2] and a new scene opened at the Imperial Court where the Kashmiri favourite Abdul Ahad Khan tried to thwart Najaf's work by making terms with Macheri and Jaipur over the Mir Bakhshi's head. Tempting the Emperor with the hope of getting the tributes of these two Rajahs himself without having to give a share to the Mir Bakhshi, he announced that the sovereign would march to that region in person. The Jaipur and Macheri chiefs sent envoys to Delhi and tried to secure easier terms than Mirza Najaf's. They were welcomed at Court and promised royal orders extending protection over their masters and repudiating the action of the Mirza. The Imperial Commander-in-Chief took quick and decided action; he sent orders to his lieutenants Najaf Quli and Afrasiyab to march from their posts to Delhi and awe the Emperor into dismissing his marplot favourite. The news of this move at once cowed the cowardly Kashmiri intriguer; he dismissed the Jaipur and Macheri envoys with empty hands and made the puppet Emperor sneak back into his palace (29th May).

The Macheri envoys, cursing the spineless double-dealing minister, went back to their master, who had no choice but to seek peace at Mirza Najaf's hands by agreeing to pay an indemnity of 33 lakhs in three years—out of which three lakhs were paid down and security given for the balance of the first instalment (c. 6th July, 1778)

The three lakhs with which the Macheri chief had bought off the Imperial generalissimo, were a loan from the Jaipur treasury, and the Naruka now tried to evade repayment of it.[3] The Jaipur diwan Khushhali Ram Bohra then called in the aid of Mirza Najaf.

An Imperial force under Zain-ul-abidin Khan (the son of a nephew of the Mir Bakhshi) was despatched and joined the Jaipur army. A confused and wavering battle followed on 8th August, 1778, in which, after an initial success, the Macheri chief was deserted by his Maratha allies, and each side fell back on its camp.

The imperialists now poured into Macheri territory, ravaging the country, capturing the fortalices and occupying the villages. It was already December and the complete submission of the Macheri chief to the Mughal invaders seemed imminent when the news came that Abdul Ahad was taking the Emperor out to Rajputana in order to rob Mirza Najaf of his command in that region. The Mirza at once patched up a truce with the Naruka, by agreeing to an indemnity of two lakhs only, and set off for the Court.

Sawai Pratap Singh Given Tika By Emperor; Later Rupture

The favourite Abdul Ahad had pointed out how Mirza Najaf had been campaigning successfully against the Jat and Macheri Rajahs for a year but had not paid a single piece of revenue or the least share of the spoils of war into the public treasury. Moreover, the new Rajah of Jaipur was bound by custom to pay a heavy succession fee, which would be swallowed up by Mirza Najaf unless the Emperor went to the scene in person. The Emperor yielded and issued from the palace in Delhi on 10th November, 1778. Najafgarh was reached on 17th December and then Rewari (where its Rajah Mitrasen Ahir interviewed and was saddled with a tribute of Rs 1,25,000). On the 23rd the camp arrived at Kanud, 28 miles west of Rewari, where the local Rajah Bhagwant Singh was received in audience and a tribute of four lakhs was laid on him. The next day the camp was pitched beyond Narnaul (15 miles south of Kanud), to which Badil Beg was posted as Imperial *faujdar*.

In Rajputana proper, several local chiefs were received at Court—Nawal Singh Shekhawat, the *thakur* of Nawalgarh on 31st December; Basant Singh, the Rao of Patan on 5th January, 1779; and Nathu Singh the Rao of Manoharpur (35 miles south of Patan) on 16th January. The furthest point reached was the village of Aminpur, in *pargana* Amirnagar, near Jaipur, on 17th January. Here the Kachhwa diwan Khushhali Ram Bohra came (19th) to arrange for his master's presentation to the throne. But Mirza Najaf himself arrived in the camp (23rd) with a strong and well-equipped army, and after some argument with his rival it was settled that these two ministers should jointly fix the Jaipur tribute.

On 19th February, Sawai Pratap Singh was introduced to the Emperor by Najaf Khan. He presented a *peshkash* of two lakhs, and his tribute was settled by mutual agreement at 20 lakhs. The Emperor with his own finger put the *tika* or paintmark of Rajahship on his own forehead, and then sent him back with many robes of honour and gifts; all his territory, including Narnaul, was restored to him. Najaf Khan undertook to collect his tribute, and leaving Himmat Bahadur as his agent for the purpose, he set out in the royal train (26th February) for the return to Delhi.

Najaf Quli, a general of the Imperial Bakhshi, Mirza Najaf Khan, leaving Delhi at the end of November, 1779, marched against Balwant Singh, the Rajah of Kanud, who had usurped many villages in the Hansi-Hisar district during the late eclipse of government. These belonged to Najaf Quli's *jagir*. The Khan, arriving on the spot, found it beyond his power to attack the fort of Kanud, because of the lack of water for many miles around it. He resorted to treachery. Pretending friendship, he released the Rajah's villages recently occupied by the invaders, sent him gifts, and invited him to a friendly meeting. The Rajah's son came in response to the invitation and the Mughal general assassinated him with the thirty Rajput nobles in attendance on him (*c.* 4 December, 1779). Najaf Quli now promptly advanced to Kanud and laid siege to the fort, after arranging for the transport of water by camels. Trained sepoys under European officers and artillery, from Begam Samru's force, joined the besiegers. Considering that most of the nobles of the state had been massacred with their prince, the fall of the place was inevitable. The Rajputs, however, made a long and desperate defence. Narnaul, from which help was expected, was looted by a detachment from the Mughal army on 5th February, 1780, and by the end of that month the besiegers had carried the sap to the edge of the moat of Kanud. On 14th February, 400 men of the garrison made a sortie and attacked the trenches of Mitrasen Ahir, the Rajah of Rewari, inflicting a hundred casualties. A week earlier, 17 desperadoes had issued from the fort separately, vowing to slay Najaf Quli and perish in the attempt; but the first to rush upon him was arrested. Nawal Singh Shekhawat, who was severely ill within the fort, was sent out in a *palki* to Singhana by mutual consent, and died there (*c*. 24th February). The Thakurani, who was holding the fort in the absence of her husband, at last capitulated on 17th March and was given a few villages for her support.

The Invasion Of Shekhawati District By Murtaza Khan Barech And Of Jaipur By Mahbub Ali, 1780

Immediately after the fall of Kanud, Mirza Najaf gained a great accession of strength for his Jaipur enterprise in the person of Mahbub Ali Khan, the Oudh general who had acted with the English brigade in repelling the Marathas at Ramghat in 1773.

Meanwhile, Himmat Bahadur had not been able to realise the promised tribute at Jaipur even after a year's stay. The Jaipur Government, with a boy of fifteen on the throne, unchecked by any strong and wise minister, was pursuing a senseless capricious course. The old diwan Khushhali Ram Bohra, by his shrewd diplomacy, had turned aside the attack of the Rao Rajah and later that of the Mir Bakhshi. After the settlement made with the Emperor in February, 1779, this minister, who had often to be absent from Jaipur on diplomatic missions, appointed Daulat Ram Haldia (the fugitive ex-minister of Macheri) as his deputy at his master's Court. The ungrateful Haldia quickly made his way into the young Rajah's heart and gained the regency for himself by ousting his patron, whom he accused of embezzlement. The Bohra, on his return to Court, was called to a harsh audit and confined in Amber fort to answer a demand for lakhs of rupees. But Daulat Ram's glory was short-lived; early in 1780 he had to flee for his life and seek asylum with Najaf Khan in Delhi. Just then Mirza Najaf received Himmat Bahadur's report that the Jaipur Government was hopelessly in default of payment.

A double invasion of the Jaipur kingdom in overwhelming force was now organized. Murtaza Khan Barech with his Afghan and Baluch followers was to force the northern route through the Shekhawati country and descend on Jaipur from its north. At the same time Mahbub Ali Khan was to follow the southern road to Jaipur, marching westwards from Agra via Hindaun and Lalsont, and strike at the Kachhwa capital from its south side. Mahbub left Delhi early in May, the traitor Daulat Ram Haldia guiding him with his local knowledge. A strong Imperial division of five battalions of trained sepoys, some under European commandants and a thousand horse with artillery, besides his own new levies, accompanied the general. By making rapid marches he advanced looting the cities in the eastern and southern regions of Jaipur State and taking many fortalices. Jhalai, Bhandarej, Basi-Toda, Lalbari, Chatsu and Watka were among his victims, till on 20th October he arrived at the gate of the Kachhwa capital, in which the Rajah had shut himself. At exactly the same time, his colleague Murtaza Khan had worked his way through the Shekhawati district to Shri Madhopur, 40 miles north of Jaipur.

Meanwhile Rajah Sawai Pratap Singh had set Khushhali Ram free and appointed him regent with supreme authority (18th October) and sent him to make peace with the Mughal Government at any cost. Mahbub Ali had quarrelled with Daulat Ram Haldia, in spite of Najaf Khan's reprimand. On 2nd November, Khushhali Ram interviewed Mahbub Ali in his tents outside Jaipur, but his offer of tribute was rejected as inadequate and delusive. The Jaipur regent even proposed to hire 6500 of Mahbub's troops for a daily subsidy and employ them in recovering certain *mahals* from the Macheri chief. The Delhi general doubted his sincerity as he had received information of Khushhali being in secret league with the Rao Rajah and of his having invited that chief to join in the defence of Jaipur. Mahbub Ali had been living all this time on plunder, constantly moving to new pastures. He next marched east from Tonk (50 miles south of Jaipur) towards Malarna (18 miles north of Ranthambhor fort) where he captured the *garhi* (probably Khirni) of Thakur Shambhu Singh (7th November) and then laid siege to Malarna. His troops captured Barwada (20 miles west of Ranthambhor) on the 9th. The woeful situation of the splendid heritage of Man Singh and Mirza Rajah Jai Singh at this time is thus described in a Marathi despatch of 10th October, 1780.

The Turks have seized 32 *parganas* of Jaipur and set up their outpost 12 kms from Jaipur city. Fourteen *parganas* of the *jagirdars* (vassals) and two of the ghanims i.e., Marathas, (together with the 32 above) make a total of 48 *parganas* lost by the Jaipur Rajah. Only four *parganas* remain under him. (*Mah. Dar.* i, 19.)

But the attempt to exact the Jaipur tribute by coercion through Mahbub Ali failed. The Rajah held out within his impregnable fortress, and the invader soon exhausted the resources of the open country, and as he could not pay his troops they began to leave him rather than die of famine in that desert land.

At last in February, 1781, Mahbub Ali, finding it beyond his power to maintain himself longer and being daily threatened by the mutiny of his unpaid soldiery, marched back to Dig, leaving most of his troops in camp there.

We shall now turn to Murtaza Khan Barech's part in this invasion of Jaipur. Early in March, 1780, his nephew was slain by the Rajputs on his way from Narnaul and his property looted. Mirza Najaf ordered him to raise forces of his own on the same terms and promises as Mahbub Ali's and sent him to penetrate into Jaipur from the north, simultaneously with the latter general's march by the south-west. Murtaza's route brought him into conflict with the Shekhawats. They barred his path at a place beyond Narnaul, but after a six hour fight with heavy slaughter on both sides, he defeated them (*c.* 20th July). Advancing further west and south, he roved about in the region around Udepur (20 miles north of Sri Madhopur), in the very heart of the Shekhawat country, and tried to secure tribute from Sikar, Nawalgarh, Khetri, Singhana and other baronies by negotiation or threat of arms. On 20th October when Mahbub Ali reached the gate of Jaipur city from the south, Murtaza Khan had made his way to Sri Madhopur, 40 miles north of Jaipur. But these 40 miles he was not destined to cross, and finally he too returned to Delhi covered with debt and failure, early in March, 1781. Mirza Najaf's finely conceived strategy, though punctually carried out by these two able subordinates, ultimately broke down on the rock of finance. The delaying tactics of the Jaipur ministers succeeded.

Bohra-Haldia Rivalry At Jaipur Court Till 1781

The 1778 expedition against Macheri had a curious after effect on the internal politics of Jaipur. Three *banias* of the Khandewal family in Kachhwa State, named Daulat Ram, Khushhali Ram II and Nand Ram, with their father Chhajju Ram, of the Haldia family, had migrated from Jaipur Court and gone to Macheri, where they had risen to the head of the administration and the charge of important forts. But by reason of their having spitefully counselled their new master not to pay his debt to Jaipur State and thus provoking the recent joint Mughal-Kachhwa invasion, he in his hour of defeat threatened to imprison and plunder them. So the entire Haldia family took shelter in Najaf's camp (*c*. January, 1779). Here Khushhali Ram Bohra took them under his protection.

From April, 1780 to February, 1781, Daulat Ram accompanied Mahbub Ali Khan in his invasion of Jaipur, while his brother Khushhali Ram II attended at Delhi. On 18th October the Rajah made the Bohra the supreme regent of Jaipur with full authority over all the sardars, great and small. (Br. Mus. Add. 25,020 f. 50*a*, f. 313*b*.)

We may here briefly narrate the course of Khushhali Ram's diplomacy towards the Imperial Government at this time. He failed to avert the invasion of his country planned by Najaf Khan, because his master was neither willing nor able to pay the enormous arrears of tribute that had accumulated. Mirza Najaf transferred the collection of the Jaipur tribute to Gosain Himmat Bahadur once again. On 27th April, 1781, the Gosain interviewed the Jaipur Rajah through Khushhali Ram I and the following settlement was made:

> Himmat Bahadur swore on Ganges water that he would never act against the Rajah of Jaipur. The Rajah made over to Himmat Bahadur *mahals* calculated to yield 12 lakhs of rupees a year, one half of which was to be remitted to Najaf Khan and the other half spent in maintaining the troops kept there for the work of collection; the imperialists were to set up their military posts there.[4]

Next month the Gosain realised Rs 75,000 and sent the amount to his master in Delhi. Daulat Ram Haldia now returned to Jaipur and was appointed army chief (*bakhshi*).

At this time Himmat Bahadur helped Jaipur State with his own contingent in defeating and capturing the Maratha mercenary Jaswant Rao Bable, who had long served Jaipur State. But being unpaid, he had tried to forcibly make himself master of Malpura and Toda on the ground that these were Solanki colonies and he was a Deccani Solanki (i.e. Chalukya, in Marathi Sulke): Bable's son Shambhuji was killed and all his war equipment and other property plundered (*Vamsha Bhas*. IV, 3889). Jaipur hostility to the Rao Rajah continued and the latter made Muhammad Beg Hamadani his patron for a money consideration.

This brings us to the middle of the year 1781. Immediately afterwards another palace revolution took place at Jaipur: Khushhali Ram Bohra was thrown into prison and Daulat Ram Haldia was re-appointed prime minister at the end of July, 1781. The Haldias governed the State for the next five years. But on 15th November, 1784, Khushhali Ram II (i.e. Haldia) was murdered in Afrasiyab Khan's camp by an agent of the Macheri Rajah. Daulat Ram fell from favour and his high office in April, 1786, and migrated with his family to Lucknow. The Bohra now became prime minister again. But his resurrection was short lived. In January next, Daulat Ram returned and became the Rajah's favourite again by pursuing a bold foreign policy. So when Mahadji arrived at the end of March, the Bohra sought refuge with him to save his life (*DY*. i, 173, 200; *HP*. 476, 468).

The Earlier Years Of The Reign Of Sawai Pratap Singh: Disorder

During the minority of Sawai Pratap Singh, the public administration was utterly neglected. The State was ruled by officers who were their own masters and selfishly quarrelled among themselves. The young Rajah gave his personal favour, with supreme power over his Government, to Roda Ram (popularly called Rodoji), because this man was in charge of the Rajah's food and drink and thus guarded him against poisoning. The second office in the State, though the first in theory, alternated between the old *brahman* diwan Khushhali Ram Bohra (whom the Rajah disliked) and Daulat Ram Haldia, a trader by caste.

As early as June, 1781, the nobles of the State had warned Sawai Pratap Singh, 'Our kingdom is going out of our hands. You should apply some remedy to set it right.' The Rajah's reply was, 'You are the pillars of my State. Carry out any plan that you consider best.' The Diwan asked the leading barons to be always in attendance at the capital, pay their due revenue, carry out the orders of the Government and serve the State. The nobles, who were for the most part their prince's clansmen and had fought loyally for his ancestors, could not bear the disgrace of taking their orders from the low men who now dominated the Court, and yet the Rajah refused to dismiss the tailor. So the nobles kept away from the capital, even as late as April, 1786, leaving the Rajah to his fate. The Shekhawat vassals took to a more aggressive course and seized his territory near their estates.

While thus abandoned by the warriors of his land, Sawai Pratap Singh also made Khushhali Bohra his enemy.

Notes

1. This should be Monday, April 13, 1778 = Vaisakha Bidi 2 V.S. 1835. (Jaipur Vansavali Ms., Sitamau Collection, p. 41). *Ed.*
2. This should be Monday, April 13, 1778 A.D. See above. *Ed.*
3. *Ibrat., i. 347*, says that Khushhali Ram (corr. Daulat Ram) Haldia, the brother of Daqlat Ram, a fugitive from the Jaipur Court, who had become prime minister of the Macheri Rajah, spitefully advised his new master not to pay! *J.S.*
4. Najaf Khan, on receiving the report of this, angrily cried out, 'Always mere words and evasive tricks! No money ever paid.' (Br. Mus. Add. 25,020, f. 221*b*) *J.S.*

XXI

Mahadji Sindhia Invades Jaipur: The Lalsot Campaign, 1786-1787

Sindhia's Efforts To Collect The Jaipur Tribute Due to the Emperor

Within three years of Mirza Najaf Khan's death (on 6th April, 1782) a complete revolution had taken place in the government of Delhi. His two successors in the high office of Regent of the Empire were assassinated and finally, at the helpless Emperor's personal entreaty, Mahadji Sindhia agreed to become Imperial Regent and Commander-in-Chief (*Wakil-i-mutlaq* and *Amir-ul-umara Mir Bakhshi*) on 4th December, 1784. Henceforth the legitimate authority of the Paramount Power came to be exercised by a Maratha chief possessed of marvellous sagacity, boundless ambition and (from 1790 onwards) irresistible armed strength. The Jaipur Court, like every other in Rajputana, had to face this altered situation and their tribal levies, fighting with out-of-date weapons and primitive tactics and under a loose casual organization, were completely mastered by the French-led professional troops and modern artillery that Mahadji had the wisdom to employ. They were now forced to pay, not blackmail to roving hordes of southern horse as before, but regular tributes due to the lawful Mughal suzerain, as demanded by his official agent. Then began the helpless hopeless agony of Rajasthan which ended only with the imposition of British paramountcy and Imperial peace 30 years later.

Mahadji Sindhia, as Mir Bakhshi of the Delhi Emperor (appointed in December, 1784), found himself burdened with the duty of collecting from the Jaipur Rajah the enormous dues of the two distinct masters. Jaipur State had, at different times in the past, bound itself to pay the Marathas large contributions, besides which quite recently (in 1779) the Rajah had promised to the Emperor 20 lakhs of rupees as succession fine and tribute, payable through the medium of the Mir Bakhshi. Mahadji had to take this claim up among the first tasks of his new office.

Throughout the three years 1782-1784 nothing was paid by the Kachhwa king, who took advantage of the internal quarrels and weakness of the Delhi Government to defy it.

Mahadji Sindhia's First Invasion Of Jaipur, 1786; The Settlement Of The Tribute

Aligarh capitulated to him on 20th November, and thus freed from anxiety, Sindhia began (on 3rd January, 1786) his march towards Jaipur, taking the Emperor with himself. Arriving near Dig he halted for over a month (10 January-15 February) trying to secure a peaceful payment through the mediation of the Naruka and the Bohra. But the hope faded away, and at last the entire camp resumed its advance (on 15th February) arriving near Lalsot on the first of the next month. The Rao Rajah of Macheri had been sent on to Jaipur in advance. He returned with the Jaipur envoys, Balaji Mahant (the spiritual guide of the late Rajah Madho Singh) and the Bohra minister on 6th March.

But the Naruka Pratap Singh, unwilling to promote a peace which would make him disgorge Narnaul and other *parganas*, cunningly set Mahadji against any reasonable settlement by advising him to rise absurdly high in his demands (to 60 lakhs), and told him that if he accepted any smaller sum after personally coming all the way from Dig to Jaipur and bringing the Emperor himself in his train, it would lower his prestige. He even suggested that, if the reigning king of Jaipur failed to find such a large sum, he should be deposed, and Man Singh set up on the throne with the Naruka Pratap as his guardian and regent, in return for which post he would pay Sindhia 50 lakhs. This selfish man's one aim was to perpetuate his hold on the Kachhwa kingdom by becoming the all powerful Maratha's agent and representative there. In the course of time Mahadji realised that the Macheri chief was a deceiver and mischief-maker, saying one thing to him and another to the Jaipur Rajah (*Ibr.*, ii, 156).

After much talk it was at last agreed by both sides that the Kachhwa kingdom should pay 63 lakhs (60 lakhs as *peshkash* and three lakhs as darbar charges), and out of this amount 11 lakhs were to be paid immediately (cash seven lakhs, jewels three lakhs, elephants and horses one lakh). Ten lakhs were to be paid in six months' time, and 20 lakhs were to be provided by the cession of land; and the remaining 22 lakhs were covered by assignments on the revenue of the fiefs of the feudal barons.

These terms being settled, the Jaipur envoys paid three lakhs in cash and kind, and Khushhali Ram took his leave (on 20th April, 1786) to collect the balance of eight lakhs and thus liquidate the first instalment. Daulat Ram Haldia then migrated to Oudh with his family.

> Khushhali Ram, on becoming regent again, restored all the former officials to their posts and imprisoned the new ones (of the Haldia Party), released the bankers and other rich people then in confinement, reassured the citizens and made them reopen their shops. (*H.P.* 476; *Aiti. Tip.*, vi, 41.)

The first quota of 11 lakhs having been fully discharged by the end of May, Sindhia left Rayaji Patil with a strong force, as well as Najaf Quli and the Macheri Rajah, in that kingdom for collecting the second instalment of ten lakhs and the assignment for 22 lakhs on the baronial estates, and also for holding the ceded districts. Then he started on his journey on 4th June.

Mahadji Sindhia's Final Rupture With The Jaipur Government, 1787

Sawai Pratap Singh had sent his ex-diwan Daulat Ram Haldia to Lucknow (May, 1786) to intrigue for the hiring of an English brigade against the Marathas. This agent spent eight months there, and though the new Governor General Lord Cornwallis definitely forbade any English intervention in the quarrels of the Indian States, some loyal British officials (notably William Kirkpatrick), out of alarm at Sindhia's designs in the Doab, encouraged Daulat Ram's hopes of armed aid from their government. Haldia returned to Jaipur in the middle of January, 1787, and installed as prime minister once more, while his rival Khushhali Ram Bohra, who stood for friendly relations with the Marathas, fell out of favour and with his partisans had to flee to the camp of Sindhia for their lives.

With the return of Daulat Ram to power, the Jaipur Government took up a vigorous policy of resistance. A close defensive alliance was formed with the neighbouring Rajah of Jodhpur, and the Kachhwa vassals everywhere were ordered to refuse payment of the assignments of revenue made on their estates in favour of Sindhia by last year's treaty. The Rajah shut himself up in his capital and prepared to stand a siege.

Rayaji Patil had been left behind by Mahadji Sindhia as his agent in Jaipur, with a force of 5000 Deccani horsemen, when he withdrew from that kingdom in June of the preceding year. This general at first gained some success and occupied some of the outlying parts of the Kachhwa kingdom. Then came the Rajput reaction. Towards the end of December, 1786, he lost 700 men in an abortive assault on a local mud-fort. The situation became steadily worse after the Haldia's return, and at the end of February, Mahadji had to send a strong force under his Bakhshi Jiva Dada to support Rayaji. Rayaji's position was rendered still weaker by the enemy's busy seduction of his faithless Mughalia contingent with promises to pay their arrears of salary which Mahadji had neglected to clear. He therefore wrote, 'daily urging his master to advance speedily to his succour'.

Mahadji's Advance Into Jaipur: The First Stage Of the Campaign

Mahadji took prompt action. Leaving Dig on 16th March, and marching daily without a halt, he reached Daosa on the 24th. This place lies 32 miles east of Jaipur city; the advanced division of the Maratha army under Rayaji stood near Sanganer, seven miles south of that capital. Envoys from Jaipur attended Mahadji's camp, discussing the amount of their tribute. On 8th April, he moved with his army to Bhankri, which is only 13 miles from Jaipur, in order to increase his pressure on the Rajah, while Rayaji advanced from Sanganer to the gates of Jaipur city.

But a settlement was rendered impossible by the stiffening of the Jaipur attitude as allies began to gather for the defence of that State.

> The Jaipur Rajah offered to pay four lakhs of Rupees immediately and demanded the surrender of Khushhali Ram Bohra, after which he would clear the balance of the tribute. Mahadji refused to set off against his claims any amount on the score of damage to crops by his troops (*pai-mali*) or to surrender Bohra. Hence a rupture took place. (*Dy. i, 220; PRC.*, i. p. 169.)

Nothing was left for Sindhia now but to throw his sword into the scale. But even for a trial of arms his relative superiority had vanished during the recent delay. Thanks to Daulat Ram's vigorous action, the Jaipur Rajah had had time to assemble his feudal levies, numbering about 20,000. His ally of Jodhpur sent to him 5000 wild Rathor horses and 5000 mercenary Naga musketeers under his general Bhim Singh. Worst of all, the Jaipur diwan was meeting with success in seducing the old Najaf Khani troops, both Mughalia horse and Hindustani trained sepoys, now under Sindhia's banner as Najaf Khan's successor. The allied Rajputs put on a bold face, and issuing from the capital (first of May) encamped some miles south of it in order to bar any further Maratha advance. Their Rajah himself joined this camp the next day. Sindhia now judged it unsafe to remain near Jaipur, and adopted the plan of seizing the forts of the Kachhwa Rajah's vassals and annexing their lands. Recalling Rayaji Patil from Sanganer, he (on May 5-7), fell back from Bhankri to Sawlia, 20 miles southwards and the same distance west of Lalsot. He publicly declared that in thus falling back his object was to draw the Rajputs into the open country, where he would be able to engage them with greater advantage. But the Rajputs were rightly exultant at this retreat of their enemy. All the country was up in tumult; outside the Maratha camp the roads could not be traversed in safety, and their caravans of provisions began to be constantly looted.

Desertion In Mahadji's Army; His Retreat

By this move Sindhia had interposed himself between the main Jaipur army (now at Sanganer) and the southern districts of that kingdom. He marched through the latter region raiding villages, levying contributions and seizing forts like Jhalai, Navai, etc., till he reached the Banas river near Sarsop, close to the Bundi frontier. Meanwhile his north Indian troops continued to desert him every day, though in small numbers at first. On 6th May, two eminent captains Zulfiqar Ali Khan and Mansur, secretly went over to the Rajputs with their contingents. The climax came on the 25th of that month when the greatest Mughalia general Muhammad Beg Hamadani joined the Jaipur Rajah, to the intense terror and despair of the Maratha army. He was promised Rs 3000 a day and given a royal welcome by his new master who made him the leader of the defence, as his unquestionable ability and fame deserved.

Muhammad Beg's defection enforced a total change of plan on Mahadji. He could not trust a single Hindustani soldier after this. It now became a question of how to save his life and the families of the Maratha generals who had come with him. He sent urgent orders to Khande Rao Hari and Ambaji Ingle to hasten to his aid from their respective stations in Bundelkhand and Karnal. He also begged the Emperor to issue from Delhi and join his camp in order to lend the prestige of his name to the acts of his Regent. Then he fell back from Sarsop to Piplai, 15 miles south-east of Lalsot, arriving there on 4th June.

As soon as the invading army began its retreat the Rajputs advanced from Sanganer, and on the 10th of that month their Rajah occupied Madhogarh, 17 miles north-west of Lalsot. Two days later they pushed a strong detachment on to Daosa, thus blocking Sindhia's northern path of retreat, via Balahari and Dig, to Agra, and menacing the kingdom of his ally the Rao Rajah of Alwar, which was thus laid utterly bare of defence. But for a fortnight after Muhammad Beg's defection, the Rajputs took no vigorous offensive and merely wasted their opportunity and slender money resources in idle talk, while a quarrel broke out with their Rathor allies about the promised war expenses. Sindhia, therefore, determined to put a bold face on it. Giving up all ideas of retreat, he counter marched towards the Rajput's position, arriving on the 15th at a Bhaia-ka-Bagh, a few miles south of the Lalsot pass. On the same day the Rajput force at Daosa pushed a detachment southwards to occupy Ramgarh, which is only six miles north-west of that pass.

But though Mahadji had boldly turned at bay, he was really not in a position to risk an action. There was an increasing desertion from his Hindustani contingent daily owing to his failure to pay their salary at a time when wheat was selling at famine prices in his camp (six seers to the rupee). His own faithful Deccani troops cherished a rooted distrust of their north Indian comrades and ever stood on the guard against any treacherous attack from that side of the camp. Sindhia was, therefore, forced to put off an action and bide his time till he would be joined by the trusty Khande Rao Hari (with 10,000 veterans and two disciplined battalions of De Boigne's sepoys and their excellent artillery) and Ambaji Ingle (with his 15,000 men and possibly a force of hired Sikhs). The Rajput army had a salutary fear of his more modern, and better served artillery and his fine sepoy battalions led by French Commandants like Lesteneau, Le Vassoult and De Boigne. Mahadji abandoned his first idea of surprising the immobile Rajput camp at night. He trusted to time for the speedy dissolution of the ill-knit Rajput confederacy; he would fight a field action when his superiority in artillery and trained musketeers would have full effect.

The Second Stage: Mahadji Assumes The Offensive

At last, on 23rd June when the junction of Khande Rao's contingent was expected on the morrow, Mahadji assumed the offensive. The strictest precaution and order were enforced by this grey veteran fighter. His plan was that his main camp should remain behind, a few miles south of Lalsot, with the baggage guard. Next Mahadji himself, surrounded by 7000 men and ten large guns, should proceed four or five miles ahead of it, with light kit, and encamp. Then Rana Khan Bhai with the main body of his army should advance three or four miles further from his master, while the vanguard, led by Rayaji Patil and Shivaji Vithal Bapu, should take post two miles in front of Rana Khan and scout for the enemy's approach. In every advance that was made, Rana Khan took up Rayaji's position of the previous night, and Mahadji similarly occupied Rana Khan's deserted camping ground. This course was methodically followed throughout the ensuing campaign.

In the course of the next day, Rana Khan occupied the Lalsot pass, which the Rajputs had evacuated a few days before. On the 26th, Khande Rao rode into Sindhia's camp with 3000 Deccani horse, De Boigne's two battalions 1300 strong, two thousand Naga monks, and some 300 foot of Rajdhar Gujar (the Rajah of Samthar). Next morning their muster was taken in Mahadji's presence and the new arrivals sent forward to join Rana Khan. On the 30th of the month the Khan advanced about three miles beyond the pass, encamping below the Jowana hill north-west of its mouth, probably at the modern village of Didwana. A wide plain lay between him and the fort of Ramgarh in the north.

The Theatre Of War Described: Lalsot

It is necessary to have a clear view of the theatre of these operations. 30 miles south-east of the city of Jaipur stands the large village of Lalsot, near the end of a long chain of low hills and outcrops that runs north-eastwards for many miles up to the Banganga river (near the modern railway junction of Bandikui) and even beyond it. The entire northern and western sides of the Lalsot district are enclosed, as if held in the tentacles of a gigantic octopus, by countless ravines which roll down tc the Morel river, a feeder of the mighty Banas. The eastern side is effectively blocked by the long diagonal chain of the

Jowana hill mentioned above. The south side is comparatively open, and through it runs the road to Kerauli (42 miles east of Lalsot) and Dholpur and Bharatpur, still further off. Lalsot village itself blocks the southern mouth of a pass bearing its name which leads by a direct but difficult path to Daosa, 22 miles due north, where the traveller takes the shortest and most frequented route between Jaipur and Agra. This road runs roughly parallel to the Banganga river and has been followed by the modern railway.

Proceeding from Lalsot through the pass immediately north of it and skirting on his left the mass of hillocks known as *Lalsot-ka-Dungar*, the traveller arrives after three miles at the village of Didwana, overlooked by two isolated peaks; then the level country begins. Turning a little to the left from Didwana, he enters, across two narrow ravines, the wide plain of Ramgarh, named after a village and mud-fort standing four miles north-west of Didwana.

From Ramgarh, four miles further to the north-west, the path strikes the Morel river at a very easy ford free from ravines and *nalas* opposite the village and fort of Bidakha. From Bidakha the path passes between two *nalas* for a mile, and thereafter begins an almost unbroken plain, dotted with human habitations for six miles till Tunga village is reached. This Tunga was now the base of the main Rajput army that had come out for the fight, their Rajah being encamped two miles behind at Madhogarh. The battle of 28th July was fought in the plain between Tunga and Bidakha, some two miles from the village of Lalsot after which it is wrongly named. The advancing Marathas had their back to the Morel river, which they guarded by their recent conquest of Bidakha fort, and their moving camp lay behind that river to the south-east near Ramgarh. Further to the south-east the long line was held by the troops guarding Mahadji Sindhia and the light field camp, and last of all by the stationary base-camp two or three miles south of Lalsot village.

Sindhia's Army Advances: Preliminary Skirmishes

The forward movement of Mahadji's army began on 23rd June, but the decisive encounter did not take place till more than a month later. To this delay both sides contributed. Sindhia was waiting till he would be joined by the unaccountably slow Ambaji Ingle, and he was also expecting to see the Rajput coalition dissolve quickly. The Jaipur Rajah, on his part, repressed the ardour of his supporters for a fight, as he was waiting for the junction of helpers from Bikaner, Bundi, Khechiwara and other Rajput centres and particularly for a large body of hired Sindhi musketeers who were fondly believed to prove more of a match for Mahadji's French-led sepoy battalions than the Rajput levies, who were mostly armed with the sword and spear. Nor was he without hopes of starving the invader out by raiding the paths of his grain supply.

On 10th July a further advance was made by Rana Khan to three miles nearer to the enemy, i.e., towards the Morel river, while Mahadji Sindhia stepped into his general's last camp, at Didwana. Contact was now established between the rival outposts and henceforth skirmishes took place almost daily, but these were barren of any result.

On the 13th and 27th of July the fights between the patrols were of a more severe character and the casualties were heavy. There was no activity in the Maratha army for four days from the 15th of that month when Mahadji's little daughter (aged two and a half years) was taken ill. She died in the night of the 16th and her fond father was stricken down by grief; he told Rana Khan, 'Act as you think fit for the next two or three days, but do not ask me, as I am not in the mood to give any reply'.

The mourning over, on the night of the 19th Mahadji received a written challenge from the Jaipur Rajah worded thus:

> You are Regent of the Empire and a veteran in war. Come out of the shelter of young guns into the open field if you dare, and fight a pitched battle with the Rajputs, and we shall see to whom God gives the victory. (*S.J. ms.* 23; *PRC.* i. p. 207.)

Mahadji then called his generals together and told them, 'If after this I make terms with the Jaipur Rajah without fighting one battle, I shall not be able to show my face in Hindustan. A man cannot live for ever. Let what will happen, happen.' They objected, saying that their soldiers would not fight unless their arrears were paid, and that up to now they had fed their followers by selling their own private property and equipment. He offered Rs 20,000 which they refused as too little; his army bill was rupees twelve and a half lakhs a month and he was already six months in default to his troops.

On the 21st, Rana Khan pushed on to Bidakha on the Morel river, which barred his road to the Jaipur camp; his vanguard under Ambaji Ingle crossed that river and raided the villages beyond, up to two miles of the Rajput camp. On the arrival of Rana Khan in full force (23rd July), the defenders of Bidakha agreed to capitulate with honour. Next day there was no movement owing to rain, but Rana Khan dismantled the mud-fort of Bidakha to make the river crossing safe for the future.

Thereafter life in the Maratha camp became unbearable owing to the total stoppage of food supply and the threatened mutiny of all sections of the army in exasperation at Mahadji's failure to pay their dues. Their starved horses were unable to carry any rider. His captains assembled in a Council of war, cried out with one voice, 'Better fight and die than perish from famine.' Mahadji agreed to stake his all on one field fight and ordered five lakhs of rupees to be paid to his soldiers (25th July) in order to hearten them for the coming battle. A second challenge was received from the Jaipur Rajah on the 26th, 'If you wish to seize my kingdom and will not accept tribute, why are you delaying to fight? Come on tomorrow; I, on my part, will be ready.' The entire Maratha army was informed that their master would take up the enemy's gauntlet immediately.

The Battle Of Tunga, 28th July, 1787; Rival Dispositions And Movements; The Rajput Charge Fails

An exceptionally severe skirmish on the 27th July prepared the ground for the decisive battle of the 28th. On that eventful day, Mahadji Sindhia, after long prayers and *puja* at midnight, slept for two hours, rose at four o'clock in the morning, and issued the orders of the day to all his generals. He ate the holy communion (*prasad*) and at break of day mounted his horse named *Desh-pujya* and rode forth to Rana Khan's camp, some two miles ahead of his own halting place. The command for the ensuing battle had been entrusted to this Khan, with whom Sindhia kept constant touch by a chain of swift couriers mounted on camels. Rana Khan marched about two miles ahead of his master with all his troops and sent his light division a mile further on. At each step that this army took to the front, Sindhia too advanced the same distance behind it, ascending successive hillocks and observing his troops through a field glass and sending forth despatch-riders with his fresh instructions. In this methodical way, giving not the least chance for a surprise by the enemy or disorder in his own ranks, the veteran went forth to seek the long looked for decision at last.

Rana Khan forded the dry bed of the Morel at Bidakha, passed clear of the ravines that skirt the two sides for a mile after the crossing, and drew up his line in the plain beyond, a mile further off. First he spread a loose screen of scouts for bringing news of the enemy's dispositions and movements. Then came the artillery, and behind it the infantry battalions which were to receive the first shock of the enemy's onset. In the third line were the Maratha horse, held in reserve for supporting any hard-pressed point in the front lines, and with this body stood Rana Khan himself. The last reserve, especially in guns and munitions, was kept under Mahadji himself, two miles behind the battle front, on the further (i.e. eastern) bank of the Morel. The Maratha artillery, on reaching the battleground, threw up a line of earth works before them by digging into the sandy soil, and thus their front was protected by an entrenchment a mile or two in length. Sindhia's army stretched west to east: the first line was formed by Khande Rao Hari with De Boigne's two battalions, the Afghan mercenaries under Murtaza Khan Barech, Ghazi Khan and other captains, and the Naga force of Motigir Gosain (left wing). Then came the discontented and passive Hindustani sepoys of the old Najaf Khani service (centre); and last, the two brigades of six battalions each under the faithful Lesteneau and Le Vassoult, together with the Rajput levies of the Macheri Rao Rajah (right wing).

The Jaipurians began their advance about the same time that they saw the Maratha army moving towards them across the Morel. They too threw up earth works before their line of guns. On their side the brunt of the battle fell on the Rathor cavalry under Bhim Singh (the *bakhshi* of Jodhpur) who had vowed in Sawai Pratap Singh's presence not to return alive without victory, and the Mughalia deserters under Muhammad Beg Hamadani, these two generals respectively leading the right and left wings of their army. Their centre was formed by the Kachhwas, who kept themselves back exactly like Mahadji's Hindustanis facing them.

After the usual light skirmishes between the rival patrols, the battle started about nine in the morning with a mutual cannonade which did more injury to the Marathas, because their guns, dragged from a more distant base and across a wide stony river-bed, were lighter pieces than those of the Rajputs whose camp was close behind. 'As the Jaipur guns were larger, their balls reached Sindhia's army, and many men and horse(s) were killed, while Sindhia's shots did not touch the Rajputs. The Jaipur balls were found to weigh from five to fourteen seers.' On hearing of it, Mahadji ordered four large guns to be taken to Rana Khan.

A little before eleven o'clock the distant cannonade ceased, as if by mutual consent. Then a tumultuous shout was heard on the Rajput right, and through the smoke screen burst four thousand Rathor horsemen at the gallop. These desperadoes, after taking a last lingering pull at their pipes of opium, drew their swords and charged the Maratha left with wild cries of 'Han! Kill them!' Sindhia's batteries ploughed through their dense ranks, opening bloody lanes at each discharge. But heedless of their fallen comrades, the survivors swept up to the Maratha guns, sabred the gunners and still advancing fell upon the supporting infantry. Their terrific impact broke the first line of the Maratha left wing; hundreds of Nagas and Afghans were slain, and even De Boigne's sepoys after firing a few volleys were forced back in confusion along with their Maratha comrades. The cool Savoyard led his disordered ranks obliquely to the rear, formed the survivors again, and reopened small arm fire, but 'the Rathors heeded it not'.

Rana Khan promptly sent up reinforcements of Deccáni horse under Shivaji Vithal (Bapu), Rayaji Patil and Khande Hari (Apa) who rallied the fugitives and renewed the combat. The bloodiest and most obstinate struggle of the day raged here. The situation at one time became so critical that the sons of Murtaza Khan Barech dismounted and fought on foot, which is the last expedient of Indian warriors when driven to bay. More guns at last came up from the rear and the Rathors retreated, but not before they had inflicted over 300 casualties, including Ghazi Khan (brother of Murtaza Khan), Shambhuji Patil and one *jamadar* slain, and Malhar Rao Pawar, Chimnaji Khande Rao (Bapu's diwan), the nephew of Bapu himself and one *jamadar* wounded. For this the Rajputs had to pay a heavy price, suffering 1000 casualties including high officers like Shivaram Bhandari and Bhim Singh's brother-in-law, besides a score of lower officers slain.

The Concluding Stage Of The Battle; A Criticism Of The Campaign

But the greatest loss to the Rajput cause was the death of Muhammad Beg Hamadani, which broke the spine of their offensive power. This general, the most famous Muslim warrior, then living in North India, had sent on his troops to attack the Maratha right wing while he sat on an elephant in the shade of a tree watching them from behind. A cannon ball struck the tree above and rebounding knocked him down to the ground, tearing one side of his body open. Then the branch, broken by the shot, fell down crushing him underneath. His advancing troops, unaware of his fate, attacked the Maratha right wing and penetrated to their baggage, but were repulsed by the Deccani horse hurried up from the reserve by Rana Khan.

The Rathors during the rest of the day made three or four advances as if to fall upon the Maratha guns again, but found no opportunity of carrying out their design. The Mughalias, deprived of their chief, did not stir again. After repulsing the first two enemy attacks, Sindhia's army stood on the defensive, the Maratha portion of it quaking in fear lest at the first successful breakthrough by the Rajputs their treacherous Hindustani comrades should join the enemy and turn their guns upon Mahadji's own! But thanks to the successful defence by Rayaji Patil and others, the traitors got no chance of doing so. But there was no further advance on the Maratha side, partly because Hamadani's death was not known to them till after nightfall, and mainly because it began to rain in the afternoon, making that sandy plain difficult for artillery movement. The Marathas were rightly afraid of the ravines in front (so convenient for ambushes), the oncoming darkness and the lack of water in that tract. So, each side fell back to its camp and resorted to random firing till an hour after sunset in order to guard against any surprise in the darkness. And the battle of Tunga, miscalled that of Lalsot, 'though sanguinary, had no decisive result', as De Boigne remarked.

The battle of Tunga has been universally acclaimed by the Rajputs as 'an entire victory'. Tactically it had no right to the claim: the Rajputs delivered successive charges on the Maratha forces in the field and failed to dislodge them; all their attacks were repulsed, and at the end of the day each side returned to its camp in the rear, as was then the usual practice. The day after the battle the Maratha army reappeared on the same field and advanced, within gunshot distance of the Jaipur camp, but none on the opposite side ventured to stir out. That is not the conduct of a victorious army. Their Rajah even begged for a two days' truce for burying and burning his dead. Nor could the Rajputs boast of having taken a single Maratha gun, and their own casualty list was much heavier than that of the Marathas.

And yet it was not a victory for Sindhia either. He had failed to crush the enemy in the field, or to rout them out of their camp. He had not captured any enemy gun. Therefore, his offensive must be adjudged a failure.

Considered in its strategy, the Lalsot campaign as a whole was a failure for Mahadji. The failure was due to his lack of a single clear objective steadily pursued and his blunder in concentrating every available soldier for the field fight, which left his line of communication with the Kerauli fatally unprotected and made it impossible for him to spare an adequate escort for the vitally necessary grain convoys. He was indeed starved out of Rajputana. He had forgotten Wellington's dictum that 'a modern army marches on its stomach'.

XXII

The Last Rajput Struggle Against The Marathas: The Battle of Patan, 1790

Sawai Pratap Singh's Character And Difficult Position

Sawai Pratap Singh came to the throne of Jaipur in 1778, at the age of thirteen.[1] His character developed as he grew older, under the stress of circumstances, and a sympathetic French observer described him (in 1794) as 'a good Prince', 'an upright Prince', who knew the evils which were ruining his kingdom but found himself powerless to remove them, because he had no honest or capable minister, no loyal baronage, no obedient subjects to support him in any attempt at driving the Marathas out of the realm. This French captain J. Pillet, who had then been six years in Jaipur, clearly proves this in his letter to Lt. Col. Peter Murray, Adjutant-General to the British Indian Army. He shows how the Jaipur Rajah's worst enemies were not the Marathas but his own subjects and servants, and how the undisciplined spirit of independence among his vassals and their selfish robbery of his lands and withholding of his just tributes ended by depriving Rajputana of its independence and making the once-victorious Rajput race subjugated and humiliated by the Deccani invaders. Against such universal moral degeneracy, the 'good Prince' Pratap Singh was powerless to effect any good. It was, as the French captain points out,

> ... this sense of his helplessness in defending his State with the poor resources then at his command, that drove Sawai Pratap Singh into the policy of placating the Marathas, as the only means of averting his own total ruin and in consequence made him seek peace and repose which he could find only in his palace, that "centre of indolence" for the monarch.

The historian who has made a minute study of the real condition of the time and place must admit the truth of this picture. (See Appendices.)

The Jaipur Rajah's worst enemies were his selfish mutually jealous ministers and his disloyal vassals even when they belonged to the same Kachhwa clan. The most notorious of the last group were Rao Rajah Pratap Singh Naruka of Alwar, Bahadur Singh Rajawat of Jhalai and Pahar Singh Khangarot. In addition to these, the Shekhawat chiefs were ever on the look-out to aggrandise themselves at the expense of their tribal sovereign in every trouble that befell him, exactly like the selfish members of the Holy Roman Empire in their attitude to their political suzerain, the Emperor of medieval Europe.

After the failure of the Lalsot campaign (July, 1787) the army of Mahadji Sindhia evacuated Jaipur territory, and it repeated its visitation there only in May, 1790. During this period of almost three years, Rajputana enjoyed freedom from Maratha ravage. The Kachhwa and Rathor kingdoms could have utilised this splendid opportunity to ensure the permanent defence of the land and keep out the Deccanis in future, if only they could have produced an extraordinarily efficient leader and a united and patriotic nobility. But it was not to be. Selfishness, discord and lack of good faith among the nobility proved the ruin of this 'land of the sons of kings', and the barons themselves were as much humbled and ground down as their young king.

From the day of Patan (20th June, 1790) to the 2nd of April, 1818, when Jaipur entered into a protective subsidiary alliance with the British Government, lay the gloomiest period in the history of the Kachhwa kingdom. As a historian who is nowhere well-disposed to the house of Amber writes,

> Throughout the twenty-five years rule of Pratap, he and his country underwent many vicissitudes. He was a gallant prince, and not deficient in Judgement; but neither gallantry nor prudence could successfully apply the resources of his petty State against its numerous predatory foes and its internal dissensions. The defection of Macheri was a serious blow to Jaipur and the

necessary subsidies soon lightened the hoards accumulated by his predecessors.

Things passed from bad to worse under his successor Jagat Singh (1803-1818), whose reign was crowded with 'foreign invasions, cities besieged, capitulations and war contributions... court intrigues, diversified not unfrequently by an appeal to the sword or dagger even in the precincts of the Court.' (*Annals of Amber*, Ch. III.)

Rajput Policy Towards The Marathas From Tunga To Patan

We now turn to the history of Jaipur from the battle of Tunga to the final triumph of Mahadji Sindhia in Rajputana. The numerous despatches in the Marathi language and the newsletters in the Persian as well as the reports of the British Resident with Mahadji, make Sawai Pratap Singh's policy and activity during this interval quite clear.

After the retreat of Sindhia from Lalsot, the Jaipur Rajah forbade any pursuit of the enemy. He considered it good riddance and was content to defend his own realm without attempting any ambitious scheme of annexing Sindhia's recently acquired North Indian territories. He wrote to the Peshwa, whose servant Sindhia avowedly was, to order the latter to respect Jaipur territory in future, out of regard for the old personal intimacy between Baji Rao I and Sawai Jai Singh and the still older cordial relation (as of father and son) which subsisted between Mirza Rajah Jai Singh and Shivaji. When Ismail Beg and other Mughalia leaders urged him to attack Sindhia's stronghold of Agra fort and drive the Deccanis south of the Narmada, Pratap restrained them, saying that he would pay these Mughalia troops as long as they remained with him for the defence of his realm, but would not undertake any adventure outside his own frontier unless formally commanded by the Emperor and backed by the legitimate forces and loyal vassals of the Imperial crown.

This was the wisest policy possible in the circumstances. The Jaipur Rajah's first task, after being freed from the Maratha menace, was to establish his authority over his refractory vassals and recover the vast territory along his eastern border usurped by the rebel Naruka of Alwar during a career of aggression for 20 years since the death of Madho Singh. But stern reality made it impossible to carry out his wise scheme. The titular Emperor Shah Alam II at once showed himself a mere shadow, powerless to protect his loyal subjects, powerless to repress the rebels against his authority, and within a year of Tunga he was robbed and blinded by the Ruhela Ghulam Qadir. Sawai Pratap Singh was therefore thrown entirely on his own resources, with a single ally in the world, Rajah Bijai Singh of Marwar, who had as much to dread from Maratha vengeance as he.

The Lalsot campaign brought no final deliverance to the Rajputs. It was public knowledge that Mahadji Sindhia, when retreating from that place, had turned his face back to the country he was being forced to leave behind and sworn, 'If I live, I shall reduce Jaipur and Jodhpur to dust.' On 29th December, 1787, the Maratha envoy at Delhi wrote to Puna 'Patil Baba's determination is to sell everything he possesses, but punish the Rajahs of Jaipur and Jodhpur and exercise his Regency of the Delhi Empire.[2] Therefore, these Rajput States had every reason to expect his vengeance if he ever recovered his power in Hindustan.

When, at the close of the year 1788, Sindhia crushed Ghulam Qadir, Rajah Bijai Singh wrote to Sawai Pratap Singh, 'Ghulam Qadir has been captured. You should now be on your guard and assemble your troops for the protection of your realm. Patil Baba is himself again. He may march against you; therefore be careful.' (*DY*. i, 374.) The Jaipur Rajah then tried hard to buy the armed aid of Mirza Ismail Beg, the nephew and successor of the dead Muhammad Beg Hamadani, in the command of the Mughalia troops and sepoy battalions that had deserted Sindhia on the eve of the battle of Tunga. But Ismail was now once again an officer of Sindhia and enjoying *jagirs* granted by him as regent in the Rewari-Narnaul-Kanaud region. Sawai Pratap Singh for a long time failed to raise the money necessary for satisfying the demands of Ismail.

At last in March, 1790, a rupture took place between Sindhia and Ismail Beg for causes entirely unconnected with Jaipur, and soon afterwards envoys from these two Rajput States reached Ismail Beg's camp near Narnaul with one and a half lakhs in cash and promises of more money, and thus induced him to join them in opposing Sindhia. The terms of the pact were: (i) the Jodhpur and Jaipur Governments would pay the Mirza seven and five lakhs respectively, namely two lakhs down and ten lakhs on the eve of the actual fighting;

(ii) the Mirza should leave his family in Jaipur as hostages for his good faith, and (iii) the Mirza should send away the *wakil* of Sindhia who had up to now been in attendance at his camp.

Mahadji Sindhia Renews War, 1790

Meantime, Mahadji had earlier realized that Mirza Ismail was an incorrigible enemy who must be crushed before he could repeat the success of Ghulam Qadir. For this coming trial of strength, the Maratha Rajah made adequate preparations, leaving nothing to chance; he had learnt wisdom from his Lalsot campaign. His forces were concentrated near Mathura by calling in all dispersed detachments. Colonel De Boigne was provided with funds and ordered to raise 13 battalions of trained sepoys with 60 pieces of artillery, and the work was effected and the new troops efficiently drilled in the course of six months.

At last, in the middle of March, 1790, he began the campaign. One large division, under the Commander-in-Chief Gopal Bhau,[3] accompanied by Jiva Dada Bakhshi and De Boigne, marched into the Rewari district, south-west of Delhi, by way of Hodal, Palwal and Pataudi, arriving at the last named town on 5th May. Another division, led by Ambaji Ingle, moved through Alwar and effected a junction with the first near Rewari. A contingent of about 4500 horse from Tukoji Holkar's army (commanded by Bapu and Kashi Holkar) tardily cooperated with this force as very reluctant partners. We may here add that one thousand horse of Ali Bahadur's force (under his *diwan* Balwant Sadashiv Aswalkar) reached Sindhia's army only on the day of the battle of 20th June. There were also two small contingents of the Rao Rajah and Najaf Quli Khan on the Maratha side.

Meanwhile in the camp, before Narnaul Mirza Ismail Beg had closed with the offer of the two Rajput Rajahs, and as the advance portion of Sindhia's army, after taking possession of Rewari and Kanti, pushed on towards Narnaul, Ismail Beg and the Rajputs hurriedly evacuated the last-named town in the face of such superior odds and took refuge near the city of Patan (in Tonwarwati) 19 miles further south, on 13th May. The Maratha vanguard came on their heels and halted four miles eastwards, their main army and camp remaining about eight miles behind.

Patan Described: The Rival Armies

Nestling in the V-shaped hollow formed by three hills over 2000 feet high which almost touch one another, lay the rich city of Patan, the seat of Rajah Sampat or Himmat Singh[4] of the Naruka branch of the Kachhwa clan. Its fort crowns the hill at 2385 feet above sea level. North-east, south-east and south of Patan the land is dotted with isolated hillocks greatly restricting access to the city. The whole of its western flank for many miles north to south is blocked by a very long chain of hills rising even higher (over 2600 feet), and separating Patan from the famous battlefield of Maonda which is only six miles due west of it in a straight line across an impassable rocky barrier So also is much of its northern side, where only a long narrow path leaving the road from Narnaul at Dabla, and winding through four successive defiles by way of Salodra and Kishorpura, can reach Patan. The main, or more correctly, the only road for access to this city is one running south-eastwards, via Rajapura to Kot-Putli, 15 miles away, across the Sota river (a feeder of the Sabi).

In this impregnable position the confederates faced the Marathas, who encamped about eight miles east of Patan, in the spacious well-watered plain from Bhopatpura to Narera,[5] outside the pass through which the road from Patan to Kot-Putli debouches, keeping the Sota river in their rear. The Mughalia-Rajput armies encamped about a mile or two outside the city of Patan and east of it, in a long line stretching north to south. There was no unity of command, nor union of hearts among the allies, or even among the two sections of the Muslim army. The Rajputs suspected the fidelity of Ismail Beg and with good reason. This general had first eaten Mahadji Sindhia's salt and then gone over to his enemies in battle; he had next joined Ghulam Qadir but fought against him in Delhi when re-engaged by Sindhia, and now he had deserted Sindhia's service a second time for a new pay-master. The Mughalia mercenaries were ever ready to sell their venal swords to the highest bidder. Within the Muslim army too, there was all but declared war. Ismail Beg's boundless arrogance, cruelty and harshness of speech had set his captains against him and his insolvency had driven them to starvation and desperation. Besides, he was known to be planning the treacherous arrest and murder of the commandants of the trained battalions under his banner, as he had murdered one commandant Muhammad Yar Khan. Hence Abdul Matlab Khan, the chief of the sepoy of artillery portion of his army, always armed in self-defence whenever Ismail rode out to battle. This section of the Muslim army pitched their camp at a safe distance from Ismail's own troops, and a Rathor force had to be stationed between them to prevent them from fighting or plundering each other! (*Ibrat.*, iii, 359 *DY* S. 26. ii. 11.)

This was the unhappy army that Gopal Bhau and De Boigne blocked up among the hills of Patan. For a week the Marathas kept their horses saddled ready day and night, to guard against surprise, and sent out their Pindari irregular horsemen to sack the villages around and cut off the Mirza's provision supply. Then, on 21st May, a letter was received from Mahadji sharply censuring his generals for their idleness and failure to secure a decision by fighting. Gopal Bhau therefore decided to send De Boigne's artillery and musketeers inside the pass in an attempt to break the enemy's line.

The Fruitless Attack Of 22nd May

Three hours before that summer dawn the drums beat to arms in De Boigne's camp. Leaving a strong force to guard his tents and baggage, he issued with the rest of his division, consisting of trained sepoy battalions and artillery under European officers and a body of Indian cavalry. His right and left wings were commanded by Major Hunter and Ashrof Beg, and his centre (which had artillery in front of it) by Michael Filoze. Behind the two wings cavalry was drawn up under Nusrat Yar Khan. From each battalion De Boigne picked out two companies of sharp-shooters and one captain and sent them ahead to engage the enemy.

The enemy took up the challenge and manned their trenches and drew up in line of battle. The force of De Boigne moving in the open, presented a sure target for Alah Yar Khan's guns which had been ranged in a line on a higher ground and tied together with iron chains, with Abdul Matlab's musketeers on guard. The hail of shots struck down many of the assailants and when at midday De Boigne abandoned the field after 'some fruitless attempts without achieving anything', he had lost two hundred men, and his cavalry leader Nusrat Yar Khan had been knocked down senseless by the wind of a cannon ball. But his artillery also replied with effect.

In another part of the field, at the south end, Ismail Beg drew up his own contingent in front of the hill of Patan, headed by artillery and sepoy battalions. The Rajput cavalry was placed in support, one half of it behind Ismail and the other behind Abdul Matlab. A force of Nagas or fighting monks in Jaipur service held their own trenches at the bottom of a hillock in the extreme north. The advance of Gopal Bhau's cavalry was checked by Ismail Beg's fire; similarly Holkar's contingent was repulsed by the Naga musketeers. Towards evening both sides gave up the useless slaughter and retired, Ismail having lost about 200 men killed and two of his battalion commandants wounded; on the Rajput side Hemraj Bakhshi and a Jodhpur *jamadar* were wounded.

The exploratory thrust failed, and Gopal Bhau decided to starve the enemy out by closing his paths of supply. Four more weeks passed in watchful inactivity, which time was used by Ambaji Ingle in inducing Abdul Matlab's corps, by a bribe of one and a half lakhs of rupees, to promise to desert to the Marathas during the next battle. Then came another stinging letter of reproof from Sindhia, and by a happy coincidence a prediction of the astrologers that if the battle was fought in the afternoon of[6] 20th June (*Asharh ekadashi*),[7] the stars would give the victory to Sindhia.

The Battle Of Patan, 20th June 1790

The Maratha army was thus drawn up: De Boigne's disciplined brigade and quick firing guns formed the spearhead of the Maratha attack and occupied the van in front of the centre; Ambaji Ingle and Balaji Ingle commanded the left wing (opposite Ismail Beg), Holkar's contingent (under Kashi Rao and Bapu Holkar) with some minor captains the right wing (facing the Jaipur Nagas); Gopal Bhau and Jiva Dada with the main body of Deccan horse the centre (opposite the Rathor cavalry). The two armies faced each other east and west in a long line; Ismail's own contingent formed the right or extreme south wing of the confederates, then came a body of Rathor horse, next Abdul Matlab's battalions, and thereafter the centre where the bulk of the Rajput cavalry was massed, and finally the left wing under the Jaipur Nagas at the north end. There were three rows of artillery in this army, one before Ismail, another before Abdul Matlab and the third in the trenches of the Nagas—a total of over 125 pieces. On the Maratha side the only artillery was that of De Boigne's brigade, whose superior mobility and greater accuracy and rapidity of fire more than compensated for their smaller number.

The battle of Patan was not fought by a simultaneous attack along the entire front so customary in Indian warfare, but began sporadically at some points and developed into a general engagement only at its end. There was no unity of command on the side of the confederates, nor any plan of battle except to watch passively for the enemy's action. Hence the Maratha army in the actual clash of arms had the advantages of surprise and initiative, for which De Boigne's eagle eye and rapid decision must bear full credit.

On the 20th of June neither side was in haste to come to grips. Gopal Bhau would not repeat his bloody offensive of 22nd May, and the Rajput swordsmen were mortally afraid of the Frenchman's guns, which they would charge only under cover of darkness or a screen of hillocks. The Maratha army took up arms before daybreak and advanced four miles westwards from their camp to the mouth of the pass leading to Patan, where they had hitherto maintained a small patrol. One quarter of the day was over before the enemy showed themselves on the heights. Then Sindhia's line of battle was formed, but there was no actual fighting for six hours afterwards. It was the *ekadashi*[8] day, and the Hindu soldiers on both sides who were observing their religious fast, felt overcome by thirst and the heat of the summer sun of Rajputana, 'and for one quarter of the day, not a shot or bullet was fired from either sides; only the Muslim troopers of both the armies galloped into the field and retreated after each such charge'. (*Ibrat.*, iii, 371.)

When the sun began to decline from the meridian, the Rajputs and their Muslim allies retired to their respective camps undressed, and engaged in cooking their meals and recovering from the heat. The Maratha army held its ground near the mouth of the pass; its generals Gopal Bhau and De Boigne sat on a hillock behind the line of their troops, keeping watch on the field and the enemy entrenchments in the distant west. The real battle was precipitated in the evening by an unforeseen skirmish. About three hours before sunset, some Pindaris from the left wing of the Maratha army, after a detour to Ismail Beg's rear, seized the transport animals of that general as they were coming back from pasture. A Muslim force hurried out to the rescue of the cattle and then Balaji Ingle with 2000 horse-men fell on the newcomers, and a severe confused fight ranged for an hour. Next Ismail Beg, in spite of his fever, which had been doubled by the sun's heat, took horse, headed a charge and drove the Marathas out of the allied lines, by his reckless personal bravery.

A general fire was now opened on Sindhia's army by all the confederate artillery, but it did little execution on account of the long range. Next Gopal Bhau sent some squadrons to skirmish against the Rathors in the centre. These masters of Parthian tactics, after a little demonstration, pretended to give way. The Rathors followed in reckless pursuit at full gallop with loud cries of victory, leaving their sheltered position on the heights. As soon as they descended into the plain and came within range, the artillery of De Boigne opened a deadly fire, mowing down hundreds among their dense masses. He had armed his sepoy musketeers with the bayonet, a weapon entirely unknown till then in Rajputana, and against it the Rajput swords clashed in vain, as the Baluchi swords were to do against Napier's bayonets at the Battle of Miani half a century later. The remnant fled back to the hills. De Boigne followed up this success by advancing at the head of his battalions and seizing the artillery of Abdul, which was completely taken by surprise and could offer no resistance.

During the confusion of this life and death struggle in the centre, Ismail Beg with his Mughalia horse and sepoy battalions had moved up against the Maratha left wing (under Ambaji) and at first carried everything before him. But De Boigne immediately after worsting the Rathor horse, turned his guns upon Ismail and raked him with a flank fire (from Abdul Matlab's captured guns, now served by his own artillery men). The Persian's artillery was silenced; his followers fell fast or fled before a murderous fire to which he could not reply; and at last he admitted the inevitable, flung away his blood-stained sword and galloped back to his tent in hopeless defeat. His commandants, Abdul Matlab and Alaya Beg sought their own safety, abandoning their sepoys to their fate.

Only in one sector of the battle front had there been no fighting worth speaking of. On the Maratha right, Holkar's contingent (about 4000 strong) were attacked by the Rathors, but saved by reinforcements hurried up to them by Gopal Bhau. Then they 'remained standing' before the trenches of the Jaipur Nagas. But De Boigne had already told two battalions to keep the Nagas in check, and now freed from the struggle in the centre and the left, turned all his force against the Nagas and routed them by a sudden onset. It was already nine at night, and the last trace of resistance died out.

The Maratha Victory And Gains

All that night and for all of the next day, a relentless pursuit was kept up by the Maratha horsemen, and the famished, thirsty tired Rajput fugitives were butchered unresisting. For Gopal Bhau had proclaimed before that he would allow every soldier to keep whatever spoils he could seize.[9] The enemy's trained battalions did not share the flight of the Rajput horse, but took refuge in Patan city, and surrendered with its surrender.

No victory could be more complete. All the property, guns and arms of the confederates left in the field or in their camps were captured. Next morning De Boigne went with some guns to the gate of Patan city and threatened bombardment; the Rajah Sampat (or Himmat)[10] Singh was powerless to resist.[11] Five of the defeated battalions' commandants fled on horseback to the hills, but all the other commandants in it capitulated and of the common soldiers nearly 2000 cavalry and 10,000 sepoys grounded arms and were sent away with only the dress they stood in. De Boigne next laid siege to the fort of Patan, which capitulated in the course of six hours, and all the vast enemy property deposited in these two places fell into the hands of the victors. For a week afterwards the Maratha army halted there and combed the villages around, recovering from them all the enemy property and guns concealed there.

The spoils of victory amounted to 105 pieces of artillery, 21 elephants, 8000 flintlocks, 1300 camels, 300 horses, besides many lakhs worth of other kinds of property. (*DY.S.* 29; *H.P.* 575; *Ibrat.*, iii. 375, mentions 6500 horses, 5300 camels, 3200 oxen etc., but I doubt these inflated round numbers.) The casualties on the side of the vanquished were five battalions and 3000 Rathor horsemen. But Ismail Beg's fine army was practically annihilated; it ceased to exist as a military unit and lost all its arms and equipment, tents, baggage and even cooking pots. On Sindhia's side, in the household cavalry (*hazurat silehdar*), 52 men were slain and 309 wounded (of these 188 by firearms), and 69 horses were killed and 104 wounded. No chief fell on either side though the report arose that Gangaram Bhandari, the Jodhpur generalissimo, had been killed. Only two of Sindhia's officers were wounded but only slightly so.

De Boigne's Achievement

It cannot be denied that the decisive part in this most decisive victory was contributed by De Boigne. His French biographer rightly praises his cool alert generalship during the swaying tides of the combat:

> The coolness of the general and the excellent discipline of his troops prevented any disorder, even when Ismail Beg's horsemen broke his line and sabred his gunners at their pieces. The ranks were dressed anew, the line was formed again as soon as it was broken, and his conserved and well-directed fire repelled that vigorous attack... Leaving his cannon in charge of the reserve, he put himself at the head of one of his battalions and ordering the other to follow, threw himself sword in hand on the batteries of the enemy; and seized the first immediately; he was master of the second at eight p.m. and the enemy were found in complete rout at nine p.m. (*Carriers*, p. 85).

The Marathas were jealous of the greater fame and favour which this foreigner enjoyed, but even their despatches are constrained to admit his brilliant achievement:

> De Boigne having secured mastery in the fight with the Marwaris on the right wing (really, the centre), fired his guns on the left wing marvellously well... The newly raised campoo of De Boigne fought magnificently, and he himself is a hero. (*HP*. 574).

That De Boigne's initiative and martial genius alone made the victory possible, will be clear from the following anecdote narrated by Faqir Khair-ud-din, the former *munshi* of the Anderson brothers (residents at Sindhia's Court):

> In the evening, Colonel De Boigne was seated on a hillock eating his lunch. On seeing the shaking among the troops of Ismail and

> the Rathors, he gave up his meal and asked Gopal Bhau to permit him to launch an attack as the enemy had no power left now to make a stand. Gopal Bhau replied, "It is the end of the day. What can you do now?" De Boigne replied that he refused to obey his General and would take full responsibility for his action... Leaving two battalions to face the Nagas and taking two battalions and ten guns with himself, he marched on the enemy's artillerly (i.e., Abdul Matlab's) and began firing on it. At this unexpected attack the order of the enemy force was broken when they tried to assemble... and after a time they took to flight...(*Ibrat.*, iii, 373).

At Patan was fought the last battle of the old style in which Jaipur troops took part. It has been described in detail on account of the misrepresentations about it. (See Appendices.)

Notes

1. But Captain J. Pillet, writing from Jaipur in 1794, says 'at the age of eleven'. The date of his birth cannot now be traced. According to *Jaipur ki Vamsavali* (ms. p. 41 received from Purohit Har Narayan Collection), Pratap Singh was born on Poush bidi 2, V.S. 1821 = Monday, December 2, 1764. *Ed.*
2. *Akh.* S.J. ms., p. 53; *DY.* i. 235. The date mentioned should be Wednesday, December 19, 1787, because letter No. 235, *D.Y.I.*, pp. 204-5, which contains the information about Mahadji's resolve was written 8 Rabi-ul-Awwal (1202 A.H.). *Ed.*
3. Gopal Raghunath, the younger brother of Aba Chitnis, one of the four confidants of Mahadji Sindhia. *J.S.*
4. The correct name is Sampat Singh (1757-1790 A.D.), who was ruling over Patan estate at the time of the battle of Patan. *Torawati ka Itihas*, by M.P. Sharma, pp. 84-87. *Ed.*
5. Six miles north-west of Kot-Putli. *J.S.*
6. Omit 'in the afternoon of' and instead read 'on'. *Ed.*
7. Omit *Asharh ekadashi* and read *Adhik ashadha sudi ashtami* (*H.P.* letter No. 574, p. 814). These two corrections are made on the basis of the correct reading of the text of the said letter II. 8-9, p. 814. The Hijri date on this day was Shawwal 6, 1204

A.H. (*P.R.C.*, i, letters No. 260, p. 387; and No. 263, pp. 369-70). This statement of Sir Jadunath Sarkar seems to be apparently based on his mistaken impression that June 20, 1790, was an *ekadashi* day. *Ed.*

8. For *ekadashi* read *Adhik ashadha sudi ashtami*, the correct *tithi* corresponding to June 20, 1790. *Shukla ashtami* is also as holy as any *ekadashi*. *Ed.*

9. *Ibrat.*, iii, 376; *H.P.* 574. *J.S.*

10. Omit 'or Himmat'. See footnote no. 4. *Ed.*

11. The Rajah of Patan immediately made peace with Sindhia, through Ramsevak (the diwan of his relative, the Rao Rajah of Alwar), agreeing to pay a ransom of Rs 60,000. (*DY. S.* 41; *Ibrat.*, iii, 378.) *J.S.*

XXIII

The Last Years of Sawai Pratap Singh, 1791-1803

The Jaipur Government's Policy After The Battle Of Patan

From the lost field of Patan, Mirza Ismail Beg fled with only 14 horsemen, and by hard riding reached the city of Jaipur on the next day. The others who shared his defeat followed the same westward path: Shovaram Bhandari and Shahmal (who had come from Jodhpur with 8000 horse) went to Sambhar; all trace of Gangaram Bhandari, the Marwari generalissimo who had brought 5000 more cavalry with him, was lost for three days, after which he too made his way to Sambhar. Sukhlal Haldia, the Jaipur representative in the battle (with 5000 horse), hastened back to his own capital. The Jaipur Rajah treated Ismail Beg very kindly, but as he could not provide the vast sum necessary for creating a new army organization out of the wreck of Patan, the Mughalia leader then left him for Jodhpur, where hurried preparations had begun for making a stand against the coming vengeance of Sindhia. There a new army was mustered under Zalim Singh and Bhim Singh Bakhshi and posted on the eastern frontier to wait for the enemy.

The Kachhwa State, which lay nearest in the path of Sindhia, concentrated its efforts on defending the capital and posted all its available troops six miles east of Jaipur. But after a time 4000 men were sent under Daulatram Haldia to join the Marwar army.

The victorious Marathas, after gathering all the spoils of war from Patan and the villages around, marched via Pragpura, south-west of Kot-Putli, to Manoharpur, 27 miles north of Jaipur, so as to be in a position from which they could threaten both Jaipur and Jodhpur, while their predatory light horse continued to raid the country for many miles. A strong detachment of 5000 horse under Lakwa Dada, with Holkar's contingent of 2000 and two battalions of Sepoys, moved through Shekhawati levying contributions from the local landlords and cities. Several of these petty chiefs secured immunity by offering a joint contribution of three lakhs through Ramsevak, the *diwan* of Alwar. The main army pushed on to Sambhar, on the Jodhpur frontier, which city was evacuated by the rump of the Marwar army. The Marathas also took the fort of Marot, 15 miles north-west of Sambhar city, and made it their base for an invasion of Marwar (end of July).

The Kachhwa territory outside the capital, especially the north-eastern districts, lay helpless before the ravages. The *zamindars* and barons (*thakurs*) of Shekhawati wrote to Rajah Pratap Singh,

> If you issue in person we shall fight under you, but we do not agree to serve under Daulatram or Ismail Beg. The Maratha army has reached our homes, while you are busy with the defence of your city. If our lands are ravaged we have no other means of living. We have, therefore, agreed to pay ransom to the Marathas. (*DY.S.* 33).

But Sindhia suddenly changed his plan of war. Leaving Jaipur aside for the present, as a settlement by negotiation seemed more promising, he ordered his generals to reconquer Ajmer district and fort first, before plunging into the sands of Marwar. Already a light force under Lakhsman Anant and Baloji Ingle had been sent on to raid the Ajmer country. The district was occupied without serious fighting, and the city of Ajmer was taken at the gallop, but the fort held out for many months. The Maratha Generals then resumed their invasion of Marwar (August) and penetrated to the environs of Merta, called 'the Gateway of Marwar'. Here a decisive battle was fought on 10th September, 1790, in which Rajput valour clashed helplessly with European science and European discipline, and machine triumphed over muscle.

But the historian of Jaipur is not concerned with this battle, nor with the campaign which ended with the surrender of Ajmer fort to Sindhia on 7th March, 1791, because no Kachhwa contingent took part in these later struggles. We only know that when Ismail Beg left Jaipur for Marwar (July, 1790), a Jaipur force of about 4000 horse under Daulatram Haldia accompanied him, and that it followed Bhimraj Bakhshi in his retreat to Nagor after the crushing defeat at Merta. (*Chandra*, ii, 82; *DY*. S, 42.)

In fact, no effort adequate for the task of confronting Sindhia's vastly superior army, now flushed with two such resounding victories, was possible for Jaipur State on account of the sad internal dissensions described in the last chapter. The Maratha despatches make it quite clear: 'The Jaipur Rajah is sitting down quietly. His ancestors left vast treasures, but though many store-rooms were opened, no money was found anywhere.' Again, 'The Rajah is penniless. In many places his brethren do not obey him. Hence Holkar is daily seizing (villages) and chastising the *garhi-bandi*. The Rajah is supporting himself by levying a war tax of 25 lakhs from the people of Jaipur.' (*DY*., ii, 393; *Chandra*, ii, 74).

The Jaipur Government thought it better to avoid plunging into the war in Marwar and to employ its forces in recovering the lands on the eastern frontier usurped by the Jats and by the Rao Rajah Pratap Singh Naruka who now lay dying. Bhusawar, which the Rajah of Baratpur had taken, was recovered early in May, 1790, by a Jaipur force under Malik Muhammad Khan, but the fight near it continued for many months after, the Jats being reinforced by Sindhia's men.

Mahadji Sindhia In Rajputana Again; Terms Made With Jaipur

The victory of Merta, though resounding in fame, proved barren to Mahadji Sindhia. As a result, the old quarrel between him and Tukoji Holkar for an equal share of his North Indian conquests burst into flame, and the Holkar contingent left the invading army in protest. Ali Bahadur was induced to side with Holkar. This open split among the Maratha chiefs neutralized the effect of the two recent victories; the Rajputs stiffened in their resistance and the hope of gaining tribute by negotiation faded into the horizon.[1] Everywhere the peasantry rose against the Deccanis, Ismail Beg's father Munim Beg took possession of Gokulgarh (the fort of Rewari) and carried his raids into Kot-Putli and other places under Maratha control. Rao Rajah Pratap Singh of Macheri, the constant ally of Sindhia, died on 24th November. and a civil war broke out among the ministers of his successor Bakhtawar Singh which paralysed that kingdom for years to come. De Boigne had great difficulty in maintaining his brigades because of Sindhia s failure to provide the necessary money. At the same time, a severe scarcity due to failure of rains raged in Rajputana, and food grains and fodder commanded famine prices.

The gathering danger called Mahadji from Mathura to the scene He arrived at Sambhar about 7th December, 1790, and then agents from Jaipur and Jodhpur reached his camp to resume negotiations for peace by payment of war contributions. Mahadji insisted that Khushhali Ram Bohra, the dismissed ex-minister of Jaipur, should come to him, and give an undertaking for the payment of the subsidy that might be agreed to. But Rodoji Khawas was then in favour, and he came to Sindhia with Pahad Singh on 8th February, 1791. (*DY. S.* 13, 14 ii, 86.) The total agreed upon was 17 lakhs, namely 15 lakhs for Sindhia and two lakhs for his ministers (*Darbar kharch*). Bankers' security for one lakh was given, and for collecting the balance and paying it by instalments the envoys left Sindhia's camp on 16th February, accompanied by Sindhia's agent Lakshman Rao. (*DY.S.*17.)

Before this the Jaipur Government had tried to make peace with the Marathas by sending their envoys to Holkar, but he would not accept even 18 lakhs, and the Rajput envoys came back in disappointment. Now, on hearing of the agreement made with Sindhia, Holkar in bitterness of jealousy began to raid the Kachhwa territory through his Pindaris, from his base at Manpur. So, the Jaipur Government agreed to pay him 12 lakhs, and Holkar promised to vacate this territory on receiving bankers' bills for the money. But this money was impossible to raise, and Tukoji (with his ally Ali Bahadur) encamped at Daosa retaining hold over the Jaipur *mahals* (such as Hindaun etc.) which he had previously attached, and keeping Rodoji in confinement. At last the only solution found was to cede Rampura[2] to Holkar (August, 1791), which reduced the money contribution still payable by Jaipur to a small sum (*Chandra.*, ii, 74). Holkar then moved to

Tonk *pargana*, seizing forts there and exacting money, and finally returning to Indore by way of Kota.

Rodoji Khawas, on being released by Tukoji, returned to Jaipur. The two heavy concessions that he had made to the two Maratha chiefs, on behalf of his master, brought about his downfall. Rajah Pratap Singh was appalled by the prospect of having to provide such huge sums. Daulat Ram Haldia and Khushhali Ram Bohra were reappointed ministers, Rodoji was dismissed (27th August) and thrown into prison, from which he could issue only after agreeing to pay a fine of seven lakhs.

With the year 1792, great changes took place in the political situation of Rajputana. Mahadji Sindhia, after re-establishing the Maharana's (nominal) authority over Chitor, got himself appointed as Regent for the Udaipur State (in addition to his Delhi Regency) and set out for Puna. He assembled all the Rajput *vakils* in his camp at Pratapgarh[3] and gave them formal dismissal with robes of honour (6th January). Ambaji Ingle was appointed as his deputy in the Udaipur kingdom, and De Boigne left to collect the tribute from Jaipur and Jodhpur. One enemy alone remained, namely Mirza Ismail Beg, but even he, after many failures in Gujarat, Rewari and Hariana, was shut up in Kanud fort, and there forced to surrender to Sindhia's French General Perron on 16th April, 1792, and finally confined in Agra fort.

Jaipur Ministers Recover Some Territories From Alwar With Maratha Help

About 18th January, 1792, Tukoji Holkar and the Jaipur Rajah met together at Daosa and came to an understanding for hiring out the brigade under Bapu Rao Holkar to the Jaipur ministers for a campaign against the Rao Rajah of Macheri.[4] Soon afterwards Tukoji himself vacated Rajputana for his own capital, due to ill health.

Peace having been made at last with the dominant invaders from the south, the restored Jaipur ministers began a vigorous campaign for collecting revenue from their refractory vassals and reconquering the territory seized by the late Rao Rajah of Macheri. In Macheri,

Khushhalgarh and several other fortalices were recovered; and Holkar's administration was set up in Kama, which had originally belonged to Jaipur State. (*Chandra.*, ii, 91; *DY. S.* 60. ii, 9.; *MD.*, ii, 235) At the same time, a Jaipur force under Chaturbhuj Haldia, assisted by Nanhe Khan (an Arab captain) at the head of 2000 horse and a French-led battalion, took the rebel stronghold of Jhilai (*Chandra.*, ii, 91). In October, 1793, we find Daulatram Haldia, assisted by De Boigne's third brigade (under Perron) attacking the refractory vassal *thakurs* and realizing the long withheld tribute from them. In the course of this internal contest the aged and faithful minister was shot dead when delivering an assault on Kalegh-garh (eight miles east of Jobner) at the beginning of January, 1794. (*DY.*, ii, 66, 116, 86, 4.)

A complete change of the leading actors now emerged on the political stage. Bijai Singh, Rajah of Marwar, died on 7th July, 1793, and the long dreaded Durrani King Timur Shah earlier on 19th May; Mahadji Sindhia died on 12th February, his son-in-low Ladoji Deshmukh Shitole on 15th April, and the Bikaner Rajah in February, all in 1794. Ahalya Bai, the most sober and capable ruler that the house of Holkar has produced, passed away on Thursday, August 13, 1795, and then followed a war of succession which broke up that kingdom. The Peshwa Madhav Rao II died on 27th October, 1795, and Baji Rao II, the destined destroyer of Maratha independence, came to the vacant throne after a year's interval. The great De Boigne retired from Sindhia's service in February, 1796, leaving his fine army in the much less competent hands of Perron. Jaipur history entered upon a placid uneventful course which continued till the death of Rajah Pratap Singh in 1803.

Dealings With Sindhia's French Generals

Mahadji Sindhia made peace in Rajputana before leaving for the Deccan in January, 1792. The Maharana of Udaipur, whose rebellious vassals he had subdued, appointed the Maratha chief as his regent or *diwan*, and this function Mahadji delegated to Ambaji Ingle, who ably controlled the affairs of that kingdom for the next nine years as '*Subahdar* of Mewar'. With the Kachhwa kingdom too, a happy settlement was made, and as a fruit of it, Jaipur forces, backed by

Sindhia's trained battalions, began to recover their lost villages and forts from the usurping Naruka of Macheri. For collecting the Maratha dues from this country, Sindhia left two armies there—one under Jivva Dada Bakhshi helped by De Boigne's third brigade (their commandant being Perron), and the second under Apa Khande Rao, which was charged with keeping order in Mewat and collecting revenue from the Shekhawati vassals of the Jaipur kingdom. Half of these royal dues had been assigned for meeting the contribution payable to Sindhia under the last treaty.

Ever since the succession of the minor Rajah Pirthi Singh (1768), the fedual nobles of Jaipur had been as refractory as those of Plantagenet England, and whenever they were called upon to pay their tribute to their sovereign they used to retire to their castles and rise in open rebellion. Thus the royal exchequer of the Jaipur kingdom was impoverished, and unintended delay in payment to the Marathas (as also to the English for five years after the subsidiary treaty of 1818) occurred.

But though there was frequent conflict between the Maratha forces and Jaipur vassals (such as the *thakurs* of Shekhawati), the Rajah himself was well treated. De Boigne and Perron were particularly respectful to him, declared themselves his friends, and paid him all social courtesies. The Jaipur archives contain a letter from De Boigne to Sawai Pratap Singh, written on 17th October, 1793, in which this General recounts how he had helped the Kachhwa king to recover his own, and never hurt, his interests. Perron too paid frequent friendly visits to Jaipur city and attended the Rajah's marriage in 1799 as an honoured guest. There was grand entertainment for this General and his staff at the Kachhwa capital (June, 1800) after the peace that followed the battle of Malpura. The aim of these two French officers was merely to do their duty of collecting money and they took care to save the peasantry from plunder or molestation by their soldiery. We possess a letter to the Kotah Darbar in which Perron rightly boasts of the discipline of his troops and assures the addressee: 'These are *campoo* troops and not Maratha light horse. If my men extort one rupee from your kingdom, I shall pay two rupees as compensation.'

In June, 1794, soon after Mahadji Sindhia's death, a proposal was made, through Captain J. Pillet (a French officer in Jaipur service), for a military alliance with the English for keeping the Marathas out of Rajputana. But it came to nothing because the policy of non-intervention then dominated the Governor-General's Council. Again, early in 1800, a Kachhwa-Rathor combine attacked Sindhia's army at Malpura, but again European science and discipline triumphed over our primitive weapons and tactics.

Thus, during the eight years 1792-1799, the Government of Jaipur continued at peace with external foes, but there were many fights on its frontiers and with its own rebellious vassals. The sickening tale of the internal feuds, heroism and treachery, murder and rapine, which ravaged the baronies of Khandela, Khetri and Sikar over twenty years may be read in the dark annals of Col. Tod (Vol. ii; *Amber*, Ch. VI and VII). These brought the foreign spoiler in. An Irish sailor named George Thomas, after serving as a mercenary captain under some Indian chiefs, was now planning to set up as a prince and carve out an independent kingdom for himself in Hariana by taking advantage of the dissolution of the Delhi Government and the endless internal discord among the Indian princes.

Early in 1798, George Thomas, in order to pay his troops, made a raid from his base at Jhajhar upon the Jaipur town of Oricha and took a ransom of Rs 52,000 from it, but the town was destroyed by an accidental fire. Soon afterwards Thomas, as the agent of Vaman Rao (the nephew and successor of Apa Khande Rao, who had died on 25 June, 1797), broke into Jaipur territory and destroyed a nest of Mina banditti about 60 miles north of the capital, in reprisal for their raids into Vaman Rao's *jagir*.

The Battle Of Fatehpur With George Thomas, 1799

The situation worsened next year. Lakwa Dada who had now become Sindhia's foremost officer in North India, ordered Vaman Rao to lead an armed force into the north-eastern districts of the Kachhwa kingdom for collecting arrears of contribution. George Thomas was offered a large subsidy and induced to join Vaman Rao with his three battalions of sepoys (400 men each), 90 horse, 300 Rohilla musketeers, 200 peasant militia of Hariana and 14 pieces of artillery. Vaman Rao's force consisted of one infantry battalion, 900 cavalry, 600 irregulars and four pieces of artillery. The combined armies set out from Kanud and entered the Shekhawati district, making collections by attacking or threatening the landowners on the way. The Jaipur royal force present in that region was at first overmatched by the invaders' superior armaments. Besides this, George Thomas was welcomed and subsidised by Bagh Singh of Khetri and other disloyal barons of that district to help them in their rebellion against their liege lord.

Thomas, after severe fighting, took possession of the fortified city of Fatehpur,[5] made it his base on account of its copious water supply in that dry sandy tract, and strengthened the defences of his camp, by keeping the town in his rear and erecting abbatis and sand-heaps with artillery to command the approaches in his front and on the two flanks. It was impossible to dig trenches in that soil of loose sand, but the abundance of thorny bushes supplied very useful *chevaux de frize*.

A large Jaipur army, consisting of royal troops and contingents of the loyal feudatories, under Rodoji Khawas (lately entitled Rajah), arrived and encamped eight miles from Fatehpur. After a preliminary skirmish for the possession of the wells outside, the Jaipur army advanced the next day to attack the invader's camp. Its right wing, composed of the whole force of Rajput cavalry, was told to attack the camp in the rear; the left wing with 4000 Rohillas, 3000 Naga Gosains and 6000 irregular cavalry, advanced against the city of Fatehpur and the only water supply of the invaders, while the centre or main body, formed by ten battalions of infantry, 22 pieces of artillery and 1600 royal bodyguards (*silah-posh*) under Rodoji Khawas, had Thomas himself for its objective.

George Thomas, leaving a part of his infantry and two six-pounders to guard his camp, and detailing four companies of sepoys and two guns to stiffen in the Maratha force behind him, marched out to meet the enemy's onset at the head of five companies of infantry and three guns. It will thus be seen that he was extremely weak in cavalry, especially as his Maratha allies stood aside during the fight. The Rajput horse advanced in close and compact order, and after a temporary check caused by the cross-fire of Thomas' artillery, made a sudden and furious charge upon his main body; its leader John Morris and several other brave men were cut down. But Thomas pushed forward two companies of grenadiers, who after firing their volleys charged the Rajput horse with the bayonet and forced it to retreat.

The Rajput movements were not properly coordinated; for while their right wing was waging this contest, the left wing delayed pressing home their intended assault upon the city, after the first attempt (made without guns) had been checked with loss by the musketeers posted by Thomas in the highest houses. The British captain, now freed from the threat of the Rajput cavalry (their right wing), immediately turned to the succour of the defenders of the city, who were now threatened with six pieces of cannon. A vigorous counter-attack by Thomas drove the enemy's left wing to withdraw their guns and retire from the attack on the city.

Rodoji now gave another example of his lack of planning and incapacity to make a simultaneous attack with all his divisions. It was only after his two wings had been foiled that he ordered a charge by his main body, which had hitherto stood idle under his precious self. But this 'main body had by this time become a confused mess, without order, regularity, or method...' Their general was not met with equal ardour by his troops; and Mr. Thomas, perceiving them at a stand, commended a heavy fire of grape shot from his guns, when after sustaining much loss, the enemy retreated.

Two 24 pounders had been abandoned in the field by the Rajputs in their retreat and Thomas tried to remove them to his camp. But a dense body of Jaipur cavalry headed by Ranjit Singh, the chieftain of Chomu, advanced sword in hand in a desperate charge for recovering the guns. The Marathas fled before the onset, and the Rajput horse, breaking into Thomas' left wing pellmell with these fugitives began to cut down a great number of his sepoys.

> The moment was critical... Mr. Thomas, with the only gun that remained, which he loaded up to the muzzle, and about one hundred and fifty of his followers, waited the event with fortitude. After permitting the enemy to approach within forty yards, he gave his fire, accompanied at the same time by a volley of musketry, with such considerable effect, that great numbers of the enemy were instantly knocked down. This first effort, being followed by two other discharges, completely routed the enemy, The brave baron of Chomu was severly wounded, Bahadur Singh and Pahar Singh (both Khangarots) fell; but the guns were saved. The Rajput casualties were said to have exceeded 2000; on the side of Thomas, Horn's was wounded, and his total loss was 300 men. (*Memoirs of G. Thomas*, London ed., 151-171. Tod, II, Ch. VII.)

Peace negotiations now began, which were promoted by the arrival of letters from Sindhia and Perron ordering the cessation of hostilities against the troops of Jaipur. Disgusted with his Maratha allies, Thomas made a painful retreat with his own contingent hotly pursued by the Kachhwa army which had lately been joined by 5000 men from Bikaner. Peace was made with Vaman Rao by paying him a small sum of money, as against his demand for several lakhs.

The Extradition Of The Murderer Wazir Ali, 1799

Only one event of importance has to be noted in the remainder of this region. Wazir Ali, who had been removed from the throne of Oudh by order of the Governor-General on the ground of illegitimacy, massacred Mr. Cherry, the Resident at Benares, along with four other European officers (14th January, 1799), and openly revolted. After being hunted by British troops he made a dash into Jaipur territory and claimed asylum. His real object was not to pass his remaining days in peace and retirement there, but to proceed to Multan, join the Durrani King of the Panjab, and returning with an Afghan army, convulse the Delhi empire and wrest the province of Oudh from British protection. Such an attempt would have been more dangerous than Ahmad Shah Abdali's invasions of 1757 and 1760, because Wazir Ali could count upon the backing of a large discontented faction in Oudh itself.

The British Government asked the Jaipur darbar to surrender the murderer. That Court could not for a long time make up its mind. On one side there was the ancient Oriental belief that when a man has sought refuge in your house, even if he is a murderer, you should not yield him up to justice. On the other hand there was the genuine fear that in the then disturbed condition of the Kachhwa country the Government could not effectively keep Wazir Ali under confinement. The Oudh prince had not been disarmed nor separated from his armed retainers, but merely lodged in comfort as a princely guest. He could have easily slipped out through neglect or corruption, and effected his escape to the Durrani king.

Failure to hold fast such a five-fold assassin after refusing to extradite him, would have been rightly interpreted as an act of overt enmity to the British Raj, and the imperialistic Wellesley who had just crushed Tipu was then on the viceregal throne. All the nobles of the

State urged Sawai Pratap Singh to purge his country of the wretch, while the *brahmans* blindly stressed the right of asylum. The solution was at last found in the British Government, through its agent Colonel John Collins, promising that Wazir Ali would not be put to death but kept in luxurious confinement in the bosom of his family. He was even allowed to retain his sword. On the Jaipur side the negotiations were thus happily concluded by Hakim Xavier De Silva and Diwan Dinaram, and Collins set out on his return with the prisoner on first December, 1799. The Governor-General made a gift of three lakhs of rupees to the Jaipur darbar.

The internal history of the State during the remainder of this reign and the first decade of the next was marked by the eternal wrangle among the different branches of the nobles of Shekhawati, and the gradual assertion of royal supremacy, but without any effective ensurance of peace and order in that storm-centre. Jaipur's intervention in the war of succession that broke out in Jodhpur after the death of Maharajah Bijai Singh (4th July, 1793), ultimately did incalculable harm to Kachhwa interests, at a time when all the State resources needed to be tactfully conserved.

The Battle Of Malpura, 1800

At last in 1800, a crisis developed in the relations between Jaipur and Sindhia's Government. The burden of money contribution was proving more and more galling to all the Rajput States, and now a new hope began to dawn in their hearts from the news of the civil war between Sindhia and Holkar in Poona, the disruption of Daulat Rao Sindhia's administration, his persecution of his old and able servants, and above all his feud with the widows of the great Mahadji (known as the Bhais' war). This last dispute threw the affairs of Sindhia in North India into the greatest confusion, while all his officers were ranged in the rival ranks and occupied in fighting one another.

Sawai Pratap Singh made an attempt to profit by these internal dissensions of his enemy. In March, 1800, he openly repudiated the money clauses of the treaty of 1791 and prepared for war. The battle of Malpura ensued. But as the Jaipur army had not yet been sufficiently modernized and trained, and lacked able tacticians, the result was the reverse of Tunga, and this appeal to the power of the sword failed.

Hearing of the Jaipur Rajah's war preparations in his camp at Sanganer, Lakhwa Dada assembled his own troops and took post four miles south of Malpura, a town about 55 miles south-west of Jaipur. His army consisted of De Boigne's second brigade (six battalions commanded by Pohlman, a Hanoverian), Chevalier Dudrence's brigade (six battalions, supplied by Holkar), two battalions of Lakhwa's own contingent, a battalion furnished by the Kota regent and a body of inefficient Maratha light horse, a total of about 16,000 men. The Jaipur army was formed by 18 battalions of musketeers, 1000 Ruhelas, 2000 Naga Gosains and more than 15,000 Rajput cavalry (including 5000 Rathor horsemen from Jodhpur led by Sawai Singh)—a total of 27,000 men, besides 54 pieces or artillery, ranging from 24 pounders to six pounders.[6] The Rajah commanded in person.

One arm of the Sohadra river (a feeder of the Banas) flowing southwards by the walls of the city of Malpura for three miles meets, almost at right angles, another arm which runs due west to east in a narrow but deep channel. South of this channel the Maratha army lay encamped near the village of Hindoli, their front to the river. The Jaipur army came and encamped north of this channel, with the town of Malpura on their left rear.

Planning to surprise the Jaipur army, Lakhwa Dada set his troops in motion at four o'clock early in the morning of 16th April. His army was drawn up in two lines, the first being formed by Pohlman's brigade (right) and Dudrence's (left), while the second, marching a thousand paces behind the first line was composed of the Maratha cavalry, these pushing forward some squadrons to the two sides of the first line to guard their flanks. The light field pieces of each brigade moved before it. The Rajput right was composed of the Rathors and the left of the Kachhwa troops.

The attempt at surprise failed, as the Jaipur troops got the alarm, through the recklessness of the cavalry patrols of the Marathas before the infantry had forded the river. A heavy cannonade was opened all along their line. On this, Major Pohlman ordered the second brigade to advance with its guns but reserve its fire till they were close to the enemy. These orders were punctually obeyed and his artillery performed well. Sweeping over the 500 yards of open space from the river bank to the line of Jaipur guns, Pohlman's infantry took 40 of them, though at some sacrifice of their own men.

But the toughest part of the battle now began. During this close engagement on the right, Dudrence's brigade (the left of their front line) was charged by the Rathor cavalry. James Skinner, who fought in this battle in Pohlman's wing, gives the following spirited description of the scene that ensued:

> The Rathors were seen approaching from a distance; the tramp of their immense and compact body rising like thunder above the roar of battle. They came on first at a slow hand gallop, which increased in speed as they approached: the well-served guns of the brigade showered grape upon their dense mass, cutting down hundreds at each discharge; but this had no effect in arresting their progress; on they came, like a whirlwind, trampling over 1500 of their own body, destroyed by the cannon of the brigade; neither the murderous volleys from the muskets, nor the serried hedge of bayonets, could check or shake them; they poured like a torrent on and over the brigade, and rode it fairly down, leaving scarce a vestige of it remaining.

Holkar's infantry is described by a European General of the time as 'ill paid, badly officered, and without sub-ordination, undisciplined, nor can they make use of their arms' (George Thomas). Besides, this was a new brigade recently raised by Dudrence and not yet sufficiently trained. The result was that the left wing of the Deccan army was crumpled up in one short onset, 320 men being slain or wounded out of a total strength of about 2400. 'Captain Paish and several other officers were killed, and Dudrence only escaped by throwing himself down amongst the dead.'

The victorious Rathors, never looking behind them or thinking of their Kachhwa comrades, swept onward in the excitement of success, covered the thousand paces up to the second line in a twinkle. Here the Maratha cavaliers did not wait to meet the shock, but 'ran away like sheep' (Skinner), the Rathors pursuing them for many miles to the rear of the battle line.

This gallant but reckless charge, exactly like that of Prince Rupert's cavalry during the Civil War in England, had a disastrous effect on their side. Pohlman's brigade, after defeating the van of the Jaipur army, was surprised to see its own left totally uncovered by the destruction of Dudrence's wing and its rear exposed by the flight of the cavalry behind it. This was the crisis of the battle: but Pohlman's skill and coolness and the discipline of his sepoys saved the day for him. He formed his six battalions into a square,[7] the bristling line of bayonets and file firing from the four faces, which prevented the enemy's cavalry from surrounding them, though the Kachhwas made onset after onset upon them. Their centre had now come into the firing line, with their Rajah in a huge *ambari* elephant, at the head of 5000 choice horse.

Pohlman's dense column, by an incessant and well directed fire of the artillery, finally succeeded in coming to close action with the enemy, of whom great numbers immediately gave way. The main body however kept their ground for an hour and a half longer, during which the action is said to have been very severe on both sides. A letter of 20th April says:

> The Rajah now approached us within two or three hundred yards, when we gave them a salvo, which brought his elephant down. The horse twice attempted to charge us, but were beaten off with great slaughter.[8] On this, the Rajah mounted his horse, and retired. The horse went off along with him. (Skinner)
>
> About 9 o'clock the field began to clear... The field was ours; but the Rathors had not yet returned from their chase; they had driven the whole Maratha cavalry several *kos*. In a few hours we saw their dust, and found they were returning in a *gol, nakkaras* beating victory... They took us for the Jaipur infantry, but they soon found out their mistake, by receiving a discharge of grape from 30 pieces of cannon. Twice they charged us; and though each time repulsed, several broke into our squares, and were bayoneted there... At last the survivors retired towards their camp. (Skinner, i, 151.)

Sawai Pratap Singh retired to Jaipur, with his army, but all his camp and baggage and guns were captured. Pohlman's brigade had 75 casualties and Dudrence's 320, but these were only the first rough estimates (*Asiatic Annual Register* for 1800). Peace was made soon afterwards.

Notes

1. In October, 1790, the Jaipur Rajah drove out Sindhia's posts from Sambhar, Parbatsar and some other places. (*DY. S.* 47.) *J.S.*
2. Rampura, situated at 25° 57′ North and 76° 4′ east, 54 miles west of Sawai Madhopur, was the headquarters of the *pargana* of that name. Later this *pargana* was granted by the Holkars to Amir Khan, founder of the Tonk State. During the reign of Amir Khan, the first Nawab of Tonk, the name Rampura was changed to Aligarh. (*Imperial Gazetteer of India*, 1908, Vol. V, pp. 207-208.) This Aligarh (Rampura) town is now the headquarters of the Aligarh Tahsil of Tonk District in Rajasthan State. *Ed.*
3. 60 miles south of Chitor. *J.S.*
4. Holkar was promised half of the conquered Macheri territory. *DY.* ii, 9. *J.S.* •
5. 75° east 28° north, thirty miles north of Sikar. *J.S.*
6. The detailed figures are taken from a letter written by an officer of Pohlman only four days after the battle but they do not make up this writer's total of 65,000 men on the Jaipur side and half that number in the Maratha army. A battalion in the Indian princes' service in those days ranged from 400 to 500 men only, the lower of these two figures being the known strength of Dudrence's battalions. I have corrected the total in the light of this fact. The absurd exaggerations of James Skinner that the Jaipur army numbered 1,10,000 men with 150 guns, and that the Maratha army lost 20,000 men among those killed and wounded, and the Rajputs 'probably double that number', have only to be stated to be rejected. *J.S.*
7. The letter from Pohlman's camp says so. But Skinner gives a different account: 'Pohlman gave the word for each battalion to form close columns of companies, in rear of the right company. He next ordered columns of battalions to close upon the centre battalion; and this manoeuvre was equally well performed; with our artillery supporting the front of our columns.' (i, 149.) *J.S.*
8. Col. Collins reported to the Governor General from Fatehgarh, on 21 April, 1800, 'Previous to the total defeat of the Rajput army, and whilst a possibility of restoring the battle still remained, Pratap Singh formed the resolution of making a vigorous charge on Mr. Pohlman's brigade with a thousand select cavalry, but he was dissuaded from carrying this spirited design into execution by his diwan Rai Chand. *J.S.*

XXIV

The British Alliance

Friendly Correspondence (Pirthi Singh's Reign)

With the British alliance (signed at last in 1818) a new chapter opens in the history of the Kachhwa dynasty and the life of the people of Dhundhar land. The age of warrior kings and conquerors is over, but Pax Britannica and modern knowledge have made Jaipur one of the most prosperous and advanced States in India, and its rulers have begun to take a distinguished part in the affairs of the new Empire of Delhi as their ancestors had done in the days of the great Mughals.

The earliest correspondence between the Court of Jaipur and British Indian Government starts with a letter from Sawai Pirthi Singh received by the Governor-General at Calcutta on 29th October, 1776, in which the Rajah says, 'Having learnt a good deal about the uprightness and amiable qualities of the Governor-General and other English men, I am anxious to open friendly relations with them.' He then requests the Governor-General to write to the Company's officers in the Delhi region to introduce the Jaipur *vakil* to Shah Alam II and give him necessary assistance, as the nobles of that Court were unfriendly to him; and concludes with the hope that 'the friendship which exists between the Company and my family will get stronger under your regime'. The Jaipur agent who bore this letter, namely Bal Krishna, was well received at Calcutta.

Warren Hastings replied, on 15th January, 1777, reciprocating the good will and in a friendly spirit advising the Rajah of Jaipur and Mirza Najaf Khan (his adversary in the Emperor's council) to make up their quarrels and live amicably in future as the English were mutual friends of both the parties. The friendly intercourse thus opened continued for many years. On 18th July, 1778, W. Hastings wrote to the new Rajah Sawai Pratap Singh condoling with him on the death of his brother Pirthi Singh, and two months later sent him ceremonial presents on the occasion of his accession, by the hands of the returning Jaipur *vakils*, Lala Bal Krishna Ram (or Rao). The Rajah returned the compliment by sending horses and other presents for the Governor-General which were received on 27th August, 1779. Next year an English agent, Mr. Fairfax, visited Jaipur for buying the best horses. In 1783, we read of another mission of Bal Krishna to Calcutta.[1]

The first advances towards a protective alliance with the British Government as distinct from friendly intercourse, was made by the Jaipur Rajah, through his minister Daulatram Haldia, when the growing power and ambition of Mahadji Sindhia, now the official Regent and instrument of the Emperor, began to menace the Kachhwa and other Rajput States. During the Lalsot campaign earnest appeals were made for English troops to aid in the defence of Jaipur. But Lord Cornwallis followed a policy of strict non-intervention, as ordered by the Home authorities. Moreover, he was not prepared to antagonize Mahadji Sindhia, as his eyes were steadily fixed on the war with Tipu Sultan which he knew to be inevitable from the overweening pride and insatiable ambition of the Mysore Sultan. In such a war, Cornwallis was determined at all costs to rope in the Marathas and the Nizam on the side of the English, and he knew that Mahadji Sindhia was the friend of the English and the medium of their relations with the Peshwa's Government. Therefore, the Marathas were given a free hand in Rajputana.[2]

Jean Pillet's Appeal For Alliance, 1794

Soon after Mahadji Sindhia's death (1794), Jean Pillet, a French captain in Jaipur service, who felt deep sympathy for the misery of

Rajputana due to baronial disloyalty, internal feuds, and Maratha aggression, made an appeal to the Governor-General, through Colonel John Murray (the Military Auditor General), for an alliance between the E.I. Company and the Jaipur State in the following words:

> Below (I give) a note of what the Prince (i.e., Sawai Pratap Singh) is in need of in order to fulfil his views; First, a defensive and offensive treaty between him and the (English) Company. Secondly, the stationing of a representative of the Company at his Court. Thirdly, the supplying by the British of arms and uniforms (as detailed), and permission to recruit for the Jaipur army in the Company's territory or in that of the Nawab Wazir of Oudh. By giving these succours, the Company will put a good ally in a condition to second their own views, however, extensive on that side, as the Rajah and his friends will in a short time second the views of the English with 50,000 cavalry and the resources of his territory, without asking for any return save a firm protection on the part of the Company and full liberty to enjoy his dominions in peace... The Company shall not upon his auxiliaries or his allies undertake any (military) measure without at the same time making grants for their subsistence.
>
> An authentic treaty, solemnised by the appearance of a representative of the British Power at this Court and sustained by adequate forces on his frontier... At the same time a smaller force, stationed as auxiliaries, with the Rajah will in combination with the Rajah's brethren, conclude the matter by chasing these strangers (i.e., the Marathas) out of his territory.

But Sir John Shore was not prepared to defy the order of strict neutrality in the affairs of Indian States beyond the Oudh protectorate, which had been repeated by the Court of Directors, and his reply was, 'a treaty offensive and defensive is out of the question'.[3] Therefore things continued in the same unhappy state for nine years more.

Wellesley Makes A Treaty Of Alliance With Jaipur, 1803

With Marquess Wellesley came the promise of a change for the better, but the promise ended in futility. When this great proconsul launched on his vigorous and India-wide warfare for crushing the

French influence in India and establishing British Paramountcy, he looked round for allies among the Indian States, particularly those which had suffered most from the Marathas.

The war with Sindhia (who was in alliance with the Bhonsla Rajah of Nagpur) began in the south on 15th August, 1803, with the storming of the Fort of Ahmadnagar by the English, and in North India on the 29th of the same month when General Lake seized Perron's camp near Aligarh. English victories followed in both theatres in rapid succession—Assaye (23 September) and Argaum (19 November), Aligarh (4 September), Delhi (11 September), Agra (18 October) and Laswari (first November). Sindhia's power was totally crushed both in the north and the south, and before the year was over he had to sign the treaty of Sarji Anjangaon (on 13th December).

Lake entered into a treaty of offensive and defensive alliance with the Jaipur *vakils* in seven articles 'duly concluded and confirmed' by that General at Sarhindi in the Agra province on 12th December after approval of the terms had been obtained from the Jaipur Rajah. It was added at the end of this document, sealed and signed by General Lake, that

> When a treaty, containing the above seven articles, shall be delivered to Maharaja Dhiraj (Sawai Jagat Singh), under the seal and signature of H.E. the Governor-General in Council, the present Treaty, under the seal and signature of H.E. General Lake, shall be returned. (*Wellesley Despatches*, iii, 637-638.)

The significant articles of this treaty are the following:

3rd Article: The Hon'ble Company shall not interfere in the government of the country now possessed by Maha Rajah Dhiraj, and shall not demand tribute from him.

4th Article: In the event of an enemy of the Hon'ble Company evincing a disposition to invade the country lately taken possession of by the Hon'ble Company in Hindustan, Maha Rajah Dhiraj shall send the whole of his forces to the assistance of the Company's army.

5th Article: As the Hon'ble Company become guarantees to the Maha Rajah Dhiraj for the security of his country against external enemies, the Maha Rajah Dhiraj hereby agrees, that if any misunderstanding should arise between him and any other side, Maha Rajah Dhiraj will, in the first instance, submit the cause of the dispute to the Company's Government, that the Government may endeavour to settle it amicably. If no amicable terms can be settled; then Maha

Rajah Dhiraj may demand aid from the Company's Govt. In the event of the above stated it will be granted and Maha Rajah Dhiraj agrees to take upon himself the charge of the expenses of such aid...

7th Article: The Maha Rajah shall not entertain in his service, or in any manner give admission to any English or French subjects, or any other person from among the inhabitants of Europe, without the consent of the Company's Government.

The ninth article of the Treaty between the Company and Daulat Rao Sindhia (13 December, 1803) recognized and confirmed all engagements concluded between the British Government and any of the feudatories dependants of Daulat Rao Sindhia. As to its effects, the Governor General wrote to the Secret Committee of the Court of Directors (on 13th July, 1804), 'By this arrangement the Rajah of Jainagar is permanently relieved from the payment of his accustomed tribute to Daulat Rao Sindhia, and from the apprehension of future exactions and encroachments on the part of that chieftain, or of any foreign State.' (*W. Desp.* iv, 150.)

How Jaipur State Helped The British In War

The terms of the treaty were honestly fulfilled by the Jaipur Government in a short time. Sindhia having been knocked out of the ring, Jaswant Rao Holkar entered into it. After the signing of the treaty of Sarji Anjangaon and that with Jaipur (on 12-13 December, 1803), Lake took post at Biana (27th December, 1803-9th February, 1804), to watch the pass leading into Jaipur and at the same time to guard the British conquests to the north. Early in February, Jaswant Rao Holkar's unfriendly attitude became manifest, and Lake started from Biana towards Jaipur, which city was threatened by Holkar. Daosa was reached 17th April. From this place, Lake deputed Col. Monson the next day to proceed with three battalions of native infantry to Jaipur city (where he arrived on the 21st). Previous to this, in the last week of March, Captain Sturrock, the Persian interpreter, had been despatched by the c-in-c from Balaheri on a mission for assuring the Jaipur Rajah of British protection. At the approach of the British army, Holkar decamped from the neighbourhood of the Kachhwa capital.

On 8th May, Lake despatched from his camp at Newai a force under Lt. Colonel Patrick Don against Rampura.[4] The place was skilfully and gallantly stormed on the 15th and Holkar fled to the south of the Chambal into his own territories.

No enemy being left within sight, Lake decided to withdraw his main army to Agra in order to escape the summer heat; he posted Monson at Kota to watch the frontier against the return of Holkar. This officer's detachment was increased to five battalions—'which were among the finest in the Bengal army', a company of European gunners, and 18 guns besides a body of about 3000 irregular horse, partly newly raised Company's *sowars* and partly small contingents from various native States. This arm (the cavalry) was commanded by Lt. Lucan (H.M.'s 74th Regiment), and W. Gardiner, a captain in the Jaipur service commanded one wing of it at the head of the Rajah's troopers. These two cavalry officers, with great courage and skill, defeated a partisan of Holkar named Tatya in a pass near Balloor Kheri (29th May), and disarmed his whole force of 2100 men and took the whole of their ordnance and stores (*Thorn.*, 350).

Monson reached Kota on 2nd June, 1804 and was joined by Lt. Col. Don from Rampura. Advancing southwards into Holkar's dominions, by crossing the Mukandara pass, he reached Sonara (19 miles southwards), and on 2nd July, captured the strong fort of Hinglajgarh (9 miles northwest of Sonara) from Holkar. Up to this point the Jaipur contingent had accompanied the British forces and done what service its small size and archaic equipment permitted it to render. But only six days later, Monson, hearing that the Gujarat army under Col. Murray had given up the attempt to join him and that Holkar had reappeared with his myriads of cavalry, began a disastrous retreat (on 8th July) in which his detachment fell to pieces and only a shattered remnant of it straggled into Agra (on 31st August). In the first night, the irregular cavalry under Lucan which served as the rearguard was enveloped by Holkar's cavalry, and routed. That officer himself was wounded and taken prisoner (later dying of his wounds). Two brave Indian chiefs Prithi-Raj, a relative of the Ballamgarh Rajah[5] and the Shekhawat Rajah's son, each with 500 horse, fought bravely to the end, and 'with all their followers were cut to pieces'. (Fraser's *Skinner*, ii, 34.)

The Jaipur Government again assisted the British in the course of this war, when Jaswant Rao Holkar after his defeat by Lord Lake near Bharatpur and expulsion to Malwa (April, 1805), collected a force of adventurers and returned by way of Rajputana to plunder friend and foe alike, and make a wild dash through the Company's new territories in North India. The Bombay division, under Major-General Jones, was ordered to move from Rampura (Tonk) and intercept him in Jaipur territory (September). At this time Sawai Jagat Singh was busy employing his army to effect his marriage with the princess Krishna Kumari of Udaipur. But when Lord Lake wrote to him to retrieve his credit with the British by a hearty cooperation with General Jones and providing the necessary supplies for that General's army, 'it was', as Sir John Malcolm testifies,

> attended with completest effect. The Resident at the Court of Jaipur (Capt. Sturrock, in a letter dated the 16th of October) informed Lord Lake that the Rajah, as soon as he received his lordship's letter, had relinquished his favourite project of marching a force towards Udaipur, and prepared a detachment, to join General Jones' army with which he cooperated in the most decided and zealous manner during the reminder of the war with Holkar... It was concluded, therefore, by Lord Lake that the Rajah of Jaipur, by his complete fulfilment of the conditions proposed to him, had fully re-established his claim to be considered an intimate and faithful ally of the British Government. (Malcolm's *Political History of India*, i, 351.)

The New Governor-General Repudiates The Treaty

But by this time a complete revolution had taken place in the Indian policy of the Home Government. Wellesley had been removed from office and Lord Cornwallis sent out as Governor-General with orders to reverse the dangerous forward policy of his imperialistic predecessor.

Even before the news of the disaster to Col. Monson and another reverse in Bundelkhand reached England, Lord Castlereagh, the President of the Board of Control (the predecessor of the Secretary of State for India) had written a despatch (21st May, 1804) crying halt to Wellesley's policy of expansion.

> The arrangement (namely the series of subsidiary alliances) carries the Company's frontier far to the north and west of Delhi... The question involves considerations of the highest moment, (one being), whether it does not swell so largely and so suddenly not only our immediate possessions, but our dependencies necessarily included within the dominion (i.e., protection) of our army, as to run some risk of rendering the frame of our Government... enfeebled and embarrassed...

He also pointed out that the European troops in India were only one-seventh of the number of 'our native army', and that while Wellesley had asked the strength of the white army in India (which had sunk to 12,211 in December 1803) to be raised to 31,000 the Home authorities could send no more than 2500 men. It would, therefore, be a military impossibility to guard all of Wellesley's new conquests and allies (*Wellesley Despatches*, iv, 224). England had then, embarked on a twelve years' war with the great Napoleon; 1805 was to be the year of Ulm and Austerlitz, and the British leaders in Leadenhall street decided to reduce their Indian entanglements to a minimum. Cornwallis came to India a second time charged with a mission to make a durable peace by removing every possible source of friction with the Marathas, and severely limiting the allied territory which the English would be bound to defend.

Lord Cornwallis assumed office at Calcutta on 30th July, 1805. He found that Lord Wellesley's 'frenzy of conquest' had

> involved the Government in extreme pecuniary embarrassment; every part of the army, and every branch of the public departments attached to it... are suffering severe distress from an accumulation of arrears, and if unfortunately it should become indispensably necessary to put the troops again in motion, I hardly know how the difficulties of providing funds for such an event are to be surmounted. (Cornwallis to Secret Committee in London, 28th August, 1805.)

Therefore, on 3rd August the new Governor-General wrote to Lord Lake stating that he considered the alliance with Jaipur to be dissolved.

> Lord Lake was instructed to transmit orders to Major-General Jones... not to give the Rajah any aid in the event of an attack from the Marathas, as the Governor-General in Council had resolved to abandon the connexion. But Lord Cornwallis stated in these instructions, that it was thought impolitic to declare to

the Court of Jaipur the dissolution of the subsisting engagements, as such a declaration... might be productive of great disadvantage to the interests of the British Government. The Resident at the Court of Jaipur was therefore to be informed of the resolution which the Governor-General in Council had taken respecting the alliance, and desired to make no communication whatever upon the subject.

Lord Lake felt the greatest embarrassment on receiving these orders; and immediately communicated to Lord Cornwallis those assurances of continued support and friendship which circumstances had induced him to make to the Rajah of Jaipur...

Upon Lord Lake's report Cornwallis had suspended the execution of the measures which he had taken regarding the dissolution of this connexion. It was concluded, therefore, by Lord Lake, that the Rajah of Jaipur, by his complete fulfilment of the conditions proposed to him, had fully re-established his claim to be considered an intimate and faithful ally of the British Government. (*Malcolm*, i, 349-352.)

Upon the death of Cornwallis (5th October) Sir George Barlow succeeded as acting Governor-General, and he carried out the policy of non-intervention to the letter. On 23rd November, 1805 he concluded a treaty with Sindhia confirming the treaty of Sarji Anjangaon (except as now modified) and ceding Gwalior and Gohud to him. A little later he transmitted declaratory articles, signed at Allahabad on 3rd December, by one of which the British treaties with the Rajput States were dissolved and Sindhia (and, by another treaty, Holkar also) were given a free hand in respect of these recent allies of the English.

The moment Lord Lake received intimation that the new Governor-General intended to dissolve the alliance with the Rajah of Jaipur, his lordship represented that... a British army under Major-General Jones had been enabled by the Rajah's aid, and the ample supplies which his country furnished, to maintain a position of great consequence to the success of the war; that, from the communication which he had received from General Jones, he did not doubt that if Holkar had attempted to retreat, as was expected, in the direction of that General's position, the Rajah's troops who had joined his camp, would have cooperated efficiently; and that the sincerity and good faith with which the State of Jaipur had acted at this crisis was most strongly corroborated by General Jones.

His arguments, however, made no impression upon the mind of the Governor-General, who continued to think... that we had obtained a right to dissolve the alliance... In conformity with this resolution, Sir George Barlow directed the Resident at Jaipur to announce the dissolutions of the defensive alliance...The Resident at the same time delivered to the Rajah a letter from the Governor-General, explanatory of the grounds upon which this measure had been adopted. The justice of these grounds, however, was warmly disputed by the Court of Jaipur. (*Malcolm*, i, 369-372.)

British Historians Condemn Barlow's Annulment Of The Treaty

The impartial British historian Horace Hayman Wilson, shows how fully the Jaipur Rajah was justified in his defence. He argues thus:

> His abandonment was wholly indefensible. It was to be controverted that a treaty had been contracted with him by which... he was entitled to British mediation and aid. When he required the fulfilment of the stipulations, he was told that "no treaty existed: it had been virtually abrogated by the non-performance of his part of the compact...". The Rajah denied the justice of the charges adduced against him. He affirmed that his troops had separated from Col. Monson with that officer's consent, and by the orders of Lord Lake; that although his forces were on their march to Udaipur, yet, as soon as their services were required, they suspended their march and joined the Bombay army under General Jones, and that General Jones and Lord Lake had both furnished him with their written acknowledgements of the promtitude and efficacy of his cooperation. Lord Lake had also given him strong assurance of the stability of the alliance. He represented that, if the British Government had been dissatisfied with his conduct at any particular time, it should at that time have expressed its displeasure and at once declared the alliance annulled. To have continued to employ the services of the Rajah until they were no longer needed, and reserved all expression of dissatisfaction until it could be used as a pretext for getting quit of an inconvenient obligation, was both disingenuous and dishonourable; to desert an old friend because the tide was setting against him, was ungenerous and unjust; and that the Powers of India could not but regard the conduct of the Government as a departure from the good faith which it had hitherto been its pride to preserve inviolate... The argument was incontrovertibly in the Rajah's favour. (Wilson's *History of British India*, first ed., i, 86-88.)

The Court of Directors, although they did not enjoin the renewal of the alliance (which might have provoked a fresh war with the

Marathas), disapproved of its dissolution, conceiving its justice extremely questionable and they warned the Governor-General to take better care of the British Government's character for fidelity to its allies in future (*Malcolm*, i, 399).

When such was the view of the generous Englishmen, we can easily understand, how,

> One of the principal agents of the Rajah of Jaipur, in a conference with Lord Lake at Delhi... had the boldness to observe, that this was the first time since the English Government was established in India, "that it had been known to make its faith subservient to its convenience". (*Malcolm*, i, 373.)

Sir John Malcolm, who was the British agent in these last settlements with Sindhia and Holkar, was so shocked by the proposed surrender of everything to the Marathas that he wrote to Secretary Edmonston offering his resignation: 'I trust to your exertions to save me from the misery of being an unwilling instrument in the accomplishment of a measure which... I most conscientiously believe will be equally disgraceful and ruinous.' (letter of 19th September, 1805.) When the surrender actually took place, Malcolm remarked, 'This is the first measure of the kind that the English have ever taken in India, and I trust in God it will be the last.' (Keye's *Life of Malcolm*, i, 337, 358.)

With this abandonment opened the most unhappy chapter in the annals of Jaipur, the story of which may be read in the sombre pages of Tod. It ended 13 years later when the protective alliance was finally concluded under the Marquess of Hastings (2nd April, 1818).

The Marquess Of Hastings Makes A Treaty Of Defensive Alliance, 1818

The policy of non-intervention of the Court of Directors, so zealously enforced in the case of Jaipur Rajah in 1806, definitely facilitated a sudden rise of vast marauder hordes of fast moving Pindaris devastating and ravishing all of Central India and the adjoining Indian States in defensive alliance with the British. In 1812, they raided Mirzapur and South Bihar, and early in 1816, they raided

Northern Sarkars. Thereafter followed their annual raids. Thereupon it was deemed that the time was ripe for a comprehensive campaign against the Pindaris and their Maratha and Pathan allies that was being planned. After the termination of the second Nepal War, in March, 1816, Lord Hastings brought the question of an alliance with Jaipur before his Council.

An alliance with Jaipur was necessary for the British Government too, as Sir John Macolm clearly points out:

> Jaipur from its local position, is to us the most important of the Rajput States... The apprehension of this danger (viz., a Pathan onrush from Tonk and Bhopal through Jaipur into Delhi and Rohilkhand)... has led the Indian Government in England to authorize a defensive treaty being concluded with the ruler of Jaipur. The necessity of altering our detached relations to Jaipur was too imperative to admit of delay. We must command the territories of this State both for operations and supplies, or they will furnish our enemies with means of attacking us in a very vulnerable quarter. (Letter to Marquess of Hastings, 17th July 1817.)

In the meantime, as early as 15th January, 1815, the Governor-General had recorded in his diary, 'The unfortunate Rajput States of Jaipur, Jodhpur, Udaipur, mercilessly wasted by Sindhia, Holkar, Amir Khan, Muhammad Shah Khan, and the Pindaris, have assailed me with repeated petitions to take them under protection as feudatories to the British Government.' But Sir G. Barlow's declaratory articles were at first considered to be a bar to such an alliance (p. 161).

But 'the question was forced upon the Indian Government, by the increasing distresses of Jaipur and by the earnest applications of Rajah Jagat Singh to be received under protection... Amir Khan was collecting the whole of his forces for the attack on Jagat Singh in his capital.' The Jaipur *vakils* at Delhi and Calcutta made pressing overtures to Metcalfe and the Governor-General respectively. Setting aside the cautious advice of his Councillors,

> the Marquess of Hastings considered the Government to be free to take Jaipur under its protection. His Lordship thought also, that the measure was highly desirable in itself... in as much it would cripple the resources of one of the predatory Powers, and save a fine and eventually useful territory from ruin and devastation.
>
> Orders were issued on 20th April, 1816 to Mr. Metcalfe

> (the Resident at Delhi) to entertain the Rajah's overtures... Jaipur was to be called upon to defray eventually the greater part of the charge to be incurred in its protection... Troops were to assemble in the neighbourhood of Muttra and Rewari sufficient for the formation of two armies of 9000 men each... It was intended that both should be ready to advance on the first requisition of the Resident at Delhi, in order to drive the Pathans (of Amir Khan) beyond the Jaipur frontier.

Other forces were posted so as to overawe Sindhia and Holkar.

At the favourable reply of Metcalfe, the Jaipur Government sent

> negotiators to Delhi furnished with full powers... Everything was soon agreed to, except the amount of the subsidy to be paid by the Rajah. Mr. Metcalfe was induced to lower his demand (originally 25 lakhs) to 15 lakhs of rupees for the permanent subsidy, with the accommodation of considerable remission during the first five years, in consideration of the impoverished condition of the territory. (*Princep.*, i. 370-377.)

But there was a hitch. Amir Khan, alarmed by the concentration of British troops at Rewari, withdrew his guns from the siege of Jaipur, in order to ensure their safety, and in July next (1816) retired from Jaipur territory. And the Jaipur side caused the negotiations to be broken off by 'brining forward a new demand, viz. that our troops should reduce Tonk and Rampura, and re-annex them to Jaipur.'

But the rupture of the treaty *pourparlers* had other and deeper causes than selfish opportunism on that part of the Rajah's agents. Firstly, it was extremely painful to a proud ancient dynasty to reduce itself to the level of a mediatised or semi-independent position by acknowledging a suzerain. Secondly, at that time the barons had parcelled out nearly the whole territory among themselves, and

> over these the Rajah had much about the same degree of influence and authority, as was possessed by the weakest of the kings of England, when the same (feudal) system prevailed in that country. The continual war of factions (among the Jaipur nobility) was prosecuted with the utmost virulence... No members of this aristocracy, however, was disposed willingly to exchange a state of things, which left so wide an opening to his hopes and ambition, for the perpetual repose and tranquillity that must result from the introduction of our (i.e. British) influence... There was reason for the aristocracy to suspect, that

> our guarantee of maintaining the Rajah's authority comprehended the enforcement of his just dues from themselves, and their suspicions made them oppose the completion of the alliance. (*Prinsep*. i, 378-380.)

The third cause was the undoubtedly high amount of the subsidy demanded (namely Rs 15 lakhs, at a time when the State income had fallen to a little over 30 lakhs).

Mr. Metcalfe broke off the negotiations at the beginning of August, 1816. On 17th November another mission from Jaipur came to Delhi to renew the discussions, but they failed as they could not agree to the subsidy. (*Prinsep*. i, 380-384. *Private Journal of M.H.* 256-263).

Stirring events followed next year, the rupture with the Peshwa after the escape and armed rising of Trimbakji Deinglia, the attack upon the Poona Residency; the India-wide British campaign against the Pindaris and the third Maratha War. In March 1818, General Sir David Ochterlony took post in Jaipur country with a reserve corps in order to overawe the Maratha-Pathan threat to the protected princes of Rajputana.

At last 'the Jaipur negotiators made their appearance at Delhi about the middle of February, 1818...' along with most of the principal people of Jaipur. After much negotiation, a treaty was at length concluded on the 2nd of April, 1818. The amount of tribute to be paid (to the British Government) as the condition to relief from further exaction from the Pathans and other depredators, was... the main difficulty. In the end the following scale was adopted: For the first year nothing; four, five, six, seven and eight lakhs, for the five succeeding years respectively; and eight lakhs afterwards in perpetuity, liable to increase by five annas in the rupee on any excess of the revenues of the State beyond forty lakhs of rupees.[6] (*Prinsep*, ii, 372; *Wilson*, ii, 428.)

Notes

1. *Calendar of Pers. Corr.*, V, 339, 342, 417, 466, 1009, 1109, 1576, 1840; VI, 344, 809. *J.S.*
2. Captain William Kirkpatrick, the famous Resident (and afterwards Wellesley's political adviser) was bitterly hostile to Sindhia and advocated armed British obstruction to his policy. But Cornwallis pulled him up short and removed him from the Residency. (See *Mahadji Sindhia and N.I. Affairs*, ed. by J. Sarkar for Bombay Govt.). *J.S.*
3. Pillet's letter and memoirs (descriptive of the society manners and political condition of Jaipur) both written in French, are preserved in the India Office, London, *Home Misc.*, Vol. 388, pp. 125-194. For an English translation see Proceedings of I.H. Record Com., Calcutta, 1939. *J.S.*
4. Tonk-Rampura, now known as Aligarh, not to be confounded with Rampura, Bhanpura, which is further south. *J.S.*
5. Ballamgarh or Ballabgarh—situated at 28° 20′ N and 77° 20′ E, is 24 miles south of Delhi, was the headquarters of the Jat estate founded by Balram Jat in the middle of the 18th century. It was confiscated in 1857, because of the complicity of the then Rajah in the great revolt of 1857. *Ed.*
6. As a matter of fact, the subsidy actually paid by Jaipur was Rs 2,00,000 (in 1818-1819), 2,54,000 (in 1820), 2,50,000 (in 1821), 5,50,000 (in 1822) and 12,50,000 (in 1823)—a total of Rs 25,04,000 against 30 lakhs according to the treaty. But we must bear in mind that the royal revenue of Jaipur had fallen very low, thanks to baronial tribulence and usurpation. *J.S.*

XXV

The Last Days Of The Ancient Regime In Jaipur

The Dark Age In Jaipur History

From the death of Sawai Madho Singh I (in 1768) to the first establishment of a British-controlled Council of Regency at Jaipur in 1839, stretches the darkest period in the history of the Kachhwa Kingdom. It would be hardly incorrect to describe this interval as a succession of minorities, for out of these 71 years the throne was occupied by minors for 46 years. Though during the remaining 25 years the reigning princes had come of age, they were still too young and too little supported by any loyal baronage or united people to recover the royal powers and the Crownlands which had slipped out of their hands during the preceding minority. It would be equally correct to say that a state of civil war with rapid changes of fortune raged throughout this long period. It was the direct supervision of the Jaipur administration by the Paramount Power under Lord Auckland's orders that ended this anarchy and at last gave again to Dhundhar Land that peace and prosperity which it had enjoyed under warrior kings and statesmen like Man Singh and the Mirza Rajah, Sawai Jai Singh and Madho Singh.

While ambitious vassals were seizing the State domains and refusing the fedual dues for their legitimate ancestral estates, ceaseless faction-fights for the regency raged in the capital and the post of Prime Minister changed hands with bewildering frequency and disastrous effect on the public administration and the economic life of the population. It was only after British blood had been shed in the streets of the capital that an end was at last put to this period of public agony.

In the reign of Sawai Jagat Singh (1803-1818) the fortunes of Kachhwa royalty touched their lowest point. The repudiation by Sir George Barlow of the protective alliance made by Wellesley, and the incapacity of the youthful Rajah and his successive ministers tempted the annual incursions of Holkar and his Pathan ally Amir Khan and aggravated the evil of internal disturbance and baronial revolt.

The great ministers of States who had helped the warrior kings to build up the kingdom and its administration, were now dead. The last two of this eminent breed, Daulat Ram Haldia and Khushhali Ram Bohra—unfortunately irreconcilable rivals owing to the diametrically opposite line of foreign policy that they advocated, were no more. The former had fallen in his master's battle in 1794, and the latter, after seeing many vicissitudes, sank under the weight of age (86 years) on 22 April, 1812. Their successors were men of much smaller calibre: Dinaram Bohra (1798), Rai Chand (1800 and 1808), Misra Sheo Narayan (1812), Purohit Manji Das (1815), Mohan Ram (1818), Rawal Bairi Sal of Samode (1819-1824), Megh Singh of Diggi (*mukhtar*, with Hukm Chand Saraogi as *diwan*, 1824), Rao Chand Singh of Duni (*mukhtar*, 1826) and Jhuta Ram Saraogi (1828-1835).

The Tragic Death Of Krishna Kumari, 1810

No history of Sawai Jagat Singh can omit to mention the tragedy of Krishna Kumari, the princess of Mewar, who cheerfully sacrificed her innocent life for the good of her father and her country. But no blame attached to the Jaipur king for the death of this Hindu Iphigenia. Her father had first offered her hand to Bhim Singh the Maharajah of Jodhpur, but that prince died before the knot could be tied (1803). The Maharana then betrothed her to Jagat Singh of Jaipur, but Man Singh the next king of Jodhpur claimed her for his bride, as if she were merely 'livestock on the estate' that he had inherited. The honour of the Kachhwa royal house did not permit Jagat Singh to give up his preferred bride out of fear of his Rathor rival. War naturally ensued between the two Rajput Houses, by which the Pathan condottier alone profited.

We pass over the wearisome tale of prolonged warfare between Rathor and Kachhwa which ended only on Saturday, 21st July, 1810, in the poisoning of Krishna Kumari as a political necessity, under pressure from Amir Khan who had gone to Udaipur to execute the deed. The following is the earliest English record of the tragedy, published on 4th November, 1810:

> The most important political event which has lately occurred in Hindustan, is the death of the Princess of Udaipur by poison... The rivalship of these two Rajahs (for her hand) produced a war... The contest, however, has at length been terminated in the manner above related. The poison was administered to the princess by her own aunt, and with the knowledge of her father. Report adds that the whole scheme was secretly contrived by Amir Khan; who, finding that the Rana of Udaipur (now entirely in his power) was too far engaged to the Jaipur Rajah to retract, and resolved that his own ally, the Rajah of Jodhpur should not be disgraced by the triumph of his rival, suggested this expedient, as the only mode of at once settling all their pretensions, and terminating the ten years' war, which this second Helen had excited. (Asiatic Annual Register for 1810-1811, Beng. Occur. p. 49).[1]

The Rivalry For The Regency Of Jaipur, 1819-1838

The signing of the treaty of alliance with the British did not immediately end the internal troubles of Jaipur, which continued for twenty-one years more. To the two evils of woman's rule on behalf of a child on the throne and faction among the nobility, was now added financial collapse. The actual collection of the State revenue fell to thirty lakhs a year, out of which the subsidy to the E.I. Co swallowed up eight lakhs, an unbearably high proportion. At the same time, the large bands of hired soldiers as distinct from the old tribal militia, raised during the preceding 20 years, clamoured for their heavy arrears of pay, which the exhausted Government treasury had no means of meeting, and yet this unwieldly force could not be disbanded without paying up its just dues. The problem for successive British Residents was how to avert public bankruptcy and keep the administration going.

This was the general political situation of the Kachhwa kingdom till 1839 and we shall rapidly pass over the interval till we reach the era of administrative reorganization under British supervision. The treaty of alliance was signed in April, 1818. The next month Sir David Ochterlony, who had been charged with the general control of British interests in Rajputana, had to proceed to Jaipur, in order, if possible, to introduce some irregularity and system into the administration. He convened a general meeting of the *thakurs* (vassals), but several of them proved refractory. To make an example of them, the conqueror of Nepal attacked and quickly reduced the strong forts of Khushhalgarh and Madho-raj-pura[2] also known as Madhogarh.)

But before the General could make any definite arrangement, Rajah Sawai Jagat Singh died[3] without issue. After some months a posthumous son was produced by one of his queens (of the Bhati clan). Ochterlony again proceeded to Jaipur, and assisted at the inauguration of the child as Rajah Sawai Jai Singh III and established a Council of Regency under the queen-mother with Rawal Bairi Sal (of Samode) as her chief minister, but the latter was obstructed by his rivals.

So the British Government in 1821 appointed a political agent at Jaipur specially to superintend its administration (the officer selected being Major Stewart). But every attempt of Bairi Sal to restore to the State the crownlands which had been usurped by the selfish barons since the death of Pratap Singh in 1803, was frustrated. In this unsatisfactory state of things, the British Government decided in 1822 to give its public support to the responsible ministers. Accordingly, Sir David Ochterlony arrived at Jaipur (on 20th January, 1823). He restored Bairi Sal to power and sent the mischief-maker Jhuta Ram Saraogi into exile at Sonagarh in Bundelkhand. (*Prinsep*. ii, 373-379. *Wilson*, ii, 429-431.)

But the removal of Jhuta Ram did not produce the expected good result. His partisans in Jaipur continued to intrigue against him and made his administration impossible, especially by inciting the unpaid troops to mutiny, while the great shrinkage in the revenue collection threatened bankruptcy to the State. So, in 1824, at Ochterlony's recommendation a new minister was appointed, and two years later Jhuta Ram was allowed to return from exile. At the end of 1826, Sir Charles Metcalfe, the Political Agent at Delhi, visited Jaipur and gave the queen-mother the privilege of conducting the regency entirely through her nominees. The new administration was as much a failure as its predecessors, arrears of pay to the troops and of subsidy to the British Government went on increasing. At last, in despair of any other remedy, the Governor General (1823) allowed Jhuta Ram to be appointed prime minister, in the hope that he might be able to act with more confidence and energy when made publicly responsible and (thereby remedy) the disorders of the State (*Wilson*, iii, 451-461).

But Jhuta Ram antagonised the *thakurs* by his extortion and threat; Ranthambhor openly defied the royal orders, and tumult and disorder accompanied by violent crimes spread throughout the country. A civil war was prevented only by the threat of British armed intervention.

Early in 1834, the Regent queen-mother (Bhatiani) died and a year later (6th February, 1835) her royal son, who had been a minor throughout his nominal reign, followed her. In the winter months of 1834-1835, a British detachment from Ajmer pacified the Shekhawati districts, by capturing and destroying the forts of the bandit chiefs of the region, with the support of the Rajah of Sikar and other loyal *thakurs*.

The Murder Of Mr. Blake, 1835

After the death of Sawai Jai Singh III, Jhuta Ram, unable to face public obloquy, resigned and the guardianship of the late Rajah's only son, Sawai Man Singh II, an infant aged 16 months, was undertaken by the British Government. Major Alves, the Political Agent for Rajputana, was sent to Jaipur to concert new administrative arrangements with the principal nobles of the State. The capital had been in a ferment ever since the death of the late Maharajah, which was popularly ascribed to poison administered by Jhuta Ram. Many of the *thakurs* with their armed retainers had assembled in the city; the numerous adherents of Jhuta Ram were in concert with the unruly mercenary troops of the palace; and Jaipur resembled the city of Verona with the armed gangs of Montagues and Capulets fighting in the streets.

Major Alves by his arrival prevented any immediate out-break of violence. Jhuta Ram was sent to the fort of Daosa and the administration was entrusted to a Council of the principal nobles under the presidency of Rawal Bairi Sal, in consultation with the Political Agent. But on 4th June (1835) the pent-up force of factious intrigue and mob fury unexpectedly burst forth in an unprecedented crime: Major Alves was severely wounded, and his assistant Mr. Blake was murdered along with several of the native servants of the Residency.

On that day, the Political Agent (Major Alves) with his party had an interview with the Queen-mother and the *thakurs* at the palace. As he was about to leave, he was attacked with a sword by a man from among the crowd and severely wounded. The assassin was seized; the Major was sent to the Residency in a palankin, and met with neither insult nor molestation in passing through the city. But later Cornet Macnaghten, his secretary, on issuing from the palace gate was assailed with all kinds of missiles from the mob outside, but escaped to safety.

> Reports had been insidiously spread among the crowd, who had assembled about the palace gates, that some undefined act of violence had been perpetrated by the British Resident, and the ferment thus excited was aggravated by the appearance of Mr. Blake, who held in his hand the blood-stained sword of the assassin (of Major Alves).

The rumour spread that he had murdered the infant Maharajah to ensure the British annexation of the State.

> As Mr. Blake left the palace on his elephant, a number of armed men, chiefly Minas, joined by the mob, attacked him... Stones and spears were also thrown at him, and finding it impossible to make his way alive through the furious multitude....he entered a temple[4] with one attendant *chaprasi* and the driver of the elephant. Two persons in the temple conducted the party to a small chamber and shut the doors, endeavouring to provide for

> their safety; but the mob forced their way in... Mr. Blake was cut down... the *chaprasi* was also killed; the elephant-driver was saved... The chiefs at Jaipur united in expressing their regret and indignation, and their determination to punish all concerned in the outrage... A minute investigation was instituted... The instigation of the crime was traced to a knot of Jain bankers of Jaipur, partisans of Jhuta Ram, and acting under his suggestions and those of his brother and nephew, Hukum Chand and Fateh Lal. The main object of the plot was to embroil Bairi Sal with the British Government... (and) to establish his inability to maintain order in Jaipur.
>
> The excitement (among the mob) was, however, the work of the moment. The city in general had remained tranquil; and the tumult round the palace was allayed by the very first efforts of the authorities. (*Wilson*, iii, 466-469.)

After a judicial enquiry, Diwan Amar Chand and Hidayetullah were hanged; Jhuta Ram and Hukum Chand's death-sentences were commuted to life-long imprisonment, but both died in Jail; Sheolal Sah and Manik Chand and minor culprits were condemned to imprisonment.

Rawal Bairi Sal, who was reapointed Regent (*mukhtar*) on 9th March, 1836, died in May, 1838. Thus the *ancien regime* ended and then commenced the modern age of Jaipur, which will be fully described in the following chapter.

Notes

1. Col. Tod who had 'witnessed the commencement and the end of this drama', confirms this. (Annals, Mewar, ch. 17). *J.S.*
2. Madhorajpura is situated at 28 miles south-west of Jaipur; 26° 35′ N and 75° 38′ E. *Ed.*
3. Tod (*Amber*, ch. III) gives '21 December, 1818, the winter solstice' as the date of the event. This is incorrect, as the news of the Rajah's death and cremation reached the Governor-General at Calcutta before 13th December; hence 21st *November* is more likely. (*Journal of Marquess of Hastings*, p. 375).

'Jagat Singh... had suffered the power of the Rajah to fall into insignificance and contempt by the immunity with which he permitted his great vassals to encroach upon the demesne of the Crown; or the imprudence with which he alienated his revenues in favour of military or religious persons, on conditions which they wholly disregarded... With the sanction and support of Sir David Ochterlony, many of the grants to undeserving individuals were resumed; and it was proposed to the *Thakurs* to assent to an arrangement by which they should consent to relinquish their usurpations. Their assent was not obtained until an example had been made of the most refractory.' (*Wilson*, ii, 429.) *J.S.*

4. A temple of the Minas in Kishanpol Bazar. *J.S.*

XXVI

The Reign Of Ram Singh II: The First Half

Birth And Education

The Sepoy Mutiny marks the reign of Ram Singh II with two clear-cut divisions, during the first of which (covering 22 years) he was a minor for all but five years, and the government was conducted under British supervision. But with the outbreak of the Mutiny he asserted his own will and moulded the policy of the State by his own statesmanly genius. With the year 1859, begins the era of modernization and progress in Jaipur and the influence of its ruler once more asserts itself in the council of the Empire of India as it had done in the days of the great Mughals.

Up to 1839, the administration of the Kachhwa Kingdom had been of the medieval oriental type. It was, by the very nature of a military State, an autocracy tempered by the counsels of the baronage, most of whom were not only the kings' vassals but fellow clansmen as well and who therefore regarded him as the head of a vast family to which they themselves belonged. In these circumstances, all the threads of the administration had to be gathered together in the Rajah's own hands and everything had to be guided by his will. The *thakurs* or barons merely tendered advice, but had to execute his orders. When they happened to assert their own will, the result was anarchy. As has been well said by an eminent historian of the Anglo-

Saxon constitution in a parallel case, 'the witenagemot governed when the king slept'.

With the coming of age of Maharajah Ram Singh, 'the king awoke' in Dhundhar Land and his reforming hand was felt in every branch of public life. Though he began to give his impetus to progress and modernization some years before the Sepoy Mutiny, yet for the sake of unity of treatment this subject will be taken up after disposing of his activities during the upheaval, which separates modern from medieval India in the British territory, no less than in the Indian States.

He was born on 27th September, 1833, and proclaimed king, on the sudden death of his father, on 6th February, 1835, in the 17th month of his infancy. The young Maharajah was, according to the ancient custom of his house, first brought before the public at the age of ten. But a vernacular (Hindi) teacher was appointed for him when he was eight, a teacher of English in June 1844, and next a master for teaching him Hindustani. In a short period he was able to read and speak English and Urdu fairly well, though he loved to talk in the Jaipuri dialect in his inner circle. In time he came to acquire a good knowledge of Hindi and could also understand ordinary Sanskrit books without the help of others.

Next Rao Jivan Singh of Duni taught him riding, and Himmat Khan gymnastics. The young Maharajah soon proved a good shot and clever swordsman as well. Nor was he indifferent to the arts; he patronised music, both instrumental and vocal, and learnt to play on the sitar and the been himself. He was not married before completing his 20th year.

Major John Ludlow, who was British Political Agent at Jaipur from January, 1844 to December, 1847, instilled lessons of political wisdom and moral culture into his mind, and as the historian Malleson noted, the young Maharajah 'benefited greatly from these lessons'. The same authority speaks of him on the eve of the Mutiny as 'extremely well educated, naturally intelligent, and fully alive to the duties which devolved upon him as ruler and anxious to perform them'. Nearly 20 years later, when this Maharajah was sitting on the tribunal which tried Malhar Rao Gaekwad, the famous English barrister Serjeant Ballantine, who noticed his speech and demeanour daily, speaks of him as 'admitted to be one of the ablest men in India, and a devoted friend of the English Government'.

How devoted, how serviceable in a supreme crisis of the Empire, that friendship was, the next section will show.

The Supreme Value Of Rajput Princes' Loyalty During The Mutiny

The Sepoy Mutiny of 1857 came as the crucial test of the loyalty of the princes and people of Rajputana, and nobly did they come out of the trial, in spite of two great disadvantages under which they laboured... their inferiority in armament and training compared with the British sepoys and the genuineness of the sepoy grievance that the Enfield cartridges were greased with cow's fat and pig's lard. If Rajput loyalty to the Paramount Power and devotion to the cause of peace and order was less spectacular and less fruitful of concrete results than the princes desired, the reason lay not in any lurking disloyalty or hesitation, but in the military weakness of their own forces at exactly this time. In 1857 the days of the medieval indigenous forces which Mirza Rajah and Sawai Jai Singh had led to victory, had passed away, and the day of the modern disciplined and well-equipped Imperial Service troops had not yet dawned. The forces of Maharajah Ram Singh lacked the efficiency of both these types of warriors; they were outclassed by the British sepoys in discipline, equipment and above all in artillery. Hence, they shrank from attacking the mutinous sepoys, especially the portion of 'Sale's Illustrious Garrison' which was posted at Nasirabad, and the superior artillery which they carried with them. The story of the greased cartridge being true,[1] the general Hindu population of Rajputana did not feel any righteous indignation against the sepoys who had mutinied only to save their religion. But they gave the sepoys no help either.

Active, self-sacrificing exertion against the mutineers, however, came from the three greatest princes of Rajputana... the Maharajahs of Jaipur and Udaipur. When the heads of the three highest clans of *kshatriyas*... Sisodia, Rathor and Kachhwa... stood by the side of the Paramount Power in the awful crisis, its moral effect on the Hindu world was incalculably great. We cannot measure it in terms of the bayonets and sabres that they brought to the field in aid of the English. This fact was acknowledged by all who could speak with authority on the subject.

Sir George Lawrence, the Political Agent for Rajputana at the time, writes: 'During the momentous period between May, 1857 and February, 1859, when our power in India was shaken to its foundation, not one of the nineteen States or princes of Rajputana wavered in loyalty or withheld a cheerful and hearty support to the Paramount Power.'

Col. G.H. Trevor, another Political Agent for Rajputana (1890-1895), bears witness to the same fact:

> What saved Rajputana was the example of the leading princes, particularly of Maharana Sarup Singh of Udaipur, Maharajah Takht Singh of Jodhpur, and Ram Singh of Jaipur, from whom the other chiefs and others outside the province took their cue. By standing fast they carried with them, for the most part, their own troops and the majority of their subjects, and thus enabled a handful of British officers to maintain order and recover the military cantonments from which they had been expelled by the mutiny of the native garrisons.

Col. Malleson, the historian of the mutiny, endorses the same view. (*History*, iv. 403) The most authoritative pronouncement came from the highest Englishman in the land, the Sovereign's representative, Earl Canning.

The Services Of The Jaipur Maharaja During The Mutiny

Sir George Lawrence, on hearing of the outbreak of the Mutiny at Mirat,

> felt ... that the maintenance of British supremacy in Rajputana... depended on the loyalty and fidelity to their treaty engagements of the native princes... With the view, therefore, of securing their co-operation, I issued on May 23, a proclamation to all the chiefs to concentrate their troops on the frontiers of their respective States, so as to be available if called upon to aid the Paramount Power. (*Reminiscences,* 279.)

In 1857, the Maharaja of Jaipur was Ram Singh, an intelligent prince, fully alive to the duties which devolved upon him as ruler, and anxious to perform them. When the mutiny broke out, he acted in no uncertain manner. He at once placed the whole of his forces, amounting to between 6000 and 7000 troops at the disposal of the Political Agent, Major Eden,

> leaving only 700 sepoys and 1880 police for the defence of the capital. (*Malleson*, vi, 158.)

The Jaipur contingent, of some 6000 men (about half cavalry and half Naga infantry) with seven guns, set out under Major William Frederick Eden (the Resident). The commandant of this army was Faiz Ali Khan (the State *bakshi*), and the second in command was Ranjit Singh, the *thakur* of Achrol. Marching towards Delhi (which was then besieged by the English), Eden reached Rewari town but found the district of Gurgaon in a terrible state of anarchy. Everywhere the unruly Meo population was up in arms, sacking villages and towns and robbing the highways.

Eden abandoned the idea of advancing north to reinforce the siege army before Delhi. He turned east from Rewari and entered Gurgaon district to suppress the banditti. Near Sohna (eight miles east of Tauru), the Jaipur *bakhshi* cut down the rebel *thanadar* of the place and burnt a number of Meo villages. At Sohna, the army was joined by about 30 Europeans fleeing from the rebels... mostly officers of the Civil service and the inland customs department. They were relieved and lodged in comfort in the moving camp.

Thereafter, this force took post for a long time between Palwal and Hodal, three quarters of the way up the great northern road from Agra to Delhi. Sir Donald Stewart, afterwards Commander-in-Chief of India, who came into the Jaipur camp near Palwal as a refugee on 19th June, 1857, and fell back with it to Hodal on the 23rd, wrote on the 27th:

> Mutiny of two or three of the Jaipur Poorbeea regiments who have made off in a body from our camp to join the rebels at Delhi. Fortunately, the national (i.e., Kachhwa) troops of the Jaipur State remained staunch... The Nagas and the Shekhawati *thakurs* converted themselves into a sort of bodyguard, and kept strict watch over the Political Agent's camp. (Elsmie's Sir Donald Stewart, p. 57.)

But the heavy rains of that year brought on epidemic fever and cholera; many of the soldiers perished, many deserted through alarm; and at last the Jaipur commanders begged and obtained Major Eden's permission to take their men back to Jaipur, as they could be of no further use at Palwal. But before their return home, a detachment from them led by Thakurs Bhupal Singh Nathwat and Sobhag Singh

Larkhani, escorted the refugee Europeans safely to Agra fort, which the Lt. Governor, James Colvin, was holding out against the rebels.

During this interval of Major Eden's absence, his wife and other Europeans of that region were housed by Maharajah Ram Singh in the Badal Mahal Palace, and laterly in the lofty Nahargarh fort towering above his capital.

The sepoy brigade at Nasirabad, mutinied on 28th May, and while passing by Jaipur, on their way to Delhi, called upon Maharaja Ram Singh to deliver up his European proteges. This he refused, and defied them to attack his capital, though denuded of his army at that time. They then hastened on to Delhi.

The destitute British officers, whose soldiers had deserted them at Nasirabad and Nimach, were sent with every necessary assistance to Agra fort, under escort of Thakur Puran Singh of Jaipur. They started from Nasirabad on 11th November, and after being relieved on the way by the kind attentions of Major Eden at Jaipur and Captain Nixon at Bharatpur, arrived safely at Agra on 3rd December, 1857.

Mr. James Colvin, the Lt. Governor of the Agra Province, requested the States of Jaipur, Bharatpur and Kishangarh to keep the Agra-Ajmer road open for the transmission of mails, as most other routes had been closed by the disturbances. Maharaja Ram Singh successfully accomplished his part of the work, and the mails arrived punctually at their destination without the loss of a single packet in transit.

When the Jodhpur Legion (composed mainly of Poorbias or Oudh sepoys) mutinied, and marched Delhiwards looting the country, the Jaipur Raj troops, along with the retainers of the Rao of Sikar (a vassal chief), tried to bar its path in the Shekhawati district (October, 1857), but the attempt failed owing to the inferior training and armament of the Rajput levies.

In 1859, Tantia Tope, the rebel leader from Jhansi, entered Jaipur territory; but found neither refuge nor encouragement there. With him were two other notorious rebel leaders the Rao Sahib and Firuz Shah. The British forces sent against these men under Brigadier Gen. Showers and Col. Holmes, received material assistance from the Jaipur Maharaja in their victorious action in Daosa (January 16, 1859) and Sikar (January, 21). As a result, this body of enemies was finally crushed.

For his eminent service during the Mutiny, Maharaja Ram Singh was given the *pargana* of Kot Qasim (with a revenue of half a lakh of rupees) in perpetuity, and highly honoured in many other ways, at the Viceroy's durbar held at Agra in November, 1859.

Early Agents To G.G. For Rajputana And Residents At Jaipur

The dawn of the modern age in Jaipur was due to the initiative and fostering care of a number of British officers of exceptional ability and generous sympathy, and it was the good fortune of Maharajah Ram Singh II to have been trained by them at the formative stage of his life and to carry to full maturity the reforms for which they had done the spadework.

After the British Indian Government had acquired control over Delhi and its titular Emperor Shah Alam II, as the result of Lord Lake's victory over Sindhia's forces (1803), an English Agent was posted at Delhi who for many years afterwards looked after the British interests in Rajputana also. Such was the position of Sir Charles Metcalfe and Sir David Ochterlony. It was only in 1832 that the post of a separate *Political Agent to the Governor-General for Rajputana* was created with Lt. Col. A. Lockett, and the Residents at the different Rajput Courts were placed under his control. The succession list was as follows:

1. Lt. Col. A Lockett, 1832-1834
2. Major Nathaniel Alves, 1834-1839

3. and 4. Lt. Col. Sutherland, April, 1839-December, 1847. But when Sutherland went to the Cape of Good Hope on sick leave (January, 1844-October, 1846), Major Thoresby officiated for him.

5. Col. John Low, December, 1847-January, 1853
6. Sir Henry M. Lawrence. February, 1853-February, 1857

7 and 8. Sir George Lawrence, March, 1857-April, 1864. But during his home leave (April, 1859-November, 1860), Major W. Eden officiated for him.

9. Col. W. Eden, ... April, 1864-1867
10. Lt. Col. R.H. Keatinge, V.C., C.S.I., 1867-1870
11. Col. J.C. Brooke, ... 1870-1873.

In order to avoid confusion, we shall always call this officer *Agent to G.G.*, while the British representative at Jaipur (and other courts) will be designated under the familiar title of *Resident,* though in official writings both categories of officers very often figured under the same title of *Political Agent*.

The first British representative at Jaipur was Capt. Sturrock (March, 1804-1805), but he was really an envoy for a particular occasion and a long interval elapsed before the post was revived. The succession list up to the Mutiny is as follows:

1. Capt. Sturrock, March, 1804-1805
2. Major Stewart (the first officer to bear the title of Political Agent, Jaipur) March, 1821-April, 23, 1824
3. Col. Raper, April, 23, 1824-November, 1825

4\. and 5. Capt. John Low, November, 12, 1825-1830. But when Low went to the hills for health reasons, Mr. George Clerk officiated for him, March, 1828-November 30, 1829.

In 1830 the political agency at Jaipur was closed by Lord W. Bentinck as a useless and impolitic expenditure, and at the same time the agencies at Udaipur and some other Rajput States were suppressed on the same ground of economy. As Victor Jacquemont found during his visit in March, 1832, 'the only officer of the Company who resides at present in Jaipur is a humble news-writer or *akhbar-navis*, who, in return for Rs 100 per month, sends daily to Delhi a couple of pages of news... He is regarded at Jaipur as a spy, which is really his official character'. (*Etat Politique et social de l' Inde du sud en 1832*, p. 46).

6. Major Ross, September 26, 1838-August 14, 1839
7. Major Thoresby, August 14, 1839-January, 1844
8. Major John Ludlow, January 24, 1844-December, 1847
9. Captain Rickards, December, 1847-1856
10. Major W. Eden, 1856.

Lt. Col Sutherland, after a visit to Jaipur in 1839 recommended to the Governor-General that the post of Resident there be made permanent. This was done.

British Generosity; Reduction Of Tribute

The troubles following the accession of the infant Rajah Ram Singh II led to the financial collapse of the Jaipur State and created anxiety about the future maintenance of the subsidiary force. At the suggestion of Col. Alves, the Governor-General deputed an officer, Major Ross, to Jaipur to report on the resources of the State. When Ross, after less than a year's stay, went away on sick leave, the investigation was continued by his successor, Major Thoresby.

This latter officer reported that in 1840, the State income was 23 lakhs and expenditure about 32 and a half lakhs, leaving a deficit of 9 and a half lakhs while the arrears of tribute amounted to Rs 31,29,000.

> Major Thoresby considered that 28 lakhs was the highest sum at which it would be safe to estimate the revenues of the country during the next ten years, and that 24 lakhs might be taken as the regular annual expenditure (exclusive of the British tribute). The tribute he considered had been fixed too high, under the impression that eight lakhs had been taken by the Marathas; though it was proved that their demand was only Rs 2,40,000, which sum was paid very irregularly.

Col. Sutherland wrote on 2nd February, 1841 to the Secretary to the Government of India, 'The tribute we now demand, in addition to the three lakhs required for the Shekhawati Brigade, and the sequestration of the revenues of Sambhar, makes a total demand on the state of nearly thirteen lakhs of rupees a year. She is therefore... in a condition of irretrievable ruin, much of which may be traced to her connection with us.' He strongly supported Thoresby's recommendation that the entire 39 lakhs of arrears of tribute should be struck off, and the annual tribute reduced from eight to four lakhs. The Governor-General agreed,[2] adding that the first of November, 1830 should be taken as the date from which the annual tribute shall be assumed to have been reduced from eight to four lakhs of rupees. At the same time the Sambhar lake was restored to the management of the Jaipur Government, and the Shekhawati Brigade was recognized and taken over as a British force, the expenses of which were to be defrayed from the tribute itself. This admitted of the total abolition of the 'unpalatable *fauj kharch*'.

The Hon'ble Court of Directors approved of these proceedings, and in addition suggested that the British tribute might be allowed to remain in arrears, so that the Jaipur Government's debt to the bankers might be at once liquidated...

'These liberal measures were received at Jaipur and throughout Rajputana with unbounded gratitude and applause... The arrears of tribute, so freely and generously sacrificed, amount to Rs 46,28,999.' (Col. Brooke's *Political History*, pp. 40-42.)

Financial Fluctuation; Equilibrium Secured At Last

Those who see the present day prosperous condition of Jaipur State and its costly activities for public good, can realise the marvellous change effected in less than a hundred years by wise and efficient administration only if they will study the following figures of the State income and expenditure during the early years of Ram Singh's reign.

	Income		*Expenditure*
1840 —	Rs 23,02,091	...	32,40,418
1841 —	Rs 25,36,262	...	20,80,972
	Plus Rs 1,50,000 (Sambhar)		Plus 3 lakhs for Shekhawati Brigade.

1844-47 (average 29 lakhs ... (average 25½ lakhs (in 1848, owing to a severe drought there was a deficit of nearly 5½ lakhs of rupees.)

	Income		*Expenditure*
1849 —	33,19,000	...	28,94,000
1850 —	29,42,000	...	30,81,000
1851 —	28,73,000	...	31,73,000
1852 —	31,73,000	...	36,08,000
1853 —	26,93,000	...	31,04,000
1854 —	32,59,000	...	31,32,000
1855 —	31,60,000	...	27,94,000
1856 —	33,01,000	...	30,44,000
1857 —	32,01,000	...	33,51,000
1858 —	34,54,000	...	33,60,000
1859 —	35,53,000	...	35,65,000
1860 —	37,65,000	...	35,75,000
1939-40 —	(1,44,67,000)[3]	...	(1,43,06,000)[3]

The component elements of the annual income were on an average (a) land revenue and Sambhar salt monopoly (half share), 20 to 25 lakhs, (b) custom duties, three and a half to four lakhs, and (c) tribute from vassals, three and a half lakhs besides a few minor sources.

The annual expenditure was at that time made up of (a) tribute to the British Government, four lakhs, (b) army, eight to ten and a half lakhs, (c) commissariat, five and a half to seven and a half lakhs, and (d) collection charges, three and a half to five lakhs.

Major Thoresby restored financial equilibrium by reducing expenditure on the several establishments of the State, as far as was compatible with efficiency. The saving on the army amounted to Rs 60,000 a year, which with the reduction of the tribute by four lakhs and the transfer of the maintenance of the Shekhawati Brigade to the British Indian army (three lakhs) meant a total reduction of expenditure by Rs 7,60,000 a year. The Sambhar Salt monopoly was leased to the British Government for Rs 1,50,000 net per annum. These facts, coupled with the discovery of Jhutaram Sanghi's hidden treasure in 1844, led to the State's debt to bankers being brought down to three and a half lakhs only, while no arrear of tribute remained due to the E.I. Company.

But in 1854, only three years after the British managers had handed over the administration to the young Maharajah, there was a deplorable relapse. The British official report runs thus,

> The Rawal (Sheo Singh Nathawat of Samode) still continued minister; and being naturally of an extravagant disposition and little inclined to business, the revenues of the State were wasted with lavish prodigality to supply his expensive habits... The troops and establishments were soon many months in arrears; the debt amounted to no less than 17 lakhs of rupees. *(Brooke*, p. 54.)

This evil state of things was remedied by the Maharajah acting firmly with the advice of Sir Henry Lawrence, the Governor General's Agent at Abu, and placing the State Council on a new footing as we shall see later.

Social Reforms Initiated

Major John Ludlow, who was Resident at Jaipur from 1844 to 1847, 'left behind him a name which is remembered with gratitude by all classes to this day,' and he was also publicly thanked by the Governor General Lord Hardinge for his social reforms. The most remarkable feature of his great work is that it was achieved with the co-operation of the indigenous Rajput nobles of the Council of Regency. As Col. Brooke justly remarks, 'In no Native State in India, had so many great and beneficial measures been inaugurated in so short a time, as were introduced by the Jaipur Council of Regency; and which could not have been carried by the power of a single British officer, acting with a Native Chief' (p. 53).

The first in point of time and importance was the abolition of sati, or the voluntary burning of a Hindu widow on her husband's funeral pyre. Soon after assuming charge at Jaipur, Major Ludlow invited the opinions of the Council of Regency on this question. Bhopal Singh Rajawat, the *thakur* of Jhilai, heir presumptive to the throne and first noble in the State, at once denounced the practice, and several other nobles were of the same opinion. In August, 1844, the Council of Regency, by an unanimous decision, declared sati penal within the limits of Jaipur territory. As the A.G.G. wrote,

> Jaipur took the lead of all Hindu States in the abolition of sati, and Bhopal Singh the *thakur* of Jhilai is deserving of immortal honour for the noble way he came forward, before any other Rajput, to denounce the custom. Other States and Chiefs followed unwillingly in the train of Jaipur. (*Brooke*, p. 45.)

Next came the rooting out of domestic slavery. Slave dealing and slavery, in its strict sense, had not been common in Jaipur, and had been suppressed by enactment in 1839. There existed voluntary bondsmen working out their debts to their creditors, and household slaves, as in other parts of India; but trading in slaves had always been repugnant to Rajput feeling. At Major Ludlow's suggestion, very stringent rules were issued by the Regency against the practice, and the very name of 'slave' was proscribed in the country.

But of even greater practical importance and of more universal benefit than the abolition of sati was the reduction of compulsory marriage expenses which lay at the foot of the practice of female infanticide among the proud Rajputs. The amount of dowry *(daeja)* and gifts *(tyag*, for bards) paid by the father of a bride rose by social custom and foolish competition to such an exorbitant extent that a single daughter's marriage left her noble father crushed with debt for the rest of his life, and yet reluctant to offer any lower sum for fear of social obloquy. Hence the birth of a female child was regarded as a curse. The great Jai Singh II had struck at the evil more than a century before this time. As his record runs:

> His Highness assembled the 53 clans of the Kachhwa, and all the nobles and foreign ministers, and having collected the pandits he explained to them that it was a serious crime in parents to destroy their offspring; and that no Rajput would be suffered in future to kill his daughters within the Jaipur State. His Highness also desired all the foreign *vakils* who were in attendance to write to their masters, in order that the same good regulation might everywhere be instituted; and explained that in the event of any Kachhwa being destitute and unable to pay the dowry and *tyag*, he must come to the town of Jaipur to celebrate the nuptials of his daughter, where he would receive some assistance from the Raj, and Raos, Bhats and Charans would be unable to levy *tyag* or other extortionate demands. His Highness also enjoined on the Charans that they were not to make any demands of *tyag* etc. from any one on a marriage taking place at the *capital* and they consented to act in obedience to this command.[4] It is worthy of remark that this custom exists in the city of Jaipur to this day, and no Bhat or Charan has the power to ask for payment on the celebration of any marriage *within its walls*.
>
> But in the course of time the admirable rules of Jai Singh II were broken through by the ostentatious vanity of individuals, who spent large sums on such occasions, in consequence of which poorer people lost dignity if they spent less. Major Ludlow tried to revive these obsolete rules. The visits of Bhats and Charans for extorting these so-called voluntary gifts, were restricted to *thakurs* (nobles) whose estates were within their home district. Subsequently, in 1847, another law was passed by the Council of Regency, restricting the demands of the Charans and Bhats to one-eighth of the yearly income of the estate of the concerned *thakur*. (*Brooke*, pp. 45-46.)

The Early Years Of Ram Singh's Personal Rule

Maharajah Ram Singh's general education has been described before. From Major Ludlow's frequent conversations he received political and moral instruction of the highest value, which left an abiding mark on his career after. The training in administrative work given to him during this minority was equally judicious and calculated to fit him fully for the high function of his life. In 1848, in his 16th year, he began to sit with the five sardars of the Regency Council to learn the work. Next, all important measures proposed by these sardars and approved by their Chairman, the Resident, were issued after explaining them to the Maharajah. In some important cases, the Resident consulted the young sovereign and learnt his wishes; His views were used to make suggestions, which were in most cases implemented. Thus responsibility in practice developed his powers and taught him wisdom and self-control.

As the result of the consistently high praise given to him, by successive Political Agents on their reports, the Maharajah was invested with full ruling powers by the Governor-General on first September, 1851. But for the next three years, Rawal Sheo Singh (the son of Bairi Sal Nathawat) dominated his young master, keeping all administrative power in his own hands and involving the State in heavy debt by his extravagance and indolence. The Maharajah, in view of his own youth and the long monopoly of power and British support which the family of Bairi Sal had enjoyed, naturally hesitated to interfere with his servant. But when the minister's misrule became intolerable, he sought the advice of Sir Henry Lawrence, now Agent to the Governor-General. Fortified with that eminent man's sympathy and support, Ram Singh dismissed Rawal Sheo Singh, and put his brother Lachman Singh (the *thakur* of Chomu), an able and more careful man in his place. At the same time, in order to counter-balance the influence of the Nathawat party, who had hitherto monopolized the high places in the administration, an independent element from outside was introduced into the Council. Pandit Sheodin who had hitherto acted as the Maharajah's tutor, was made *diwan* with charge of the Revenue Department, while a separate and independent officer, Faiz Ali Khan, was appointed to command the army (with the title of *bakhshi*.) 'There was room for all at Jaipur, as Sir Henry Lawrence truly observed, and the counter-balancing influences to the

Nathawat party then introduced (1855), liberated the State from thraldom.' (*Brooke*, p. 54.) The harmful concentration of power in one sole ruler's hands was prevented by the creation of departments under heads who were responsible directly to the sovereign (in 1854).

The new order introduced in 1854-1855 took some time to get into full stride, but within two years the Sepoy Mutiny intervened, which engrossed every ruler's attention to the exclusion of all other affairs. It was only after India had passed under the Crown (1858) that the era of reform began in right earnest. No doubt, several modern improvements in Jaipur owed their beginnings to British officers during this prince's minority, but it is necessary to treat the subject in one place along with Ram Singh's own reforms, lest the interest and instructive value of the story be lost to the reader by the dispersion of the subject over different chapters. This literary arrangement cannot, in fairness, be taken for an attempt to ignore or belittle the work of these great and good British pioneers among the makers of modern India.

Notes

1. This is borne out by Sir G. Forrest in his official history, Capt. Prichard (*Mutinies in Rajputana*, pp. 28 and 287), Gen. Seaton (*Cadet to Colonel*, ii, 80), P.E. Roberts, O, Malley (*History of Bengal, Bihar and Orissa*) and other authorities. *J.S.*
2. Secretary to Govt.'s letter to Col. Sutherland, dated 8th July, 1842. *J.S.*
3. These figures are quoted from the Government of India publication *Memoranda on the Indian States, 1940. Ed.*
4. The noble example thus set by the Jaipur Rajah was followed by a Jodhpur sovereign who reigned some years after him, and who issued a similar prohibitory order. *J.S.*

XXVII

The Reign Of Ram Singh II: An Era Of Progress

Administrative Reorganization

Before the year 1859 ended, the last embers of the Sepoy revolt had been quenched with liberal statesmanship no less than with blood and iron. India had come under the direct care of the British Crown and Parliament, and the Indian princes who had nobly stood the ordeal, had been recognized as protected allies of the British Sovereign with permanent inalienable rights and as members of a far-flung British Empire whose parts were connected together by the bond of freedom and cooperation. A new era opened before our princes and their peoples as the repercussion of the rapid modernization and progress in British-governed India in the political, economic and educational fields which came as the best after-effect of the Sepoys' failure. In this work Jaipur took the leading part in Rajputana and the credit for it belongs to Maharajah Ram Singh and the able instruments that he had the wisdom to choose.

The young Maharajah was by this time firmly in the saddle, and his first task was to set his own house in order, before he responded to the call to share in Imperial councils outside his realm.

First of all, the administrative machinery at the centre was remodelled; the concentration of work in one hand and absolute rule gave place to departmental specialization and individual ministerial responsibility. At the same time the clear separation of functions which is at the root of administrative efficiency, was accepted in principle and steadily pursued.

In 1854-1855 the *diwan* and *bakhshi* were given independent charge of the Revenue and army departments respectively and thus the prime minister's work was lightened. A year later the Maharajah had established his own Private Secretariat (*Khas Daftar* or *Huzuri* work), which was another corrective to the Prime Minister's monopoly of power. The reform went further in 1854-1855, when four new departments were created for greater facility of work, namely, (1) the Police, under an Inspector General, (2) the Medical Department, under a civil surgeon, (3) the Education Department, and (4) the Survey and Settlement Department.

At the same time the kingdom was divided into five districts (*nizamats)* in imitation of the districts of British India, each with its own magistrate (*nazim)*, collector, judge and police chief.

On 31st August, 1867, the Maharajah formed a Royal Council, composed of eight members, among whom the departmental portfolios were distributed; but each department was put in the joint charge of two or three of these ministers, as a safeguard against slackness or corruption. The Maharajah himself presided over the Council, for which a big hall was built in the Jaleb Chowk. The administrative subdivision of the kingdom was later carried further, by marking it out into ten districts.

Law And Justice

Major Thoresby (1840) established Civil and Criminal Courts on the British Indian lines, and introduced the system of charging court fees in civil suits. The defeated party had to pay the court expenses to the winning party. Litigants were allowed to engage legal practitioners to conduct their cases.

At the capital, all civil suits below Rs 3000 are tried in the *munsif's* (subordinate) courts, and suits above that amount come before the *Sadar Diwani Adalat* (or Chief Civil Court). Criminal cases at the capital are tried in the court of the City Magistrate, termed the *Faujdari Adalat.* There is also an appellate court at the capital, and over it stands the highest tribunal in the State, namely the Council. But in the twentieth century a High Court has been established, which has taken over this supreme jurisdiction. In the districts, the Magistrates or *nazims* are vested with the powers of judges in civil suits as well. The prefect of police (*kotwal*) tries petty criminal cases at the capital.

The Police And Jails

In the capital, the police chief was named the *kotwal*, who worked under the supervision of the magistrate *(faujdar)*. In 1836, police arrangements were introduced in the districts also, and police headquarters were established in the Shekhawati division for better control of lawlessness. In 1858 four new police posts were set up in the district towns. Police rules were framed in 1860 and revised in 1874, and in 1865 a new General Superintendent of Thugee and Dacoity for the State was appointed for this special work.

The police of the State, as reorganized in Ram Singh's reign, was composed of two separate bodies: (a) the rural police, consisting of *chaukidars* and *tahsil sepoys* who acted under the orders of the magistrates in their respective districts, and (b) the general police who exercised independent powers in all police matters within their respective jurisdictions, and were directly subordinate to the darbar and its agents.

Formerly, prisoners were kept in forts. Later, the city prisoners were lodged in the Naharbara (Ramganj). In November, 1840, the city jail was removed from the Naharbara to Loon Karan Natani's *haveli* in which the city *kotwali* had already been established. The present Central Jail was constructed in 1854. It stands outside and south of the city walls. Major C.A. Baylay in 1878 reported on it as 'very well conducted, and a great credit to the State. The average number of prisoners, male and female, is over a thousand'.

Education

Modern education began during the incumbency of Major Ludlow in 1844. What was achieved in 15 years by Maharajah Ram Singh's zeal for progress will be seen from the following British Agent's report in 1875:

> In Jaipur, public instruction has made greater progress than in any other State in Rajputana, during the administration of the present Maharajah Ram Singh... The College at the capital, which was opened in 1844 with about 40 pupils, had in 1875 a daily class attendance of 800 (including the oriental and High School departments). The annual cost of maintenance is borne exclusively by the Maharajah. The college was affiliated to the F.A. (i.e., Intermediate) examination of the Calcutta University in 1873.
>
> There is also at the capital a well-attended "Rajput school" for the instruction of the sons of the *thakurs* and higher officials of the State, (established on 15th June, 1861). There is also a Sanskrit College (founded in 1845) attended by about 250 pupils; and a school with several local branches for the education of girls[1] which has an attendance of 500 pupils.
>
> In the districts there are 33 elementary schools wholly supported by the State, and 379 indigenous ones, all more or less so supported, with an aggregate class attendance of nearly 8000.

In June 1867, the Maharajah by the advice of Sir Charles Trevelyan, opened a School of Arts. The branches taught were plain and ornamental carpentry, carving in wood, bone and ivory, plain and ornamental blacksmith's work, pottery (both in the Indian and European styles), coach-building and upholstery, drawing and book-binding. In 1875 it had seven teachers and 25 pupils.

A medical school was opened in Jaipur City by the State in 1861, but in the course of a few years it was found that a more efficient supervision and a more thorough education could be secured at much less cost by sending the Jaipur pupils to the Agra Medical School at State expense. This has been done since 1868, when the local medical school was closed down.

On 26th March, 1869, the Maharajah founded a Society called the 'Social Science Conference' with the aim of removing social evils and introducing reforms by means of deliberation and consent. The Society suggested many new sanitary measures, new materials and implements of agriculture, mass education, and improvements of schools and colleges and similar instruments of public upliftment. Many of these were carried into effect, when no insuperable difficulty presented itself. One of the most useful was the revival and extension of the primitive practice of trial by *panches*, for disputes among the members of the same caste or community.

Hospitals

The present day's greatly extended arrangements for medical aid throughout the State will be described in the chapters on the now ruling prince. The splendid Mayo Hospital was constructed by Maharajah Ram Singh at a cost of Rs 1,63,000. Its foundation stone was laid by the Viceroy Lord Mayo, during his visit to Jaipur, on 15th October, 1870. Ram Singh also established and maintained dispensaries in most of the towns in his dominions, besides outdoor dispensaries in several wards of his capital.

An educational institution of the deepest significance to Rajputana, in the foundation of which Maharajah Ram Singh took a leading part, is the Mayo College for Princes at Ajmer.

> In the latter part of the year 1870, the Earl of Mayo visited Rajputana, and in a darbar held at Ajmer suggested to the princes and chiefs there present that a college should be founded at Ajmer, where the future rulers and nobles of Rajputana might receive such an education as would fit them for their high position and important duties.

It was to be maintained at the joint expense of the British Government and its feudatories. The chiefs subscribed nearly six lakhs of rupees, out of which the Jaipur State contributed Rs. 1,25,000—besides building boarding-houses for the pupils from their respective States. The Government granted 150 acres of land and built the College and the teachers' quarters.

The College was opened for teaching work in 1877, though the buildings took some more years to be completed.

The Capital

A survey and census of the city of Jaipur was undertaken in 1867. Roads and *pucca* drains were made in 1869, and other measures were adopted for improving its sanitary condition. A regular municipal committee was nominated. Kerosene lamp-posts were placed in different streets and bazars. In 1874 gas replaced kerosene oil for city illumination.

During Major Ludlow's incumbency the first attempt was made to provide the city with pure water. The Aman-i-Shah *nullah*, which flows about a mile and a half to the west of the city, was dammed up by Lt. Morton, and a masonry aqueduct was built for conveying the water to the city. But the embankment was of faulty construction and it gave way in 1855, on the water first rising to the height required for flowing into the aqueduct. 'Access had been levied on the townspeople for its construction, but whole labour and work was destroyed.' Later, Captain Swinton Jacob took the work in hand; he constructed a *cutcha* dam and set up an engine[2] which pumped the water into iron pipes for transmission to the city (1874).

In 1879 the Ram Prakash Theatre was constructed for the entertainment of the city. A public library with a large and valuable collection of English and Oriental works was founded in 1871. The other additions to the amenities of the capital such as public gardens and museums will be described later.

Communications

In Ram Singh's reign Jaipur was connected with Agra by rail, and two other lines, one leading to Delhi and another via Ajmer and Ahmadabad to Bombay, were constructed. To this work Jaipur State gave every assistance, and orders were issued to cede the land needed for the railway without charging any price.

The greatest service of this Maharajah to the cause of economic progress was the construction of metalled and bridged roads, with good staging bungalows at intervals, which were absolutely necessary for travel by road before the spread of railways.

(1) The portion of the Agra-Ajmer road lying within this territory is a first-class metalled road, 127 and a half miles in length, running east to west and touching the capital of Jaipur about midway. This road, together with staging bungalows throughout at convenient intervals, was constructed by Maharajah Ram Singh, the British Government contributing one-fifth of the cost. The eastern portion alone cost the Maharajah eight lakhs.

(2) The Jaipur-Tonk Road, second class, with 48 miles in Jaipur territory.

(3) The Karauli-Mandawar road, 49 miles long, passes through two large towns in the Jaipur State. It became an important artery of trade, because of its connecting the Mandawar station[3] on the Rajputana Railway[4] and the town of Hindaun,[5] which is the principal mart for all the cotton, grain, oilseeds, raw sugar, tobacco, etc., grown in the south and east of Jaipur State (1875).

The British Imperial postal system was introduced into the State in this reign and it was supplemented by the Maharajah's Rajput post-offices scattered throughout his dominions. In 1875, there were 38 Imperial post-offices in the Jaipur territory.

Telegraphic connection with the rest of India by way of Agra was opened on 8th April, 1864, and the line was later extended to Bombay.

Famine Relief

The great Rajputana Famine of 1868-1869 was a fiery ordeal for our ruling Prince's statesmanship and humanity, and most nobly did Maharajah Ram Singh come out of it. As the A.G.G. wrote in his report[6] on the famine, on 9th December, 1870, 'The first ruler who took a decided course in the matter, not on account of any pressure which was put on him, but solely for the purpose of benefiting his subjects, was the Maharajah of Jaipur, a Chief conspicuous alike for liberality and benevolence.' In the end, 'the acknowledgements of the Government of India were conveyed to the Maharajah of Jaipur for the active interest he had manifested in the cause of humanity'. (*Famine Report*, paragraphs 171 and 188.) His personal salute was raised from 17 to 19 guns.

Now for the history of the famine and the measures for the relief of its victims, 'The rainfall of 1868 was unfavourable from the commencement, being only one-third of the average in the course of the year.' The *kharif* yield in 1868 was only one-fourth of the normal... The *rabi* harvest of 1869 was fair in Jaipur, though blight partially affected it. The *kharif* of 1869 was attacked by locusts.

At Jaipur measures of relief were adopted under the very eyes of the Maharajah. 'In the city of Jaipur itself,... the population as a rule is much richer and the charities are more numerous and opulent than in other towns in Rajputana.' Jaipur before all other States took the lead in a liberal policy. The Maharajah of his own accord, as early as 20th September, 1868, abolished forever the duty on (the transit of) grain throughout his territories.[7] His Highness sanctioned the construction of many famine relief works, on which 15,000 people were employed daily. Loans were granted to agricultural classes and two lakhs of rupees were given to *zamindars*, while large remissions of revenue were made to all who needed them. Relief houses for the helpless poor were provided, and were most efficiently organized.

> The commencement of the rainy season of 1869 was very unfavourable to Jaipur... In August a meeting of the principal inhabitants was convened, at which the Mahrajah himself presided and promised to double any subscriptions which might be raised. The donations amounted to Rs 15,000, and the monthly cost of relief at the capital was Rs 700. In September 34,408 adults and 19,491 children received relief, and next month 23.189 adults and 17,819 children.

The cost of the relief measures to the State was very high as will be seen from the following figures. In two years two lakhs of revenues were excused to the peasantry; the relief works (in the form of buildings, road, bunds etc.) cost Rs 1,82,693 (*ibid*. paras, 185-89)—besides food to the value of Rs 1,31,652, freely distributed to the poor.

'The Best Friend Of The British Government'

Maharajah Ram Singh of Jaipur was one of the first Indian rulers to realize that a higher stage had been now reached in the evolution of the indigenous political system of the country. On 19th November, 1866, Sir John Lawrence as Viceroy of India had appealed to the ruling princes of India, at his Agra Darbar, in these clear and ringing terms:

> The standard by which the Paramount Power would henceforth estimate the worth of each one of the princes, was not his long line, his wealth, or his power, but his determination to govern well. The Chief who made his people happiest would be the best friend of the British Government.

His successor, Lord Mayo (1869-1872) also,

> in his personal and social relations with the Feudatories, made them realize that the one path towards the viceregal friendship was the good government of their territories... He gathered round himself a circle of chiefs whose character he personally admired, and in whose administration he took a well-founded pride...

as his biographer Sir William Hunter writes (1.213 and 233). On 23rd November, 1870, Lord Mayo in a private letter to a member of the British Cabinet, declared, 'with some (of the Feudatory princes) such as Jaipur, Bhopal and Patiala, we are on terms of intimacy and friendship'.

We here see how Ram Singh's liberal policy and spirit of progress in his internal administration, won for him the personal friendship and trust of successive Viceroys. Lord Mayo's visit to Jaipur in October, 1870 was one of the glorious events in the history of the State and it led to the creation of institutions which are a source of enduring benefit to the people.

So, too, Sir William Howard Russell, the chosen chronicler of the Indian tour of the Prince of Wales (afterwards King Edward VII), after his visit to Jaipur in February, 1876, writes,

> The Maharajah of Jaipur has the reputation of being one of the most enlightened of Indian Potentates.[9] He was invested with the badge of the G.C.S.I. by the Prince of Wales personally.
>
> The great England lawyer, Serjeant Ballantyne, wrote of him, "the Maharajah of Jaipur, admitted to be one of the ablest men in India, and a devoted friend of the English Government". (*Some Experiences*, ii, 244.)

In 1875, Maharajah Ram Singh was appointed to the bench of six commissioners nominated by the Viceroy, Lord Northbrook, to investigate the charge brought against Maharajah Malhar Rao Gaekwad by Col. Phayre, the dismissed Resident at Baroda, of an attempt to poison him. The five other members were Maharajah Jayaji Rao Sindhia, Sir Dinkar Rao, and three Europeans, Sir Richard Couch (Chief Justice of Bengal), Sir Richard Meade (ex-A.G.G. for Central India and Chief Commissioner of Mysore), and Mr. Philip S. Melvill, I.C.S.

After a long trial, the English members declared in favour of all the charges against the Gaekwad having been proved; while the Indian Commissioners found the charges not proved, His Highness of Jaipur even declaring Malhar Rao to be 'not guilty'. Maharajah Ram Singh urged, in his judgement, 'that Damodar Pant, Raoji, and Musoo, whose testimony is supposed to form the basis of this grave charge against the Gaekwad, are accomplices, and their evidence is not corroborated by a single respectable witness'. If the charges are not proved by satisfactory evidence, an accused person is entitled to an acquittal, whatever one's suspicions may be. This is English law.

In fairness to the memory of Maharajah Ram Singh it is necessary to mention that Lord Northbrook himself wrote to the Secretary of State for India, on 28th June, 1875, pointing out 'the incapacity of the Residents at Baroda for many years and Phayre's (reprehensible and refractory) conduct' for which the Viceroy had to dismiss him from the Residency at Baroda *before* he brought the charge of poisoning. As the great English Lawyer Serjeant Ballantyne writes:

> Col. Phyre's mode of giving evidence was not satisfactory. It was not until reprimanded by the President that he admitted his conduct in Sindh... My own deliberate and well considered belief is that Col. Phyre was subjected to no real attempt to be poisoned. I cannot think that the weighty reasons given by the Maharajah of Jaipur, and substantially agreed (to) by his (two Indian) colleagues, are met by any of the arguments used by the English Commissioners. (*Some Experiences of a Barrister's Life,* ii, 237-247.)

After this equally balanced divergent judgement had been given, the Government of India by a proclamation dated 19th April, 1875, deposed Malhar Rao on the ground of maladministration, previous to and not connected with the inquiry into the charge of poisoning and declared, 'Her Majesty's Government have not assumed that the result of the inquiry has been to prove the truth of the imputations against His Highness (the Gaekwad)'.

After India had passed under the Crown, by the Indian Councils Act of 1861, the Governor-General was empowered to nominate from six to twelve additional members to form his Legislative Council, of whom one half must be non-officials. Maharajah Ram Singh was so nominated from 1869 to 1873.

But the legislation which he helped to frame affected British India, and his weighty speeches in the Council may be read in the *Gazette of India*; they do not concern the history of Jaipur, except to mark the high position earned by its chief in the Senate of the Indian Empire.

The Glories Of Modern Jaipur

The free contact of the Jaipur Rajahs with the wide world outside their own realm, which had been interrupted since the death of Ishwari Singh (1750) was revived under Ram Singh II. The extraordinary natural intelligence with which this last named Maharajah was endowed, made him keep his eyes open and derive the fullest benefit from the cultured progressive society into which he was thrown in his many visits to the great cities of British India and during his long stay in Calcutta as a member of the Imperial Legislative Council. Calcutta was then the intellectual capital of British India no less than the political, and Maharajah Ram Singh was so fascinated by the cultural amenities of that city and its Indian society that he conceived the plan of making Jaipur a second Calcutta. Sawai Jai Singh II had founded the Kachhwa capital, Ram Singh II adorned it and made it the jewel and pride of Rajputana in the *modern* age.

We have already seen how he supplied his capital with schools, colleges, gas light for the streets and pure water supply through pipes, without which no city can be considered civilized. In imitation of the Eden Gardens (named after Lord Auckland's sister the Hon'ble Emily Eden) he planted the Ram-nivas Garden, covering an area of 2200 feet by 1500 feet, with a very beautiful hand-stand in the centre, where the State-band played every Monday evening. The Calcutta Zoological Garden found its counterpart in a fine collection of birds and animals at Jaipur. The total cost was nearly six lakhs of rupees.

The Medical College Hospital of Calcutta suggested the Mayo Hospital, and Maharajah Ram Singh induced Lord Mayo to lay its foundation-stone on 15th October, 1870. It cost Rs 1,63,000 during this reign, which figure does not take account of the additions made later.

The Maharajah's Public Library (founded in 1871), Museum and Ram Prakash Theatrical Hall (1879), were intended to benefit the Rajputana public like the Calcutta Public Library (Metcalfe Hall), Indian Museum, and the Great Bengal Theatre of the then capital of British India.

His Royal Highness, the Prince of Wales, laid the foundation-stone of the Albert Hall in Jaipur (6th February, 1876), which was constructed to serve the purpose of the Town Hall of Calcutta. Above all, a modern palace was built outside the city, amidst extensive grounds and shady trees, and named Rambagh Palace, as an improved residence for royalty.

With all these varied and useful additions to the attraction of the Kachhwa capital, it was only natural that Sir William Russell, who accompanied the Prince of Wales in the royal visit to Jaipur should write, 'We passed through a gateway, and Jaipur lay before us, *a surprise and wonder forever*.' During this visit the Prince shot his first tiger—a full-grown female eight and a half feet long (on 5th February, 1876).

Notes

1. The High School (or Matriculation) section of the Girls' School was opened in 1867, with an English headmistress. *J.S.*
2. The water is pumped up by steam-pumps about 104 feet high into service reservoirs, which command the city, through which water is delivered in iron pipes under 50 feet pressure. *J.S.*
3. Mandawar Station — Now known as Mandawar Mahwa Road. Mandawar — Situated at 27° 10′ N, 76° 49′ E; one mile North of Mandawar Mahwa Road. *Ed.*
4. Rajputana Railway — Now the Bandikui Agra section of the Western Railway (Metre Gauge). *Ed.*
5. Hindaun — Situated at 26° 44′ N. 77° 2′ E; 11 miles north of Karauli. Now a railway station of the Bayana-Sawai Madhopur section of the Western Railway (Broad Gauge). *Ed.*
6. 'Famine in Rajputana', published in the *Gazette of India* of the 25th February, 1871. *J.S.*
7. 'This decided action on the part of the Maharajah of Jaipur materially strengthened Col. Keatinge's hands. All the Native States met at a conference at Ajmer on 16th December, 1868 and agreed to abolish or reduce those duties during the famine.' (*Report*, para. 171). *J.S.*
8. *The Prince of Wales' Tour: A Diary in India*, 2 Vols. (1877) ii, 357.

XXVIII

Sawai Madho Singh II

His Policy And Achievements

On the death of Maharajah Ram Singh (17th September, 1880) without issue, Kaim Singh of the Isarda branch of the royal house, who had been adopted by the late sovereign, succeeded to the throne, under the title of Maharajadhiraj Sawai Madho Singh Bahadur II. The direct line of Maha Singh, the eldest son of Kumar Jagat Singh (the latter being the eldest son of the great Man Singh I), which had ruled Jaipur from the time of Mirza Rajah Jai Singh II for two centuries and a half, now ended. The succession passed by adoption, to the line of Maha Singh's younger brother Jhujhar Singh (the baron of Raisar). Isarda represents one branch out of the numerous descendants of Jhujhar, who are known collectively as the Rajawat branch of the Kachhwa royal house, and who hold numerous appanages, such as Jhilai, Siwar and Ranoli.

The ceaseless faction-fights between rival local nobles or *bania* ministers had ruined the Kachhwa kingdom ever since the death of Madho Singh I. The terrible act of bloodshed with which these selfish party-feuds had heralded the accession of Ram Singh II at the capital itself, had left an ineffable mark on this Maharajah's memory. He was determined to be no longer the slave of any domineering noble or to give a monopoly of power to any local party; he must balance them with an outside element. Moreover, Jaipur could not afford to dream the dreams of the middle ages and maintain a conservative existence in isolation amidst the India of the Crown which was rapidly becoming modernized. Civilized administration and modern popular progress require agents and tools of a higher intellectual level and of a more varied training than conservative old-time Rajput society can supply.

Therefore, Maharajah Ram Singh II, and following him Madho Singh II, cast their nets far and wide and picked up the ablest and most unselfish ministers that they could find anywhere in India, and yoked them to the administrative team with those local nobles who gave any promise of capacity to serve the needs of a modern government. The history of Jaipur today is the best testimony to Ram Singh's insight into character and power of choosing the fittest servants. As Sir Henry Lawrence had said (in 1854), 'there is room for all at Jaipur'. (*Brooke*, p. 54.)

Having selected the ablest and most faithful ministers, Madho Singh (like Ram Singh before him) gave them his confidence and left them free within the limits of their respective departments to carry out his general policy. Unlike Philip II of Spain and Aurangzib of Delhi, he never made the mistake of dictating the minute details of the administration or interfering with the day-to-day business of the State; he merely laid down the broad principles of the Government he wished to be followed in his State. This has been the secret of the success of every wise 'ruler of men'. Trust begets trust, and responsibility calls forth all the latent capacity of a servant.

Speaking in general terms, we can say that Ram Singh gave Jaipur light, and Madho Singh gave it wealth while extending light at the same time. Ram Singh had fostered his finances with care, so that in his reign the State income rose from 30 lakhs or even less to 61 lakhs a year. Under Madho Singh the economic resources of the country were so skilfully developed and the administration was so economically conducted by an honest Indian agency, that by the time of his death his income had reached a hundred lakhs per annum, with no increase of taxation but rather repeated and heavy remissions of State demands on the peasantry on joyous occasions. He left behind him an accumulated reserve of about two crores in spite of his lavish donations for countless works of public benefit in and outside his State throughout a long reign of 42 years.

Planned Economic Development

In 1883 the Maharajah started a cattle and horse fair at the capital (near the Aman-i-shah *nullah*), which has been continued ever since. The success of this annual institution was greatly promoted by the abolition of custom duties on the commodities consumed by the persons and animals that took part in the fair. Stallions are kept at Jaipur to encourage the breeding of high class animals. On 5th April, 1884 the transit duties levied on the feeder roads leading to stations on the Rajputana Railway[1] were remitted (except in the case of opium).

As early as August, 1881, he started the collection of articles of arts and industries, as well as antiquities. These formed the nucleus of an Economic and Industrial Museum. It held before the eyes of craftsmen the best specimens of local manufacture as well as the finest works of art in India. A collection of the raw products of the State was also formed, in order to open the eyes of the people to the natural resources of the country and the necessity of developing them scientifically.

In 1883 an exhibition was held, when for two months the Museum was kept open for general inspection, and it was largely attended by all classes of people. Its lasting result was an expensive standard book entitled *Memorials of the Jeypore Exhibition of 1883*, with colour illustrations, published at the Maharajah's expense. All the interesting exhibits of this year were purchased by the State, and these were ultimately housed in the Albert Hall, after its completion at a cost of over five lakhs of rupees in 1887, under the supervision of Colonel S. Swinton Jacob, C.I.E. This Museum is a permanent source of instruction to visitors and local craftsmen alike, and in a few years Jaipur art objects and Jaipur curios became extremely popular all over India, thus benefiting the artisans of the city, whose trade had been languishing in the machine age.[2]

Another very expensive and extremely useful work, named *Portfolios of Indian Architectural Details*, with a number of full size plates in colour and black and white, was published by the Maharajah, with the object of instructing and inspiring architectural artists, by displaying before them the most charming examples of Indian architecture found in the early buildings of Rajputana and Mughal India.

A cotton press was constructed at Jaipur (1882-1885) and a

ginning factory in 1912. Another cotton press was opened at Mandąwar (1892) at a cost of over two lakhs of rupees.

We may here mention that by the treaty of 7th August, 1869, the Jaipur half-share of the Sambhar Salt Lake was perpetually leased to the British Government on the following conditions: (a) Rs 2,75,000 should be paid to the State as royalty, against one and a half lakhs according to the agreement of 1840. (b) 1,72,000 maunds of salt are to be supplied per annum for the needs of the kingdom of Jaipur. (c) 7000 maunds of salt to be supplied per annum for the use of the Maharajah and his household.

Railways, Canals And Roads

The State has one railway of its own connecting Jaipur with Sawai Madhopur on the B.B.C.I. Line,[3] 73 miles in length, which cost nearly 24 and a half lakhs and was opened fully in 1907. Another line from the capital to Palsana[4] via Reengus,[5] a length of 61 miles costing 24 lakhs, was opened in 1918. Since then it has been pushed on to Jhunjhunu[6] in Shekhawati, a further 57 miles. The portion of the Nagda-Muttra trunk line (B.B.C.I.), from Sawai Madhopur to Hindaun via Gangapur[7] was purchased by the Maharajah's Government advancing 85 lakhs of rupees as the cost of its construction (1916).

The Public Works Department of the State was reorganized by His Highness and supplied with very skilled heads and a larger number of subordinates in order to cope with its vastly extended activities, and to utilize the huge capital expenditure to the best advantage. Some of these works, though begun under Ram Singh, were brought to completion under Madho Singh. There are 224 State irrigation *bunds* with distributory canals, on which Rs 38,60,952 have been spent. Leaving out works with a capital expenditure of Rs 2,70,500 which yield no net revenue, the remaining works, on a capital outlay of nearly 36 lakhs, give a gross annual return of Rs 2,91,212 or a little over eight per cent.

On roads Maharajah Madho Singh spent over 12 lakhs, leaving out of account minor undertakings and the city of Jaipur. The main road from Jaipur, eastwards to Agra and westwards to Ajmer, was thoroughly renewed and improved at a cost of Rs 3,85,000. The

Jaipur-Tonk and the Hindaun-Kerauli roads accounted for Rs 5,68,000 between them. An important internal road, very useful for administrative purposes, is the one from Jaipur to Lalsot which has cost a lakh and a quarter, while the path running due north from Lalsot to Dausa[8] has opened up a hitherto neglected region and supplied an alternative route.

Education And Public Health

The Jaipur Maharajah's College was opened in 1844, as a school where no fees were charged. In 1865 it was placed under Babu Kanti Chandra Mukherji as Headmaster, and he effected a remarkable improvement in it. In 1867 it sent up its first batch of candidates for the Entrance (i.e. Matriculation) Examination of the Calcutta University. In 1873 it became a college in the true sense of the term, when it was raised to the Intermediate (then called F.A.) standard of the University. Three years later, Sir William Russell, the companion of the Prince of Wales, recorded, 'the great progress which has been made in ten years does honour to Mr. Kanti Chandra Mukherji, the Principal of the Maharajah's College' (ii, 460). B.A. Classes were opened in 1888 and M.A. in 1900. The College so far had had no provision for science teaching. But a lump grant from the Maharajah enabled it to secure the necessary apparatus, and affiliation for the Bachelorship of Science degree was granted by the University[9] in 1905. Three years later, when the LL.D. degree of the Edinburgh University was conferred on the Maharajah *honoris causa*, he made a most gracious return for it by increasing the annual grant of his college by 10,000 rupees.

The Maharajah's College has an Oriental department attached to it, where Sanskrit is taught. These institutions are liberally endowed by the State, and in addition to these centres of higher education, there is a network of primary and secondary schools all over the Jaipur territory. Education in the State is entirely free; besides which, meritorious students are given stipends and prizes. In the Girls' School situated in the middle of the capital, daily doles are given to needy pupils to enable them to carry on their studies without distress.

The State bears the entire running cost of the Mayo Hospital at the capital and of the free dispensaries in all important towns. The

Mayo Hospital has ample accommodation for resident patients, and was provided in this reign with electric installation, an X-ray apparatus, and a bacteriological laboratory. In fact, His Highness spared nothing to make it a modern and up-to-date institution. A Zenana Hospital, named after Lady Hardinge, has been constructed and endowed, with one floor entirely set apart for ladies who live in seclusion *(purdah)*. Lord Curzon has described it as 'one of the best equipped in India'. The Sanitary Department, created in 1895, looks after the public health of the country, and there is a veterinary branch for the care of animals.

We may here add that the needs of the capital were attended to by the installation of a new pumping plant at the Aman-i-Shah water-works in 1906, at a cost of Rs 30,000. Gas works were started in 1878 for city illumination, but at first the gas was generated from crude petroleum. In 1916 coal gas was introduced at a cost of Rs 1,14,818.

A Share In The Defence Of The British Empire

Maharajah Madho Singh's contribution to the defence of the Indian Empire was as conspicuous as his assistance to every good cause for public uplift and the relief of human suffering in any form. The Imperial Service Troops (first created in 1889) mark a laudable advance in the status of the Indian States. As Professor Dodwell has well observed,

> The subsidiary forces established by Wellesley and (Lord) Hastings were garrisons installed at a hostile capital; the Imperial Service Troops are maintained by the States for the protection of the common country. The first marked the mistrust of the Paramount Power; the second the union of interests between the States and the Empire. Indeed these troops... mark the Empire's new willingness to take the Princes into partnership.

This designation was given to certain bodies of the States' forces which were placed for training under British officers, but were to remain entirely under the control of the States which raised them and were only to fall under the orders of the Commander-in-Chief (of British India) when they were employed on active service. The maintenance of such bodies was later entirely at the discretion of the princes themselves, the chief condition being that they should always be kept effective and ready to serve whenever called for.

The Penjdeh[10] affair (1885) created in the minds of the Viceroy Lord Dufferin and his advisers deep anxiety about India's military defence, and consequently the British Indian army was entirely reorganized and improved, and a new policy of trust and equal partnership was adopted towards 'Indian India'. The Maharajah of Jaipur was among the first to respond to the call. In 1888, when the Black Mountain expedition sent to punish the tribe that had killed Major Battye and Captain Urmston, was complicated by a domestic rebellion against our friendly Amir Abdur Rahman,[11] Maharajah Madho Singh paid to the Viceroy fifteen lakhs of rupees 'towards the cost of the defence of India's north-west frontier and also placed all the resources of his States at the disposal of the British Government in the event of war'. The next year he raised the Jaipur Imperial Service Transport Corps, because Lord Roberts, the Commander-in-Chief, had impressed upon His Highness the necessity of maintaining such a corps as 'the highest military talent and the most capable fighting strength are of no avail without transport trains service, which supplies the sinews of war'.

The Jaipur Imperial Service Transport Corps had (in 1919) a strength of 1200 ponies, 16 *tongas*, 560 carts and 792 personnel. The Corps also has ambulance arrangements for the immediate removal of 500 sick or wounded men at a time. It is a complete self-contained unit, with its own workshops ready to start at a moment's notice. Lord Roberts has publicly acknowledged 'the valuable help afforded to the Chitral expedition by the transport trains organized by the Maharajahs of Gwalior and Jaipur'. *(Forty-One Years,* Ch. 67.)

The record of this Jaipur Corps has been brilliant. It was on active service throughout the expeditions of Chitral (1895-1896) and Tirah (1897-1898). During the Great War (1914-1918) it gave continuous service in the front line in Mesopotamia and Persia, and in 1919 on the north-western frontier during the Indo-Afghan invasion.

We may here add that besides his frontier force donation of 15 lakhs in 1888 and the Transval War gift of one lakh in 1900, Maharajah Madho Singh contributed over 14 lakhs to various funds and towards the cost of the war, during the World War of 1914-1918. At the same time his sardars, officials and subjects subscribed to War Loans for nearly 14 and a half lakhs of rupees. The Maharajah presented a battery of ten machine guns as a thanksgiving for the recovery of George V from his accident in France (1915). In addition to the above Imperial Service Troops, Jaipur State maintains a local force consisting of 6000 infantry, 1000 cavalry, 6000 Nagas and some pieces of artillery. The police force in the capital is 855 strong and in the districts about 7000, besides the Mina watchmen in forts and stores.

The Maharajah Attends The Coronation In London, 1902

Maharajah Madho Singh's visit to England stands forth as a memorable event in the history of the British Empire and of Hindu society alike. Here was an orthodox Hindu prince of the high 'twice-born' *kshatriya* caste, crossing the 'black waters' and yet observing all the rites of his religion and performing the customary worship of his deity everyday throughout those months, whether afloat or in that far-off foreign soil, as scrupulously as in his native Rajasthan. His 124 Hindu officers and attendants did the same. Thus they all came back without forfeiting their caste by any breach of the ancient rules about food and daily rites. This example did incalculable good to Hindu society in its aspiration to seek progress and light by direct intercourse with the west. It should be remembered in this connection that orthodox *brahman* leaders of Hindu society like Pandit Madan Mohan Malaviya and Mr. B.G. Tilak visited England without losing caste, only after the Kachhwa Maharajah had set the example.

To the world at large this visit proved the bonds of an Empire, where an orthodox Oriental ruler, on his free will dared to take his place in the gathering of notables from all the Dominions to do homage to their common suzerain at the Imperial capital. And he did all this without being denationalized or repudiating the ancient creed and traditions of his race. The unifying force of such an Empire rises above caste, creed and locality.

His Highness sailed from Bombay in May, 1902, in the *Olympia*, a new ship of the Anchor Line which he had chartered. This ship flew the *Panch Rang* or Five Coloured flag of his house, which was now reflected on the bosom of the Thames, after having floated over the Oxus in Central Asia under Mirza Rajah Jai Singh in 1644. His Highness took with him the image of his household deity, Gopalji, and all necessary supplies for four months (including hundreds of casks of holy Ganges water, and even Indian earth), so that nothing foreign or 'unclean' need be used. Moray Lodge, Campden Hill, was the Maharajah's residence in London, and his staff and retainers occupied another large building near it. The people of England had never before seen a Hindu King who lived and moved about in strictly orthodox Hindu style, and he was greeted with enthusiastic cheers.

At Dover he was welcomed to English soil by the Mayor and Corporation of that historic borough, and as he entered London (3rd June) in a procession headed by his deity and rendered picturesque by the oriental costume and arms of his party, it presented a sight never to be forgotten.

Maharajah Madho Singh witnessed and took part in the coronation procession of King Edward VII and the scene of his crowning in Westminster's Abbey, and also attended the Court held at Buckingham Palace, as an honoured guest, accompanied by his sardars and officials. Leaving London on 22nd August, he arrived in Jaipur on 14th September, 1902.

We need hardly add that His Highness attended the coronation darbars at Delhi in 1903 and 1911 and took his seat close to the Viceroy. In the State entry into Delhi, which preceded the Coronation Darbar for Edward VII, the Maharajahs of Jaipur and Gwalior, riding side by side, headed the long lines of Rajputana and Central India chiefs respectively.

To the King Hospital Fund in London, he donated Rs 75,000 (in 1902) and to Queen Alexandra for hospitals in London one lakh (in 1908), besides the one lakh sent to Her Majesty by Maharani Jadunji in 1907 for distribution among charitable institutions in London.

Famine Relief

The great famine which devasted Western and Central India in 1899-1900 did not spare Jaipur. His Highness took very energetic and effective measures to meet this natural calamity. The actual relief work cost 80 lakhs, and in addition large remissions of outstanding revenue demands were made. The severe scarcity of 1915 made him spend a lakh and a half on relief.

The Famine of 1899 made Maharajah Madho Singh realise how necessary it is for the Government of India to have funds at hand which can be used *at once* to combat the calamity and supply food grain, and thus the idea occurred to him of founding a permanent All India Famine Fund, which would be set apart for this purpose in advance of any such natural visitation. He laid his scheme before the Viceroy, Lord Curzon, who cordially approved of it. Thus the Indian People's Famine Trust was created in 1900, and the Jaipur contribution of 25 lakhs (paid between 1900 and 1906) formed its kernel. The interest on the corpus of the Trust Fund is available for helping famine-stricken people in any part of India, without having to wait for passing budget grants through any Legislature.

Royal And Other Eminent Visitors

The picturesque aspect of the city of Jaipur and the fame of its arts and crafts, combined with the Maharajah's widespread reputation, drew many visitors to his capital. We have seen how King Edward VII, when Prince of Wales, visited Jaipur in 1876, during Ram Singh's reign. King George V in 1905, and Edward VIII in 1921 (before their respective accessions) did the same. Queen Mary travelled from Agra to Jaipur in September, 1911, and the Maharajah did her the honours of his capital. In order to signalise the occasion, he delighted his subjects by remitting 50 lakhs of arrears of revenue, and opened a new road, named after Her Majesty, which runs to the Jhotwara palace and gardens, some distance north-west of the capital.

The Duke of Connaught, after conducting the Delhi Darbar on behalf of his eldest brother King Emperor Edward VII, paid a visit to Jaipur (January, 1903) along with his Duchess. A darbar was held in the Jaipur Palace at which His Royal Highness decorated the Maharajah with the Grand Cross of the Victorian order (G.C.V.O.) in the name of His Imperial Majesty.

Every Viceroy of his time has visited Jaipur and so have many Commanders-in-Chief. Lord Roberts, when retiring after his 'forty-one years in India' (1893), passed via Jaipur on his way to Bombay and was 'royally welcomed by the Ruler of the State... and given excellent sport amongst the wild boar' as he tells us in his autobiography.

The then Crown Prince of Germany in his Indian tour of 1911 visited Jaipur and conferred on the Maharajah the Grand Cross of the Prussian Crown (G.C.P.C.).

Public Benefactions

Maharajah Madho Singh's public benefactions were too many to be enumerated in detail. His judiciously applied charity transcended the bounds of his own country and creed. He contributed to the cost of a Roman Catholic Church at Phulera (1905) and a Protestant Church at Jaipur (outside the Chandpole Gate, 1913). His immediate predecessor on the throne had built a Roman Catholic place of worship outside the *Ghat* Gate (at a cost of Rs 5884 in 1868). Muslim mosques also continued to enjoy his liberal charity. As for the Hindu places of worship, not only did he maintain and adorn those in his State, but also made considerable endowments to the great shrines and *tirthas* venerated by all Hindus. The Gangotri temple at Uttar Kashi (in Tehri Garhwal), the *ghats* and tanks at Soron[13] were repaired and adorned at his expense and the Pushkar Lake was cleaned (1892). On the Vaishnav temples at Vrindavan and Barsana—especially the Radha-Madav shrine in Vrindavan and the Kushal-Bihari Mandir in Barsana he spent two lakhs in cash, besides conferring on them a perpetual endowment of Rs 6000 each per annum. The temples in Jaipur will be dealt with later.

Of education His Highness was a liberal but judicious patron. Besides making lump grants to the Raj College at his capital and increasing its recurring annual aid from the State, he gave five lakhs to the Hindu University of Banaras (1916-1919), a quarter of a lakh to the Rajput College at Lucknow (1920), half a lakh to the Endowment Fund of the Mayo College, Ajmer (1908), and Rs 8150 for the Hall of this last institution (1884). B.M. Malabari's Seva Sadan in Bombay, received Rs 10,000 from him in 1908. Smaller donation are passed over for want of space.

On medical education and hospitals, he was even more munificent. To the Lady Dufferin Fund for the medical relief of Indian females (especially women in *purdah* he contributed Rs 1,35,000 (1885-1902), to the Lady Hardinge Hospital and Medical College for women at Delhi he paid three lakhs (1912), besides Rs 10,000 to Lady Minto's Nursing Fund (1918), and his Maharani Jadunji one lakh to the last named Fund (1907). The Gwalior Hospital received one lakh from him (1919), the King Edward Hospital in London Rs 75,000 (in 1902) and other London Hospitals (through Queen Alexandra, in 1908) one lakh, the Red Cross Fund Rs 25,000 (in 1918) and King George V for charitable purposes Rs 15,000 (in 1915), besides one lakh sent by his Jadan Queen to the Empress for charitable distribution in 1907. The medical improvements within the State have been referred to earlier.

The Imperial Institute, London, was given three lakhs by the Maharajah (1891) and the Victoria Memorial, Calcutta, three lakhs and a half (1901-1905 and 1921) while the Jaipur public subscribed Rs 32,768 to the latter institution.

His Death Monuments

Maharajah Madho Singh lived the life of a simple believing Vaishnav, as he had been a devoted worshipper at the Raj temple in Vrindavan before his accession. He made frequent pilgrimages and loved to feed *brahmans* and religious mendicants every year. Honours came thick upon him in recognition of his loyalty to the Crown and catholic spirit of liberality. His salute was increased to 21 guns, of which four were personal to him. Among the titles he received were G.C.S.I. (1888), G.C.I.E. (1900), G.C.V.O. (1903), G.B.E. (1919), besides the rank of Major General conferred on him at the Coronation Darbar of 1911, the German Grand Cross of the Prussian Crown (1911), and above all the Honorary LL.D. degree from the learned University of Edinburgh (1908).

Rich in honours, richer still in the gratitude of a contented and prosperous people, Sir Madho Singh died on 7th September, 1922 after a reign of 42 years. As he had no issue by his Queens, he adopted some time before his death Kumar Mor Mukut Singh, the younger grandson of his own eldest brother, of the house of Isarda (Rajawat

Sept, Mansinghwat branch). This prince is now reigning as His Highness Sir Sawai Man Singh II.

A noble cenotaph of white marble, built at a cost of Rs 1,82,476 covers the mortal remains of Sir Madho Singh at Gaitore, amidst the *chhatries* of the other rulers of his house. His name is also enshrined in the very large and beautiful Madho Behariji temple outside the Chandpole Gate on the Station Road, built after his demise by his devoted queen of the Tanwar clan.

One range of palaces was built in this reign, at Sudarshangarh (popularly known as Nahargarh in 1883-1892), at a cost of nearly three and a half lakhs of rupees. But the best monument to Madho Singh's fame in the learned world will be the four astronomical observatories built by Sawai Jai Singh II, which had fallen into ruin during nearly two centuries of political turmoil, and which Maharajah Madho Singh entirely renovated, strengthened and protected with infinite care and great expense. He completed this work by publishing a learned work in English, describing fully the instruments and their operations, written by Chandra Dhar Sharma Guleri and A.H. Garrett.

In an allied branch of the science of the skies, a meteorological observatory has been erected at Jaipur (1881) and equipped at considerable expense, and it is deemed a first class institution of its kind.

Notes

1. Rajputana Railway—Later known as B.B. and C.I. Railway, and now known as Western Railway. *Ed.*
2. The collection and publication were due to the supervision of Surgeon Col. Thomas Holbein Hendley, C.I.E. *J.S.*
3. B.B.C.I. Line — Now known as Western Railway (Metre Gauge). *Ed.*
4. Palsana situated at 27°29′ N and 75°22′ E; is 14 miles north-west of Reengus Junction. This line was later further extended to Churu via Sikar, thus connecting it with Rewari Bikaner line of the Northern Railway. *Ed.*
5. Reengus — Situated at 27° 22′ N and 74° 34′ E; is 32 miles

north-west of Jaipur. It is an important junction on the Rewari-Phulera chord line of Western Railway. *Ed.*

6. Jhunjhunu — Situated at 28° 7′ N and 75° 24′ E; 35 miles south-west of Loharu, now the headquarters of the district of that name in Rajasthan State. This Railway line has now been further extended from Jhunjhunu to Loharu, a junction on Rewari Churu line of the Northern Railway. *Ed.*

7. Gangapur — Situated at 26° 29′ N, 76° 44′ E; 38 miles south-west of Sawai-Madhopur. Gangapur city is an important station on Sawai Madhopur Bayana line of the Western Railway (B.G.) because of its big railway loco shed. *Ed.*

8. Dausa — Situated at 26° 54′ N, 76° 21′ E; 38 miles east of Jaipur. The earliest capital of the Kachhawas in Dhundhar. *Ed.*

9. Following the enforcement of the Universities Act, 1904, territorial adjustments were made in 1905 and the Maharaja's College, Jaipur, was thereafter affiliated to the University of Allahabad. *Ed.*

10. Penjdeh — a village in Russian Turkistan, situated at 36° 10′ N and 62° 30′ E, on the junction of the rivers Murghab and Kushk, which was the scene of a Russo-Afghanistan boundary dispute in March, 1885. *Ed.*

11. Abdur Rahman—Amir of Afghanistan from 1880 to 1901. *Ed.*

12. The Hindi book *Jaipur Naresh ki England Yatra*, ed. by Shiv Narayan Saxena, Jaipur, 1922, gives a detailed illustrated account of this memorable visit. *Ed.*

13. Soron — a well-known centre on the southern bank of Burhganga (Ganges) situated at 27° 54′ N and 78° 45′ E; 27 miles north of Etah. *Ed.*

XXIX

Sawai Man Singh II: Education And Share In Administration

Education

This prince was born on 21st August, 1911, as the second son of Thakur Sawai Singh, the Chief of Isarda, who was the nephew of Maharajah Madho Singh. Since the Maharajah was childless, he adopted this prince on 24th March, 1921, and changed his name from Mor Mukut Singh to Sawai Man Singh. On his death (on 7th September, 1922) he left the throne of Jaipur to him. During the young Maharajah's minority (1922-1931) the administration was carried on by a Council of Regency, which was dissolved when His Highness was invested with full ruling powers by the Viceroy on 14th March, 1931.

Maharajah Man Singh went through the full course of Education at the Mayo College for Indian Chiefs at Ajmer, under the guardianship of Mr. J.W.C. Mayne and Lt. Col. C.C.H. Twiss, and passed the Diploma Examination. Thereafter he was sent to England in July, 1929 to undergo a course of military training at the Royal Military Academy, Woolwich. During the period of his training (in 1937)[1] he put in some weeks' duty with the Life Guards in London. At present, His Highness holds the honorary rank of captain in the British Indian Army (January, 1934), and was created a G.C.I.E. in June, 1935, being invested by His Majesty George V.

In 1933 Maharajah Man Singh took his Polo Team to England,

where it set a record by winning all the eight open tournaments: The Hurlington Club Champion Cup, The King's Coronation Cup, The Prince of Wales' Empire Polo Cup, The Roehamption Challenge Cup, The Ranelagh Open Challenge Cup, The Rugby Cup, The Indian Empire Challenge Shield, and The West Somerset Cup.

His Highness is a good pilot and has laboured much to develop aviation in his kingdom, for which a fine aerodrome has been built near the capital and six landing grounds outside important towns. The Jaipur Flying Club was started in March, 1937 under the patronage of the Maharajah who presented a Tiger Moth Aircraft to the club for instructional purposes. The affairs of the Club are managed by a committee, which enjoys a State subsidy.

Under the latest administrative arrangement the Maharajah is President of the Council of Ministers, and also Minister for the Army. Lately, during the Prime Minister's absence on sick leave (7th August, 1939-December, 1939) His Highness also discharged the duties of the Prime Minister. His punctuality, strenuous application to duty, and readiness to meet his subjects have been noticed by all who have come in contact with him.

The New Model Administration Of Jaipur; The Central Directorate And How It Was Formed

As early as 1878, that far-seeing statesman Sir Henry D.Daly wrote:

> There is an increasing tendency in the administration of the Native States to conform to the general pattern of Government in force in British India. The Native States of which Tod and Malcolm wrote, exist no longer, the days of strife have passed away, and with them the tyranny and oppression which made life insecure and property the prize of the strong. All the great States are penetrated and swayed to some extent by public opinion; and even where this finds more expression on paper than in acts, the feeling is not less real.[2]

Twenty-one years before the above was written, Maharajah Ram Singh had made a beginning in this direction. He had adopted the principles of decentralization of the ruler's power and division of functions among ministers by the creation of departments. But each department was 'put in commission', to borrow a phrase from British constitutional usuage, or in other words, placed under a committee of two or three members instead of a single responsible head. This council was replaced in 1921 by one called *Mahakama Khas* — consisting of six ministers and one secretary, in which only one minister was given charge of a department and invested with wider powers than the old State Council. This arrangement continued with the necessary changes of personnel during the minority (1922-1931) following the death of Maharajah Madho Singh II.

The present day administration of the State is conducted by a Council of State or *Mahakama Khas*, consisting of (1) the Maharajah as President, (2) the Prime Minister as Vice-President, and (3) a certain number of ministers appointed by the Maharajah from time to time. At present (1940) there are five such ministers incharge of the Education, Finance-cum-Public Works, Judicial, Home and Revenue departments. The sixth, the Army department is in the hands of the Maharajah himself, and the seventh, the Political department in those of the Prime Minister.

The Council of State is competent to pass final orders on all matters except the investment of State funds and treasures. The ministers have been given the power to make appointments in their respective departments, subject to the recommendation of the State Public Services Commission.

Army Reform

As the New Model Army of Jaipur has been created and nourished under the personal care of His Highness, and he has all along been in charge of the military portfolio in the Council, his subject is best described in the present chapter.

Administrative reform and economic development had been initiated and carried very far by Maharajahs Ram Singh II and Madho Singh II, but the army had its turn only in the reign of Sir Sawai Man Singh.

Under the Mughal Empire, the Jaipur soldiery had measured

swords on more than equal terms with Uzbaks and Persians, Afridis and Baloches, Bijapuris and Marathas. Then had come, in the middle of the eighteenth century, the downfall of the old order in society and that revolution in the art of warfare which enforced a complete change in the organization of Indian armies. For various reasons, the Jaipur Government could not give effect to this change throughout the nineteenth century, though it modernized its civil administration. The first dawn of a change came in 1888, when the Viceroy, Lord Dufferin, in a speech at Patiala declared, 'I intend to ask those Chiefs who have especially good fighting material in their armies, to raise a portion of their armies to such a pitch of general efficiency as would make them fit to go into action *side by side with Imperial troops*.'

The Jaipur Maharajah promptly responded to the call and set up his own quota of Imperial Service troops. But it was urged by the British military authorities that his kingdom could not supply men of the type that can be trained into first class modern infantry and that a transport corps instead would be more serviceable in the need of the empire. So, the Jaipur Government supplied only muleteers and stretcher-bearers, but no infantry or cavalry. But much water has flowed under the Thames since then; the era of mutual trust and cooperation has succeeded that of suspicion, and it has been left to his present Highness Sir Man Singh II to remove this slur on the Rajput race and remodel that army as can form disciplined infantry fit to 'go into action side by side with British troops'. If we continually examine the condition of the Jaipur forces with their sorry plight as above or even in 1868, as described by competent European observers, we shall realize the marvellous transformation that has been effected in the confidence of the Paramount Power, and—we must not omit to add—the assistances so ably rendered by trainers from the British army.

The eminent French *savant*, Victor Jacqumont, draws this doleful picture of the Jaipur army as it was in 1832:

> This kingdom maintains 2000 cavalry in the pay of the State, and the *thakurs* (feudal barons) are bound to supply 5000 more. The infantry of the Rajah does not consist of less than 20 battalions, but only two of them are complete, the rest have 300, or 200, or 150 men each. The stronger battalions are commanded by men of colour (i.e., Feringis), undoubtedly Portuguese, but reputed to be Frenchmen. The other battalions are generally commanded by Musalmans who have learnt a little of Euro-

> pean discipline in the armies of Sindhia or Holkar. The infantry is armed with *rejected* English muskets and dressed in red rags in the shape of coats. Their pay is Rs 5/- monthly, but the pay is always much in arrears, and at the time of payment some deductions are almost always made in it. The position of the officers, Europeans or mostly (native) Christians, is equivocal; they will not be received by the English officers. There is no intercourse between them and the English who pass (through the country). They are ill paid, but live comfortably in the manner of the Indians. (*Etat Politique et Social de L'Inde du Sud en 1832*, p. 39).

Col. J.C. Brooke, wrote as follows in 1868:

> The Army of Jeypore consists of ten Regiments of Foot, each 600 strong; and 4000 Nagas, men ill armed and without discipline; besides a small body 700 cavalry, divided into seven Ressalahs, and 4250 Jagheerdar horse. There are besides 1500 men employed in guarding the several forts within the territory. The Regiments of Infantry are composed of the same classes as filled the late Bengal Army. The men are badly appointed, and neither the old or unfit men are weeded out of them.
>
> The Nagas are a body of religious mendicants, who are trust-worthy and true to the State. They receive the small pay of Rs 2 a man per month, and Re one for each child, averaging Rs 3 per fighting man. In the roll, children are counted as well as adults. They are armed with matchlocks, and will not undergo any discipline. (*Political History*, p. 12.)

To this the only addition was the Imperial Service Transport Corps (1889) already described in the chapter on Maharajah Madho Singh II.

In 1932, the Jaipur State forces were completely reorganized under the personal direction of H.H. the Maharajah, who is its chief commandant and also the minister in charge of the army portfolio. For general service, in any part of the British Indian Empire, he maintains the bodies, namely:

(a) the Jaipur Lancers, 530 strong,[3] at an annual cost of about four lakhs and a half of rupees,

(b) the First Jaipur Infantry, 779 strong, at an annual cost of over three lakhs of rupees, and

(c) the Jaipur Transport Corps, 282 men at a cost of Rs 1,84,601.

For internal security, he maintains a B class, consisting of

(d) the Sawai Man Guards, 684 strong, at a cost of over three lakhs of rupees and

(e) the Second Jaipur Infantry, 323 strong, at a cost of Rs 85,227.

The artillery is classed as Irregulars, and consists of 35 muzzle loading guns drawn by bullocks, used for saluting purposes only. The strength of this arm is 132 officers and its annual cost Rs 31,177.

Feudal contingent: Originally the field-holders of the Jaipur kingdom were bound, by the terms of their tenure, to supply 5600 mounted soldiers for the service of the Maharajah every year. Owing to royal favour, lapses and so on, this number fell to 4225. But following the example of the Angevin kings of England, this armed service was commuted into money payment (scutage) in 1925, and by the year 1937, as many as 3941 troopers had been thus commuted, while 238 others were exempted from service for other reasons, thus leaving a net balance of only 46 due for service to the State.

Another step in the same direction taken in 1935-1936, was the dissolution of the Naga irregulars, which was commenced in 1936. These are of a quasi-religious military order, followers of the saint Dadu Dayal, who used to be borne on muster pay-rolls of Jaipur State in recognition of their services in Mughal times and even as late as the Mutiny of 1857, and two and a half lakhs of rupees were spent on them every year. In 1936, recruitment into their body was stopped. On a muster being taken (1936), their actual strength was found to be 3190 men. Of these 1047 were retired during 1937, leaving 2143 on the rolls.

Their transition from martial to peaceful avocations has been assisted by State grants. 495 Nagas have been settled on land. 1322 detailed for police or guard duties, and 120 trained for the regular army (1937).[4]

The Jaipur army in all its branches now forms a compact modernized force of 2730 men, or just under two per thousand of the male population of the kingdom of all ages. This may be contrasted with the unwieldly number of irregulars in Mughal times and pre-mutiny days. At the same time that this efficiency has been secured, by preferring quality to quantity, the military budget has been actually reduced. In the middle fifties of the nineteenth century the army consumed thirty per cent of the State revenue every year; today it is just twelve and a half per cent (leaving out of the debt and investment figures of both sides of the balance-sheet).

But mere numbers of men enrolled and amounts of money spent cannot give a just estimate of the quality of the army. In this respect the modern Jaipur Kingdom has been happy in securing some highly qualified organizers and trainers for its army. Its Chief Commandant, the present Maharajah, secured the best possible opportunity for military training by entering the Royal Military Academy, Woolwich, in 1929 and also by being attached to the Life Guards (London) for some months in 1938. Distinguished officers of the British Indian Army (both Indian and European), who won crosses and medals in the Second World War have been commandants of the various regiments of Indian State forces, and many Raj officers were under training with the army in England and British army in India. The State has also liberally utilized the services of Indian Commissioned officers on loan from the British Indian army.

In addition to the annual recurring expenditure on the army (including the Military Hospital), modern barracks have been built for the Sawai Man Guards at the capital and a first-class aerodrome has been constructed six miles outside it (at Sanganer), with six landing grounds within the State territory.

Notes

1. A unique honour came to him in 1937, when His Majesty the King (George V) selected him for appointment to his Life Guards. Appointments to the Guards are made personally by the king and no other Indian had achieved the honour before him. (*A brief sketch—H.H. the Maharaja of Jaipur*, by A.N. Alal, p. 19, para 45.) *Ed.*
2. *Memoirs of General Sir Henry Dermot Daly*, by Major H. Daly, p. 317. *Ed.*
3. Including cadets, vets, etc. *J.S.*
4. There were 2142 Nagas on the rolls of the department on the first of September, 1937. 18 were settled on cultivation and 967 were reduced, leaving 1157 on the rolls on the August 31, 1938. The total expenditure of the department amounted to Rs 1,54,919. (Extracts from *Report on the Administration of the Jaipur State for 1937-38 (Samvat 1994)*, p. 53, paras 333-4.) *Ed.*

XXX

Jaipur Administrative Activities Today

Heads Of Income And Expenditure

The policy and trend of the modern administration of Jaipur can be easily seen if we examine the sources from which it raises its income and the ways in which it spends that income. The figures below are for a normal year, 1937.

Leaving out the income and expenditure on the 'Debt Heads' which nearly cancel each other, the total income from 'Revenue Heads' was Rs 1,46,95,850, and the total expenditure on the same Heads, Rs 1,29,76,566; the capital expenditure on electrical installation and railway materials etc., was an addition of Rs 12,48,513 to this latter figure, but we must exclude it here as a sort of investment.

On the income side, land revenue brought in nearly 45.5 lakhs; tribute 6.16 lakhs (from which four lakhs payable to the British Government must be deducted), the *jagirs* which were granted in lieu of military service yielded 7.61 lakhs in commutation. Customs duties and excise yielded 23 lakhs and administrative expenditure of two and a half lakhs on the same; stamps 3.77 lakhs (but deducting 2.79 lakhs as the expenses for law and justice, the net gain was a trifle under one lakh); Railways yielded 13.20 lakhs (against a recurring expenditure of 8.32 lakhs); interest on the State's past investments aggregating over five crores, yielded 21.22 lakhs; and salt eight lakhs.

In forests and electricity the income and expenditure nearly balanced each other. Mines yielded a little over one lakh.

We thus see that land revenue (both direct from tenants and indirect in the form of tribute and scutage from vassals) contributed forty per cent of the total annual income of the State: royalty on natural resources i.e. salt minerals and forests 7.3 per cent, indirect taxes on consumption (i.e. customs and excise) 15.5 per cent. Much of the remainder came from the business enterprises of the State and past savings.

Hence the taxation is extremely light on the people. Many a modern State would envy Jaipur in this respect.

On the expenditure side of the budget we have out of a total annual outlay of Rs 1,29,76,565:

Military	15.89 lakhs
Police	7.74 lakhs
Jails	1.86 lakhs
Or total for protective service:	25.49 lakhs, or nearly twenty per cent.
Sovereign's family	14.80 lakhs
General Administration	5.90 lakhs
Capital Municipality (which is tax-free)	2.04 lakhs
Or total for administration:	22.74 lakhs or 17.6 per cent.
Education	6.83 lakhs
Medical	4.32 lakhs
Religion & Charity	2.71 lakhs
Total on Public benefit:	13.86 lakhs
Karkhana-jat	6.95 lakhs
Pensions	3.62 lakhs
Total:	10.57 lakhs

This amount was clearly apportioned ordinarily, as classified above.

Legislation And Justice

A Legislative Committee consisting of officials and non-officials was established in 1923 for the purpose of making recommendations as to the existing legislation and of recording opinion on any legislative proposal referred to it by the Jaipur Government. Since then a large number of laws have been placed on the statute-book giving effect to the recommendations of this Committee. At present the Committee consists of a Chairman (the Finance Minister) and two official and three non-official members.

In addition to the above body, a committee of sardars was formed in 1925, as a purely consultative body, to advise the Council of State on such matters as may be referred to it, particularly those relating to the rights and privileges of the Sardars. It is composed of six of the leading barons of the kingdom.

The laws now in force in the State have for the most part been framed in the spirit of the laws of British India and sometimes bodily borrowed from the latter.

The Council of State is the highest tribunal corresponding to 'His Majesty in the Privy Council' in the English Constitution. Appeals lie from the Chief Court to the Council of State, in civil cases of a certain standard of importance. On the criminal side, the orders passed by the Chief Court are final, but all sentences for capital punishment or life-long imprisonment are subject to confirmation by the Council of State. Capital sentences are not inflicted in the State now.

Below the Chief Court in due sequence on the civil side are: (a) the District Judge's Court (one); (b) Subordinate Judges' Court (seven); (c) Nagim's Court *(Kot-Qasim)* (one); (d) Munsif's Court (eleven); and (e) Tahsildars' Courts (nineteen) in number which entertain original suits valued up to Rs 50 where one party is a cultivator.

On the Criminal side, below the Chief Court are: (a) the Sessions Judges' Court (one); (b) Assistant Sessions Judges' Courts (five in number, with no appellate jurisdiction); (c) District Magistrates' Courts (two in number, with both original and appellate powers); and (d) Courts of Magistrates, of First Class, Second Class and Third Class rank (6, 10 and 21 respectively) all with original powers only.

The Chief Court (four in 1924) is at present constituted of the Chief Justice, Sir Seetla Prasad Bajpeyi, Kt., C.I.E. and three puisne judges. In 1937 they decided a total of 788 cases of various categories.

The Police And Jails

The Police Force of the State was entirely reorganized in 1925 and rendered more efficient by proper training, modern equipment, provision of houses and reasonable pay. Attempts are being made to reclaim the members of the criminal classes by settling them on the land with State subsidies, giving them employment in the Police and the P.W.D., and educating their boys.

At present the Police Force consists of an Inspector General, two D.I.G's, eight Superintendents (plus one probationer), 19 Inspectors, 86 Sub-Inspectors, and 2176 constables of different grades, besides clerks, *jamadars*, *chowkidars* etc. The total annual expenditure is over five and one fourth lakhs of rupees.

The special Armed Police has been reorganized and expanded in strength to meet the requirements of modern days. By the provision of motor transport the mobility of the force has been greatly increased. Three Sub-Stations have been opened outside the city to supplement the work of the Prefect City Kotwal.

The Police Training School was opened in 1932 for the training of officers and men. An authoritative reference book for the training and working of the Police, entitled *The Police Guide* was printed in 1933.

The Central Jail, Jaipur, had an average population of 1237 persons out of which half were employed in the prison factories, producing goods of the gross value of Rs 43,226. The average cost per prisoner is about Rs 97.8 per annum.

Land Revenue And Agriculture

For the purposes of land revenue administration, the territory is divided into two divisions—the Eastern consisting of five districts *(nizamat)*, 16 collectorates (*tahsils*); and the Western, consisting of six districts with 13 collectorates. Each Division is in charge of an officer called *diwan*, who has one deputy *(naib diwan)*.

The crownlands *(khalsa)* form 39,220 square miles out of the State's total area of 16,682 square miles. In this portion there are 2124 villages with 1.66.426 *bighas* under the plough, irrigated by 31,641 wells and 403 tanks (after excluding a large number, nearly one half of the above, which are now out of use).

Remissions of State demand on the peasantry have been liberally granted by the Jaipur Maharajah at every time of scarcity or other natural calamities, and arrears have been written off on joyous occasions. Thus in the 16 years from 1922 to 1937, a total of over four crores and twenty-eight lakhs of rupees has been written off from the State demands due from the crownland cultivators and the barons enjoying fiefs *(thikanas)*.

Only the briefest account can be given here of the activities of the Agricultural Department (founded in 1928 and reorganized in 1938). There is an experimental farm at Basi, where good results were obtained in different crops, especially in wheat and cotton. Efforts at popularizing the cultivation of groundnuts were continued, and about 500 maunds of groundnut seeds were distributed. Improved Coimbatore crops were tried out with promising results. Above all, an exhibition lorry toured the countryside, awakening farmers asking for improved implements.

A school for the training of the agriculturists in improved methods of cultivation and improving the breed of cattle did much useful work. Deeper boring all over the state resulted in 234 wells in the course of 1937. In 1938 a scheme was sanctioned for providing wells in villages where no one had attended to this predicament, and wells were dug in certain rural areas to remove the scarcity of drinking water. The whole scheme is to be completed by stages in coming years, and Rs 50,000 was spent in 1940 on it. Experiments by administration under departmental agency were continued. The work of cadastral survey and periodical assessment of land clearly showed that the tendency has been to commute metayerary rights by rent. Local candidates are trained in the State Farm and most of them are taken up into the State service. Settlement operations were completed in 1940 at a cost of Rs 20 lakhs.

Village Upliftment

The measures for improving village sanitation and mass education will be dealt with in these sections on medicine and education respectively. By the Jaipur Village Panchayat Act of 1938, panchayats entrusted with army administrative functions are being regularly established in the villages. The cultivator's milchy cattle and his stored agricultural produce have been exempted by law (subject to certain conditions) from attachment for debt. Facilities are also afforded for the distribution of *taqavi* and the plantation of trees.

The destruction of pigs and bucks, which do so much damage to crops if left to breed unchecked, has been allowed in the cultivated area within a radius of ten miles around Jaipur city. A fee of two rupees has to be paid for every head of animal shot. At the same time the forest laws have been relaxed by (a) abolishing the cess levied on loom, dhank and bamboos, from reserved forest tract, and (b) keeping the State forest over a total area of 343 square miles open for cattle grazing during the famine of 1939, and in certain other cases.

Begar (French *corvee* or forced labour) was prohibited throughout the state and the ancient but vexatious petty all possible *log-bags*[2] (cesses) have been abolished.

A representative committee of officials and non-officials was formed in 1938 for Rural Development and funds have been provided by the State (without any fresh levies) for their work. In addition to this specific agency, the Collectors (*tahsildars*) hold monthly meetings in various central places in their respective jurisdictions. Villagers and their collectors assemble for the free discussion of all questions requiring the attention of the authorities; in this way real local grievances can be speedily known and remedied.

The Maharajah has recently ordered the establishment of District Advisory Boards at the headquarters of each district, and a Central Advisory Board in Jaipur. Non-officials will constitute from 67 to 92 per cent of the members of the District Boards and 73 per cent of those of the Central. These non-official members will, at the outset, be nominated from a panel of persons elected by the different classes and interests among the public of the area concerned.

The Boards shall meet at least once in three months and are authorized to make recommendations to the Government on a large number of subjects of public utility, such as medical relief, public works, social legislation, education, rural uplift, taxation trade, agriculture and industries.

Municipalities

A revised Jaipur Municipal Act was enacted in 1938, in which half the seats on the board were filled by election. (The same pattern was adopted in district Municipalities too.) A representative of the capital was nominated to represent the Municipality in the Central Advisory Board of the State. The Municipality, so constituted in its various sub-committees, thus duly enjoyed full freedom in the administration of the municipal affairs of the capital.

The Town Improvement Committee, consisting of officials and non-officials, was constituted in 1931, for devising schemes for housing areas in the city. Developing suitable schemes have been already completed, and a number of houses designed on modern lines with the usual amenities have been constructed. The Jaipur Municipality has now an area of eight square miles and a population of 1,44,179 souls. The Municipal Board has 29 members (only five of whom are officials), with the Director of the State Medical Services as its Chairman.

The Municipality had an income of Rs 93,823 (in 1937), which was made of (a) the rent of land and buildings (Rs 38,866), (b) license fee for vehicles (Rs 44,114) and a few other items, but no conservancy tax, no road tax, while drinking water and electricity are supplied and charged from the State. Its total expenditure in the same year was Rs 2,16,521, and the deficit of Rs 1,22,697 was as usual borne by the State.

The water supply from the Aman-i-Shah reservoir having proved inadequate for the needs of the growing city, water was brought from the Jamwa-Ramgarh bund, by means of new water works completed in 1931 at a total cost of 40 lakhs. The demand for this pure drinking water is steadily increasing, and the water consumed was nearly 13 lakhs of gallons during the year 1937. The streets and houses are now lit by electricity, generated and sold by the State; in the year 1937-1938, 24 miles of road were thus illuminated in Jaipur city and its environs. Electricity superseded gas lighting.

The increased supply of water to the citizens from other sources enabled the Municipality to do the needful. In the city the drains have been greatly increased in breadth, and all of them have been cemented. Special attention is being paid to improving the conservancy arrangements by cleaning the lanes for this purpose in the houses of the city, and the methods for removing refuse has been modernized and made easier.

The Man Prakash talkies were opened by His Highness Maharaja Man Singh II as a private concern. The natural amenities of the city will be described under education.

Education

At the end of the year 1938 the State had 1215 educational institutions, and 64,258 students. The total expenditure on education was nearly 13 lakhs. (The above figures combine Government and private undertakings.)

At the top of the educational ladder is the Maharajah's College which is now first-grade, teaching up to the M.A. and M.Sc. degrees of the Agra University, with a roll strength of 463. It has recently been housed in a new palatial building, with a splendid airy hostel for inmates, the two together costing the State ten lakhs. Extensive playgrounds surround the college, and in respect of all these amenities it stands unsurpassed in Upper India.

Jaipur is the home of a large commercial community, whose activities range over all parts of India. In order to afford facilities for higher commercial education, B.Com Classes were opened in the Maharajah's College in July 1939. There is an Intermediate College for Arts, Science and Commerce of G.D. Birla at Pilani, with 62-63 pupils.

The Sanskrit College has 458 students. Of the 13 schools in the State, four are maintained entirely by the State, three by *thikanas* and six by private persons (strength 75), one for girls and two for boys in the capital.

For female education there are: one normal school (10 pupils), two secondary schools (strength 244) and 24 primary schools (945 pupils). The State spends Rs 45,179 on them. But there has been general apathy and only three per cent of the total female population of the State is enrolled and there under instruction; 18 per cent of them get English education and the rest receive classical knowledge at home. There is an average of one school for every eight villages. Primary education is free throughout the State.

The Maharajah's School of Arts and Crafts had 216 scholars in 1937, and it cost Rs 27,297.

For the training of teachers there are two Training Schools, at Jaipur and Paota, and one Central Training School at Paota. Private educational institutions receive some grants. Scouting and physical training are making steady progress, and drill-masters are being trained for work in the schools. The Junior Red Cross Movement has also been introduced into a large number of schools. The Boy Scouts have been given a boarding house by the State (costing Rs 10,000) and an annual grant of Rs 2000, being the pay of the organizing Secretary.

Seven Adult Schools have been started (with 956 pupils) in villages selected by the Rural Development Committee in order to remove adult illiteracy.

Nine women teachers have been appointed as an experimental measure, in co-educational primary schools.

In the revised curricula, handicrafts such as spinning, weaving, tailoring, carpentry, gardening and agriculture are being given greater emphasis, so as to reduce the evil of the purely literary course.

An Education Code was promulgated for the organization and conducting of educational institutions. An Educational Survey Committee was formed in 1938 for the purpose of framing the expansion of primary and secondary schools. It has produced a report after its completion. The scheme of compulsory attendance after their enrolment has been introduced as an experimental measure in schools in three district towns. The result is being observed with interest by all.

Certain other educational agencies may be mentioned here. Among other institutions, under the Department of Education is the Public Library, which is open to the public (except on Sundays) and possesses a large collection of books. This is entirely financed by the State. In 1937, it was used by 41,936 persons.

The Museum, located in the Albert Hall of the Ramnivas Gardens, presents one of the notable architectural features of Jaipur. In 1937 it was visited by nearly three lakhs of persons. On Fridays it is reserved for women after 12 noon and the women visitors are shown round by female attendants. A genuine old Persian carpet, depicting garden scenes, 29 feet by 12 feet, probably woven at Isphan about 1600 and purchased by the celebrated Mirza Rajah Jai Singh in 1632, is the latest rarity added to the collection. It is an exquisite piece of work.

The Meteorological Observatory founded in 1881, which is quite distinct from the indigenous Astronomical Observatory built by Sawai Jai Singh II, (and thoroughly repaired and renovated by Sawai Madho

Singh II), has been now turned into a first class observatory of international standards. Its equipment has now been updated by adding instruments of present day importance and it has been closely linked with the Chief Aviation Forecasting Centre, India (Karachi), by training its officers in the meteorological observations necessary for aviation.

The State Archaeological Department is proud of having for its first director Rai Bahadur Dayaram Sahani (1935-1939), who has completed his recent excavation work in general, as well as in Sambhar. A report has been issued describing the excavations at Sambhar.

Medical Treatment

The State maintains dispensaries at the headquarters of the districts, to which must be added ten maintained there by individuals but supervised by the Directors of Medical Services. The expenditure on this Department was four lakhs.

The Mayo Hospital is the central hospital of the State. It has 170 beds for males and 50 for females. During the years 1936-1937, 73,570 outdoor and 6191 indoor patients were treated in it.

The State Zenana Hospital (opened in April, 1931), has been designed for eventual expansion to 160 beds. In 1937 it treated 8830 out and 1782 in-patients. The Lady Willingdon Hospital, which will be one of the most modern and up-to-date hospitals in India, and the King George V Sanitorium (for tuberculosis patients) are nearing completions. In 1939 six new medical officers were appointed for special work, viz., one F.R.C.S. for surgery, one D.O.M.S. for eye diseases, one officer for children's cases, one for ear, nose and throat, one additional Public Health Officer, and one extra Chemist for the State Laboratory.

The State grants an annual subsidy of Rs 1800 to an Ayurvedic dispensary (i.e., indigenous Hindu dispensary), named the *Dhanwanturi Aushadhalaya*, founded in 1919 and maintained by public subscriptions.

The analyses carried on in the State Central Chemical Laboratory and the pharmaceutical preparations made there, the State veterinary, vaccination and sanitary branches, training of midwives and nurses, the medical examination of the school population etc. need not be described here

Public Works And Railways

This department spent Rs 36,39 lakhs. The main items were:

building:	15. 6 lakhs
roads:	4.31 lakhs
irrigation:	4.53 lakhs
imarat:	1.11 lakhs
electrical and mechanical:	4.00 lakhs
water works:	1.93 lakhs

New constructions include the Sawai Man Guards Barracks Hostel, Maharaja's College (1.60 lakhs) include and Lady Willingdon Hospital. The first two have been completed. Extensions were made at the Sanganer Aerodrome, and a number of new bunds constructed and old canals remodelled. The existing water tanks are receiving constant attention for their assistance to agriculture. A new tank at Khandar at an approximate cost of seven lakhs was begun in 1939.

There are some 513 miles of metalled and 233 miles of unmetalled roads in the State.

Out of the more than 500 miles of railway running through Jaipur State territory, the Maharajah's Government owns 181 miles. Up to 31st March, 1937, this latter railway was worked by the B.B. and C.I. Company, but after that date the State has taken over the working of it. The line is being extended from Jhunjhunu to Churu (36 miles) and Sikar to Bissau (48 miles).

Men are being trained for appointments in the different departments of the railway, mechanical workshops for undertaking all sorts of repair work equipped, and stores and stock of sleepers built up for the State. During the first complete year of State management, the railway yielded a net income of 6.77 per cent on a capital outlay of eighty-three and a half lakhs of rupees. A further capital expenditure of six and a half lakhs is proposed in 1937.

The Jaipur Darbar has contributed Rs 85 lakhs towards the construction of the Nagda-Mathura line which passes through the territory. On this the State received nearly Rs 7,92,180 as net earnings in 1937.

Industry And Commerce

His Highness, after noticing the immense development of trade and commerce in England during a recent visit, has given special attention to industry and commerce in his State, appointing Mr. N.S. Rahalkar as the expert director. The proposals of the administration will be watched with much interest, for there can be no more promising field for economic development on modern lines than the Jaipur kingdom.

Constitutional Problems For The Future

The material progress and modern administration of present day Jaipur have been described above. But these very successes have brought to the front two problems which can no longer be solved, though their right solution is extremely difficult and is hidden in the womb of futurity. These are the Political relations of the sovereign with his barons on the one hand and with the intelligentsia of the State on the other.

The food problem had been very clearly presented by that exceptionally gifted Political Agent Lt. Col. R.H. Keatinge, V.C., C.S.I., in his Report for 1867:

> The nobles are practically far more independent of their Chiefs than the latter are of the British Government. There are few great nobles who will permit a revenue or police officer of their Chief's to enter their estates except as a mere traveller, who will respond to any calls for returns or statistics, or will acknowledge his civil or criminal jurisdiction. One great link is thus missing from the chain of authority which to ensure good order, should necessarily connect the Government with every grade of the people.
>
> Absence of responsibility, such as I have above described, is, as must be expected, abused by the great majority of the nobles. Numbers of them maintain bands of plunderers who, in return for the protection given, are always ready for any emergent service. Trade is trammelled by every conceivable exaction by which a small present profit can be made, and the cultivators and poorer classes are degraded to the condition of serfs.
>
> Stagnant as no doubt the condition of society is in Native

> States, there are Chiefs who desire reform, but the opposition they meet from their nobles is so serious that they can seldom accomplish much.
>
> I am convinced that the ancient feudal system of the Rajpoots cannot exist in close contact with the civilization from the west which now surrounds it. Before long it will, I apprehend, be necessary for Government to recognize openly this difficulty, to collect reliable information on the subject, and to promulgate general rules regarding the extent to which it expects nobles in their different degrees to render obedience to their Chiefs. (Keatinge's *Reports on the Rajpootana States for 1867-1868,* Genl. Rep. paras 80-84.)

This state of things exactly resembled the condition in Medieval England, when the robber barons with their hordes opposed the king's officers in the duty and maintenance, prevented the king's writ from running there and broke the king's peace within the limits of their fiefs. It required the strong arm of Henry VII to curb them, and construct the beginning of a modern and free England. Col. Keatinge's suggestion was not carried out by the Paramount Power, and Jaipur State, like many other States, still has to face this vexatious problem, in the middle of the twentieth century.

At the other end of the scale, the 'pathetic condition' of the population in Indian States too is being disturbed by the 'time spirit'. As Mr. E.S. Montague and Lord Chelmsford by their knowledge wrote in 1918:

> We know that the States cannot be unaffected by constitutional development in adjoining (British) provinces... We need not conceal our conviction that the processes at work in British India cannot leave the States untouched and must in time affect even those whose ideas and institutions are of the most conservative and feudal character. (Report, paras 300 and 312.)

Notes

1. This Chapter was written in the year 1940, and it describes the details of the system and activities of Jaipur State on the eve of the Second World War. *Ed.*
2. This order regarding *Log-Bag* excludes the abolished *bab* of the revenue department. For the immense variety of these taxes (under the name *abwab*) in the Mughal Empire, see J. Sarkar's *Mughal Administration*, Chapter V. *J.S.*

Mirza Raja Jai Singh I

Sawai Jai Singh II and his ***navaratna,*** *including Vidhyadhar and Kriparam*

Vidhyadhar, the architect of Jaipur

Ground plan of Jaipur City, with a report on the progress of its construction

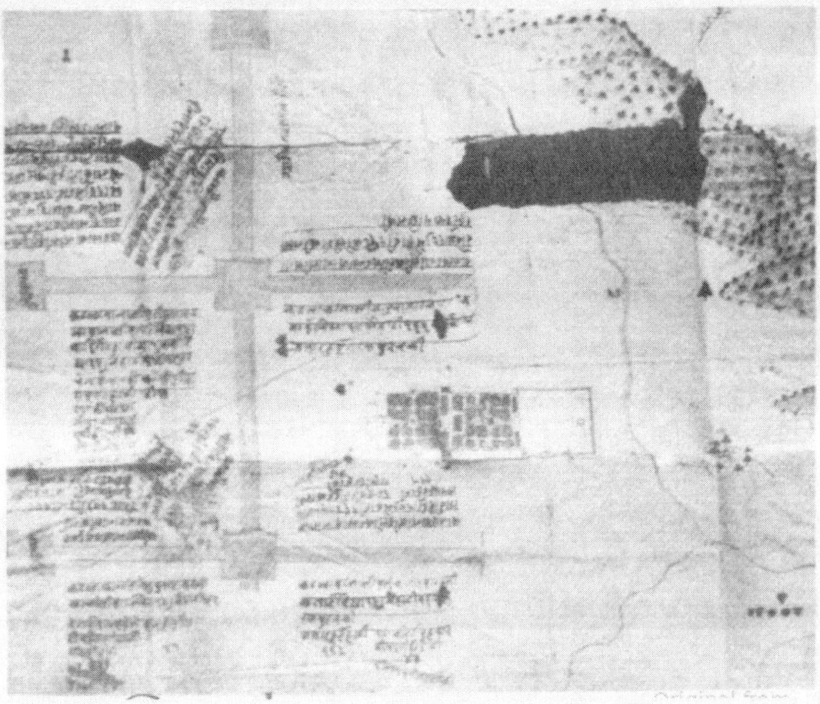

The assembly of rulers of Amber and Jaipur (up to Sawai Ishwari Singh, seated on the lower left foreground)

Vidhyadhar, the architect of Jaipur

Ground plan of Jaipur City, with a report on the progress of its construction

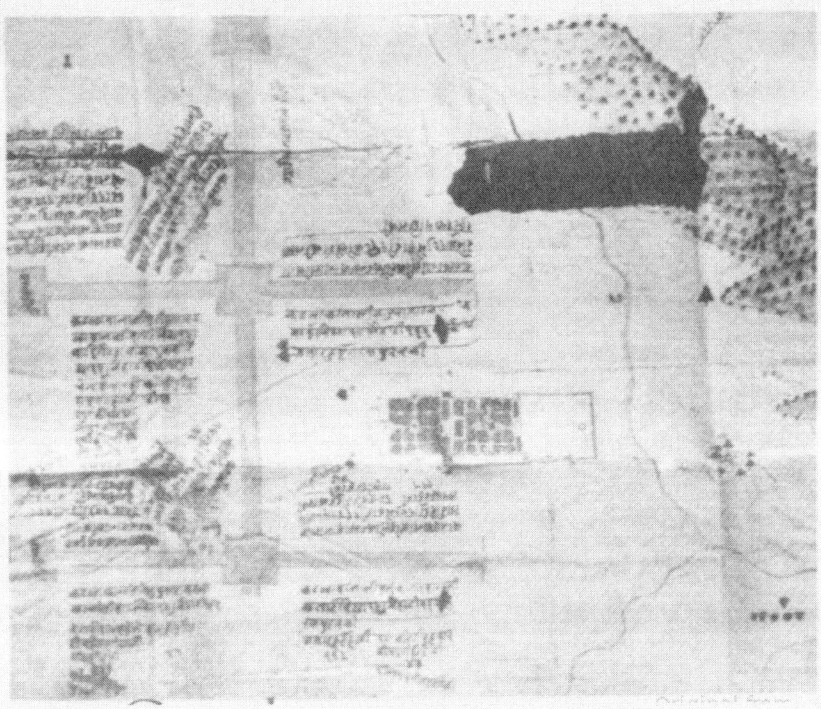

The assembly of rulers of Amber and Jaipur (up to Sawai Ishwari Singh, seated on the lower left foreground)

Sawai Ram Singh II

Sawai Man Singh II

Appendices

I

From Letter Of Nizam-ul-mulk Asaf Jah I To Sawai Jai Singh II (Jaipur State Records, No. 466)

... 'I repeatedly wrote to Shahu by way of advice that the going of the Marathas for plundering Malwa and Gujarat was not good but opposed to the desire of His Majesty, and that he should urge his troops not to cross the Narmada. But my urging and insistence proved of no avail; the troops of Shahu, who do not listen to his words nor obey the control of anybody, did not desist from their raids... (So, Nizam called Shambhuji of Kolhapur, the rival of Shahu to his side and began to seduce Shahu's officers like Santaji &c.)...

At no time is it expedient to make a rupture with the Marathas. In spite of the fact that in Aurangzib's reign and former times, they had not so much strength, dominance and number, what a large amount of treasure had to be spent in the enterprises against them and how many Rajahs and high *mansabdars* (both paid by cash and by *jagir)* with the necessary equipment had to be appointed: Today the Marathas have permanently fixed the roots of their disturbance in all the Empire, and their strength and power has exceeded all limits...'

From the dying advice of Asaf Jah to his son Nasir Jang *(Haidarabad Daftar-i-Mal* Ms.)

'It is necessary for the ruler of the Deccan to remain friendly to the Marathas, who are the landholders of this country, and contrive for concert and cooperation with them...' (f. 50 *b)*

★ ★ ★

'As far as possible never consent to waging war... Try patience and peace (*i.e.*, diplomacy) to the limit of possibility and betake to war only when there is no other remedy.' (f. 52 *a)*

★ ★ ★

Since I wrote on the Maratha conquest of Malwa in my portion of William Irvine's *Later Mughals*, Vol. II. (1921), the printing of the original despatches of Peshwa Baji Rao I's reign and the critical researches of Maharaj-Kumar Raghuvir Sinh, D. Litt., of the Rathor house of Sitamau, have conclusively proved the forged character of the 'Nandlal Mandaloi letters' which impute the death of Girdhar Bahadur and the Maratha victory in Malwa in 1728 to Nandlal's treasonable collusion, and describe Jai Singh II as exulting at the success of this disloyal conspiracy. These *Hindi* letters (not Dingal nor Persian, the only two languages in which Jai Singh's genuine correspondence was written as the Jaipur State archives prove), — were all fabricated nearly a *century after* the event and passed off on Sir John Malcolm as genuine in order to give the Mandaloi an importance which he never had as a mere village revenue collector *(chaudhuri)*. Nandlal was too small a fry to have influenced Indian history as alleged in these letters, and still less to have been a bosom friend and confidant of Jai Singh in the Imperial politics of Delhi.

II

Was There Kachhwa Treachery At Patan?

Authentic accounts of the fighting at Patan and the intrigues that preceded it have come down to us from (a) the Marathi despatches of Mahadji's and the Peshwa's agents in Hindustan; (b) the news-letters of William Palmer, the British Resident attached to Sindhia; (c) the detailed Persian narrative of Faqir Khair-ud-din who had friends and relatives in high posts under De Boigne, and (d) the French memoirs of De Boigne himself, put together before his death in his native town of Chambery. Not one of them alleges that the Jaipur generals were bribed by Mahadji Sindhia to 'keep aloof during the fight' and treacherously leave the Rathors to fight and perish unaided, as Tod asserts in the following passage:

> An unlucky stanza which a juvenile Charan had composed after the battle of Tunga, had completely alienated the Kachhwas from their (Rathor) supporters, to whom they could not but acknowledge their inferiority... This stanza was retained in recollection at the battle of Patan; and if universal affirmation may be received as proof, it was the cause of its loss, and with it that of Rajput independence. (Kachhwa) national pride was humbled; a private agreement was entered into between the Marathas and the Jaipureans, whereby the latter, on condition of keeping aloof during the fight, were to have their country secured from devastation. As usual the Rathors charged up to the muzzles of De Boigne's cannon, sweeping all before them, but receiving no support, they were torn piecemeal by showers of grape, and compelled to abandon the field. Even the women, it is averred plundered the Rathors of their horses on that disastrous day; so heart-broken had the traitorous conduct of their (Kachhwa) allies rendered them... Both these ribald strains are still the taunt of either race; by such base agencies are thrones overturned, and heroism rendered abortive.

The contemporary record of eye-witnesses proves that the mercenary drilled sepoys and artillery, commanded by Abdul Matlab Khan and Alayar Beg, that had entered Ismail Beg's service were so exasperated at their pay being long in arrears that they agreed to be neutral in the coming fight as soon as Sindhia paid them one and a half lakhs of rupees. Ismail Beg knew of this discontent and had, for sometime before the battle, planned to seize Abdul Matlab by treachery, but without success. Treachery there was at Patan, but it was between the two Muslim groups of the same army and not between the two Rajput clans.

If the Jaipur rajah came to terms with Sindhia after this battle much earlier than the lord of Jodhpur, it was primarily because his kingdom lay directly in the path of the victor, while Marwar was at a safer distance. The French life of De Boigne which Col. Tod had read *before* he wrote his annals of Amber, distinctly says this: 'Le raja de Jypore, quise trouvait le plus voisin de l'armee mahratee, fit quelques offres de submission; mais celui de Joidpour concentra ses forces...' (The Raja of Jeypore, who found himself the most neighbouring of the great army, made some offers of submission; but that of Joidpur strengthened his forces...) Secondly, the Jaipur Rajah was merely a defaulter of tribute to Sindhia, while the Jodhpur Rajah had in addition robbed him of the fort and *subah* of Ajmer and was unwilling to give them back; therefore his offence was unpardonable, and these two Rajput kingdoms did not stand on the same footing in the eyes of Sindhia.

No student of war can doubt that the Rathor swordsmen would have been butchered as helplessely by De Boigne's highly disciplined and European-led musketeers and quick-firing guns, even if ten thousand Kachhwa cavalry had pushed them from behind; the latter would only have swelled the number of the victims.

There was a rupture between the Rathors and the Kachhwas after the battle, but money was at the root of it. Bijai Singh had promised to help Pratap Singh with his Rathor cavalry on condition of their full expenses being borne by the Jaipur Government. Sawai Jai Singh II was popularly believed to have left behind him many crores of treasure; but in reality his vassals were withholding their annual tributes and his war-wasted fields were yielding no revenue. This fact the Rathor contingent would not recognize and they at last abandoned the Jaipur cause in anger.

Thus the 'universe' whose 'affirmation' Tod has received as 'proof' excludes all the impartial contemporary witnesses and records, and comes, in the ultimate analysis, to be reduced to the opium-eaters who are 'still' (to use Tod's own language) wrangling over the question whether the Rathors are more heroic than the Kachhwas.

III

Capt. J. Pillet's Account Of Sawai Pratap Singh

'Le Prince rempli d' integrite ...' (p. 11)

Again, 'Voila le perspective actuel de cette Cour gouvernee par an bon Prince, entoure d'idignes sujecs qu'il connoit, et qu'il souffre par un effet de son moderation et de sa prevoyance sur l' impossibilite qu'il a de less ameillieure et de leur succeder de plus capables de tenir les reines d'une Government qui a besoin de tetes seines, justes, equitables et plus que sage et cetera.' (p. 13). 'Mais ce jeune Prince, sans experience dans un cas de cette importance, sans conseils de competence, sans chefs et sans finances, d'un temperament natural pacifique, ennemi du travail, amateur des plaisirs et da sa tranquilite, qu'il ne trouvoit que dans son palais...'[1] (p. 14 of transcript from India Office London ms., Home Misc. Vol. 388.)[2]

Notes

1. 'The prince full of integrity...' (p. 11) Again, 'Here is the real perspective of this court governed by a good Prince surrounded by the unworthy subjects that he knew. He suffered for them as a result of his moderate temperament and for his foresight regarding the impossibility of making them better and providing them with the most capable persons to hold the reigns of a government that needed wise, impartial, just and cool persons (p. 13). But this young Prince in such an important matter was without experience and competent advisers, without military chiefs and finance. He was by temperament a natural pacifist, an enemy of labour, an amateur who found pleasure and tranquility only inside his palace...' (p. 14 of transcript from India Office London Ms. Home Misc., Vol 388.)
2. Home Misc. No. 388, item No. 8, pp. 125-194, J. Pillet to Murray with an account of Jaipur and the situation and proposal of Pratap Singh in French. *Ed.*

Index

Abdul Ahmad Khan 261-262
Abdullah, Wazir 169-170
Abdul Matlab 291-294, 297
Abdul Rahman, Amir 371, 378
Abdul Razzaq Mamuri 83
Abhai Singh 195-198, 233
Abul Fath 68
Abul Fazl 65, 69; on Raja Bhagwant Das 72; on Raja Man Singh 77; murder of 87, 91
Adil Shah 135, 138
Afghan: ruling families 75; revolt of 76, 78-79, 81, 101, 148, 163-165, 168, 235, 244, 257
Afghanistan 65-67, 70-71, 100, 104-105, 148-149
Afridis of Tirah 70; letters of 73-74; Darya Khan 150
Agra 115, Shivaji's visit to 130; escape from 133, 320
Ahmad, Crown Prince 234, 245
Ahmadnagar 89, 101; Fort of 318
Ahmad Shah Abdali 250
Ain-i-Akbari 146
Ajit Singh 148, 161-162; murder of 195
Ajmer 36, 37, 149, 200, 248, 300-301
Akbar 36; Rajput Marriage Policy 37-38; won rajput devotion 39-40; 45-47, 52, 56-57, 64-70, 72; with eastern chiefs 75-76, 82-3; death of 85, 92, 219, 225
Akbarnamah 71, 93
Ali Mardan Khan 104
Alves, Major: murder of 334-336
Alwar 1, 172; Rao Raja of 276
Amar Singh 46-47, 83
Amarsor 220-221
Amber: Dassehra festival in 17; conquest of 24; disputes in 34, 36 97, 99, 162, 172, description of by French scholar 208-209, 218-219
Amir Khan 149-50, 326-327, 331-332
Apa Khande Rao 305; death of 306
Arnold, Sir Edwin 210
Arracanese 85
Asad Khan 162
Asaf Jah I 174, 176, 178, 183
Asaf Khan 101-102
Ashrof Beg 291
Assam 146-147
Astronomical instruments constructed by Jai Singh II 212
Astronomical Observatory of Jai Singh II 205, 211-216
Attock 65, 68, 148
Auckland, Lord 330
Aurangabad 139-142
Aurangzib 105-107, 113-116, 124, 131-132, 135, 140, 142, 145, 148, 150, 152-153, death of 154, 157, 159-160, 225
Aya Mal 183, 233, 239
Azam Khan 101, 129-130

Babur 32
Badakshan 66; invasion of 105-106
Badayuni: on Battle of Haldighat 51, 53, 69
Bagru, battle of 237-238
Bahadur Khan 118-119
Bahadurpur, battle of 114
Bahadur Shah I 161-163, 203
Bairi Sal, Rawal 333, 335-336
Bajaur: country of Yusufzai settlements 67
Baji Rao: second Peshwa 175-176; visit to Rajputana 182-183; raid on Delhi 184; death of 185
Baji Rao II 304
Bakhtawar Singh (Macheri) 302
Bakht Singh, Raja 195-201, death of 202; 236
Balaji Rao, Peshwa: visits Jai Singh II 185, 237
Balaji Vishwanath: first Peshwa 175
Balkh: invasion of 105-106
Ballantyne, Sergeant 339, 362
Bal Krishna Ram, Lala 315-316

Banas 4, 8, 48, 275
Banganga 2, 3, 5, 277-278
banias 10, 16
Bar Gujar 23-24
Barlow, Sir George 323, 326, 331
Barwara 249-250, 265
Baylay, Major C.A. 355
Beg, Mirza Jan 115
Bengal 75-76, 83-85, 115, 146-147
Bentinck, Lord W. 345
Berar 133
Bhagwant Das, Raja 36-37, 46-47, 56-57, 64-70, 72, 91-92, 219, 227
Bhanpur 80
Bhils 168
Bhima: region of 139
Bhonsla, Kanhaji 165
Bhonsla, Shahji 103
Bhum 139-140
Bida 51, 53
Bidar Bakht 157-158, 160; death of 161
Bidhaka 278, 280-281
Bihar 71-72, 75-76, 115
Bihar Mal, Raja 33-36
Bijapur: Sultan of 102-103, 124; invasion by Jai Singh of 136-138
Bijapuri 100, 124, 136-137, 139-140
Bijay Singh (Chimaji) 157, 161, 193, 246-247, 249, 254-255, 288, 304
Bikaner: invasion of 198, 247
Birbal, Raja 68
Bishan Singh 150; Jat wars of 151; last days of 152-154
Black Mountain Expedition 371
Bohra, Khushhali Ram 259-260, 262-265, 267-269, 271, 273-274, 302-303, 331
Boigne, Col. De 276-277, 281, 283, 291-295; achievement of 296-297, 302-305, 311
Boudier, Claude: French Jesuit 214
brahmans 9, 132, 310
British Empire 353
British Government 286, 309-310; Jaipur enters into protective alliance with 316, 323, 325-326, 333-334, 336
British Imperial Postal System 359
British Indian Government 315, 344
British Museum Persian manuscript Or. 1271 221
Brooke, Col. 349; on Jaipur army 383
Browne, Maj. James 221-222
Bund Boochara: masonry dam 5
Bund Moran: irrigation works 4
Bundi 189-190, 192, contest for throne of 232-233; 238, 244
Burhanpur 89

Canning, Earl 341
Castlereagh, Lord 321
Central Asia: Shah Jahan's invasion of 106
Chagtai Khan 36
chamars 10
Chambal 8
Chand Bardai 25
Chandrasen 41, 44
Chandrawat, Gopal Singh 164
Chaprwara Bund 4
Charar Gulzar-i-Shujai 204
Chatsu 103
Chaturbhuj 33
Chauhan, Harnath 138
Chauhan, Prithviraj 25
Cherry: Resident at Benares 309
Chisti, Khwaja Muinuddin: shrine of 31, 42
Chitor 46, 48, 110
Collins, Col. John 310, 314
Colvin, Lt. Governor James 343
Cornwallis, Lord 273, 316, 321-323
Council of Regency 330, 333, 349-350, 379
Council of State (of Jaipur) 381, 388
Court of Directors 317, 324-325, 346
Curzon, Lord 370, 374
Cuttack 79

Dacca 84-85
Dadu 17, 384
Dadu Panthis: origin of 16
Dalel Singh 232

Dara Shukoh, Prince 105, 108, 110-111, 113-114, 116; defeat of 117-118; made captive 120
Daulatabad 103
Dausa 6, 23, 274, 276, 278, 302
Deccan 89, 100-103, 105, 124, 135, 149-150, 153, 157
Delhi: Ahmad Shah Durrani's threatening of 234-235; invasion of Marwar by 238, 245-246, Court of 250; 267; Govt. of 270; Empire of 315
Deorai 117
Deoti 24
Dharmat 114-115, 122
Dhola: scion of House of Kachhwa 21
Didwana 247, 278-279
Digamsha Yantra: astronomical instrument devised by Jai Singh II 215
Dilir Khan 117-118, 126-127, 136, 140
Dinaram, Diwan 310
Din-i-Ilahi 91
Dodwell, Professor 370
Doly, Sir Henry D. 380
Don, Lt. Col. Patrick 320
Dudrence, Chevalier 311-313
Dufferin, Lord 371, 382
Duraha, Treaty of 184

East India Co. 317, 319, 321, 332, 348
Economic and Industrial Museum 367
Eden, Major William Frederick 341-342
Edmonston 325

Fairfax 316
Farrukhsiyar 163, 167-168, 170, 190-191, 202, 219, 225
Fatehpur, Battle of 307-308
Figueiredo, Padre Manoel de 212-214
Filoze, Michael 291
Firuz 259-261

Gabelsperger, Antonne: Bavarian Jesuit 214
Gaekwad, Maharaja Malhar Rao 361-362
Gangadhar Tatya 237-238, 240
Gangapur 6
Gangwana, battle of 200
Gardiner, W. 320
Garrett, A.H. and Guleri, C.: book of 214, 377
Gidhaur 77
Girosias 168
Goa 125
Gogunda 48-49, 55-56, 58
Golkonda: 124; Sultan of 103, 135, 138, 140
Gond 103, 112
Gopal Bhau 291-295, 297
Gopal Singh Rao 165, 189
Gosain Himmat Bahadur 267
Government of India 346, 359
Grierson, Sir George 21
Gujarat 40, 57, 118-119; Maratha occupation of 174
Gwalior 185

Hada, Anand Singh 197
Hada, Bhim Singh 168, 191
Hada, Budh Singh 168, 190; death of 194; 204, 232
Hada, Dalel Singh 193-194
Hada, Durjan Sal 191, 232-233, 237
Hada, Pratap Singh 194
Hada, Raj Singh 197
Hada, Ummed Singh 193-194, 232-233, 237-238, 244
Haft Anjuman: extracts from 141-142
Haldia, Chajju Ram 267
Haldia, Daulat Ram 264-268, 272-274, 300-301, 303-304, 316, 331
Haldia, Khushhali Ram II 267-268, 272
Haldia, Nand Ram 267
Haldighat, battle of 49-53, 57
Hardinge, Lord 349
Hastings, Lord Warren 315-316; Treaty of Defensive Alliance with Jaipur 325-326, 370
Heber, Bishop 208, 210, 211
Himmat Bahadur 264, 268

Himmat Singh 81-82, 93
Hindaun 6
Hingane, Mahadev Bhat 183
Hirji Sarhand 132
History of Shah Alam II (Muna Lal) 221
Holkar, Ahalya Bai: death of 304
Holkar, Bapurao 303
Holkar, Jaswant Rao 319-321, 327
Holkar, Khande Rao 232, 240
Holkar, Madhav 246
Holkar, Malhar 180-181, 194, 230, 233, 236-238, 243-244, 248, in Jaipur territory 249; victory at Mongrol-Bhatwara 250-251; death of 252
Holkar Tukoji 301, 303
Holmes, Col. 343
Hunter, Dr. W. 214
Hunter, Major 291

Idar 56
Imperial Service Transport Corps 383
Imperial Service Troops 370
Inayet-ullah 225
Indian Councils Act 1861 362
Indian Peoples Famine Trust 374
Ingle, Ambaji 275-276, 279-280, 289, 292, 303-304
Ingle, Baloji 292-293, 300
Isa Khan Bhati 81-82; death of 83
Ishwari Singh 202; accession of 229, 231-239, suicide of 240
Islam Shah 34
Ismail Beg, Mirza 288-292, 294-296, 299, 301, 303
Ismail Quli 70

Jacob, Capt. S. 358, 367
Jacquemont, Victor: French Scholar on Jaipur and Amber 208, 345
Jadav Rao 136
Jafar Khan 130
Jagannath: son of Bihar Mal 58
Jagannath Pandit: Hindu astronomer 213
Jagat Singh 77-80, 82-83
Jagat Singh, Maharana 230, 233
Jagat Singh, Sawai 321, 326, 331; death of 333
Jahandar Shah 163
Jahangir 87-88, 97-98; death of 100, See also Salim, Prince
Jainiwas 205
Jai Prakash: astronomical instrument devised by Jai Singh II 215
Jaipur 6, 9; festivals in 15; as trading centre 15, 91-92, 156-157, 173, 181; Baji Rao's visit to 183; foundation and growth of 205-206; streets of 206-207; account by foreigners on 207-209; palaces in 210; State archives of 218; expansion of 219-220, 236-238; Maratha invasion of 239-240; 246-249, 255, 257; under Prithvi Singh 259, 261, 264-266; Bohra-Haldia rivalry at 267-268, 270-271, 273, 287-289, 300-302; archives of 305, 306, 309-310, 313, Raja of 316; state of 317; treaty with British 318-319, 320-324, 326-328; last days of Ancient Regime in 330-336; service of Maharaja of Jaipur during Mutiny 341-343; Residence at 345; reduction of tribute in 346; social reforms initiated in 349-350; era of progress in 353-360, 363-364; developments under Madho Singh II in 366-374; royal visitors to 374-375; new model adm. of 380-381; army reform in 381-385; modern adm. of 386; income and expenditure in 386-387; Legislation and justice in 387-388; police and jails 389; land revenue and agr. in 389-390; village upliftment 390-391; municipalities in 392; education in 393-395; medical treatment 395; public works, industry and commerce 396-397; constitutional problems for future 397-398.
Jaipur Imperial Service Transport Corps 371

Jai Singh, Mirza Raja I 39, 98; character of 99; work in Deccan 100-103; campaigns beyond n.w. frontier 104-106; at three sieges of Qandahar 107-109; in war of Mughal succession 110-111, 113-116; pursuit of Dara 118-119; years at Court 120-121; against Shivaji 123-127, 128-132; in Deccan 135-138; campaign in Bhima-Manjira region 139-140, 141-142; misery & death of 143-145
Jai Singh, Sawai Raja II 39, 153-154, accession of 156-157; under Bidar Bakht 158-160; in reign of Bahadur Shah I 161-162; First Viceroyalty of Malwa 163-166, 167; against Churaman Jat 168-171; received titles 171, 172-173; dealings with Marathas 174-177; third viceroyalty in Malwa 178-184; befriends Peshwa Balaji Rao 185, 187-188; policy in Rajputana 189-190, 191-192; defeat of Budh Singh Hada by 193-194, 196-200; death of 201, 202, construction of city of Jaipur 205-207; observatories 211-216; character and achievements of 218-225; social reforms of 226-227; 229, 253, 350
Jai Singh, Sawai Raja II 333-334
Jaisinghpura 305
Jajau, battle of 190
Jalor 55, 197
Jamrud 150
Jaswant Singh Chundawat 259
Jaswant Singh, Maharaja 100-111, 113, 116-117, 119, 123, 130-131, 133; death of 148
Jat 9, 151-152, 237, 243, 246; state 253, 254-256, 301
Jat, Badan Singh 171-172, 253
Jat Churaman 152, 167-168; death of 170, 191, 202
Jat, Jawahar Singh 252-255; death of 256
Jat, Suraj Mal II 237, 245; death of 253
Jaunpur 75
jaziya: abolishment of 39; imposition of 149, 224-225
Jhotwada: river supply of water to Jaipur 206
Jhunjhunu 221, 378
Jhuta Ram Saraogi 333-336
Jodhpur 181, 189, 198-199, 238; Maratha siege of 247; Maharana of 257; Raja of 273, 300, 310
jizya see jaziya
Jones, Maj. Gen. 321, 323-324

Kabul 65-68, 70, 106-107
Kachhwa (Kachhawa, Kachhawaha) 20, 22, 39, 53, 58; Rajas of 63, 67, 72; barons of 92, 102, 156, 158; marriage of royal Houses of 197; territorial expansion of State of 219-220; army 251, 252-253, 257, 259, 272-273, 286, 299, 300, 310-311, 315, 330-333, 338, 340
Kachhwa, Bhau Singh 89, 97; death of 98
Kachhwa, Durjan Singh 81-82
Kachhwa, Gaj Singh 168
Kachhwa, Madho Singh 53, 65-66, 68-70
Kachhwa, Maha Singh 84, 88; death of 97-98
Kachhwa, Raj Singh 259
Kachhwa, Suraj Singh 64
Kalekh Bhund: irrigation work 5
Kakil 24
Kama 253, 256, 304
Kam Baksh 161-162
Kanud 16, 263
Kashmir: conquest of 69
kayastha 16
Kaye, G.R. 213-215
Keating, Lt. Col. R.H. 397
Kedar Rai 85
Kelwara 57
Khair-ud-din, Faqir 296

Khajwa, battle of 116
Khanderao Hari 375-377
Khanderao Dhabade 165
Khandela 16
Khandesh 57, 133, 159
Khan-i-Dauran 103 (Nusratjang) 104
Khan Jahan 169-170
Khanua, battle of 32, 34, 42
Khawas Khan 136
Khelna 157; siege of 158
Khyber Pass 66-68, 149-150
Kirat Singh 109-111, 121, 126-128, 143, 145
Kirkpatrick, William 273, 329
Kishangarh 2
Kishan Singh Kumar 148-149; death of 150
Kotah: festivals in 15, 190, 251
Kot Qasim 6, 9
Krishna Kumari: Princess of Mewar, death of 331-332
kshatriya 16, 20
Kumbha, Maharana 31, 33
Kumbhalgarh 55, 57
Kusathal Pancholas 193-194
Kushal Singh, Raja: Shahu's adopted son 176, 186

Lahore 234-235
Lake, Lord 169, 318, 320-325, 344
Lakhwa Dada 306, 311
Lakshmi Narain: Raja of Cooch Behar 82
Lalsot: campaign of 271, 275, 277-284, 286, 288
Lawrence, Sir Henry 348, 351, 366
Lawrence, Sir John 360
Leitao, Petro da Silva 214
Lesteneau 276, 281
Lockett, Lt. Col. A. 344
Lohri, Battle of 138
Lucan, Lt. 320
Ludlow, Maj. John 339, 349-351, 355, 358

Macchiwara 235
Macheri 261-262, 267, 272; death of Raja of 302, 303
Macnaghten, Cornet 335
Madec, Rene 254-255
Madhav Rao II (Peshwa): death of 304
Madho Singh, Maharaja Sawai 190, 202, 219, 222, 229-231, 235-237, 242; accession of 243, 244-245, 248-250, 252, 254; death of 256; estimate of reign 257
Madho Singh, Sawai II: policy and achievements 365-366; eco. dev. under 367-368; communications, education and public health 368-370; in defence of Br. Empire 370-372; attends coronation of Edward VII 372-373; famine relief 373-374; royal visitors 374-375; public monuments built by 377
Mahbub Ali Khan: Oudh General 264-266
Mairta 118
Malarna 220, 228, 265
Malcolm, Sir John 321, 325-326
Maldeo 41
Malesi 26
Malikambar 89, 90, 98, 100
Malpura 6, 9, 237, 249, 268; battle of 310-311
Malwa 56, 149, 163-166, 174-178, 180; *chauth* of 182; Baji Rao appointed Deputy Gov. of 184; surrendered to Balaji Rao 185, 321
Malleson 39, 341
Mandsaur 180
Mandu 178
Mangalvide 136, 140
Mangrol 251
Manjira: region of 139
Manoharpur 220, 222, 251, 300
Man Singh, Maharaja of Jodhpur 331
Man Singh, Raja 36-37, 39, 46-50, 52-58, 64-68, 70-71; receives title of Raja 72-73, 75; appointed viceroy 76; first conquest of Orissa 77-80, campaign in East Bengal 80-85, 86-88; in the Deccan and death of 90, 219
Man Singh, Sir Sawai II 377; education 379-380; army reform of 381-385

Manucci, Niccolas 144, 150, 223
Manupur 235-236
Maonda, battle of 255-256
Maral, Bhai Khan: letter to Jai Singh I of 73-74
Marathas 124, 126-127, 163-164, 166, 176-180, 233, 236-237, 239, 243-244; in Jaipur 246-251; 252-253, 257, 260, 270-271, 282, 286, 290, 293-294, 300-302, 307, 316, 321, 325-326
Marwar 2, 13, 40-41, 148-149, 161-162, 194-195, 197-199; invasion of 238, 246-248, 300
Mathura 132
Mau 105
Mayo College 357; education of Man Singh II at 379
Mayo Hospital 357, 370, 395
Mayo, Lord 357; on Ram Singh II 361
Mello, Diogo de 125
Mello, Francisco de 125
Memorials of the Jeypore Exhibition of 1883 367
Meo 10, 110, 341
Merta 41, 57, 197, 300-301
Metcalfe, Sir Charles 326-328, 333, 344
Mewar 1, 2; Dassehra festival in 17, 20, 34, 45-46; Kingdom of 48, 53, 55, 58, 83, 162, 179; Baji Rao's visit to 182-183, 232
Mewat: brigand population of 109, 263
Minas 10, 13, 335
Mohi 56
Monson, Col. 319-321, 324
Montague, E.S. and Chelmsford, Lord 398
Morel 277-281
Morris, John 307
Mughals 50, 100, 103, 126, 136; capture of forts in Bhima-Manjira region 139, 140, 147, 151; disintegration of 187-188, 260
Muhakam 169-171
Muhammad Akbar, Prince 149
Muhammad Beg Hamdani 275, 281, 283, 288
Muhammad Hakim, Mirza: ruler of Kabul 63-67
Muhammad Khan Bangash 174-176, 187
Muhammad Mehdi: Muslim astronomer 213
Muhammad Shah 170, 172, 177, 181, 185, 192, 212, 221, 225; order of 226, 229, 234
Muhammad Sharfuddin Hussain Mirza 35-36, 76
Muhammad Sharif: Muslim astronomer 213
Muazzam, Prince 141
Munhot Nainsi 59
Murad Baksh, Prince 104, 106, 113-115
Murray, Col. John 317, 320
Murshid Quli Khan: house of 188
Murtaza Khan Barecht 265-266, 281-282
Mutiny (Sepoy) 338-341, 351

Nadir Shah 184
Nadot 55
Nagor 196-198, 247-248
Nagpur: siege of 103
Najafgarh 262
Najaf Khan, Mirza 224, 260-267; death of 270, 316
Najaf Quli 263-264, 272
Najib-ud-daulah 252-254, 262-263, 266, 271, 289
Najmuddin Ali Khan, Sayyid 187
Nariana: Headquarters of Dadupanthis 17
Narivalaya Yantra: astronomical instrument devised by Jai Singh II 215
Narnol 355
Naro 33
Naruka, Himmat Singh 290
Naruka, Pratap Singh 222, 260, 271-272, 286, 301

Naruka, Sardar Singh 250
Nathawats: noble clan group of Kachhwas 259, 351
Netaji Palker 131, 136; desertion to Bijapuris 138; return to Mughal side 139
Nizam Ali 252
Nizam of Hyderabad 175
Northbrook, Lord 361-362
Nusrat Yar Khan 291

Ochterlony, General Sir David 328, 333-334, 344
Orissa 77, 115

Pachayan 32
Pajvan 25
Palkhed campaign 175
Panhala, Fort of 138, 157
Panipat, Battle of 250
Panipat, Second Battle of 35
parganas issued to Ram Singh 146
Parenda, siege of 102-103; Fort of 150
Parviz 89
Patan 250-251, 289-291; battle of 292-295
Pathans: revolt of 148, 326-327
Penjdeh Affair 371
Pere de la Hire: tables of stars 212
Persia 104
Perron, General 303-305, 308, 318
Peshawar 64-65, 70, 234
Phaltan 140
Phayre, Col. 361-362
Pillet, J. 223, 227, 305, 316, 329; letter to Lt. Col. Murray on Sawai Pratap Singh 285, 297
Pirthi Singh, Raja 305; reign of 315-316
Pohlman, Major 311-314
Polier, Col. 211
Portfolios of Indian Architectural Details 367
Pratap Singh, Maharana 46-47, 49-56, 57-58, 242
Pratap Singh, Sawai 261, 263, 265; earlier years of reign 268-269, 273; character and difficult position 285-286, 287-288, 300, 303; death of 304, 310, 313, 316-317
Prithvi Singh, Raja 259-260; death of 261
Prithvi Raj Raso 25
Punjab 63-65
Purandar 125; siege of 126; treaty of 132, 135, 136
Puran Mal, 32-33, 77
Pushkar: Lake 200, 375; territory 254

Qaim Khan 221
Qamruddin Khan: wazir of Muhammad Shah 187, 221, 234-235
Qandahar 104-105, 107-108, 112, 120, 148
Qasim Khan 114
Qutbuddin Khan Koka 88
Qutlu Khan Lohani 78

Raghunath Dada 245-246; invades Rajputana 248, 249, 252
Raipur 78
Rai, Raja Dulha II 22-23
Rajaram 151; slaying of 152
Rajasthan 218-219, 250, 271
Rajawats: noble clan group of Kachhwas 260, 365
Raj Mahal 81, 115, 232, 236
Rajputana 1; peasants in 13; festivals of 14-15; traders and bankers of 15; Kachhwa migration to 22, 149, 161-163, 178; local hegemony of 188-189; Maratha penetration into 194, 201, 219, 238, 244, 248, 250, 252, 263, 286, 302-304, 341; agents to Gov. Gen. for 374; famine in 359
Rajputs: origin of name 20, 66, 255-256, 282-283, 290, 293, 301, 307; Princes during the Mutiny 340
Rajrup, Raja 117-118
Ram Chandra Dev, Raja 79-81

Ramgarh 247, 276-278
Rampura: State of 189-190, 302, 314, 320-321, 327
Ram Rao: eldest son of Maldeo 41
Ram Singh (son of Jai Singh I) 121, 128-133, 141-142; succession to throne 145; in Assam 146-147; in Afghanistan 148-149; death of 150; 218, 220
Ram Singh (son of Abhai Singh) 238, 244, 246, 248, 257
Ram Singh, Sawai II 334; education 338-339, 340-344, 346; income and expenditure during early years of 347; early years of personal rule 351-352; adm. reorganisation 353-354; law, justice and police 354-355; education 355-356; hospitals 357; capital 357-358; communications 358-359; famine relief 359-360; friend of British 360-362, 363-364, 380
Ram Yantra: astronomical instrument devised by Jai Singh II 215
Rana Khan 277, 279, 280-283
Rangamati 147-148
Ranthambor 46, 190, 218, 222, 245, 251, 334
Raona (Pipar), Battle of 238
Ratan Singh 33
Rathor: marriage of Royal houses of 197, 199-200, 247, 254, 281, 283, 286, 294, 297, 311-312, 332-333, 340
Rathor Durgadas 148, 162
Rathor, Ramdas 51, 53
Raverty, Major 28
Rawshaniya: Sufi sect 68, 71-72
Rayaji Patil 272-274, 277, 282-283
Regency Council 351
Reinhard, Walter 254-255
Rewari 289
Roberts, Lord 371
Rodoji Khawas 302-303, 307-308
Ross, Major 346
Ruhelas 168, 176
Rupa 152, 155, 169, 170
Rupsi, Baron of Daosa 36, 42
Russell, Sir William Howard: on Ram Singh II 361, 369

Sadat Khan 18; house of 188
Sadullah Khan 107, 110
Safdarjang 244-245
Said Khan: Subehdar of Punjab 63-64, 66, 76-80
Salabat Khan (Mir Bakshi) 238
Salim, Prince 66, 80, 83-84, 86-87
Sambhar 6, 7, 189, 195, 237, 300, 302, 346; salt monopoly at 348, 368
Samrat Yantra: astronomical instrument devised by Jai Singh II 214
Samugarh 115
Sanga, Rana 32, 34; death of 42
Sanganer 274-275, 311; aerodrome constructed at 385, 396
Sangram Singh Maharana 179
Sansaní: siege of 151; capture of 153
Sarbuland Khan 181
Sarji Anjangaon, treaty of 318-319,323
Sarup Singh, Maharana (Udaipur) 341
Saswad 125
Sawai Madhopur 6-8, 257, 368
Sayyid, Abdullah 167
Sayyid, Husain Ali 167
Shadman Beg 64
Shah Abbas II 107
Shah Alam II 288, 315, 344
Shahbaz Khan (Mir Bakshi) 57-58
Shah Jahan 100; campaign in the Deccan 101-103; campaign beyond n.w. frontier 104-105
Shah Nawaz Khan 117-118
Shahu, Raja 174-176, 178, 183, 236.
Shaista Khan II 159
Shambhuji 130, 149
Sharza Khan 136-137
Shekhawat 26, 221-222, 232, 249, 263, 266, 269, 286, 306, 310, 355
Shekhawat, Nawal Singh 264
Shekhawati 2, 3, 5, 6, 9, 27; invasion of 265, 300, 334, 343, 346-347

Sheogaon, Treaty of 175
Sher Shah 34
Shivaji 111, 123-125; submission of 127-128; visit to Agra 129-131; captivity and escape from Agra 132-133, 136, 138
Shivsingh, Kumar: death of 202, 229
Shore, Sir John 317
Showers, Brig. Gen. 343
Shuja, Prince 102, 104, 111, 113, 115; defeat of 116
Shujaet Khan 148
Shuja-ud-daulah 251
Siddi Masaud 137
Sikhs: rising of 162, 253, 256
Silva, Hakim Xavier De 310
Sindhia, Dattaji 246-250
Sindhia, Daulat Rao 310, 319, 327
Sindhia, Jankoji 249
Sindhia, Jayappa 243, 246
Sindhia, Mahadji 252; appointed Commander-in-Chief 270; first invasion of Jaipur 271-272; final rupture with Jaipur Govt. 273, 274-284, 286-289, 291-294, 299-305, 308, 316
Sindhia, Nar Singh 247
Sindhia, Nima 159
Sindhia, Ranoji 180, 194
Sirhind 234-235
Sirohi 55
Sisodias: descent from 20, 53, 58, 189, 257, 340
Skinner, James 312-314
Smith, V.A. 28, 63
Soghor 152-153, 171
Solanki 268
Stewart, F.: British traveller 13
Stewart, Sir Donald 342
Strobl, Father Andre: Bavarian Jesuit 207, 214
Sturrock, Capt. 319, 321
Sulaiman, Mirza 70-71
Sulaiman Shukoh 108, 114-115, 121
Sultanpur 137-138
Suraj Mal Mishran: eulogist of Court of Bundi 191, 204, 227
Surtan 32
Sutherkand, Lt. Col. 345-346
Swat 67

Takht Singh, Maharaja (Jodhpur) 341
Tantia Tope 343
Tazkhirat-us-Salatin-i-Chaghtai 196
Teg Bahadur 146
Thomas, George 306-309, 312
Thoresby, Major 348, 354
Thun 170
Tieffenthaler, Father Joes: Tyroless Jesuit 207, 214
Timur Shah: death of 304
Tod, Col: description of Dassehra in Udaipur 17; Kachhwa conquest of Minas 27-28, 47-48, 60-61, 87; on death of Jai Singh 144; on Congress of Rajas of Rajasthan 194, 204, 211, 217, 219, 226; on Ishwari Singh 242, 306, 325; on murder of Mr. Blake 336, 380

Toda 146, 230, 233, 237, 268
Todar Mal, Raja 47, 68; death of 72
Tonk 1, 145, 219, 230, 237, 302, 327
Tonwar, Pratap 52-53
Tonwar, Ram Sah 51, 53
Torawati 6
Tori Sagar: irrigation work 4
Trevelyan, Sir Charles 356
Trevor, Col. G.H. 341
Tunga: Battle of 281-283

Udaipur 58-59; Maharana of 149; Baji Rao in 183; treaty of 229; Maharana of 236, 243, 304
Udairaj 142-143
Udai Singh, Maharana 41, 45; death of 46
Ujjain 163-165, 168, 178
Uniara: Fort of 222
Usman 84
Uzbaks 106

Vijragarh 125; capture of 126
Vaman Rao 306, 309
Vamsa-Bhaskar 195, 202-204, 223-224
Vasault, Le 276, 281
Vidyadhar Bhattacharya 206, 216, 239-240
Vyankaji 136

Warid Teharani: Persian historian 223
Wazir Ali 309-310
Wellesley, Marquess 309, alliance with Jaipur made by 317-318, 321-322, 331, 370
Wendel, Father F.X.: Belgian Jesuit 172
Wilson, Horris Haymen 324

Yusuf Khan: Sultan of Kashmir 69
Yusufzai: clan of Afghans 67-68, 70

Zain Khan Koka, 68, 71
Zakariya Khan 188
Zij-i-Muhammad Shahi: table of stars 211-213

Zorawar Singh, Raja 198